GOD ENCOUNTERED

OTHER WORKS BY FRANS JOZEF VAN BEECK:

Christ Proclaimed: Christology as Rhetoric
Grounded in Love: Sacramental Theology in an Ecumenical Perspective
Catholic Identity After Vatican II: Three Types of Faith in the One Church
Loving the Torah More than God? Toward a Catholic Appreciation of Judaism

GOD ENCOUNTERED

A Contemporary
Catholic Systematic Theology

Volume Two/1:
The Revelation of the Glory

Introduction and Part I:
Fundamental Theology

FRANS JOZEF VAN BEECK, S. J.

A Michael Glazier Book
THE LITURGICAL PRESS
Collegeville, Minnesota

Grateful acknowledgment is made for the use of the following materials. A first version of the Introduction (§56) appeared as "Tradition and Interpretation," in *Bijdragen* 51(1990): 257-271. Most of §§61-64 appeared, under the title "Professing the Creed among the World's Religions," in *The Thomist* 55(1991): 539-568, and most of §§94-95, under the title "Divine Revelation: Intervention or Self-Communication?" in *Theological Studies* 52(1991): 199-226. Excerpts from *The Body and Society*, by Peter Brown (copyright © 1988 Columbia University Press, New York) are reprinted with the permission of the publisher. Excerpts from *The Habit of Being* by Flannery O'Connor (copyright © 1979 by Regina O'Connor) are reprinted by permission of Farrar, Straus & Giroux, Inc. Excerpts from "The Catholic Novelist in the Protestant South" by Flannery O'Connor, as it appeared in *Viewpoint*, Spring 1966 (an essay later published in slightly different form in *Mystery and Manners* by Flannery O'Connor; copyright © 1966, 1969 by the Estate of Mary Flannery O'Connor), are reprinted by permission of Farrar, Straus & Giroux, Inc. Excerpts from *The Violent Bear It Away* by Flannery O'Connor (copyright © 1955, 1960 by Flannery O'Connor; copyright © 1988 renewed by Regina O'Connor) are reprinted by permission of Farrar, Straus & Giroux, Inc. The illustration on the dustjacket, fol. 112r of *Codex Sanhippolytensis* N° 1 (15th cent.), is used once again by kind permission of the *Bischöfliche Alumnatsbibliothek*, Sankt Pölten, Austria.

Imprimi potest: Very Rev. Bradley M. Schaeffer, S.J., Provincial, Chicago Province. May 8, 1992.

Nihil Obstat: Rev. Charles R. Meyer, S.T.D., *Censor Deputatus*

Imprimatur: Most Rev. John R. Gorman, Vicar General, Archdiocese of Chicago. June 8, 1992.

The *Nihil Obstat* and *Imprimatur* are official declarations that a book is free of doctrinal or moral error. No implication is contained therein that those who have granted the *Nihil Obstat* and *Imprimatur* agree with the content, opinions, or statements expressed.

Cover design by Ann Blattner.
FIRST EDITION

Library of Congress Cataloging-in-Publication Data

Beeck, Frans Jozef van.
    The Revelation of the Glory. Introduction and Part I. Fundamental Theology.

    (God Encountered; v. 2/1)
    Bibliography: p.
    Includes index.
    1. Theology, Doctrinal.   2. Catholic Church—Doctrines.
I. Title. II. Series: Beeck, Frans Jozef van.
God Encountered; v. 2/1.
BX1747.5.B4 vol. 2/1
ISBN 0-8146-5498-3

For Hans-Georg Gadamer.

"Whole countries have admired you for your interpretations."

(Sirach 47, 17)

Das Christentum hat mich immer nur am Rande gestreift und mir immerhin die Offenheit gewährt, nicht den Wahnideen der Aufklärung ganz zu verfallen.

Christianity has never touched me more than peripherally and provided me all the same with the openness not to be completely enslaved by the delusions of the Enlightenment.

(Letter of January 29, 1989)

O admirabile commercium!
Creator generis humani,
animatum corpus sumens,
de Virgine nasci dignatus est:
et procedens homo sine semine,
largitus est nobis suam deitatem.

What admirable exchange!
Humankind's Creator,
taking on body and soul,
in his kindness, is born from the Virgin:
and, coming forth as man, yet not from man's seed,
he has lavished on us his divinity.

(Antiphon at vespers, January 1,
Feast of the Holy Mother of God)

Contents

Preface   x

Abbreviations   xx

Introduction. Tradition and Interpretation   1
   [§56]   Theologizing in the Presence of the Great Tradition, 1

Part I. FUNDAMENTAL THEOLOGY

Chapter 1. Interpreting the Creed   21

  Preliminaries
    [§57]   The Profession of Faith: Systematic Dimensions, 21

  Universalist Perspectives
    [§58]   Interpretation, 27
    [§59]   Christian Universalism Undergirded by Natural Universalism, 32
    [§60]   The Created Order in the Text of the Creed, 36

Chapter 2. Professing the Creed Among the World's Religions   41

  The Horizon of Humanity and the World
    [§61]   The Creed, the Created Order, and the Religions, 41
    [§62]   The Creed as a Mandate for Interreligious Dialogue, 49

  Interpretation and Dialogue
    [§63]   Excursus: Participative Knowledge, 53
    [§64]   Again: the Christian Dialogue with the World Religions, 60

Chapter 3. Gateway to Contemplation   72

  Retrospect and Outlook
    [§65]   Two Coordinated Universalisms, 72

  Professing the Creed Before God
    [§66]   The Mystery Beyond the Creed, 74
    [§67]   Educated Ignorance, 78

  Educated Ignorance Today: Which Agenda?
    [§68]   A Modern Issue in Theological Interpretation, 89
    [§69]   The Catholic Tradition, 92

Chapter 4.   The Creed Torn Apart   99

The Nature of Christianity: The Issue
   [§70]   Keeping the Creed and Its Perspectives Together, 99
   [§71]   The Nature of Christianity in the Great Tradition, 103

Just What is Christianity?
   [§72]   Dissociation and Disintegration, 114
   [§73]   The Impasse Personified: Lessing as a Modern Prophet, 125
   [§74]   Closing Meditation: Establishment and Identity, 130

Chapter 5.   The Portrayal of the Divine Nature   134

Again: The Nature of Christianity
   [§75]   *What Does the Christian's Profession Mean?*, 134
   [§76]   Christianity as Transitional: Two Conclusions, 139
   [§77]   Interpreting the Creed: Retrospect and Outlook, 146

Catholicity: Symbolism and Sacramentality
   [§78]   A World of Symbols, 149
   [§79]   "If God is for us...." (Rom 8, 31), 162

Chapter 6.   "Charity Perfects Nature"   175

Again: the Faith Professed Before Humanity and the World
   [§80]   Introduction: Aquinas on Natural Tendency, 175
   [§81]   Natural Theology: Two Applications, 181

Graced Nature and Reason Enlightened by Faith
   [§82]   Nature Rationally Discerned in Faith, not Autonomy, 183
   [§83]   The Catholic Tradition and the Reformation, 188
   [§84]   The Catholic Tradition and Enlightened Humanism, 196

Chapter 7.   Humanity's Natural Desire for God   204

The Catholic Tradition and the Modern Struggle for Authenticity
   [§85]   Blondel: Catholic Faith Sponsoring Freedom of Thought, 204
   [§86]   The Failure of Rationalist-Historicist Apologetics, 211

Reason and Nature Aspiring to Faith and Grace
   [§87]   "Immanence": A Native Preparedness for the Supernatural, 230
   [§88]   Summary: Grace and Nature Intertwined, 239
   [§89]   Immanence in the Experience of Prayer, 241
   [§90]   The Face of Christ in the Mirror of Human Nature, 246

Chapter 8. Christian Faith and Credibility: Three Basic Issues   258

The Problem of Fundamental Theology Today
   [§91]   Retrospect and Outlook: Natural and Positive Religion Again, 258
   [§92]   Fundamental Theology a "Separate" Discipline?, 264

An Apologetics of Immanence
   [§93]   Interpretative Apologetics, 273

God Encountered?

[§94]   Revelation: Divine "Intervention"?, 283
[§95]   Revelation and its Anthropological Infrastructure, 295

Notes   318

Bibliography   334

Subject Index   353

Names Index   356

Scripture Index   359

Preface

In a second volume, *God Encountered* takes for its theme "the radiance of God's glory" (Wisd 7, 26; Heb 1, 3), both in the creation of humanity and the universe and in its gracious re-creation. This is the theme of the divine *exitus*—in Blessed Jan van Ruusbroec's idiom, God's "outflowing." In an all-encompassing (and hence, ungraspable) design of profuse liberality, so Christians believe and profess, God freely reaches out. This occurs in a divine self-extension that is unabated and indefatigable, in a self-communication that gathers urgency as it goes, in a creative activity that produces and generates an imperfect, yet dynamic universe, while at the same time inspiring that universe to offer its response in turn, in wonder and awe at the Glory revealed to, in, and beyond itself. Thus the *exitus* results in a universe of finite beings meant to be both relatively subsistent in themselves and ecstatically seeking an eternal home with God; thus the world and humanity become the very ground upon which God is encountered in place and time; thus, in the perspective of an ultimate union with God, the creature is readied to become the very stuff of the manifestation of the Holy One. For the *exitus* does not show its true nature till the *reditus* it initiates and supports and encompasses is manifested, too; the divine outflowing includes, as its own ongoing fulfillment, an ingathering; the revelation of the Holy One aims at drawing into holiness all that ever comes to be; the revelation of the Glory is designed to glorify—to embrace and divinely bring home to God whatever finds itself being produced and generated by God.

God's *exitus*, it will be explained specifically, is archetypally, historically, and consummatively embodied and actualized in the faith of

Israel, and especially in its principal offspring, the person of Jesus of Nazareth, who is the Christ, risen and present in the Spirit to as well as in the community that bears his name. Around the edges of this manifestation of God in Jesus Christ, and in it, and beyond it, the Christian faith ultimately discerns, often only by peripheral vision as it were, but sometimes with astonishing directness, God's transcendent, Threefold Self, sovereign beyond all that exists, all the more hidden for being so manifest, all the more awesome for being so intimately present: Fullness of ineffable Life everlastingly communicated in ever self-renewing outflow and return—God and the Word and the Spirit.

One very authoritative response generated by God's *exitus* is the trinitarian profession of faith, most strikingly embodied in the Christian Creed. Accordingly, in this second volume, the Creed offers itself for theological treatment. It does so in a twofold manner.

First, it raises *fundamental* issues: the Christian faith engages the dynamics of tradition, of interpretation, of intercultural and interreligious dialogue, of ultimate theological reference, of historical process and historic existence, of the relationship between humanity and God, and hence, of anthropology and theology. The second volume of *God Encountered* treats these matters in an Introduction and eight chapters; together these comprise Part I—a *prima secundæ* dedicated to *fundamental theology.*

Secondly, the Creed raises theological issues that are positively *doctrinal* and *mystagogical*—most of all, the understanding of the person of Jesus Christ and God's Blessed Trinity. This latter array of distinctively Christian doctrines, however, is intelligible only on the basis of two clusters of theological themes of wider reference: Israel's conceptions about God and creation, as well as their impact on Christian culture (especially in the West), and a baffling mystery universally acknowledged in a bewildering variety of ways: humanity participates in a cosmos laced with evil and even with sin of its own making. Parts II-IV of the second volume of *God Encountered*, therefore, will explore these three clusters of themes—a *secunda secundæ* devoted to *the central Christian doctrines.*

Needless to say, given the organic unity of the Creed and of the catholic theology that reflects on it, it is impossible to separate fundamental theology from the central Christian doctrines and *vice versa.* Any physical separation of the two, therefore, is predicated, not on the need for a separate *understanding*, but on the need for orderly *exposition*; and the latter must be kept firmly subordinate to the former (§7, 2). Separate courses in Fundamental Theology or Central Christian Doctrines, in other words, do not imply affirmations about separate realms of Christian truth or even theological inquiry. Accordingly, the reader will find the Introduction and Part I laced with Christian doctrine, just as Parts II-IV will be shot through with fundamental theological issues.

In orchestrating the Christian profession of this divine *exitus*, this second volume will, naturally, continue and build upon the first. From a different point of view, however, it will merely restate the first volume, albeit in a fuller form. That is, the second volume will be somewhat like a transparency superimposed on the first volume—particularizing it and showing lots of fresh doctrinal and theological detail. This new detail will especially (but by no means exclusively) enhance and orchestrate the five final chapters of the first volume, which (it will be recalled) offered a broad map of the Christian faith as a positive religion.

Despite the greater depth of exploration undertaken and the greater wealth of detail offered (or perhaps, precisely because of this depth and wealth), this second volume will show, even more clearly than the first, that *God Encountered* is a *basic* systematic account of catholic faith and theology and no more. Ever so many *quæstiones disputatæ* are mentioned rather than disputed; some are not even mentioned. While this certainly betrays the limits of the author's knowledge, it also reflects his commitment to *catholic openness*.

The reason for this is that a most characteristic feature of the catholic theological tradition is concern with unity and broad coherence, and hence, with *connections*. The unity of both the Christian faith and Christian theology demands that, in the constant search for a configurative balance between Faith and Culture, the Church and its theologians cultivate openness, by attempting to establish dynamic relationships with humane, secular concerns, especially those of the present day. For catholicity's devotion to the historic Tradition is basically subservient to the achievement of this ever so desirable balance in the present moment; the ideal of lasting unity remains catholic only so long as the present Christian community remains committed to openness—as long, that is, as it frankly engages the particularities of present temporal and local contexts (§§2; 14; 15). Accordingly, catholic theology tends to view the history of the Christian community as the record of organic unity constantly, respectfully, and patiently being forged out of raw, but exciting multiplicity. The systematic theological elucidation of historic Christian faith is an ongoing object lesson in the *embracing* of such multiplicity in the very act of offering to *structure* it, by turning (to borrow Shakespeare's portrayal of the poet's role, in the fifth act of *A Midsummer Night's Dream*) "the forms of things unknown ... to shapes," and to give them a "local habitation and a name" in the universe of Christian doctrine.

One real strength of this type of approach to systematic theology is that it operates from inside the historic faith-Tradition; it agrees to interpret both Faith and Culture from a stance of committed involvement rather than attempting to judge them from a higher, allegedly impartial point of vantage. This can be put differently. Despite serious lapses into totalitarian ideologizing (a fairly recent Roman Catholic one will be examined in §86), the catholic tradition in theology has been content to operate *from a particular viewpoint within history and the cosmos.* If there should exist such a thing as an Archimedean point of leverage from which the earth and its fullness can be moved, the catholic tradition holds that God alone has a handle on it. (Saint Thérèse of Lisieux, in the story of her life, reflects how only Almighty God can be the Archimedean fulcrum, and only prayer the lever; in lifting up the world with their prayer, she adds, the saints have succeeded in doing the impossible.) And as for human nature, the catholic tradition holds that it is not available in pure, totally fixed form. Catholic theology at its truest and best, therefore, has been *discretionary*: it has viewed Christianity as an ongoing encounter between an infinitely resourceful God and an endlessly flexible cosmos. Hence, it has tended to defend the Christian faith by offering, not a free-standing, absolute, ideological account of it and of its critique of non-Christian positions, but an *interpretative* one—one that *participates* in the historic Tradition, in its wealth as well as its vicissitudes (§56).

To be more believable, these fine explanations should perhaps be restated in a manner a little less sanguine. *God Encountered* is committed, as a matter of deliberate choice, to a positive, ecclesial bias in systematic theology (cf. §4; §31, 1-3), without, however, disparaging fundamental theological pursuits in any way. Not surprisingly, therefore, its commitment to fundamental theology draws its principal warrant from the profession of Christian faith itself (cf. §23, 3), as this book will abundantly show. In other words, the development of a theological anthropology, by means of a careful reflection on the depth of human self-awareness, is neither a concession to the Enlightenment nor an exercise in liberal, agnostic modernism. On the contrary, it is a fundamental requirement of the need for human integrity in believing—an integrity created and cherished by God. Taking human self-awareness seriously guarantees that the *positive* elements of the Christian faith are appreciated as they should be, namely, as historic instances of true divine self-communication to humanity and the world—a self-communication that prompts, not credulity, but true faith-responses (§25, 2). Accordingly, *God Encountered* recognizes, as a matter of positive Christian theological principle, that critical, transcendental reflection, both on Christian faith and on human experience, is fully legitimate. The great Tradition recognizes such reflection as integral to the Christian faith because it is owed to humanity and the world by virtue of their natural, God-given integrity—an integrity acknowledged, treasured, and indeed enhanced, by faith.

Arguably, all of this holds true nowadays more than ever before. Christian faith, as Karl Rahner and Bernard Lonergan, in their various ways, never tired of emphasizing, encourages native human integrity to affirm itself in its enjoyment of the search for meaning, especially amid the enormously differentiated demands of life in a bewilderingly pluralistic world.

However, not even these brave declarations of principle should be too readily swallowed. Eager as we Christian theologians may be to justify critical reflection on humanity and the world by recourse to the Christian faith itself, we must not overlook the fact that much of the culture that surrounds us is quite determined to think for itself anyway; it obviously does not feel any great need for the Church's seal of approval in doing so. In fact, many elements in our culture suggest that the shoe is, rather, on the other foot. For there is a sometimes discouragingly wide chasm between two positions. On the one hand, there is the fairly *unified*, structured humanism of the *Christian* Tradition represented by the Church; on the other hand, there is the *secular* insistence (integral to the cultural climate of the United States, where the insistence has the endorsement of national heroes like Lincoln and Jefferson) that human freedom and integrity are, in practice and in the long run, better warranted by *dispersal*—that is, by the intentional cultivation of the widest variety of ways of thinking and living. Principled pluralism, in other words, is widely regarded as a more reliable guide to truth than Christian faith.

Quite frequently, those who speak for Christianity sincerely extend a cordial welcome to pluralism. But they often fail to convince. In the eyes of many libertarian inhabitants of the "real world," there is liable to lurk, behind such appealing professions of Christian openness, a lack of critical realism, of the kind frequently found among religious persons too naively comfortable with authority and too reluctant to engage in free exploration. Worse still, many of our contemporaries remain wary of a purposeful, authoritarian ecclesiastical obscurantism posturing as candor, but in reality intent on helping cast an unholy spell on humanity and the world—a "design of darkness to appal" (Robert Frost, "Design").

No wonder that there have arisen, in Christian churches, responsible theologians whose thinking has been shaped by the pragmatic, critical pluralism that surrounds us. Accordingly, some of them have chosen, in fundamental theology, to take a consistently critical stand, well clear of any unified ecclesiastical tradition. This move puts fundamental theology in a rather sharply polarized relationship vis-à-vis Christian doctrine, of course, but the gain in public credibility (so its practitioners appear to think) is well worth the ecclesial inconvenience. Part I of volume 2 of *God Encountered*, while acknowledging the credibility problem, has chosen not to adopt this solution. And there's the rub.

I have long found this whole issue an uncomfortable one. In this book, which offers a full-size fundamental theology, I must finally face it. My brief encounter with David Tracy in Part I (§92), therefore, represents a watershed. Honesty demands that I add at once that my treatment will fall short of doing justice to either the integrity or the learning of Tracy's work. But a word of explanation is appropriate, since it will also help me restate the fundamental options behind *God Encountered* as a work of systematic theology.

The issue is not whether there is flat disagreement between David Tracy and myself; there isn't. Nor is it whether there is room for argument, for there is. The issue, as I see it, is far more elusive. As I measure the latitude for reasoned agreement and disagreement between David Tracy and myself, my eye finds itself drawn in the direction of an area of less arguable concerns. I suspect that what tells the two of us apart is a wider area of divergent commitments, predicated on tastes, experiences, and perspectives, and hence, an area less easy to chart, let alone to take definitive positions in. Where Tracy appears to favor a critical *epochē* as the way to reliable understanding, I am predisposed to abandon; consequently, while

Tracy's thought is often austerely formal and dialectical, mine tends to delight in drama and expressiveness. In keeping with this, I would suggest, Tracy expects more from the critical approach to religion and culture favored by modern social science than I do; I tend to get absorbed by the aesthetics of it all first and to think later. Hence, I am liable to overstate where Tracy (it would seem) will understate; in the end, therefore, I may have to draw nearer to the Truth by subtraction and pruning and *apophasis*, Tracy by addition and letting be and *cataphasis*. Also, as a fundamental theologian, Tracy typically approaches the correlation between modernity (and postmodernity) and catholicism from the angle of the former; characteristically, too, he views the correlation as precarious. Consequently, he views the relationship between fundamental theology and Christian doctrine as an "uneasy alliance." I approach that same relationship from an eschatological point of view—that is, from the angle of explicit Christian faith and especially hope; characteristically, I view the correlation in the perspective of reconciliation—that is, as basically positive. Finally, Tracy would appear to conceive of the theologian primarily as a single *individual* who has several contending *publics to address*—the church, the academy, and society at large. I certainly prefer to think of the theologian as *one among many* in a *particular community* of worship groping for intellectual integrity—a community, too, that helps shape, to a significant extent, the common culture. My view makes of the theologian primarily a conscience and a memory and a voice of both the historic Christian community and the academic tradition—that is, a mind and a soul formed and informed by the variety of historic experience, of conflict, and of such resolution as has been achieved.

For all these differences, what makes both David Tracy and me typically catholic (and even Catholic), I suggest, is our acceptance of a dialectic of provisionality—the deliberate *patience* with which we approach theological reflection on the world and humanity, on grounds that are both foundational and eschatological. So those issues between us that I feel unable, for now, to explore I happily entrust to the continuing catholic theological tradition. That broad stream can be trusted to accommodate them.

Meanwhile, in writing this volume, I have not been without other companions and sparring-partners. Like the first, this second volume owes a debt of gratitude to a handful of good friends and reliable critics of substantial parts of it: Eamon R. Carroll, O. Carm.;

Charles Hallisey; Francis X. Clooney, S.J.; John McCarthy; Jill N. Reich; Virginia M. Ryan; George Schner, S.J.; and James J. Walter (if a collegiality is defined in terms of sustained interest and assistance, Jim is a superb colleague). There was also a quiet variety of occasional conversation partners, critics, and supporters: Charles Brannen, S.J.; Jan Maarten Bremer; J. Patout Burns; Susana Cavallo; Louis Dupré; Ernest L. Fortin, A.A.; Timothy A. Howe, S.J.; Dennis K. Keenan; David J. Livingston; Vilma Seelaus, O.C.D.; Thomas H. Tobin, S.J.; David Tracy; Urban C. von Wahlde; John L. White. Without their competent and often quite discerning advice and criticism, this book would have been much less reliable in many areas of detail and far more given to unwarranted generalization. Odds are, too, that without their interventions (and without close to three weeks in Sicily in June, 1990) I would have felt a great deal more often alone and lost *in una selva oscura*, trying to recall what the point of the whole enterprise was in the first place. I also fondly recall my generous friends in the parish community of St. Clement's, Lancaster, Wisconsin, and especially the pastor, my friend John Urban, at whose hospitable rectory many pages of this book were revised. And last but not least, there was my graduate assistant, Michele Langowski, who put the indices together with the speed and the dexterity that are the privilege of youth. She was joined, on the home stretch, by Nancy Johnson, of the Fine Arts Department of Loyola University, Chicago, who did the typesetting with an energetic commitment to speed, accuracy, and elegance, and by Father Michael Naughton, O.S.B., and Messrs. Mark Twomey and Peter Dwyer, of The Liturgical Press, three capable men embodying a quiet, reassuring friendliness.

There is one more person to whom I am much indebted, except in his case the indebtedness is subtler as well as more pervasive. Before I ever started work on *God Encountered*, when I was still a member of the Roberts House Jesuit community at Boston College, I enjoyed, in the course of many a Fall semester in the years 1977-1984, the daily privilege of Hans-Georg Gadamer's urbane, learned, and encouraging company. Invariably, when the occasion arose, he showed interest in, and respect for, every kind of knowledge, wherever and at whatever level of sophistication it occurred; he showed it by the twin arts of attentive listening and asking, not intentionally "hermeneutical" questions, but genuinely inquiring ones. In this way, he demonstrated that he had his eye on the object of his conversation partners' interests far more than on his own; that is, he was practicing hermeneutics by actual encounter at least as much as he must have been theorizing about methods of inquiry in his own mind. I am grateful to him for accepting the dedication of this second volume, and I hope that some of his polite presence and his thoughtful and thought-provoking habit of searching and probing has shaped the discussions in it.

A final piece of advice to the reader. *God Encountered* is becoming a large work—one larger than originally envisaged. But its size has less to do with the *volume* of doctrinal statements and theological positions it contains than with the charms and complexities of the *journey* it has taken to move from statement to statement and from position to position. By hindsight, this adds up to an object-lesson in systematic theology as well as a guide to the proper use of this book. Part of what this book (and indeed all of volume 2) means to offer to the reader is the suggestion that the Tradition is better understood as an *exercise in movement* than as a *museum of monuments*. Let us turn Newman's image of Revelation as a country enveloped in twilight (§15, 3) into a little allegory, in order to state what this book very much wants to convey. Catholic systematic theology is less a redrawing of existing maps of those portions of the Land of Revelation and Reason that enjoy the light of day, than a careful journey of exploration through darker, more enigmatic regions, in search of the more hidden mysteries that connect the well-known and manifest parts. Accordingly, it will eventually be proposed in Part II of volume 2 (§110, 5) that the living Tradition is greater than its brightest moments, teachers, and establishments, simply because it represents the ongoing test of Christian faith rather than its temporary triumphs. Tradition has a lot in common with *drama*, and the wisdom of a play comes across *in the process of performance* rather than in the *tableau* achieved just before the final curtain drops, let alone in the published text.

At the end of the first part of this second volume, therefore, not all will be said and done. The reason for this is only partly that there remains a *secunda secundæ* to be finished and a third volume to be started—scarcely an irrelevant fact from an author's point of view. It is that the value of this book will depend, not so much on the reliability of the account it gives of the *state* of Christian doctrine and catholic theology, as on the degree to which it will turn out to enable readers to go on and become participants in the *living tradition* of both. And even beyond that, this book has been written in hopes of suggesting how Christian doctrine and catholic theology ultimately live off and commend what monuments can only recall and movements can only approximate: the never-ceasing, worshipful silences and songs of praise and thanksgiving and supplication of Christian communities as well as individual Christians, in the actual presence of the living God—the One Who Was, Who Is, and Who Is to Come.

Frans Jozef van Beeck, S.J.

Abbreviations

AF	*The Apostolic Fathers.* Edited and translated by Kirsopp Lake. *Loeb Classical Library.* 2 vols. London: William Heinemann; New York: G. P. Putnam's Sons, 1930.
AG	*Ad Gentes:* The Decree on the Church's Missionary Activity (Vatican II).
AristBWks	*The Basic Works of Aristotle.* Edited by Richard McKeon. New York: Random House, 1941.
Barry	*Readings in Church History.* Edited by Colman J. Barry. Rev. Ed. (3 vols. in 1). Westminster, MD: Christian Classics, 1985.
Bettenson	*Documents of the Christian Church.* Second edition. Edited by Henry Bettenson. London, Oxford, and New York: Oxford University Press, 1967.
CC	*Corpus Christianorum.* Turnhout: Brepols, 1953-.
CF	*The Christian Faith in the Doctrinal Documents of the Catholic Church.* Edited by J. Neuner and J. Dupuis. New York: Alba House, 1982.
CSEL	*Corpus Scriptorum Ecclesiasticorum Latinorum.* Vienna: F. Tempsky, 1866-.
DH	*Dignitatis Humanæ:* The Declaration on Religious Freedom (Vatican II).
DictSp	*Dictionnaire de spiritualité ascétique et mystique: Doctrine et histoire.* Edited by Marcel Villers and others. Paris: Beauchesne, 1932-.
Dods	*The Works of Aurelius Augustine: A New Translation.* Edited by Marcus Dods. Edinburgh: T. & T. Clark, 1971-76.
DS	*Enchiridion Symbolorum Definitionum Declarationum de Rebus Fidei et Morum.* Edited by H. Denzinger; revised by A. Schönmetzer. 32nd Edition. Freiburg: Herder, 1963.
DV	*Dei Verbum:* The Dogmatic Constitution on Divine Revelation (Vatican II).
FC	*The Fathers of the Church: A New Translation.* Washington, DC: The Catholic University of America Press, 1948-.
Goodspeed	*Die ältesten Apologeten.* Edited by E. J. Goodspeed. Reprint. Göttingen: Vandenhoeck & Ruprecht, 1984.
GS	*Gaudium et Spes:* The Pastoral Constitution on the Church in the Modern World (Vatican II).

HG	A. C. Cotter, *The Encyclical "Humani Generis" with a Commentary.* Weston 93, MA: Weston College Press, 1951.
Jaeger	*Gregorii Nysseni Opera.* Edited by W. Jaeger and others. Leiden: E. J. Brill, 1921-.
LG	*Lumen Gentium:* The Dogmatic Constitution on the Church (Vatican II)
LThK	*Lexicon für Theologie und Kirche.* Edited by Josef Höfer and Karl Rahner. First Edition. Freiburg: Herder, 1957-1965; suppl. vols. 1967-1968.
LXX	The Septuagint version of the Jewish Scriptures.
MT	The Masoretic text of the Hebrew Scriptures.
NA	*Nostra Ætate:* The Declaration of the Relationship of the Church to Non-Christian Religions (Vatican II).
NPNF	*A Select Library of the Nicene and Post-Nicene Fathers of the Christian Church.* New York, 1887-1892; Oxford, 1890-1900.
PG	*Patrologia Græca.* Edited by J. P. Migne. 162 vols. Paris: 1857-1866.
PGL	*A Patristic Greek Lexicon.* Edited by G. W. H. Lampe. Oxford: Clarendon Press, 1961-1968.
PL	*Patrologia Latina.* Edited by J. P. Migne. 221 vols. Paris: 1844-1864.
PlatoCDia	*The Collected Dialogues of Plato.* Edited by Edith Hamilton and Huntington Cairns. *Bollingen Series,* LXXI. Princeton: Princeton University Press, 1961.
RW	Jan van Ruusbroec. *Werken.* 4 vols. Edited by J. van Mierlo, J. B. Poukens, L. Reypens, M. Schurmans, and D. A. Stracke. Mechelen: Het Kompas; Amsterdam: De Spiegel, 1932-34.
SC	*Sacrosanctum Concilium:* The Constitution on the Liturgy (Vatican II).
SC	*Sources chrétiennes.* Paris: Cerf, 1940ff.
SchrzTh	Karl Rahner, *Schriften zur Theologie.* 16 vols. Einsiedeln, Zürich, and Köln: Benziger Verlag, 1954-84.
TheoInv	Karl Rahner, *Theological Investigations.* 21 vols. Baltimore: Helicon/New York: Herder and Herder/Seabury; London: Darton, Longman & Todd, 1966-88.
UR	*Unitatis Redintegratio:* The Decree on Ecumenism (Vatican II).
VatIIPr	*Acta et Documenta Concilio Oecumenico Vaticano II*

	Apparando. Series II (*Praeparatoria*). Rome: Typis Polyglottis Vaticanis, 1964-69.
VatIISyn	*Acta Synodalia Sacrosancti Concilii Oecumenici Vaticani II.* Rome: Typis Polyglottis Vaticanis, 1970-80.
Vg	The (Latin) Vulgate text of the Scriptures.

Tradition and Interpretation

[§56] THEOLOGIZING IN THE PRESENCE OF THE GREAT TRADITION

[1] Writing a systematic theology that honors the great Tradition of the undivided Christian Church can be, disconcertingly at times, an exercise in irresolution.

After the happy completion of the first, daybreak volume of *God Encountered*, such a melancholy move to open the second volume may seem out of place. A case, perhaps, of the noontide devil—the *dæmonium meridianum[1]*—plaguing an author who has by now become the slave of his own enterprise and come to the realization that he is going to get the heat of the midday to bear in putting together the second volume? Is he taking out insurance against future failure, or is he bent on focusing on the dark side of attainment, afflicted by the mechanisms of self-defeat, of the kind that psychologists have come to associate with "the success-fearing personality"?[2] Perhaps. Or perhaps not, for the sentiment does have objective reference. Ambiguity, and the irresolution it tends to produce, one discovers in due course, lurk out there, in the very concept of writing a systematic theology animated by the great Tradition.

The ambiguity begins with the realization that *scripta manent*—what is written stays around. Books, in and of themselves, are like monuments; they are made in order that they may endure and attract notice. Even the humblest paperback lays claim to being memorable; projected three-volume works trumpet the claim. But what is *ambiguous* about this?

[2] Accepting the understanding of the great Tradition and its advancement (cf. §14, 4; §55, 4) as the true measures of good catholic theology means deferring to a formidable tribunal, and one of very long standing. Before it, quite a few books of theology have wilted and been rated less than memorable. To the extent that they have been so judged, they have also fallen short of their professed pur-

pose—that of commending the great Tradition. If such books have at all succeeded in honoring the Tradition, they have done so only feebly, or even unintentionally—that is to say, *sub contrario,* by contrast, in a negative fashion, by *not* living up to it. *Scripta manent,* indeed; but many of them do so by standing, penitentially, on library shelves, offering dusty apologies for a job not very convincingly done.

But then again, if books that fall flat do little good, they happily do not do much harm either, at least ordinarily and in the long run. The dignity and the authority of a trade may not be shown to advantage by the work of journeymen, but they are not measured by it either. To the extent, therefore, that authors turn out to be journeymen, their works prove to be little more than marginal comments, often wide of the mark, transient period-pieces, remembered by only a few (again, at least in the long run), and justly so. Or to change the metaphor, much as mediocre theology is welcome to applaud the great Tradition from the sidewalks, it fails to become part of the march. If it honors the parade, it does so by being relevant to it only in passing. In the meantime, the Tradition itself continues, sovereign and unabridged, if momentarily shortchanged, despite the well-intentioned applause.

But there *are* books that turn out memorable. The problem is, though, that to the extent they do, no matter how deep the devotion that animates them, they *also* tend to become seductive. In proportion as authors prove to be masters of sorts—committed witnesses to the great Tradition and capable interpreters of it—they are *also* likely to obscure and detract from the very thing to which they succeed in testifying. The finger which the master points at the moon will become part of his disciples' view of it, and to that extent it will *also* deprive the disciples of the more single-eyed (that is, the fuller, more integral) vision.

At the mere thought of this, a shadow of inadequacy will settle on every section one writes, even the most satisfactory, tempting one to rewrite and, eventually, to unwrite. True, one remembers that in the best of cases a work of theology will succeed in generating new understanding despite its partiality. In such cases, the whole of the Tradition will be set astir and come alive, if ever so slightly; and in the process, it will advance by one short but intrinsically authoritative step (cf., again, §55, 4). But some loss remains unavoidable even there. A memorable work, precisely by being memorable, *also* obtrudes itself on the memory; in the very act of furthering the Tradition, it also draws attention to itself; and in so doing it at least partly obscures or narrows the Tradition.

And so it is that by dint of pondering the unsettling alternative between irrelevance and seductiveness, the systematician devoted to the Tradition can get caught—caught between the desire for success and the fear of it, and between the fear of failure and the desire for it.

[3] In this predicament, if it is permitted to compare the little with the great,[3] it helps to go to that same great Tradition for relief, in the form of medicinal analogies, and to come, thankfully, to the discovery that things have never been otherwise, really.

The example of Augustine comes to mind. His profound, ardent, and highly personalized theological vision has turned out to be one of the West's most reliable bridges to the tradition that preceded him. But it has *also* served to alienate the Church of the West from the East, and to blind it to some essential theological and humane elements of the patristic past—elements of which Augustine himself was still broadly aware (despite his limited Greek), but which he did not champion as forcefully as his favorite themes. In this way, it can be said that "to Roman culture at the time of the fall of the Empire, Augustine gave a prayerful soul, but to the Middle Ages he gave a series of problems."[4]

To cite a more telling example, the West's growing reliance on Aquinas' genius has *also* served to confine and constrict the understanding of the Christian faith; in fact, this has happened more than once in the course of time. Thus, in proportion as the sheer talent resident in Aquinas' *Summa* succeeded, over time, in gaining acceptance, it also increasingly came to obstruct scholasticism's view of much of the preceding theological tradition (with the exception of Augustine, of course). Where Thomas the *Doctor* was remembered, Thomas the *Sententiarius* tended to be forgotten; consequently, the West's last surviving anthology of patristic thought, Peter Lombard's *Sentences*, already thickly encrusted with the comments of Aquinas and other scholastics, entirely disappeared from view (cf. §80, 1). On another score, as Michael J. Buckley has so ably shown in his book *At the Origins of Modern Atheism*, Aquinas the philosopher was remembered so well at the dawn of the modern era that Christian theology began to appeal to him in the interest of abdicating its responsibility for the fundamental question of God's existence, so as to relegate it to philosophy (cf. §68, 1, [*l*]; §84, 2, a, [*u*]; §99, 3, a). Aquinas' genius had negative side effects even as late as the nineteenth and twentieth centuries, in the wake of the

Thomistic revival introduced by Leo XIII's encyclical *Æterni Patris* of 1879 (DS 3135-3140).[5] It is true, twentieth-century neo-Thomism largely succeeded in rediscovering the full scope of Thomas' "intellectualism"; accordingly, it managed to shake off the rationalist prejudices that had infected its ancestry in the eighteenth and nineteenth centuries (cf. §87, 2, a). Still, even this open variety of Thomism repeatedly turned out to be surprisingly resistant to the retrieval and advancement of important parts of the great Tradition, especially Scripture, the Liturgy, and the Church Fathers. And so on.

[4] All of this is beginning to suggest conclusions. First of all, the great Tradition must in any case be respected, if it is to be advanced at all. Secondly, given the Tradition's depth and breadth and especially the holiness that resides in it, it is not inappropriate to sigh, with Hans Urs von Balthasar, for *confessores* rather than mere *professores* for the accomplishment of the theological task. But thirdly, not even *confessores* are an unshakable guarantee that the Tradition will be represented in its full compass in every circumstance. Nor even will the authoritative *magisterium* avail, no matter how central its role in keeping the Tradition true to itself. For the faith resident in the Tradition is dependent on *continuing interpretation* for its continued life, and, interpretation being what it is—a mixture of perception and overlooking, of mindfulness and forgetfulness—*the Tradition cannot help being beset by oblivion and loss as well as cheered by recovery and gain.* This holds regardless, whether the current confessors and professors fail or succeed.

Stating this is not an exercise in liberal, modernist relativism. Even less is it an exercise in reactionary cynicism, of the kind that seems to delight nowadays in insinuating that any theologian's interpretation of the Tradition is as plausible as any other's, and that, therefore, none of their theologies make any *real* difference. (Our only assurance of *really* understanding the Christian faith-tradition, it is then sometimes added, with a fraudulent appeal to catholicity, lies in following the *magisterium* alone.) Rather, being aware of the presence of both loss and gain in the Tradition involves an act of faith, albeit one in the tradition of Ecclesiastes. For better for worse, the Tradition must be carried forward, just as Jesus Christ must continue to be proclaimed whatever the proclaimers' motives, whether they preach from envy and rivalry or from good will (cf. Phil 3, 15ff.). And just as the living Christ remains greater than the proclamation he alone authorizes, so the Tradition

remains greater than any current renditions of it, even the most authoritative. For that reason, those do most to carry it forward who
most allow themselves to be carried forward by it, which is the work
of grace. Not surprisingly, the second Vatican Council taught that
the *magisterium* is—that is to say, that it should be—at the *service* of
the Word of God as it lives in Scripture and Tradition (DV 10).
Theologians need not be part of the authentic *magisterium* to take
this to heart as well.

[5] In our own century, we have witnessed this issue several times,
and at close range. Karl Barth has been praised for having restored
the Christian *confessio* and blamed for having proposed a narrow-
minded version of it, constricted and constricting. But it must be
recalled that any constriction was caused, not so much by Barth's
weaknesses (though some of them were glaring indeed) as by the
magnificence and the creativity of his prophetic, confessional retrieval of many great themes from the Reformation as well as from
the undivided Tradition. Fascinated by the compelling splendor of
Barth's system (and especially by its inner unity), and beguiled by
Barth's own disavowal of the Tradition's theological authority, many
Barthians, quite unaware of the depth of the master's attachment
to the Tradition, came to credit him for what he had really found
elsewhere. In so doing, they showed how much less deeply and
broadly they themselves understood the Tradition than Barth, who
had struggled to understand it; accordingly, they came to render
and develop his alleged thought less reliably. No wonder Barth's
grand thunder was frequently turned into mere stridency.

Of late, charges of narrowing the Tradition (though on rather
different grounds) have been laid at Karl Rahner's door in certain
quarters—again, it would seem, unfairly so. It is pointless, of
course, to deny that Rahner's thought suffers from substantial weaknesses—the most notable, perhaps, being his lack of affinity with
Scripture and with the theological wealth of the Church's liturgical
tradition, and his overconcentration on the human person as the
potential rather than the actual recipient of God's self-communication (§14, 4, a, [k]; §31, 3; cf. §22, 3, d). But his wonderful
gifts—his deep rootedness in, and loyalty to, the great Tradition;
the sheer passion and radiance and depth of his synthetic talent in
dealing with the fundamental issue of Christian faith and human
integrity; and most of all, his indubitably mystical bent—all of these
mark him as a *confessor*, no matter how professorial he often sounds.

Still, if the modern Church's understanding of the great Tradition has been decisively advanced by Rahner's vision, it has also been eclipsed, in part, by its power and attractiveness. But that was only to be expected. Consequently, saying that his theological account of the Catholic faith is incomplete is a truism, not a legitimate accusation. It simply amounts to saying that it cannot stand entirely by itself; that for that reason it must not become the object of fascination; that, if it is to be fully understood, it must be placed in the context of the Catholic Tradition that inspired it in the first place. Suggesting that his account of the faith, solely by reason of its incompleteness, is misleading or even fatally flawed amounts to blaming the teacher for the (alleged) sins of (some of) his somewhat less discerning disciples [a]. It also implies, insidiously, that it is within the power of anyone, theologian or magisterial authority, to represent and interpret the great Catholic Tradition in any given situation in explicit doctrinal language in a way that is not in some way partial.

In this context, of course, Hans Urs von Balthasar is bound to come to mind. No modern theologian, not even Henri de Lubac, has so emphatically claimed catholicity, *both in its integrity and in its openness*, as the specific feature of his thought, and not without justification. There is ample warrant for respect and even admiration here, for von Balthasar is a true catholic master. But while he may have reorchestrated large segments of the great Tradition left untouched by Rahner's reflections, his own version of it, no matter how strikingly catholic, is partial, not comprehensive. His work, by virtue of its indisputable spiritual and cultural depth and breadth, certainly serves to enliven and advance the Tradition; but it *also* eclipses it in part, if only by attracting so much attention to its own, sometimes disproportionate virtuosity. And there are substantial weaknesses, too—mostly, it would appear, of the "symptomatic" kind (cf. §22, 3, c). Thus, von Balthasar's characteristic slogan "whoever says yes to more will be proved right" (cf. §8, 6, a, [*f*]) overlooks the real possibility of immaturity and naiveté in believing becoming a threat to faith. *Cordula* and pieces like it are irritating, if elegant, exercises in caricature born of anxiety and scholarly fastidiousness; they do an injustice to the magnanimity of the catholic Tradition by casting aspersions and raising specters [b]. Contrary to

---

[a] As Hans Urs von Balthasar comes close to admitting he is doing: *Cordula oder der Ernstfall* (2nd ed.), pp. 124-125. Cf. also §14, 4, a, [*l*].

[b] In the case of *Cordula* (ET *The Moment of Christian Witness*), the epilogue

impressions created, von Balthasar's far-flung ontological and
sacramental theology of the sexes, proposed with such finality, is
covered, neither by patristic precedent, at least not in the
Cappadocians and Maximus the Confessor, nor by explicit magisterial teaching.[6] His arrogant, uninformed disparagement of
"Eastern" forms of prayer, lumped together for mere polemical
convenience, is best forgotten. And finally, the manner in which
Adrienne von Speyr is accorded such great authority is not reminiscent of the rather more sober-minded affective relationship practices that have, in the Tradition, proved theologically reliable.

[6] All of this has consequences. If, for example, there should be
concern, in some places, that the great Tradition is being made to
suffer oblivion or constriction in our day, there is wisdom in not
blaming the problem only on incompetence, dissent, or heresy. Incompetent and dissenting theologians, or even heretical ones, may
very well exist and be at fault, but the great, capable, orthodox
teachers, too, must shoulder part of the responsibility, for the holy
intensity of their vision has disabling effects on the Tradition as
well. Not even the most sacred resolve, on the part of the *magisterium*, to guard the deposit of faith and hand it on entire can succeed

---

added, by way of *apologia*, to the second German edition shows symptoms of
rationalization; it does not succeed in dispelling the impression that the book is
largely the product of anger born out of anxiety. Von Balthasar concedes that
Cordula may have overstated its case, by presenting readiness to suffer martyrdom
as the decisive criterion of fidelity to the Catholic faith. However, he explains, the
book's purpose in doing so was serious: it meant to issue an *exhortation to holiness*
(p. 127) and a badly needed *warning* against creeping naturalism (p. 125). There
is a threefold problem with this justification. First of all, seriousness of purpose
is not in itself (that is to say, out of context) a reliable way to truth. For example,
there simply is no dependable answer available to the person who "seriously" raises
the completely hypothetical question if Saint Thomas Aquinas would have stood
the test of martyrdom, regardless whether such a person means to suggest that he
would have stood it or not. And conversely, professed eagerness to suffer martyrdom *may* be a sign, not of faith, but of fanaticism, as we have known (not since
modern psychology, but) at least since Clement of Alexandria. Secondly, ends do
not justify means. To be acceptable, warnings must be fair, even if they are inspired by concern about the integrity of the faith; warnings drawn from caricature
are unfair, and betray a different, unacknowledged agenda. Thirdly, there is the
problem of the medium interfering with the consciously intended message. What
does a diatribe bristling with broad overstatements, written in the immunity of a
study, have in common with martyrdom in such a way as to commend it? Do
words— especially words designed to sting, provoke, and even hurt—really add to
the appeal to martyrdom that emanates from Christ crucified? Could they, perhaps, detract from it?

in not drawing at least some attention to itself—again, at some expense to the very Tradition it is seeking to uphold and advance.

> [a] This especially applies whenever it is insufficiently emphasized that the Christian does not really believe "in" the Church, since the Church is not God (as, for example, Henri de Lubac is at pains to explain in his book *Christian Faith*). Thus whenever magisterial teaching focuses on the Church's, or the churches', *own* ecclesial fidelity in believing; whenever teaching is magisterial and apologetic rather than liturgical and kerygmatic; whenever the emphasis of the teaching is on *means* to living and proclaiming the gospel and the creed rather than on the gospel and the creed themselves (cf. §23, 4, c)—then the great Tradition is especially likely to suffer the kind of oblivion and loss that are the inevitable by-products of renewal, recovery, and gain.

[7] Given this situation, how can anyone, but especially catholic systematicians, continue to attempt to continue the Tradition, let alone to build monuments to it? How can anyone face the dilemma: mediocrity irrelevant to the Tradition *versus* merit that directs attention away from it? Face it, that is, without having one's sense of purpose in living and in writing dislodged by an irresolution from which there is no exit?

The threat of irresolution, though unsettling, is not necessarily debilitating in the end; it can be chastening, too, and in that case it tends to be liberating as well. Like all Christians, theologians must make their peace with the limitations of their times and places as well as their own personal ones, become carefree, and —most of all—learn that while it is wise to be devoted to the Tradition, it is unwise and unnecessary to feel too responsible for it. The New Testament warns against anxiety and worry (*merimna*), because they will inhibit free speech in the Spirit and suffocate the seed of God's word (Mt 10, 19 par. Lk 12, 11; Mk 4, 19 parr.). Those warnings apply here. No matter how carefully theologians must try to do justice to the great Tradition as it offers itself to their view, they will do well to remain carefree at heart, for the Tradition as a whole will forever be greater than all its interpretations and renditions, even the greatest. Hence, while the Tradition must command the respectful devotion of all in the Church, no one in the Church needs to claim control over it, and no one owns it—in fact, no one can be required to own it, that is to say, to comprehend it. And since no one in the Church owns the living Tradition, no one should attempt to gain control over it (cf. §55, 3) [c].

[8] To make all these points is to imply an understanding of the
fundamental theological dynamics of the Tradition's capacity for
ongoing regeneration and reformation, and especially of the source
of that capacity. There are, we have explained, themes and empha-
ses of the Christian faith that are obscured and pushed into reces-
siveness and even oblivion under the influence of the Tradition's
lapses as well as its great and creative moments. Would it be fair to
say that they go into abeyance and become dormant, though only
to await retrieval, in some new way, elsewhere and at another time?
And could it be that in thus being consigned to the recessive part
of the deposit of faith—that is, in Newman's image, in receding into the darkened parts of the landscape of Religious Truth—they revert, so to speak, to the company of the unstated mysteries that
subterraneously connect the manifest ones (§15, 3)? And could it
also be that there, in that obscurity, they get an opportunity (so to
speak) to recover from the overexposure they suffered while they
were prominent? And could that recovery consist in their losing
the brittleness of signification and the all-too-definite sharpness of
reference they had while they were prominent, and in their regain-
ing their inner integrity as well as their organic connections with
the other elements of the great Tradition? In other words, are
prayers, practices, and pronouncements that are eclipsed by new
developments in some fashion recycled? Do they become, as it
were, the Tradition's dead leaves? And do they, *precisely by having
been eclipsed*, enrich the dark soil of mystery that must always sustain
the explicit profession of the Christian faith? And could this
process account for the spring-like bursts of *living faith* that usually
accompany, at the watershed points in the Tradition (in the idiom
of the *nouvelle théologie*, in the 'fifties, its moments of *ressourcement*),
the retrieval of long-forgotten Christian prayers, practices, and pronouncements, and most especially the great retrievals that are the

---

[c] Cf. Nicholas Lash, *Easter in Ordinary*, p. 259: "... 'doctrine' is the name of an
activity, lest we be misled (by the more widespread use of the term as a
substantive) into supposing that the Christian doctrine of God is some substance
or 'thing' to which some group ... might lay claim as their *possession*. But nobody
owns the identity-sustaining rules of Christian discourse. As Christians, we
acknowledge *responsibility* for their use because we acknowledge, or confess, their
use to be 'authorized.' And even though it was people like us who *made* the rules,
they did so in the conviction that they were authorized to do so. Neither the
Fathers of Nicea, nor the authors of the Westminster Confession, supposed
themselves to be simply 'making up' the rules that they made."

historic reinterpretations of Scripture? Is it part of the great Tradition's dynamic that the living faith of the moment is always pushing some of the comforting faith of the past into oblivion *in order that it may get renewed to function once again, but in the service of the Church's revival, elsewhere or in the future* [d]?

[a] All of this involves not only the theological understanding of the *dynamics* by which the great Tradition moves, but also, inseparable from it, the understanding of its *boundaries*. During the third session of Vatican II, in the course of the discussion of the draft Dogmatic Constitution on Revelation *Dei Verbum*, Cardinal Albert Meyer of Chicago raised both of these issues. He began by observing that the draft presented "the life and the cult of the Church entirely under a positive aspect," and by noting, with approval, that the draft did not limit the Tradition to the explicit pronouncements that result from its authentic interpretation by the infallible *magisterium*. However, he went on to point out, with refreshing realism, an important consequence of this latter definition of Tradition, and to request that it be explicitly recognized, namely, that *the Tradition encompasses negative elements*. He explained, "such tradition is subject to *the limitations and defects of the Church Militant, which is the Church of sinners and which knows divine realities through a mirror darkly*." In fact, the cardinal added a few days later, "this living tradition *does not always and in all things advance and grow*. For when the Pilgrim Church contemplates divine matters, it can fail in some respects and actually has failed."[7] Both issues invite a brief reflection.

[b] To start with Cardinal Meyer's second suggestion, it was not adopted by the Council, but neither does the conciliar text exclude or disavow it. First of all, *Dei Verbum* explicitly states that

---

[d] And, it should be added, could this not all the more strongly apply to those doctrines, practices, and forms of worship referred to earlier in this section (§56, 6, a)—those that are further removed from the normative center of the Christian faith? If the answer to this question should be affirmative, then two ecumenically important conclusions would seem to follow. First of all, Fries and Rahner would be right in recommending that it is both necessary and sufficient towards ecclesial communion for member churches *to refrain from denying* the special doctrines of any church that honors the Nicene-Constantinopolitan Creed (§48, 3, b). Secondly, it would seem to be possible *intentionally* to consign to benign neglect very partial doctrinal affirmations and definitions made in the past, trusting that they will be retrieved once the churches that used to profess them with a vengeance have allowed them to recover their organic connections with the wider context of doctrine, conduct, and worship.

the "heritage of the faith" is "the one sacred deposit of the Word of God," which is "formed by sacred Tradition and sacred Scripture." In other words, the bearer—in technical terms, the "integral subject"—of the Christian faith tradition is "the entire holy people united with their shepherds in the teaching of the apostles, in the common life, in the breaking of the bread, and in prayers" (DV 10; cf. Acts 2, 42). That is, the great Tradition is simply the historic Christian community *insofar as it has persevered, and continues to persevere, in the Christian faith under the conditions of its pilgrimage* to the eschaton, under the guidance of its apostolic witnesses.

These conditions, of course, also include *sin*, so the question arises if sinful failures are part of the great Tradition. It is obvious that sin—in the twin forms of personal and systemic sin— has led (and will continue to lead) the Christian community to lapse occasionally, or even regularly, from its loyalty to the faith entrusted to it. These sinful lapses are not likely to be always quickly overcome, nor even are they likely to be immediately identified, except (perhaps) by prophets, who unfortunately, are not numerous, and in any case, not often instantly or generally recognized as prophets. Usually, therefore, it takes pastoral judgments, however precarious, to denounce and correct apparent sinful failure—judgments sometimes confirmed as sinful by the long retrospect of history, sometimes not. In any case, to the extent that lapses in the Tradition are reliably identifiable as sinful, they do not, it would appear, *as such* qualify as part of the great Tradition. In other words, it would seem reasonable to distinguish between the Church's factual *history* (which encompasses everything, including sinful departures from faith and their consequences) and its genuine *faith-tradition*. But even here too much clarity can be mistaken. Have the Christian community's recoveries from past sin not become part of the wisdom of the great Tradition? And hence, is not all sin, thanks to the merciful grace that embeds it, embraces it, and uses it as a goad to repentance, a *felix culpa*, and thus, part of the great Tradition, even while it occurs, and even in advance of its occurrence?

The dynamics of the positive advancement of the great Tradition under the conditions of the Christian community's earthly pilgrimage also encompass other elements of failure—elements that are not sinful in themselves, but simply a matter of the unavoidable *limitations* that go with the very process of tradition.

After all, the great Tradition does not exist apart from the tradition*s*; in fact, it might be said to subsist in them. But these tradition*s* are ambiguous; they both carry the great Tradition and narrow it. Even the most authoritative actors in the Tradition, including the *magisterium* (§56, 6), have obscured and eclipsed authentic elements in the Tradition in the very act of vigorously contributing to its development. It would seem to be as naive to ignore these lapses as it would be artificial to exclude them from the definition of the great Tradition. It is unnecessary to maintain that the Tradition travels the road of unqualified progress alone.

[c] These reflections, finally, help clarify the issue of the great Tradition's *boundaries*. Vatican II's identification of the entire Christian community as the bearer of the faith tradition prevents us from drawing these boundaries too narrowly. Thus it would be a lapse from catholicity to confuse the great Tradition with particular traditions, Yves Congar has explained.[8] Thus it would be a lapse into integralism to restrict the great Tradition to its manifest, magisterially defined elements (cf. §19, 1), if for no other reason than that these elements, as Newman well saw, convey their integral meaning only to the extent that they are interpreted in connection with elements less accessible to demarcation and definition: the recessive elements of "mystery" (§15, 3). In other words, it is part of the limitations inherent in the Church's pilgrim state that the outlines of the great Tradition must always remain somewhat indeterminate owing to the fact that it takes *interpretation* to establish both their true meaning and their authority. If this holds true for the Tradition as it is expressly proposed by the *magisterium,* then *a fortiori* the integral Tradition—that is, the Tradition as it embodies *both* the *sensus fidelium* and the witness of the apostolic *magisterium*—must be ultimately indeterminate. The great Tradition's boundaries, therefore, are not "clear" [e].

---

[e] These points attempt to meet a question formulated by Joseph A. Colombo, in his review of the first volume of *God Encountered.* To his own critical query, "what is the scope of the 'Great Tradition'?" Dr. Colombo adds (sensibly, I think), "While its core may be intuitively clear, its boundaries are not." I would have to say, in agreement, that the great Tradition's boundaries are indeed not *intuitively* clear in the sense of being not *intuitively* establishable as definite; but I would have to add they are not "clear" at all, *except in an interpretative sense* (that is, in a provisional, operationally adequate, discretionary sense: §63). This clarity, however, is

[9]   If this is how the great Tradition operates [f], then theologians, by respecting as well as trusting the tradition as a process that operates on a dynamic of both gains and losses, can more effectively interpret it in properly *theological* terms. That is, they can profess that the great Tradition of faith is *fundamentally* the embodiment of *God's* self-revelation, and hence, that it is *ultimately* to be entrusted to the safekeeping of God:

> See now: I, I am the One,
> and there is no God except Me;
> I bring about death, and will bring about life,
> shatter, and I will heal;
> and there are none that force anything from my grasp.
>
> (Deut 32, 39)

In the Christian Church, this profession of faith in God as the encompassing milieu of the living faith-tradition, along with all its vicissitudes, takes the form of the remembered promise of the risen Christ's presence till the close of the age (Mt 28, 20).

[10]   Against this stable backdrop of divine assurance, theologians can be carefree as well as responsible in dealing with the worrisome proximate aspects of Tradition. There, at close range, revelation remains a matter of manifestation set in mystery, of light combined with darkness; accordingly, revelation manifests itself, in the course

---

sufficient, both epistemologically and theologically.   In other words, it is incumbent (especially on the *magisterium*, but also on theologians, not to mention saints) to set genuinely intelligible boundaries to the Tradition, but this is done interpretatively—that is, by determining *in every here and now* the boundaries of the great Tradition. The latter, however, will essentially and forever transcend every determination and hence, continue to invite further interpretation. Thus it will always remain possible (and indeed theologically imperative) to seek for new "definitions" of what the great Tradition involves, by (re)interpreting the data of the great Tradition in the areas of worship, life, and teaching (cf. Frederick Lawrence, "Method and Theology as Hermeneutical"). This explanation, incidentally, entails a related point as well. The *Tradition* is to be distinguished (though never separated) from *Revelation*, the latter being the formal, generative element ("the soul") of the former. Yet they have this in common that they resist reduction to definition, and hence, to definitive boundaries. The issue of Revelation is to be taken up in §94.

[f] That is, on a dynamic that is non just progressive and cumulative, but partly cyclical: §13, 1, [e]; §51, 4, b, [s]. The reader familiar with the writings of Hans-Georg Gadamer (especially *Wahrheit und Methode* [ET *Truth and Method*] and some of the essays in the collection *Philosophical Hermeneutics*) will have noticed broad analogies between the conception of Tradition proposed here and Gadamer's treatments of tradition, respectively, as the game that *encompasses* the players, and as a process marked by both disclosure and concealment.

of history, in a succession of patterns of prominence and recessive-
ness (cf. §15, 3). Systematic theologians (among others) can indeed interpret and explicate it reliably, *as a tradition that truly involves God*, and thus help advance it in the world of place and time;
but they can do so only on condition that they develop a keen
sense of *partiality* and *conditionality*.

[11] The *partiality* involves the issue of *catholicity*. The *integrity* of
the catholic faith requires, as a corrective to every theologian's
inevitable partiality, an eager *openness* to the plurality of theological
systems and the acceptance of appreciative, interpretative, critical
communication among these systems as *theologically* meaningful
goods (§22, 1-2).

[a] Again, therefore, the great Tradition's catholicity requires a
consistently *hermeneutical attitude* (cf. §21, 4; §23, 5). *All* visible
church structures (including, for example, stated doctrinal commitments) are religiously meaningful as well as defensible as
catholic only insofar as they are placed, ultimately, in the perspective of *mystery*—that is to say, presented and commended as
essentially and constantly (re)interpretable.

[b] On this score, Hans-Georg Gadamer's insistence on the nev-
er-ending nature of the interpretative conversation is deeply
compatible with catholicity's reverence for the great Tradition.
It does not entail a commitment to principled relativism of the
agnostic variety; while it does encourage the ongoing reflection
that modern pluralism demands, it does not advocate continuous
discussion—that wearying means of avoidance—to sidestep commitment;[9] rather, it has affinities with the contemplative, devout
skepticism of Ecclesiastes. That is to say, it helps keep alive the
sense for "the mystical element in religion" (Baron Friedrich von
Hügel), which is inseparable from Christianity's eschatological
perspective.

[c] Heinz-Günther Stobbe, a vocal critic of the favorable recep-
tion Gadamer has enjoyed in recent Catholic theology, has
added a caveat to this. Modern social and behavioral sciences,
he explains, have amply shown how the will to attain the truth
(*der Wille zur Wahrheit*) can remain self-centered and turned inward, and thus destroy, or at least hinder, community rather
than establish it. Consequently, it would be a mistake, in accepting Gadamer's hermeneutical theory, simply to take for

granted, on the part of all involved in the conversation, an effective will to attain the truth—the ingredient that is so critical
to any hermeneutical process, as its foundation and motor force.
In making this point, Stobbe has underrated and even misunderstood the philosophic depth of Gadamer's commitment to
dialogue, mutuality, and circularity in hermeneutics; still, his
warning can profitably be integrated into the hermeneutical attitude, especially insofar as it is required in ecumenical dialogue.[10]

However, in his rather overstated doctoral dissertation *Hermeneutik—ein ökumenisches Problem*, Stobbe sadly moves from critique
to diatribe. On the one hand, he unfairly charges that Gadamer's insights have been used, in recent Catholic theology and
exegesis, to further a revival of the dated, old-fashioned Catholic
appeal to the decisive authority of Tradition; thus Gadamer has
contributed, in his view, to an undesirable "reconfessionalization
of exegesis" in Catholic circles.[11] On the other hand, and more
importantly, he brutally mischaracterizes Gadamer's hermeneutical theory itself. He does so by calling it the "exact theoretical
expression of the disintegration of civilized bourgeois consciousness," shaped as it is by "modern" philosophy and social theory.
This interpretation of Gadamer's work enables him to attack it,
with more savagery than understanding, as a *symptom* of the contemporary socio-cultural impasse rather than as a *response* to it.
Not surprisingly, in Dr. Stobbe's grandiloquent exposition, Gadamer's basic intentions are distorted: his emphasis on the role of
dialogue in the process that leads to understanding and his "relativistic trust in the conciliatory power of language" simply turn
out to mirror the structure of a society uncritically devoted to a
pluralism of purely opinionated points of view and to a relentless
differentiation of piecemeal functions, leading to specialization
and professionalization.[12]

In his impatient zeal, Stobbe does not appear to have enter-
tained the possibility that *Truth and Method* is precisely an attempt to help *interpret as well as heal* the socio-cultural situation
he so deplores: the fragmentation of understanding caused by
post-Enlightenment dogmatism of scientific-historicist origin. He
fails to see that Gadamer's plea in favor of tradition is intended
to *liberate* us (as well as the convictions we profess to live by),
both from our subjective prejudices and from the objectivist authorities that claim dominion over us. Stobbe's obvious failure
to appreciate this discredits his wholesale, dogmatic rejection of

Gadamer's patient hermeneutic as logically contradictory, radically committed to suspense of judgment (*durchgängig aporetisch*), and historicist [g]. Prejudice has blinded him to the contribution that Gadamer's work has made (and will, it is hoped, continue to make) toward a renewal of the catholic understanding of Tradition.

[12] The *conditionality* involves the issue of scholarly *method* and of the intellectual *attitude* it is predicated on. The attitude required here is a profound devotion to the Tradition—one rooted in an even deeper respect for it. There, in the respect that underlies the response, lies the difference between two basic styles of interpretation: those that honor the Tradition by *responding to it* and those that show admiration for it by *using it*—often, it would appear, as *an object*, that is to say, as *material upon which satisfying intellectual operations can be performed.*

[a] The distinction between response and use owes a debt to Martin Buber's distinction between relation (*Beziehung*) and experience/use (*Erfahrung/Gebrauch*) in *Ich und Du* [h].

Walter J. Ong has made a related point. He observes that modern culture, fascinated by print-literacy, promotes *objectivity* as an ideal of understanding (cf. §7, 1, a-b; §17, 1, a). Such objectivity "becomes possible when one envisions the world as essentially neuter, uncommitted, and indifferent to the viewer. Study of such a world is felt to be *not a response to the world but a*

---

[g] And so on and so forth, with a vehemence that is symptomatic. The unspoken issue would appear to be—what else?—*authority;* underneath all his vehemence, Stobbe seems to be clamoring for the restoration (by an effort of the will?) of a simpler, more "logical" world, in which the truth of the tradition can be established in a fashion that is both crystal clear and widely compelling. In the heat of battle, he mistakes a judicious friend for an enemy and lashes out at him. Somehow, I seem to have heard the tone of voice before.

[h] For Buber, "experience" (*Erfahrung*) connotes involvement with oneself rather than encounter with the other; hence, it implies that the other is approached as a thing (an "It"), and hence, *used.* Accordingly, Buber can commend the habit of "extricating oneself from the kind of intercourse with reality that consists in *experiencing and using* it [*sich aus dem erfahrenden und gebrauchenden Umgang mit den Dingen zu lösen*]." The reason for this is that the attitude that seeks experience is opposite to that of readiness for encounter: "Only the one who craves to use things can be the captive of any of them; the one who lives on the strength of present encounter can only be united with them [*Verhaftet etwelchen unter ihnen ist nur, wer Gier trägt, sie zu gebrauchen; wer in der Kraft der Vergegenwärtigung lebt, kann ihnen nur verbunden sein*]." Cf. *Ich und Du*, p. 123 (ET p. 152).

an operation upon it" (cf. §102, 6; §103, 2) [*i*].[13]

Andrew Louth, in his elegant monograph *Discerning the Mystery*, has made the point once again: not "objective" procedures, of the kind that wrap themselves in the authoritative mantle of "scientific method," give the mind access to the mystery that is the substance of the great Tradition, but truly participatory ones, of the kind that consistently attempt to understand the phenomena of faith as they beg to be understood, namely by participation.

[13]   A responsive, participatory style of interpreting the great Tradition is very much like reading a great story (or at least sizable, representative parts of it) to others, with interpretative commentary added to the reading. Good story-readers add to the story, but this is so only because they have put themselves at its service; they never allow their listeners to forget that they are really listening to someone else's text. Sound interpretation requires (and produces!) that height of chastened self-expression, which is disciplined transparency [*j*]. Now there's a standard for the practice of catholic theology! The astringency of scholarly method in the service of a response that does justice to the wealth of the other! No wonder systematic theology raises the issue, not only of method, but also of purity of intention (cf. §13, 1, b, [*g*]; §22, 3, c).

[14]   For the great Tradition will always be greater, animated as it is by two ultimately incomprehensible infinities: God living and faithful, and God's mirror-image, the ever-longing human spirit (cf.

[*i*] In the West, *geometry* (or mathematics) became the principal tool for this neutralization of the world (cf. §96, 4; §99, 4) in the service of complete, totally objective *realism*. Geometry was adopted even by artists, as demonstrated by the wholesale introduction of the laws of optical perspective as *costruzione legittima* ("legitimate construction"), first developed by Leone Battista Alberti in 1435, and presented as simply normative by Albrecht Dürer in his *Unterweisung der Messung* (ET *The Painter's Manual*) in 1525 (cf. §94, 5). For a characteristic example of "geometric neutralization," cf. the illustrations in *The Painter's Manual*, p. 434.

[*j*] On this theme (and on a rather more personal note) I recall a moment of instructive embarrassment many years ago. My violin teacher interrupted my deeply-felt rendition of a Mozart piece by gently holding my bowing-arm. "Listen," he said, "try just playing what's on the page—you know, the stuff Mozart wrote. Don't put so much feeling into it. There is enough feeling there already. Mozart put it there." It was to be years before I began to realize that what he was trying to teach me was that I must *interpret* Mozart's work, instead of *using* it— using it, that is, *for the purpose of my own self-expression and self-affirmation*. In light of this anecdote, a question arises. Could it be, curiously, that there is a self-serving agenda hidden behind some well-intentioned scholarly method, too?

§66, 3, a). Of these infinities, the latter is natively proportioned and attuned to the former, just as the former desires to meet and embrace the latter in a final "admirable exchange"; for the time being, however, they are involved in a struggle for mutual encounter and integration as immemorial as humanity. On this perspective, it becomes clear that it really takes witnesses—*martyres!*—to do the great Tradition justice. In the felt presence of such witnesses, it will also become obvious that systematic theology is, ultimately, the record of a *history of salvation*—the story of both the recovery and the fulfillment of the deepest aspirations of human integrity (cf. §38, 1; 4-5).

Even more deeply, therefore, systematic theology will have to be a form of *mystagogy*: it must lead the way into the mystery (cf. §55, 2). This means that it will be convincing to the extent that it is sensed to proceed from, and to lead into, worship—that is, the praise and thanksgiving (*confessio*) which is carried by God's Spirit (cf. §45; §34, 5). That Spirit of Truth, then, is the true soul of the great Tradition; it is also the soul of the Tradition's potential for regeneration—of recovery of whatever will inevitably get lost, whether by human failure or by human attainment. In this way, the Spirit leads us on the way, in the whole truth (Jn 16, 13). That Truth will also inspire (though, obviously, in varying degrees) theologies memorable and theologies forgettable, as well as theologies in between, and put all of them in their places, time and time again.

[15] It is against the background of these realizations, as sobering as they are reassuring, that this second volume of *God Encountered* sets out to elaborate its understanding of the substance of the Christian profession of faith. It will do so by offering a theological interpretation of the central affirmations of the great Tradition of the undivided Christian Church, or perhaps, in cases, a reinterpretation of them. And in all likelihood, it will do so without being able, in every case, to tell the difference between interpretation and reinterpretation—such are the tricks historical and cultural perspective tends to play on the understanding.

Part I

FUNDAMENTAL THEOLOGY

CHAPTER 1

Interpreting the Creed

PRELIMINARIES

[§57] THE PROFESSION OF FAITH: SYSTEMATIC DIMENSIONS

[1] Sometime in the mid 'fifties, at the beginning of an academic year, an unusual editorial appeared in *Propria Cures* ("Mind Your Own Business"), the student newspaper of the City University of Amsterdam in the Netherlands. It appeared over the signature of a new associate editor, who had written the piece to introduce himself to the paper's large, varied, and mostly undergraduate readership. If the editorial was a bit of a *coup*, this was in character with a far more remarkable fact: its author was a Catholic—the first ever to be appointed an editor of *Propria Cures*, it was rumored.

After demonstrating, in a few brisk paragraphs, that he had both the bite and the irreverence required for the job, the new editor closed with a reference to the most delicate aspect of his appointment: his religion. He declared that he was indeed a Catholic, and to let his readers know what this involved, he explained:

> I believe in God the Father Almighty,
>   creator of heaven and earth;
> And in Jesus Christ, his only Son, our Lord,
>   who was conceived by the Holy Spirit,
>   was born from the Virgin Mary,
>   suffered under Pontius Pilate,
>   was crucified, died, and was buried,
>   descended to hell,
>   on the third day rose again from the dead,
>   ascended into heaven,
>   is seated at the right hand of God the Father Almighty;
>   thence he will come to judge the living and the dead;
> I believe in the Holy Spirit,
>   the holy Catholic Church,
>   the communion of the saints,
>   the remission of sins,

>   the resurrection of the flesh,
>   and everlasting life. Amen.

Earnest sermonizing, with more than just an edge of irritation, is a national tradition in the Netherlands. Thus it was hardly surprising that the editorial aroused much principled venting of opinion, especially among non-students. Had the sacred Creed been profaned by the pagan page, or the agnostic page by the sectarian Creed? Or both by an upstart? Fortunately, there was much unprincipled amusement, too, especially among students. After all, the Apostles' Creed is not very often quoted by way of provocation in these martyrless days, nor do papers proud of their irreligious heritage generally allow themselves to be outwitted, least of all by their own staff. In any case, the new editor, having introduced and identified himself to his own satisfaction, had simply signed off, leaving his readers to make of it what they wanted—both of his gesture and of the Creed. He must have realized that by printing the text of the Creed as part of his editorial self-portrait, he was giving his readership a completely accurate definition of what it means to be a Christian, while at the same time, of course, carefully avoiding either saying what it meant or, what boils down to the same, what it meant to him and to the community he had professed to be a member of. At the very least, our Amsterdam undergraduate must have sensed that a Creed publicly stated yet left uninterpreted has great potential for provocation.

The particular incident aside, it is a matter of long experience that traditional formulas of commitment like the Creed, in and of themselves, harbor meanings that exceed particular uses. Even when used to take an individual stand, the Creed's affirmations are liable to elicit deep-seated responses in a wider circle. It takes an effort to dismiss the profession of a creed; even the most agnostic among us know the curious power exercised by traditional faith-conviction articulately expressed. Minimally, creeds will tease people or provoke them to contradiction; not infrequently, they will give rise to thought. No wonder the Creed is among the favorite texts used as points of departure in systematic theology.

[2] It was promised, in the first volume, that the divine *exitus* would be the subject-matter of the second volume of *God Encountered* (§23, 4). This was tantamount to promising that the present volume would give a reasoned, theological interpretation of the undivided Church's original profession of faith, that is to say, of the

expressive account the Church gives of its direct encounter with the divine condescension (§23, 4, c).

At an early date in the history of Christianity, it was explained, this original profession of the Church's faith took shape in two types of authoritative statements, both of them closely connected with the Church's worship as well as with the Christians' commitment to community: rules of faith (*regulæ fidei*) and baptismal creeds. The former reflect the process by which liturgical formulas developed into reliable, flexible guidelines for community catechesis as well as for the public profession of the faith in the encounter with non-believers (cf. §43, 4, a). The latter reflect, especially by virtue of their textual stability, the solidity of the faith-commitment celebrated and entered upon at the heart of the baptismal liturgies (§52, 1-2).

Towards the end of the first volume, it was also pointed out that it is necessary, both for the sake of the renewal of the Church and from a theological point of view, that the *teaching* of the *Christian faith* retrieve its connection with *community worship*. This, it was added, could be expected to restore the *baptismal profession of faith*—and hence, the faith of *all* members of the Church—to the center of the Church's teaching. It could also be expected to retrieve an organic understanding, rooted in worship, of *salvation history*, and in the context of that narrative, of the *hierarchy of truths* (§52, 8).

In focusing on a theological treatment of the Church's original profession of faith, the present volume is attempting to honor all those promises. In practical terms, it will do so by undertaking, as its central task, the development of a *systematic theological commentary on the Creed*.

[3] Four comments already made, or at least suggested, in the first volume may serve to delineate some of the dimensions of this project.

[a] First of all, the relationship between the *exitus* and the *reditus* is one of *asymmetry*. Both the natural order and the order of grace are governed by the dynamics of an encounter that is divinely initiated—of a partnership that is entirely of God's making (cf. §23, 4, b and notes). Hence, the commitment of *God Encountered* to the exposition and interpretation, in this second volume, of the divine *exitus* involves a proposal about the understanding of the *hierarchy of truths*.

The Church's basic profession of faith, played out in the *regulæ fidei* and stabilized as well as summarized in the authoritative creeds, conveys the Church's immediate response to the divine *exitus.* For this reason it is the central core of the undivided Church's great Tradition; in fact, though expressed in human language, it is the formal, operative element—the element directly prompted and enabled by the Holy Spirit (cf. §34, 6-7)— of the account of the *reditus* of the world and humanity to God. The account of God's *exitus*—the central profession of faith— must, therefore, be considered the foundation of the Christian faith, and consequently the standard against which all other doctrines are to be measured (cf. §23, 4, c).

It follows that the present volume, in taking the Creed for its theme, proposes to offer a theological account, both catholic and ecumenical (cf. §1), of *the content of the undivided Christian Church's profession of faith*, and in that sense, of the *normative nature of Christianity.*

[b] Secondly, it must be remembered that the separate treatment of the *exitus* and the *reditus* to be offered in *God Encountered* owes a debt to the need for elegant exposition (cf. §23, 4, a). In light of what has just been explained, it will be recalled that in reality the divine *exitus* and the *reditus* of humanity and the world occur simultaneously, not sequentially. Consequently, the theological account we must give of the all-enfolding and all-empowering divine self-extension in the *exitus* cannot be adequately distinguished from the theological account of the *reditus* of humanity and the world, which will be the proper subject matter of the third volume of *God Encountered.* In fact, any account of the *reditus*—the process of elevation, by way of worship, sacrament, Church community, mission, and Christian ethics, of humanity and the world to full participation in the divine nature— is doomed to being an exercise in sectarian irrelevance if it is divorced from the account of the *exitus*—the divine condescension. That is why it was explained that the traditions to be discussed under the rubric of *reditus* "orchestrate and organize and protect the Church's central act of faith in God only in an *indirect* fashion. Consequently, they depend on the fundamental doctrines for their meaning, and hence, they have to be interpreted and evaluated accordingly" (§23, 4, c).

[c] Thirdly, the profession of faith must be understood in its full scope. In the creeds, the divine *exitus* is spelled out in the *entire* sweep of salvation history. This implies, first of all, under the metaphorical rubric of *cognitive retrospect*, that God's self-com-

munication in salvation history is permanently and indefeasibly anchored in God's original self-communication in creation, as the precondition of the gracious amplification and deepening of God's *exitus* in the Christ-event. Secondly, salvation history, under the metaphorical rubric of *cognitive prospect* this time, is inalterably oriented to the divinely-promised absolute fulfillment: the final transformation, by an ecstasy that is the pinnacle of grace, of humanity and the world [*a*].   The divinely-given warrant for this total fulfillment—the center of salvation history as well as the key to both past and future— is the revelation of Jesus Christ as risen, which also involves the revelation of God's eternal Trinity (cf. §40, 1; §43, 4, b).

[d] Fourthly and finally, the point just made will have reminded the reader of another promise made in the first volume. *God Encountered* is committed, under the rubric of *exitus*, to the interpretation of the Christian faith in terms of *grace and nature*. The two orders, it was explained, will be *treated sequentially*, in the interest of elegant exposition (§23, 4, a). But they must be *understood as mutually related*, and hence interpreted *in dialectical terms*. Though antecedent to the order of grace, the order of nature is not simply augmented, or added on to, by the order of grace; if such were the case a sequential treatment of the two orders would do complete justice to their real relationship. As it is, however, the orders of grace and nature are intertwined, not juxtaposed. In that intertwining, the order of creation, far from being replaced or overwhelmed by the order of the incarnation, retains its integrity; in fact, it is intrinsically enhanced by it (cf. §26, 2, a). Not surprisingly, in the act of uncovering this enhancement, theological reflection will also rediscover, at the heart of the order of creation, its prior, native openness to the order of the incarnation.

All of this means that the relationship between nature and grace must be understood in terms of mutual priority, or *perichōrēsis* (cf. §23, 4, b; cf. also §29, 2; cf. §25, 3, a; 7; §26, 1; 3). However, in this *perichōrēsis*, the two elements, though equally

---

[*a*] On "cognitive prospect" and "cognitive retrospect," cf. the explanation of the mutually related experiences of the present *sub specie præteriti* and *sub specie futuri*, in F. J. van Beeck, *Christ Proclaimed*, pp. 265-93.

constitutive, are not equal in ontological rank any more than the orders of *exitus* and *reditus*. The order of the incarnation comprises the elements of the Christian faith insofar as it is a positive religion; that is, it is the concrete form of grace as it is already taking shape in place and time [*b*].   Consequently, it must be recognized as inclusive of, and superior to, the natural order, including the religious aspirations that are integral to it (§29, 2; cf. §25, 3, a; 7; §26, 1-3).   In the remainder of the present volume, therefore, and especially in this first part, it will come as no surprise that the relationship between grace and nature will be consistently presented as mutual but asymmetrical.

[4] Towards the end of the first volume, it was elaborately argued that the Christian community understands and uses the Creed in a web of dynamic links that relate it to other elements of the Christian faith, which are integral to the Creed itself and serve to verify it (cf. §44, 1-3; §47-52). These other elements are the communally accepted standards of Christian conduct and the normative forms of Christian worship. In light of its connection with these two immediately related elements, the profession of the Creed was shown to be a commitment to fidelity in the community and an entitlement to the worship entered upon in Baptism.

In this fashion, it became clear that the Creed is not a free-standing, self-sustaining structure. Hence, it should not be counted on to be able, by virtue of its inner conceptual logic alone, to deliver its meaning, let alone to compel anyone's intellectual assent. The Creed, to put it crudely but effectively, is *relative*, in the sense that it comes not without a proximate agenda in the related areas of Christian life and worship.

In this first part of the second volume of *God Encountered*, that argument from the first volume will be decisively expanded and deepened. Once again the Creed will turn out to be relative, but this time the relativity will not be proximate but *ultimate*: the Creed is dependent on realities so deep that even conduct and cult can only respond to them and point to them. The Creed's ultimate relativity lies in its being set between two universalist perspectives

---

[*b*] This expression "the concrete form of grace as it is already taking shape in place and time" is to be understood as a clarification, and in that sense a correction, of the simpler formula "the concrete shape of grace," used repeatedly in the first volume (cf. §26, 2).

which, though intelligible, are incomprehensible—perspectives which, taken together, in their proportion to each other, form an *absolute*: the height of grace held out by God, and the depth of nature upheld by God and open to God.

UNIVERSALIST PERSPECTIVES

[§58] INTERPRETATION

[1] This second volume of *God Encountered*, it has been stated, is committing itself to the development of a systematic theological commentary on the Creed. In doing so, however, we are involving ourselves in fundamental theological issues. Why?

No commentary on a document is ever offered simply by way of reiteration, rewording, or restatement. *To comment is to convey meaning* to others who presumably seek, or should seek, to understand. But this means that *to comment is to interpret*, for to interpret is to attempt to come to, and communicate, a *fresh understanding*. This implies three related things.

> [a] First of all, the very act of interpreting a document implies the claim that it *can* be interpreted—that the meaning of a document like the Creed is not definite and unequivocal in such a way as to coincide, conclusively and exhaustively, with its explicit wording. Interpretation usually also implies that a document *needs* to be interpreted—that the document, given a particular situation, raises questions that require commentary. Interpretation, therefore, always implies the recognition that there are alternative, and in that sense new, ways of stating or orchestrating a document's meaning—ways that exceed the precise limits of the text. Hence, offering an interpretation of the Creed for the purposes of understanding implies that there is at least a choice of answers available to the simple yet fundamental question, *What does the Creed mean?*

> [b] Secondly, the affirmation that the meaning of the Creed can be established (or at least illuminated) by means of interpretation implies that there are answers available to an important normative question. The Creed is clearly not intended, like a Rorschach inkblot, to elicit purely projective, individual interpretations; it cannot be made to mean just anything that anyone might say it means. Thus the question about the meaning of

the Creed entails a second question. Granted that there is a choice of answers, how are we to choose from among them? Or—what comes down to the same—which answers are relevant, real, legitimate, responsible, truly illuminating?

To resolve this issue, we must recall that interpretation is in the service of understanding, and that the method of understanding must be determined by the matter to be understood (§8, 6). Interpretation, therefore, must imply a basic commitment to recognize the Creed for what it is: the profession of faith of a particular, historic community that has brought the Creed home to us as a central piece of its tradition. The proposition that the meaning of the Creed can be understood by interpretation, therefore, warrants the expectation of legitimate answers if only we ask the question, *What does the historic Christian community mean by the Creed?*

[c] This immediately leads to the third implication. From a literary and linguistic point of view, the Creed is a clear instance of *idiom*. Idioms are *loosely coherent systems of usage at once restricted and public.* An idiom can be described as the whole panoply of available linguistic and literary expedients that have authoritatively served, and continue to serve, a particular cultural group in expressing its vital concerns, in the interest of *both* living by them *and* bearing witness to them before the common culture. That is to say, *an idiom helps a sub-culture identify itself* while at the same time *keeping it related to the wider linguistic world* that shares its language but is not adequately familiar with its particular concerns [c]. The commitment to interpret the Creed to bring out its meaning,

---

[c] From a linguistic point of view, the term "idiom"—like the term "grammar"—implies a point well made by George Lindbeck in *The Nature of Doctrine,* namely, that the language of Christian doctrine is *conventional.* Consequently, like anything else that is "cultural-linguistic," doctrine has to be *learned* in order to be understood and used intelligently and appropriately. However, I wish to suggest that the term "idiom," with its explicitly *cultural-communal* connotations, is preferable to the term "grammar" in discussing the nature of doctrine. Unlike "idiom," "grammar" sums up the strictly morphological, and thus rather more objective, intractable features of the *general* language—that is to say, those features that are less likely to meet the need for inventiveness and freedom in expressing the experiences, ideas, and aspirations of sub-cultures within the encompassing language-community. (Note, incidentally, that the difference is in the *degree of free manipulability,* not in the *possession of meaning.* Grammatical elements do *not* differ from idiomatic ones in that the latter are meaningful and the former semantically vacuous; with very few exceptions, even the most "mechanical" grammatical elements are carriers of identifiable meaning.)

therefore, implies a commitment not to assume that its language can be readily understood by anybody who knows how to read. Rather, those who wish to interpret the Creed must agree to pay attention to the range of ways in which it is *used* by the community that presumably knows, from experience, how to use it. It follows that the decision to interpret the Creed implies a third affirmation, namely, that there are reliable answers available to the question, *How is the creed appropriately used?*

[d] It is time to return to the Creed. Interpreting it under the guidance of these three questions will turn out to be a profoundly theological enterprise [d], which will bring to the surface two theological perspectives that are integral to the Creed as well as intimately related to each other—perspectives, too, of a roundly mystical nature. This requires a full explanation.

[2] The Christian faith, it was pointed out long ago, is concretized and practiced between religion and world, neither of which comes in chemically pure form. They come in a variety of *structures*, in complexes of religious practice and beliefs, in complexes of cultural practice and convictions, and in the interplay between the two (cf. §10, 1). The Creed is one such structure, and interpreting it to the culture (whether inside the Church or outside it) is one of the forms the interplay must take.

Interpreting the Creed, therefore, is *meant to mediate* between religion and world. This means, first of all, that the interpretation of the Creed in response to questions and concerns that come from the world is an essential part of the Church's *witness*. For much though the Creed has its roots in worship, its proper function is in the Church's life of witness. Like the *regulæ fidei*, the Creed represents, both to the faithful and to the outside world, the Church's prophetic account of the meaning of life in Jesus Christ. It presents itself as the symbol of a public life commitment that appeals, ultimately, to the authority of the revealing God (cf. §51, 4, [q]).

No wonder such a symbol provokes responses and gives rise to thought; it is meant to do so. No wonder such an appeal elicits encounters—many of them in the form of questions and outright challenges—between the great variety of concerns current in the

---

[d] For a fundamental discussion of interpretation, as it functions in contemporary theology, cf. Frederick Lawrence, "Method and Theology as Hermeneutical."

common culture and the central faith tradition represented by the Christian community. In representing the authority of God, there-fore, the Creed appeals to the world. In doing so, however, it im-plicitly appeals to a truly fundamental worldly concern, namely, the natural human quest for *integrity in believing*. More importantly, in the very act of appealing to this quest it *endorses* it —the quest is theologically legitimate.

In this way, the interpretation of the Creed serves a twofold theological agenda. Far from being an exercise in modernism or relativism, interpreting the Creed is witnessing, in public, to the Christian profession of faith; at the same time it serves to recognize and meet the fundamental human need for integrity in accepting and understanding the Creed.

In the very act of interpreting the Creed, therefore, abyss calls to abyss (Ps 42, 7): the profession of the mystery of God's design, in Je-sus Christ, for humanity and the world appeals, in and of itself, to that human thirst for integrity which is the immediate consequence of humanity's fundamental attunement to the mystery of God. For this reason, interpreting the Creed is a theological enterprise, not just by reason of the Creed's transcendent origin and subject-matter, but also on account of the depth of receptiveness immanent in hu-man persons to which the act of interpretation addresses itself [*e*].

[a] From the above it is easy to see how intimately the decision to interpret the Creed is related to the fundamental issue of *catholicity* (§1). This is so because in managing the encounter between Creed and culture, theology has two equally undesirable extremes to avoid.

On the one hand, there are those who, fearful of even the semblance of accommodation, insist on presenting the Creed as simply ("literally") true and undebatable. "The Creed means what it says," they will insist—often with the suggestion that those who ask really critical questions are probably doing so because they are resisting a full faith commitment. In this way, they wholly identify the *meaning* of the Creed with its *authoritative wording*, and accordingly, they tend to insist that it is to be ac-cepted and understood entirely on its own explicit terms. But in thus bravely refusing to *interpret* the Creed, they forget two

---

[*e*] Cf. the analogous point made in the first volume about the practice of theo-logical understanding (§8, 8).

things. First, turning the profession of faith into a windowless fortress means using it to block access to the living God—the God who is neither ensconced nor embattled. Secondly, in presenting the Creed for acceptance only, they rob it of its divinely mandated *appeal.* This amounts to dismissing, not only all challenges and critical questions, but also the questioners that bring them up, along with the concerns that animate them. It amounts to demanding slavish conformity where the faith calls for a fair hearing and for the kind of obedience and abandon that comes from a generous and open heart touched by the living God. Finally, in turning the Creed into a totally objectivized, opaque set of tenets, in an integralist vein, they turn the Church into a closed society. The *openness* of catholicity is gone.

On the other hand, there are those who, fearful of even the semblance of sectarianism and intolerance, do indeed present the Creed as true, but with a proviso: it is only "symbolically" true —its real truth is exhaustively reducible to a variety of interpretations of it. They, too, in their own way, fail to interpret the Creed; instead, they *replace* it by (allegedly equivalent) *opinions* about it (cf. §19, 1, [*d*]). This, first of all, robs the Creed of its divine authority. But by showering cheap acceptance and understanding on all questions and challenges addressed to the profession of faith, this approach also takes the human bite out of the Creed; it loses its power to challenge—that is, to elicit responses. By thus being interpreted out of existence (except as an interesting document), the Creed is turned into a public park area with unlimited access. That is to say, if it offers questioners any welcome at all, that welcome makes no real difference. Thus, too, the Church ceases to be a community united by a profession of faith; the *integrity* of catholicity has been dissipated.

Both approaches fail to do justice to the Creed as one of the principal carriers of the Christian community's vital tradition; consequently, they refuse to allow the Creed to govern and challenge and put at risk *their own understanding.* They turn it into a thing—an entity as objective and unrelated and impersonal and intractable as the weather. Those who refuse to *interpret* the Creed turn it into an impenetrable local fog. Those who forget that it is *the Creed* that is to be interpreted turn it into an all-pervasive but barely perceptible vapor.

[§59] CHRISTIAN UNIVERSALISM UNDERGIRDED BY NATURAL UNIVERSALISM

[1] Our resolve to interpret the Creed implies the recognition that it is addressed to the world, and thus that it will raise questions. In fact, one consequence of the assurance of Christ's presence to the Church till the close of the age (Mt 28, 20), as the warrant for its proclamation, is that there will be no end of questions. All these questions are invitations extended to Christians to give an account of the hope that is in them (cf. 1 Pet 3, 15) [f]. From a theological point of view, such questions deserve answers that seek to achieve "discretionary fit" (§14, 2): they must attempt both to interpret the Creed and to meet the concerns that prompt the questions.

[2] The curious thing, however, is that the search for meaningful interpretations, while initially undertaken to satisfy questioners, will invariably end up involving those questioned as well, to the point where they will discover to how large an extent they are questioners themselves. This tends to be so because questions, at root, are always more than mere *requests* for solutions, explanations, and clarifications of particular *problems*; this applies especially where the Creed is concerned.

Asking *particular* questions, in fact, is in and of itself a radical act with a *universal* significance. It unites the questioner and the respondent at a level far deeper and against a horizon far broader than is suggested by the particular question that is asked and the particular answer that is elicited. For behind every particular question stands a questioner—a human person. There is one feature which this person has in common with all human persons: *a native, intrinsically enjoyable penchant for asking questions, and for acknowledging no boundary at which to stop doing so.* That is to say, the human person is *the universal questioner.* This is true not only in the sense that nothing whatever is immune from being questioned by at least somebody. It also means that asking questions, even embarrassing or explosive ones, is something that all human persons somehow have in common. It is an urge whose persistence, depth, and breadth suggest that its roots strike more deeply than either human intelligence or human freedom. No efforts will ever completely succeed in controlling and restraining, let alone squelching, the

[f] Except, perhaps, those that are patently intended as provocations. These call for martyrdom of one kind or another—at least from the point of view of the Christian life considered as the imitation of Christ.

human urge to ask questions convenient and inconvenient, no matter how discouraging or hostile the climate, whether public or private. Even in the privacy of the most tightly self-controlled individual consciousness the stir of the inner sea will wash ashore a steady supply of questions; in fact, such questions tend to become more enigmatic and intractable the more they are suppressed. Nor is all this questioning simply a perverse habit; it is aimed, at least in original intention, at *understanding*. Not surprisingly, therefore, Aristotle opens his *Metaphysics*—his inquiry into realms of reality that lie beyond the boundaries of the observable—with the acknowledgment: "All human persons *by nature* desire to know."[1]

At root, therefore, all *particular* questions about the Creed are expressions of, as well as appeals to, this *universal* feature of humanity—one as native to all human persons as a birthright: a spontaneous, *natural urge to understand*. The human person is defined by this urge. Its stubbornness conveys the extent both of the human need for understanding and of the human person's radical, if not always effective, capacity for it.

There is something else to this urge as well. Since the urge to question is universal, it relates all human persons to all that exists. That means: it is as constitutive of their resemblance to God, the Creator of all that is, as it is essential to every person's integrity as a member of the human family (cf. §2, 1).

[a] As a result, few questioners are more infuriating than those who insist on getting only *particular* (or, as they tend to say, "straight") answers to the particular questions they ask about the Creed ("No, all I want to know is this...."). They are asking legitimate questions, but they refuse to get them answered against the only horizon against which both the questions and the answers make sense.

[3] Consequently, in insisting on interpreting the Creed—the communal Christian profession of faith in God—the present treatment is implicitly making, along with the great Tradition, two intimately related, vital affirmations about the relationship between the Christian profession of faith and humanity at large.

The first affirmation is the following. Inasmuch as the Creed sums up the Christian *kerygma*, it is fundamentally meant to appeal to Christians and non-Christians alike, and to appeal to them at the level where they are most *radically and authentically human*. The second is that even beyond that, the Creed is meant to meet all human persons where they are most *radically attuned to God*. But in stating this, we are also affirming that the Creed implicitly acknowledges universal *humanity's native orientation to God as a positive given*. Such a native orientation, in turn, invites *fundamental theological reflection*. This is important enough to warrant further analysis.

[4] The proposition under investigation is that the Creed, in requiring—and indeed encouraging—interpretation, implicitly acknowledges humanity's native orientation to God as a given that invites theological reflection. In other words, implicit in our resolve to interpret the Creed, we have shown so far, is the presumption that *the Creed itself is compatible with, and indeed invites, a natural theology with a universalist appeal* (cf. §25, 4, a).

This presumption has such important consequences for Christian theology that it must be checked off against the explicit Christian profession of faith itself. If our presumption should indeed be supported by, say, the text of the Creed itself, the construal of a natural theology with a universalist appeal would clearly prove to be an integral element of systematic theology's total task, which is to give an account of the Christian profession of faith, both to the Christian community and to the culture that surrounds and in many ways pervades it. Our presumption, therefore, is important enough to merit careful additional reflection.

[5] The Creed, of course, *thematically* (and hence *primarily*) professes God's universal salvific design as revealed in Jesus Christ risen from the dead. That is to say, it primarily professes not the immemorial order of nature but the historic order of the Christian dispensation, often dubbed (in convenient, if sometimes misleading, theological shorthand) as "the revealed order" or "the order of grace." Consequently, the universalism most explicitly professed by the Creed is based on this positive profession of faith. This is another way of saying that the Creed is a piece of Christianity insofar as it is a *positive religion*: it primarily reflects the worship that identifies the Christian community, as well as the eschatological aspirations alive in it (cf. §38, 2-4; §52, 2).[2]

If, therefore, the Church professes the Creed in every place and at all times, it does so because it aspires, on the strength of the present gift of the Holy Spirit that unites it with God, to the fully actualized union of humanity, along with the world, with God. This union with God has always been, is now, and will forever remain, a matter of pure grace—design, gift, and promise of a sovereignly free, incomprehensibly gracious God (cf. §32, 2; §34, 2). Seen in this perspective, the Creed is principally characterized by its eschatological orientation—an orientation which is, of its essence, *universalist* (cf. §38, 1-5; §39, 2).

> [a] It is not surprising, therefore, that even those primitive trinitarian creeds that lack every trace of christological narrative (and thus also every reference to Christ's coming to do justice to the living and the dead) still include a profession of at least a few eschatological articles of belief at the end. The most notable among these features are the universal church (which represents and anticipates the final gathering of the saints), the (definitive) forgiveness of sins, the resurrection of the flesh, and the life that lasts forever (cf. DS 1-6; CF 1).

[6] But there is found in the Creed itself, though almost implicit, another, *subsidiary universalism* as well. This universalism is *protological*, and it represents the universal order of *nature*. In the catholic interpretation of the Christian faith, this natural universalism is understood to be harmoniously coupled with the universalism of grace, which it undergirds. It is indeed true that the Creed primarily addresses itself to all of humanity with the eschatological message that lies at the root of the Christian faith. Yet it *can* do so only *on the basis of nature*: humanity's native, God-given potentiality for union with God as it has taken shape, and is taking shape, in history [g]. This deep source of evolving natural potentiality not only tolerates, but positively *demands*, *natural* theological reflection with an appeal no less universalist than the resurrection of Christ itself.

> [a] The traditional catholic profession of the relative integrity of the natural order is, therefore, *ultimately* undergirded by the fact that the Creed, which is parasitical upon Christian worship, is prompted by the risen Christ (cf., again, §38, 2-4; §52, 2). It was explained that the profession of Christ's resurrection from the dead involves, as an immediate consequence, a new, conclusive reinterpretation of the entire *history of Israel,* but beyond that, a new, conclusive interpretation of the *history of the world*

---

[g] Into this universal union, it must be added at once, humanity is natively called to draw the entire world as well, being its natural representative and fiduciary. Hence, the fundamental theological universalism proposed here must be both anthropological and cosmological—just like, for that matter, the Christian profession of eschatological faith itself (cf. §9, 1, [i]; §40, 1).

(§40, 3), that is, of the entire natural order, and especially—it should be added—of Israel's vision of it [h]. This protological perspective, which is integral to the profession of Christ's resurrection, involves a theology of history and (going back behind and below history) of the aboriginal nature of all things created. It is true, of course, that such a theological reflection on past history and on the natural order *also* serves to meet humanity's natural demand for intellectual integrity in believing, which is a legitimate feature of human autonomy. But from a catholic point of view, this reflection is not simply a concession to human autonomy, and certainly not to self-willed, sinful human autonomy, as much of the Reformed tradition has tended to suspect (cf. §81, 3). *It is mandated by the Christian faith itself—* an essential point well made once again by Frances Young, in the introduction of her recent *The Making of the Creeds.* No wonder that this Christian awareness of the natural—that is, the created—order can be found in the very *text* of the Creed, in two ways.

[§60] THE CREATED ORDER IN THE TEXT OF THE CREED

[1] Firstly, practically all extant creeds open with the profession of God the Father as *pantokratōr.* God is "Father Almighty," which has connotations of absolutely transcendent majesty. God is the Power that transcends all the powers that be; God is the ruler of all that is and all that counts. In Paul Tillich's arresting idiom, the living God is the "God above God."[3]

[a] An analysis of the literary pedigree of this title reveals that it continues Israel's profession of faith in God as the God of the created universe in all its splendor, along with all the powers that animate and (often) dominate it. The Septuagint renders the Hebrew expression *YHWH tsᵉbā'ôth* ("Lord of the [heavenly] hosts") by *[Kyrios] pantokratōr* in the vast majority of cases. The remaining cases fall into two categories. The Book of Psalms renders *YHWH tsᵉbā'ôth* literally, by *Kyrios tōn dynameōn* ("Lord of the powers"); so do Zeph 2, 9 and Zech 1, 3. LXX 1 Kings (= 1 Samuel in the Hebrew Bible) and Isaiah simply transliterate *tsᵉbā-*

---

[h] The expression *tôlᵉdôth haššamayîm wᵉha'arets*—"the generations of the heavens and the earth" in Gen 2, 4—sums up "the way all things came to be." Thus it is the semantic equivalent in Hebrew of what we call "the natural order." On the entire subject, cf. H. Renckens, *Israel's Concept of the Beginning.*

'*ôth* as *sabaōth*; this creates a foreign, mysterious-sounding proper
name for God ("Lord Sabaoth"), which is apt to convey majesty.[4] Finally, *pantokratōr* often occurs in the LXX version of the
Book of Job, where it consistently translates Hb. *Šadday* ("Almighty"). The deuterocanonical writings of the Septuagint show
a number of comparable instances of *pantokratōr* in apposition
to *kyrios*; used absolutely, it consistently occurs in 2 and 3 Macca-
bees. In the New Testament, apart from one occurrence at the
end of a composite quotation with uncertain reference (2 Cor
6, 16-18), *pantokratōr* is found exclusively, as well as frequently,
in the Apocalypse. There it occurs in apposition to "the Lord
God," in the formula *Kyrios ho Theos ... ho pantokratōr* (Rev 1, 8;
4, 8; 9, 16; 11, 17; 15, 3; 16, 7; 21, 22); in two cases, the formula
is simply *ho Theos ho pantokratōr* (Rev 16, 14; 19, 15).

All of this justifies the conclusion that the divine title *pantokratōr* must be taken to be the linear successor, in the Christian
idiom, of the title *YHWH ts⁽bā'ôth* in the Hebrew Bible. There
the phrase conveys the awe-inspiring, absolute transcendence of
Israel's God, exalted, as the Only True God professed in the *Shema* (Deut 6, 4), above the assembled heavenly powers (cf., e.g.,
Ps 89, 6-9), to whose governance the gentiles, distant as they are
from the living God, have been entrusted by divine design (Sir
17, 17); this partly explains why they mistake them for divine
beings (Deut 4, 19), in their various pantheons.[5] In the Apocalypse, this long-standing connotation of absolute transcendence
over the powers that move the universe is protologically and eschatologically enhanced and orchestrated, in keeping with the
book's apocalyptic theme: "'I am the Alpha and the Omega,' says
the Lord God, the One who Is and who Was and who Comes,
the *Pantokratōr*" (Rev 1, 8).[6]

[b] In the textual development of the creeds, the title *pantokratōr* has furnished the point of linkage for more developed
professions about *the nature of the created universe in relation to God.*
These developments interpret the universe, first of all, as created
by God in its entirety; hence, God's Lordship over it is marked
by comprehensiveness and universal awe: the world ruled by God
includes both "heaven and earth"; all that is—realities both "seen
and unseen"—must acknowledge God as Lord (cf. DS 1-5, 10-64;
CF 1-13). In this regard, Christianity emphatically continues
Israel's profession of faith (§97, 4; §98, 1, a; 3)—a position that
became of the highest importance when, especially in the sec-

ond century, the Christian Church had to define its view of the universe over against many forms of spiritualist gnosticism (cf. §78, 2, a); eventually, this was to yield the concept of "creation out of nothing."[7]

[c] It is not unimportant to pay attention to some further consequences of the profession of God as the Creator of the universe. In the creeds, the word *pantokratōr* (Lat. *dominator omnium* or *omnipotens*) functions as a *title*, or a *name*, of God. That is to say, it operates *liturgically*, it acknowledges God as the living, transcendent, and all-inclusive *Presence*, and it does so by *addressing* and *naming* God—metaphorically of course.[8] Thus "God Almighty" professes that in transcendently and creatively ruling the universe, the living God has been, is, and will always be at work, in sovereign power, in and behind everything that is ever being done, by no matter what power in the world. On the other hand, the English expression "the Almighty" (like Lat. *omnipotens*, which it renders), is liable to be understood in a purely *adjectival* sense. Hence, it tends to be taken to express a divine *property* or *attribute*. This will often occasion a loss of contact with the experience of awe and worship. That is to say, the word "omnipotent" will turn into a *term* and invite *abstract, logical* discussions about the *possible* implications of the predicate "almighty" as it applies to God—a problem squarely recognized by Aquinas.[9]

This in turn *may* lead to a well-known phenomenon: interminable, unprofitable, and ultimately irreverent discussions about the *possibilities* conceivably open to the Creator to exercise power. Such discussions usually end with the conclusion that the creation of beings whose definition contains an internal contradiction (like a square circle) is not open to God. Not infrequently, however, in the course of such debates, the reference to the living God is imperceptibly replaced by a purely logical *concept of god*, and thus the debate itself turns into a game of chess the mind plays with itself. Eventually, the mind will then run into a checkmate of its own devising, and be wearily forced into a mulish affirmation of God's *potentia absoluta* ("there is nothing of which the human mind can affirm that God cannot do it"), which turns the power of the living God into a surd to be put up with rather than a mystery to be thankfully acknowledged in *docta ignorantia* [i].

---

[i] This nervous preoccupation with divine omnipotence is not a little fueled by

[2] Secondly, in most of the developed creeds (one of them even antedates Nicaea: DS 40; CF 6) the profession, in virtue of the resurrection, of Jesus Christ's consubstantiality with the Father in divinity ends with a pointer to the created order as well [j], commonly by means of the phrase: "through him all things came to be." In this way, the Creed extends the "inextricable and mutual bond between Jesus Christ and the living God" (§33, 1), revealed in Christ's resurrection, so as to include his divine activity, with the Father, in the creation and governance of the world [k].   Thus the expression also serves to anchor the risen Christ's eschatological victory over the powers of sin and death in his sovereignty over the powers of the universe as their Creator (§40, 2; 3, c).

[a] This creedal profession of Christ's protological significance endorses a doctrine that has its roots in the New Testament (1 Cor 8, 6; Col 1, 16-17; Heb 1, 2-3; Jn 1, 1. 3. 10; 17, 5; 1 Jn 1, 1-2; cf. §40, 2), and beyond it, in Jewish Wisdom literature (cf. §40, 3, c). It was canonized, in a very explicit form, as early as the second and early third centuries—the upshot of the Christian apologists' sustained dialogue with contemporary philosophy in establishing the role of the *Logos* in creation (DS 40-60; 71; 125; 139; 150; CF 6-14).[10]

[b] Immediately below the surface of the Creed's affirmation of Jesus Christ's role in the creation of the world lies a related claim of the highest importance, to which we will have occasion to come back, especially in the fifth chapter (§78, 2-4). In entering the created world by becoming Incarnate in Jesus Christ, the Creator-*Logos* came into his own (cf. Jn 1, 11). The Christian faith, therefore, belongs squarely and verifiably in this world; it is

---

the characteristically modern, yet deeply mistaken, assumption that omnipotence is the *principal* attribute of God. We will come back at length to this theme, in the course of the treatment of the doctrine of God, in the second part of this volume. Cf. esp. §§106-111.

[j] Romans 4, 17 provides a scriptural model for this perspective: Abraham "believed in God who makes the dead come alive and who calls into existence what does not exist."

[k] It is worth noting that the seventh-century Northern Irish "creed of Bangor" (DS 29) presses the title *Deum omnipotentem* ("God Almighty") into service for this purpose, by predicating it of the Son. In so doing, the creed is using *omnipotens* in the same way as the Greek patristic tradition, which had long used *pantokratōr* as a predicate applicable to each Person of the Blessed Trinity.

not the esoteric secret of a society of initiates cultivating the advent of the New Age, as Marcion and similar gnostics of all times have claimed it is. It is not a privileged, sectarian, totally "spiritual," totally "liberated" way into the intimacy of an allegedly only true God, who—unlike the Demiurge of Greek philosophy and the Creator-God of the Jews—is totally unrelated to the world as the common run of humanity knows it (cf. also §40, 3, d).

[3] In this way, in *professing the living God, and Jesus Christ, the Word of God, as integral to the world in its created, natural condition*, the Christian communities, from the second century onward, have expressed their determination, on the authority of God, *to remain faithful to nature*. That "nature" is the one true world reliably created, through the divine Word, by the one and only true God—the God who has called them from their particular corner of the world to faith in Christ the Lord of all. This God and the Christ sent by God are now sending them back into the whole world, in order to evangelize it. The world of the Creed, therefore, is the world that the Christian community naturally shares with all of humanity, even though its horizons are immeasurably expanded.

[4] The world of the Creed is the world to which the universal Gospel message addresses itself—that is, the whole world shared by all of humanity. When reading expressions like this, we must recall at once that the Gospel message does not find the world in a stable, *tabula rasa* state. The natural world is, first of all, an *evolving* world. But more importantly for our present argument, it is always and everywhere a world already *transformed* as well as *differentiated*, in the most natural of ways, by a humanity whose unity is as striking and raises as many problems as its diversity. The natural world, in other words, is a world that turns out to have lent itself, in the most natural of ways, to *culture* in all its variety of forms. Given humanity's native attunement to the mystery of God, it is not surprising that culture has, in part, taken the form of *religions*.

Consequently, for the Christian Church, faithfulness to nature—to the world created by God—must take the shape of an encounter with the great religions. The next chapter must explore this fundamental dimension of the public profession of the Christian faith.

CHAPTER 2

Professing the Creed Among the World's Religions

THE HORIZON OF HUMANITY AND THE WORLD

[§61] THE CREED, THE CREATED ORDER, AND THE RELIGIONS

[1] The task of interpreting the Creed in light of its universalist perspectives has led us to the issue of Christianity's relationship with the world's great religions. In taking on this issue, however, we must begin by reminding ourselves of an important fact—one heavy with consequence, as will become clear in the course of this chapter.[1] It is a fact that first began to contribute significantly to the reshaping of the self-consciousness of the West in the eighteenth century, when an increasing fascination with the variety of religions and cultures in the world first led to their interpretation in a Deist perspective—as shapes and manifestations of one and the same natural human religiosity (§28, 4).

The fact is this. All of the great world religions make universalist claims. None of them content themselves with purely local or regional relevance; they all offer an encompassing interpretation of human life in the world, and of the world itself—which is, of course, what makes them transplantable to other areas in the world. In other words, Christianity (along with the Judaism to which it owes the faith in the One True God that remains its root commitment [a]) is not alone in relating a *particular* profession of faith

---

[a] Gerd Theißen has made a point of stressing the relevance of the specifically

to a natural world-order *universally accessible to humanity.* Nor is
Christianity alone in professing that there prevails, by transcendent
design, a deep *coordination* between, on the one hand, that all-inclusive world order, and on the other hand, the particular profession
of faith shared among its members.

The great religions are very much with us today, and in much
sharper relief than two centuries ago, when they first began to make
their presence felt. In the global village of the twentieth century,
it has not only become impossible to overlook the world's great religious traditions; their *complexity* is only just beginning to dawn on
us. It is wise, therefore, to acknowledge the world religions early on
in this fundamental theology, and to do so, at least initially, simply
for the sake of realism and fairness—that is, without immediately
entering into much busy theoretical argument or jumping to conclusions of allegedly historic importance.

[a] While commending the encounter with all of the world's
great religions, the Second Vatican Council's Declaration on the
Relationship of the Church to Non-Christian Religions *Nostra
Ætate* gives Judaism pride of place, by placing it at the climactic
point of the document. This implies a double recognition. On
the one hand, it acknowledges "the spiritual bond that connects
the people of the New Covenant with the race of Abraham. For
the Church of Christ recognizes that, in God's mysterious plan
of salvation, the roots of its faith and its election lie with Abraham, along with the other Patriarchs, and with Moses and the
Prophets" (NA 4). On the other hand, it recognizes (though
not without a fair amount of residual hesitancy; confessions of
sin are rarely made with as much abandon as professions of
faith) that Judaism has been the target of Christianity's most
egregious sins of interreligious intolerance.

Because of this double-edged relationship, a deep sense of
mutual affinity and a deep awareness of mutual hurt have continued to enhance each other in Jewish-Christian relationships
everywhere to this day. This neuralgic situation must at least

---

Jewish tradition of monotheism to modern Christianity: "An introduction to the
Jewish faith is objectively necessary to make Jesus' preaching intelligible today. It
is to Judaism that we owe the faith in the One and Only God. For a long time this
faith was self-evident. Today it is a minority opinion. Since it is, historically and
objectively, the most important presupposition of Jesus' preaching, it must be
made accessible anew today" (*Der Schatten des Galiläers,* p. 55; cf. ET *The Shadow of
the Galilean,* p.36).

serve to drive home a twofold realization of fundamental significance. Not only is it essential for Christian theologians to engage in scholarly efforts to understand the Jewish traditions so
as to overcome centuries of deep alienation [b]; it is also imperative for all Christian churches systematically to try to restore
their own full Christian integrity by making sustained efforts (no
matter how painful at times) to bridge the gap that separates
them from *contemporary* Judaism in all its forms, by engaging in
genuine (and often repentant) dialogue. Only in this way will
it be possible for Christianity today to be honest in retrieving its
root connection with Israel and with the Judaism Israel generated—a task to be attempted in the beginning of the second
part of this volume (§97).

[b] In the present context, therefore, it is of fundamental importance to recognize that the Jewish-Christian dialogue can rely
on deep parallels in the area of their several interpretations of
the relationship between particular revelation and the universal
order of nature. In his book *Jewish-Christian Dialogue: A Jewish
Justification*, the Jewish theologian David Novak has explicitly
broached this important issue. He has done so by offering us a
fine analysis of the Jewish tradition of interpreting the relationship between the knowledge of God by virtue of particular divine
election and the recognition of God in the universal natural
order. The first and fundamental set of theological arguments,
Professor Novak explains, are to be derived from the concept of
"Noahide law," which "mediates between Judaism and the non-
Jewish world in both time and space." From the perspective of
the Jewish nation, divinely chosen to observe the Torah in its
fullness, the Law as imposed on Noah undergirds the Torah revealed to Israel at Sinai. This earlier Law imposes on all of humanity the observance of a number of fundamental precepts that
are "inherent in created human nature, *the same nature that made
possible the revelation of the Torah to Israel.*"[2] Even though Novak
has developed his theme primarily in the interest of offering
positively Jewish theological warrants for the Jewish dialogue with
Christianity, his treatment would seem to have the potential for
a more universalist application.

---

[b] Here lies the great merit of Paul van Buren's *A Theology of the Jewish-Christian
Reality*, a book capable (like other works by the same author) of changing in-
grained habits of Christian theological understanding and reflection.

[2] Consequently, the Christian mission to the world must acknowledge some basic *structural parallels* between itself and other great religions. They are the following. The (Judaeo-)Christian tradition is not alone (1) in distinguishing between *the particular order created by the "revelation"* (or its functional equivalent) that is the content of its own special profession of faith and *a universal order of "nature"*,[3] (2) in having conceptions about *the integrity of the natural order and its relativity*, (3) in recognizing, on the basis of this order, *a natural comparability between itself and other great religions*, and hence, (4) in thinking that there is *a natural basis for encounter and debate among the great religions*, while (5) at the same time continuing to think that *the natural order provides the basis for a natural, non-sectarian apologetics to establish the credibility of its own particular profession of faith* (cf. §91, 1-3).

All these points, but especially the last three, lay bare the far-reaching consequences of the fact that the Christian Creed is not the creed of a sect (cf. §40, 3, d). Rather, the Creed implies what we have termed a subsidiary, protological universalism, based on the fact that the Christian community acknowledges an all-inclusive natural order—one which it shares with all of humanity.

[3] Let us now consider a few examples that will enable us to detect structural parallels between Christianity and other religions in the area of the relationship between particular doctrines and precepts and universal significance. Let us do so by drawing three vignettes of the relationship as it appears in some of the world's great religions. That is, let us do so by overlooking, for the moment, the distortion conveyed by the labels put on these religions by nineteenth-century Christian missionaries: "Hinduism," "Buddhism," "Mohammedanism"—a distortion that suggests that these religions are organized orthodoxies like Christianity. Finally, let us do so simply by way of a preliminary exercise—one that may assist us in considering an argument that will lead to a conclusion vital to the interpretation of the Christian Creed.

[a] We begin with an example from the world of Mahayana Buddhism. Here we encounter the relationship between universalist perspective and confessional particularity in a striking configuration. Much as the attainment of enlightenment, with its infinite horizon, is the goal of the individual life, the life of faith cannot but start with concrete particulars. Travelers must board the raft of doctrine that will take them on their voyage to the distant, still invisible shore of the truly real. In doing so, they can-

not but experience the first, painfully particular phase of faith: a distressing awareness of the myriad ways in which they are hobbled by the world they have decided to leave behind at the dock. Then comes the second phase, which carries with it a first, decisive broadening of the horizon. In the passage, travelers begin to abandon themselves, bravely, to the historic tradition, unsteady as it may be. "I take refuge in the *Buddha*—the fact that there was an explorer who made this trip and proved to us that it is possible. I take refuge in the *dharma* ['teaching'], the vehicle of transport, this boat to which we have committed our lives in the conviction that it is seaworthy. I take refuge in the *sangha*, the Order, the crew that is navigating this trip and in whom we have confidence." Finally, the further shore has been reached. At that point, there is reason indeed to be thankful for pioneer, ship, and crew; still, it would be foolish to express that thankfulness by insisting on carrying them along any further; they have served their purpose. Travelers who have arrived no longer depend on the particularities of their voyage through the world. They do not even need the assurance of continuity implicit in the experience of their own individual identity any more, for they now recognize the latter as extremely feeble [c]. Having been enlightened by moving through appearances and beyond them, they themselves now begin to reveal, *in* the world in which they are still moving around, the true—if hidden—nature of this world. Having been made perfect by moving through transience and beyond it, they now help bring to perfection this world, painfully mired in particularities that pass away. They do so by revealing its essence—that is to say, its impermanence—against

---

[c] The Dutch novelist Jan Willem van de Wetering (*The Empty Mirror*, pp. 136-140) has a charming account (under the caption of the *koan* "Is a cloud a member of the sky?") of one way in which many of these realizations dawned on him. While staying in a Japanese monastery, he decided to press his desire for formal induction into Buddhism. He wished to do so by means of a ceremony in which he was to vow publicly that he was taking refuge in Buddha, in the Teaching, and in the Brotherhood. However, in a garden conversation with a simple fellow-monk, it became clear to him that an individual—being always in process—can no more reliably be "a Buddhist" than a cloud can reliably be a part of the firmament. The ceremonial specifics of his desire to be a Buddhist, he thus found, were not so much something to be carried out as something to be gotten over and left behind. In the process, he found, his desire for the induction had been both fulfilled and transcended.

the day when they will be ready to enter into *nirvana*, in union with all that lives and moves [d].[4]

[b] Traditional Hinduism, in its many forms, recognizes a fundamental structural congruence between the natural world order and the scriptural-ritual world order revealed in the central Vedic writings. Thus the Veda, in orthodox Hinduism, makes available to the believer the key to all of reality. That key is *ātman*— that is, recognition of, and access to *brahman*—that is, the ultimate, all-encompassing reality in its wholly transcendent unity. Using the Veda as the absolutely superior touchstone of orthodoxy, traditional Hinduism could feel justified in sorting out all the known Hindu sects, and in lining them up (by means of "doxographies") in an ascending order of correctness.[5] It also felt justified in similarly evaluating the sects extraneous to the Hindu world—the various kinds of Buddhism and Jainism, and even, in a few isolated missionary contexts, some of the newly discovered foreign religions.

India's historic encounter with nineteenth and twentieth century colonialism produced a new, and characteristically princi-

---

[d] It is hard to miss the striking parallels of the Mahayana account of the road to Enlightenment with the Christian tradition of the three stages—purgative, illuminative, and unitive—of spiritual progress (§§53-54). However, on closer inspection, the very parallels serve to put the considerable differences in even sharper relief. Most notable among these differences, it would seem, is the Mahayana account of the preparatory stages of spiritual enlightenment as purely instrumental, and hence, as ultimately dispensable. In the Christian tradition, on the other hand, complete spiritual maturity—life in consistent union with God—never involves leaving the stages of immaturity completely behind. Even the most mature mystics remain to some extent pistics in that they remain indebted to the Church, which continues to pre-exist their faith and ground it; it is the community that both symbolizes and conveys that faith is and remains a *gift*. Mystics remain residual charismatics, too, in that they will never leave behind the patient pursuit of perfection; no Christian is ever wholly "beyond virtue." Behind this distinctively Christian tradition, it would appear, ultimately lies the Jewish understanding of the Lord God as Maker and Savior of humanity and the world—an understanding to which the Christian idea of the Incarnation is thoroughly indebted. Israel's God is both utterly transcendent and utterly immanent, and thus prompts a faith-response that combines the profoundest awe with the deepest intimacy (cf. §34, 7). Awe of such a transcendent God forbids that anyone should ever attain complete, assured spiritual maturity, let alone think of it as a personal property. Intimacy with such a present God demands that the present structures of faith should be cherished as carriers of the divine presence, and hence as symbolic and sacramental (cf. §78); they should not be dismissed as a matter of unsubstantial, ultimately expendable appearances, and hence, as alienating because ultimately deceptive (cf. §10, 1, a; §77, 3).

pled, version of Hinduism known as neo-Hinduism. Neo-Hinduism became especially prominent in those centers in the Indian subcontinent where Christianity had become an influence to be reckoned with. With regard to neo-Hinduism, therefore, it is very important to recognize that its agenda, and hence its shape, is largely determined by the need for Hindu self-representation and self-defense in the face of cultural and religious pressure of European, and in that sense Christian, provenance. Precisely for that reason, neo-Hinduism also came to base itself primarily on *Vedānta*—the most recent, most reflective, and especially most universalist layer of the Vedic tradition. This combined indebtedness to, on the one hand, foreign culture and, on the other, strongly philosophical traditions sharply reduces neo-Hinduism's reliability as a guide to traditional Hindu orthodoxy. Only in a very indirect fashion, therefore, does neo-Hinduism give access to classical Hinduism, and the fact that most of neo-Hinduism's authoritative writings were originally composed in English ought to serve as a warning.

For all that, neo-Hinduism's affinity with traditional Hinduism is obvious, even though it seems to have made a point of countering Western dogmatism and superiority with rather robust claims of its own devising. Thus neo-Hinduism simply objects to being considered a religion. Rather, it professes to be the adequate representation and orchestration of the coherence and meaning of the natural order in its integrity—the order that remains absolutely sovereign over all the visible differentiations it encompasses. In making this affirmation, neo-Hinduism is implying that all the religions (such as Christianity, Islam, and Buddhism) are *sects*, and to that extent on a par with the gamut of sectarian traditions within Hinduism itself. Over against all these sects, neo-Hinduism defines itself as the embodiment of the one universalist, unifying, concordant religious faith that accounts for all religions. It can make this claim because it considers itself, on the basis of *ātman*, reliably (because essentially) attuned to the absolute, and hence of universal validity in and of itself.

Consequently, neo-Hinduism volunteers a critique of all the particular, positive religions that exist everywhere, to show that they are essentially unsatisfactory. However, it is also prepared to recognize the religions as aspirants to a higher unity, and indeed happy to do so and to integrate them as such in its picture of the world of religion. In this way, neo-Hinduism succeeds in combining a truly missionary fervor with a capacity for philosophical, patient (if somewhat weary) tolerance. It knows how to appreciate and even commend legitimate forms of religion—especially those within the Hindu tradition—as partial approaches to the absolute that are appropriate in certain times and places [e].[6]

[c] Unlike Mahayana Buddhism, and Hinduism and neo-Hinduism, Islam shows some of the family features of the three main branches of Western monotheism (§67, 4, b) in the way in which it conceives of the relationship between itself as a positive religion and humanity and the world at large. The relationship takes the form of a firm awareness that God's original, universal Will and God's eventual, universal Judgment provide the religious life with its two truly ultimate perspectives. Thus the Qur'an recognizes that "submission" to the Holy Will of God, or *islam*, is written into all of creation; the whole universe is naturally *muslim*. God's Will is also written into the human heart, by way of an original, primordial Covenant. Consequently, all human beings, in their several religious communities, owe it to God as well as to their own nature to submit, consciously and freely, to the divine Will and to perform good deeds. Among these communities, Islam as a historic religion can claim to represent the best, fullest manifestation, by God's own design, of God's Will. Yet at the same time, because of the distance between God and creatures, which must remain infinite, those who profess Islam are not

---

[e] Both the missionary zeal and the emphatically universalist tolerance of neo-Hinduism are strikingly evident in a place like the Vedanta Asrama in Marshfield, Massachusetts. There, in a tasteful temple building, four separate sculptured shrines incorporating the images and symbols of, respectively, Buddhism, Judaism, Christianity, and Islam, are placed in arched recesses at the center of each of the four walls. To the present author, the total effect is one of both peaceful mutual recognition and deliberate mutual cancellation; not surprisingly, the Temple has succeeded in keeping him suspended between reassurance and confusion on more than one occasion. The strongly missionary universalism of the neo-Hinduist Vedanta Society would appear to have features in common with the type of principled religious pluralism to be criticized further on (§64, 6-7; cf. esp. §64, 6, a and [r]). To mention another example, Eric J. Lott's interesting *Vedantic Approaches to God* argues that ultimate reality in Vedantic Hinduism admits of a personalist-theistic interpretation; but the preface by (not surprisingly) John Hick suggests—a bit hastily, it would seem—that this shows that Hinduism and Christianity can be accommodated under the same universalist-theist umbrella. Finally, there would appear to be parallels between neo-Hinduism and ancient Stoicism (cf. §27, 4, b-c; §32, 5).

automatically assured of the divine favor; in fact, God will abandon them if they abandon God. God remains free even to abandon the community of Islam itself if it should abandon God. For
that reason Islam is surrounded by other religious communities,
in which people practice *islam* according to their own prophetic
traditions. Other religions, therefore, must be interpreted as a
divinely ordained incentive; Islam must compete with them in
goodness.[7]

[d] Needless to say, these three thumbnail sketches do not even
come close to doing justice to the complexity of the world's
great religions, and thus, to the daunting dimensions of the
issue under discussion. But at least they may serve to make the
essential point made before (§61, 1) in a fashion that is somewhat more concrete and not entirely theoretical: several great
non-Christian religious traditions, especially missionary ones like
Islam and Buddhism, relate their positive, particular professions
and expressions of faith to all of humanity and the whole world
in their natural integrity.

[4] The Christian Creed, we have shown, evidences an analogous
approach: it, too, defines its particularity in relation to humanity
and the whole world. In the Christian profession of faith, we have
explained, this particularity enjoys pride of place. The Creed's
primary profession is *positive* (§59, 5): the Creed thematically formulates the Christian faith in its concrete, historic specificity, which includes an eschatological, universalist perspective.

Now it was explained long ago that this primary profession of
faith, in virtue of its eschatological perspective, defines and authorizes the *Christian mission to the whole world* (§42, 1, a; §50, 3). More
recently, we have explained that the explicit profession of Christian
faith is undergirded by a commitment to humanity and the world
in their natural integrity, by means of what we have termed a *subsidiary universalism* (§59, 6). Taken together, these two theses lead
to very important conclusions about Christianity's relationship to
the created universe, to be elaborated at length later on (§§77-79).

[§62] THE CREED AS A MANDATE FOR INTERRELIGIOUS DIALOGUE

[1] In the present context, however, we must draw a first, fundamental conclusion. It is the following. *The Creed itself implicitly invites and mandates a Christian dialogue with humanity's great religions.*

Why? If respect for the universal order of nature undergirds the Christian profession of the order of grace, then this respect must naturally extend to the ways in which other religions have acknowledged and interpreted that natural order. Consequently, *respectful dialogue with world religions, precisely inasmuch as they make their particular claims in a universalist perspective, must undergird the Christian mission.* Since it is important to understand this thesis accurately, let us clarify it in some detail.

[a] First of all, what is asserted is that it is *the Creed* that mandates a respectful dialogue. The thesis, in other words, is presented as a *theological* proposition predicated on positively *Christian* warrants. It is not proposed in deference to any allegedly superior general principle, to which all the world's religious traditions would supposedly owe obedience on grounds that naturally command universal acceptance. This is in character with the fact that the Catholic Church, at Vatican II, acknowledged *positively Christian* grounds for professing itself as vitally as well as respectfully related to the great religions (NA 3; cf. GS 92).

Not surprisingly, our thesis is ultimately anchored in two interrelated *christological* affirmations, namely, that God is not set against creation (§79, 2-4), and that, in being united with the divine *Logos*, human nature—and the whole natural order along with it—is not diminished but dignified (cf. §78, 4, a; §82, 1, a). In other words, Jesus Christ is professed as the Son of God and as the Savior of all of humanity and the whole world because he embodies and includes and welcomes all ways and all souls, assays and chastens them, and perfects them by putting them in an ultimate perspective.[8] He is *not* so professed because he (or faith in him) *displaces* all other ways to God, along with the great souls that have found, lived, and taught them. Very importantly, Christ incorporates the natural order by virtue of *sovereignty*, not by dint of *superiority*; it is misleading, therefore, to characterize the classical Christian profession of Christ's *sole* Saviorship as "exclusivist" [f].

---

[f] Consequently, I am forced to suggest, despite the urgency of the issue of religious pluralism, that Paul F. Knitter's proposal, in *No Other Name?*, to make some kind of distinction, in the Christian faith, between a universalist *theological* focus and a particularist *christological* profession of faith is premature; it creates more problems than it solves. From a Christian point of view, it comes close to compromising the "inextricable and mutual bond between Jesus Christ and the living God" (§33, 1), both in the order of grace and in the created order (§60, 2; cf. also J. Dupuis, "Le débat christologique dans le contexte du pluralisme reli-

[b] This point having been made, it must be added at once that the proposition that the Creed mandates the respectful dialogue with world religions has been heeded at least as much in the breach as in the compliance. Hence, affirming it as integral to Christianity calls for a firm *mea culpa*, on the part of both the Christian Church and the Christian theologian. The problem has roots in a misguided christology. In interpreting Christ's victory over sin and death in triumphalist terms, and in uncritically aligning itself with political power (cf. §76, 4, [*j*]), the Church has often professed the Creed—and hence, Christ's universal Lordship—in *exclusivist, intolerant* terms totally unwarranted by either the example of the historical Jesus or the true sense of the conciliar definitions.[9]

This error came to be compounded by dubious developments in the cultural shape of Western Christianity. Undue deference, on the part of the simple faithful, to ecclesiastical-political establishments became the norm; an increasing preoccupation with salvation from sin as the central theme of the Christian faith contributed to the development of an ever more starkly adversary relationship between Christendom and non-Christian cultures.[10] In time, these developments provided spurious theological warrants for the "conversion" of the non-Christian world by means of missionary campaigns that were as intolerant and aggressive as the inquisitorial and administrative vigilance with which the "defense" of the Christian faith was frequently pursued at home [*g*].

---

gieux"). If that bond is loosened, Jesus Christ ends up being entirely defined by the particularity of his humanity. But in that case, any truly universalist claims made on his behalf amount to an offensive exercise in Western superiority and prejudice (cf. §72, 4, d, [*p*]). Reluctantly, therefore, I conclude that *both* Christ's uniqueness *and* his inclusiveness are jeopardized in Knitter's proposal. The proposal made here makes no concessions in the area of Christ's uniqueness in regard to both God and humanity and the world, but it argues that in presenting itself as exclusivist, Christianity has misunderstood both Jesus Christ and its own normative profession of faith, and hence, the significance of the great religions as well. Implicit in our proposal is the contention that the profession of Christ's uniqueness is substantially a matter, not only of eschatological perspective, but also of a way of life congruent with that perspective (cf. §42; §64, 5; cf. also F. J. van Beeck, *Christ Proclaimed*, pp. 507-18). That is, the understanding of Christ's uniqueness is substantially dependent on *practice* an insight supported by Knitter in a more recent essay ("Making Sense of the Many," p. 207).

[*g*] One very serious blot on the history of the Catholic Church in the Western hemisphere deserves specific mention. Unlike the slave traders, who made only the feeblest of attempts at offering a religious justification for their crimes against

[c] It must be noted that the affirmation intended by the thesis has a limited target area. The thesis states that the acknowledgment of the natural order—an acknowledgment that Christianity shares with the great religions—furnishes the interreligious dialogue with its *foundation*; it does not state that it furnishes it with its all of its *content*.

In fact, when it comes to the *content* of the interreligious dialogue, *God Encountered* is committed to a much broader (that is, much more catholic) proposition, namely, that the religions' *positive elements* should be the principal content of the interreligious dialogue, for several reasons.

First of all, the agenda of any real dialogue between religions must take into account the positive elements. It is a rationalist mistake to think that natural religiosity exists separately (§26, 3); in fact, an appreciative understanding and interpretation of a religion's positive elements is capable of laying bare, in an indirect fashion, its true nature as a *religion* (§25, 3; cf. §24, 2, a).

Secondly, good Christian theology interprets the positive elements in Christianity (and, arguably, in other religions as well [h]) as the concrete shape of the human response to God's self-revealing graciousness—that is, as the concrete shape of grace (§26, 2; §35, 1, b; §57, 3, d and [b])—and consequently,

---

humanity, the leadership of the Spanish *Conquista* explicitly used Christ's victory over the demons as the rationale for the brutal treatment of the native Americans and the destruction of their culture. The protests of Christian prophets like the Dominican friar and bishop Bartolomé de las Casas (1474-1566), the author of *The Only Way to Draw All People to a Living Faith* and many other splendidly indignant writings, were largely disregarded. The problem, of course, could come to the fore so virulently because it was as widespread—if dormant—as Christendom itself. Thus the rise of Christian and post-Christian Deism must be, to a significant extent, laid at the door of the aggressive ecclesiastical triumphalism that once prevailed in Europe (§28). And while it is unfair to exaggerate the links between colonialist imperialism and the Christian missionary endeavor in the nineteenth and twentieth centuries, it is unwise to deny them altogether. The efforts of contemporary scholars like Wilfred Cantwell Smith, John Hick, and even Paul Knitter to reinterpret the Christian faith and its relationship to other religions in "inclusivist" or "pluralist" terms may well have to be judged theologically unsatisfactory in the end; what cannot be denied is that the scandals of the past cry out for the *kind* of remedial theological reflection they offer.

[h] Cf., Heinz Robert Schlette, *Die Religionen als Thema der Theologie*, pp. 43-65 (ET *Towards a Theology of Religions*, pp. 41-61). The acceptance of the concept of "natural sacraments" (§78, 4, b), by which non-Christian believers meet and worship God, and in doing so experience God's gracious blessing, is one consequence of the sort of theological (as against merely comparative) interpretation proposed here.

as superior to natural religion (§31). It would, therefore, be a theological mistake of the first magnitude to exclude the great religions' positive elements from the agenda of the dialogue, no matter how intractable they may seem.

For, thirdly, even from a humanistic, purely anthropological point of view, it a mistake to want to subdue the concrete particulars of a different religion by fitting them into some large, overarching framework that claims to explain everything. A far more reliable test of the seriousness of any encounter is a genuine, unprejudiced interest in the concrete particulars of other people's convictions and practices, no matter how particular and partial they may be. For it is a sign, not of respect, but of prejudice and a false sense of superiority to belittle and disregard the specific meanings, practices, and intentionalities of any positive religion. This warning applies no less whenever it is proposed, however politely, that we can account for these specifics by regarding them as conventional differentiations of one allegedly universal—i.e., natural—religion (cf. §28, 3).

In other words, our thesis *affirms* that the great religions have an awareness of a universal order of nature in common, and that this awareness provides the interreligious dialogue with a common point of departure. Our thesis implicitly means to *dispute* the proposition that the dialogue among the great religions is justified in aiming at mutual understanding by insisting that each religion agree to having itself be exhaustively interpreted within the framework of one, allegedly all-inclusive, naturally accessible order (cf. also §95). We will shortly argue this proposition at greater length (§64).

[2] At this point, our thesis about the Christian mandate for the dialogue with the great religions requires some careful undergirding, by means of a reflection of a rather more philosophical nature. This reflection, in fact, amounts to a full-scale, detailed *excursus.* Cumbersome though this procedure may be, it will at least serve to drive home the delicacy of the task in hand.

INTERPRETATION AND DIALOGUE

[§63] EXCURSUS: PARTICIPATIVE KNOWLEDGE

[1] Let us begin by going back to the basic question. Christian respect for the all-encompassing order of nature, it was stated, must

extend to the ways in which *other religions* have acknowledged that universal natural order (§62, 1). Why exactly is this so?

The answer to this question is as profound as it is obvious. No human group or individual can claim to have an *objective, comprehensive* grasp of the all-encompassing order of nature, for the simple reason that they are all part of it. Human persons can no more grasp or comprehend or be objective about humanity and the world in their totality than fish can about the water that sustains them, or, for that matter, individual persons can about the very persons they are. Just as we are unable to adopt a point of view *outside* ourselves in order to grasp ourselves in our totality as whole persons (which is why all precise self-knowledge remains ever so precarious), so we are unable to adopt a point of view *outside* our personal relationships with others, and even more, *outside* humanity and the world, in such a way as to get them in clear focus in their totality.

[a] To realize this may be at first disconcerting. The idea of the world and humanity as constituting a given, all-inclusive order of reality "out there" comes so naturally to the thinking mind, and it is such an indispensable ingredient in all the great cultural and religious traditions in the world as we know it, that we naturally assume that "we know what we are talking about" when we say "humanity and the world," or, for that matter, when we say "I" or "me" or "you" or even "us."

Yet critical reflection, as Immanuel Kant has so conclusively shown in his *Critique of Pure Reason*, compels us to accept the fact that our cognitive grasp of certain realities is subject to serious limits (cf. §8, 2 a). These realities are our own selves and other persons, and humanity and the world in their totality (not to mention—as Kant does—the transcendent reality of God). Whatever it may be that corresponds, "out there in the real world," to the *ideas* we have of ourselves and of other persons, and of humanity and the world, we cannot but agree that we do not know them as (judging from the definite way we talk about them) we *appear* to know them. That is, we do not know them *as objects of knowledge.*[11]

[2] Does this mean our knowledge of ourselves, other persons, and humanity and the world is a complete illusion? That it amounts to nothing? Of course not.

First of all, it makes little sense to say that we have an idea, but no real knowledge, *of* realities *about* which we can, and do, in fact know so much objectively. After all, in our quest for understanding, we approach humanity and the world in a great variety of distinctive (if partial) ways, all of which are in some way rational. By means of these approaches, we do succeed in grasping a thousand particular, objective things, *about* ourselves, *about* others, *about* humanity and the world. All the while, of course, we realize that not even the largest accumulation of such particular items of knowledge *about* ourselves, others, and humanity and the world will ever add up to *exhaustive comprehension.* Yet we will insist, despite this essential provisionality and incompleteness of our knowledge *about* ourselves, others, and humanity and the world, that we somehow really *know* them. Is this insistence merely naive, or does it stand up to critical examination? This question leads to a second, more important point.

[3] In understanding ourselves, others, and humanity and the world, we rely, not only on detailed, objective, rational (and sometimes even purely rational) knowledge, but also on knowledge of a different sort. A realist like Thomas Aquinas, for all his esteem of knowledge of the precise and rational kind, is fully aware of this second type of knowledge. The most succinct formulation of his understanding of this issue occurs in the context of an ethical discussion in the *Summa theologica,* but the concept itself occurs throughout his mature work, where it has a wide variety of applications. He explains:

Right judgment can come about in two ways. The first way follows the path of the accomplished use of reason [*perfectum usum rationis*]. The second way is based on a certain natural affinity [*connaturalitatem*] with the things about which, as it happens, we have to form judgments.[12]

In other words, knowledge—especially the knowledge that is a reliable guide to the lived life and in that sense "practical"—is not limited to the rational kind. When the occasion arises, knowledge is also available on the basis of *familiarity* or *participation.* Saints know about God from their experience of love—*caritas*—in prayer and practice, people faithful to their marriage vows know about chastity from the experience of the pains and joys of loyalty, and cobblers know about leather from the experience of working with it every day. All of this is so true that saying that *they* are the ones that *really* know is not just an unpleasant attempt at edification or moralizing, or an instance of the romantic idealization of old-fashioned craftsmanship. *They obviously know.* Only prigs and rationalists will maintain that saints and chaste folks and cobblers "don't really *know*," just because they have not studied either faith or ethics, or the physiology of the animal skin and the chemistry of the tanning process, or just because *they do not succeed in explaining, in articulate, objective terms, what they do know.*

It is true, of course, that many people who know by familiarity are conservative—they often resist the findings of rational investigation. But on the other hand, even without being prigs or rationalists, intellectuals (and other smart people out to win an argument) tend to be so impressed by detailed, objective knowledge ("the facts" or "the state of the art") that they end up, in practice, considering it the only "real" knowledge. Even more importantly, they tend to be unaware of the extent to which detailed, objective, articulate, rational ("objectifying") knowledge of every kind is and remains *dependent on participative knowledge*—the sound understanding implicit in the relationship of familiarity with the (for lack of a better word) "object" of knowledge.

[4] This last proposition, which will be crucial to our argument, can be further explored and clarified under three rubrics: *perspective, convergence*, and *interpretation.*

[a] The pursuit of particular pieces of detailed, objective, rational knowledge is never entirely self-justifying, not even in strictly academic endeavors. Establishing, say, whether there is ammonia on the planet Jupiter assumes, at the very least, that the researcher *cares*—no pursuit of academic knowledge without some type of *interest.* That interest, and the grounds for it, are not entirely amenable to articulation, yet they are not, for that reason alone, altogether irrational. Educated interest of some sort motivates every particular scholarly inquiry and gives it a provisional sense of direction; if everything goes well, that sense of direction improves as the inquiry moves along and as the data confirm or modify it. Thus there results a dynamic process. On the one hand, as the detailed data accumulate, they contribute to the researchers' broad, participative familiarity with the problem and make it more assured; on the other hand, the pursuit of detailed, objectifying knowledge is increasingly guided by the perspective furnished by this broad, initially unthematic, participative knowledge. Only to the extent that researchers develop sounder participative judgment will their particular theoretical pursuits make more sense; without such judgment, the objec-

tifying research will "fall apart" and disintegrate, or simply become insignificant. We conclude that objectifying knowledge needs the *perspective* offered by participative knowledge if it is to make sense, and that participative knowledge gains in assurance as it is thematized and articulated by objectifying knowledge.

[b] Participative knowledge also accounts for something else: the sense that what I know is coherent. Research will reward and confirm the researcher's initial interest according as the particular data begin to arrange themselves into *patterns*; here if anywhere the whole again and again proves to be more than the sum of its parts.

A good analogue of this is found in the everyday experience of *conversation*. In ordinary, everyday communication situations, the experience of the dynamics of speech (the "rhetoric") makes intelligent listeners of us. We understand the drift of the conversation better as we become better *participants* in it, and we are better participants if we do *not* bore each other to tears by insisting on complete explicitness about every last detail. Understanding a conversation is indeed dependent on knowledge of the objective meaning of words and the precise subject-matter of the conversation, but our ability to "read" what people are saying to each other in the situation is far more important.[13] For the understanding achieved in live speech is not dependent on the participants' awareness of the discrete linguistic *elements*, even though the precise meaning of all those (phonetical, grammatical, syntactic, lexical, idiomatic, etc.) elements can be analytically established. Understanding depends on the lived experience of *relevance*. Relevance is dependent, among other things, on the experience of *convergence* of all (or at least most) of the elements in a speech-situation; and that experience is primarily a matter, not of attention to details but of participation in the process as a whole. If the speech-situation comes off, all (or at least most) of the objectifiable elements of speech conspire to function as "pointers," and from the way they point we will spontaneously infer what the story is [*i*]. The opposite happens when the

---

[*i*] John Henry Newman has been both subtle and emphatic in explaining that this also applies to learned discourse. Knowledge arrived at by the various forms of inference (for which our native "illative sense" equips us) is neither less certain nor less truly knowledge for being less than completely rational and definitive. Cf. esp. *An Essay in Aid of a Grammar of Assent*, chaps. 8 and 9 (pp. 209-99).

speech-situation fails to come off. To the extent that we *don't* get the story, discrete elements in the conversation will become prominent in a haphazard way, only to distract and confuse and mislead us, and further explanation or accumulation of detail (especially of the "helpful" kind) may only serve to make matters worse. Not until "the penny drops" (often at the drop of the "right word")[14] will we get reconnected and catch up, and thus begin to understand again—the broad meaning (i.e., the "point") of the conversation in the first place, and in that context most of the details, too, though only as necessary, against the horizon of the broad meaning of the conversation.

[c] All of this, finally, constitutes *interpretation.* The two kinds of knowledge mentioned by Aquinas are indeed distinguishable, but not doomed to remain forever separate; normally, they function in interplay. Let us take a literary example. "Genuine poetry," T. S. Eliot wrote in his great essay on Dante, "can communicate before it is understood."[15] The broad, intuitive, participative understanding which the first encounter with a poem awakes in me remains inarticulate at first, but that understanding, no matter how unthematic, does furnish me with a first *perspective* to guide my critical investigation by. Subsequently, according as the objective, detailed knowledge that I acquire about the poem falls into a *convergent* pattern, I will proceed, thanks to my "illative sense," increasingly to *interpret the poem as a whole in the light of its details, and the details in the light of the poem as a whole.* Thus in the process of interpretation the poem—and my own spiritual world along with it—gets both more complex and more unified. Delightfully, my inner world gets both furnished and organized; it develops into a broader, more coherent landscape, with more patterned, cherished detail. In the process, my horizon is expanded and my perspective is enlarged to make room for even more reality. Thus I grow and find both enrichment and enlightenment, in virtue both of what I come to know in the way of objectivity and of what I come to understand by participation.

[5] Let us sum up this analysis and come to a first set of conclusions. The fact that things and persons resist complete comprehension by means of objectifying knowledge does not prevent us from truly knowing them, for we can also understand them in a more integral (if less articulate) way, by participative knowledge. Far from being irrational, such participative knowledge serves to inspire and

guide and lend perspective to objectifying knowledge, while objectifying knowledge in its turn serves to structure and articulate participative knowledge [j].

In being known in this twofold way, *reality reveals its structure.* There is both unity and multiplicity to everything that exists—both to individual persons and things, and to humanity and the world in their totality. The multiplicity in them allows us to approach and appreciate them by means of detailed, objectifying knowledge; yet we realize that they are more than a conglomeration of objectifiable elements; for a fuller understanding of their integrity—that is, their unity—we remain dependent on participative knowledge.

The pursuit of knowledge of every kind thus invariably turns out to be an exercise in *interpretation*; put differently, it is interpretation that mediates between reality and ourselves. On the one hand, things and our own selves and other persons and humanity and the world can indeed be known in their integrity, but only *interpretatively*—that is, according as our participative understanding of them increasingly makes sense of, accommodates, and integrates objectifiable elements arranged in significant structures. And on the other hand, all the details we objectively know *about* things and ourselves and other persons and humanity and the world are indeed a matter of true knowledge, but they acquire meaning only to the extent that they, too, are known *interpretatively*—that is, in their relevance to the whole.

[a] In mentioning *structure* and *unity and multiplicity*, the present digression has evoked themes treated in a fundamental fashion long ago (§§10-11, esp. §11, 3; cf. also §58, 2). In that context, the issue of *interpretation* and its relationship to perspective ("horizon") came up, too (§11, 5). It stands to reason that some of the other issues that surfaced then should turn out to be relevant to the present discussion, too. This holds especially for *encounter and dialogue*: we know reality by interpretation, also in the sense that we share our different perceptions and perspectives with one another, both as individuals and as groups (§11, 4). And our assurance that, while interpreting, we are indeed in touch with *reality* reveals that, if we know the truth, we know it

---

[j] Readers of Martin Buber's *Ich und Du* (ET *I and Thou*) will have noticed, in this analysis, a transposition of his treatment of the appropriate interplay between knowledge by relationship ("I— Thou" knowledge) and knowledge by objectification ("I—It" knowledge).

in *hope*, as we share our always provisional, always perspectival interpretations (§11, 6).

[6]   Our analysis has shown that comprehensive, totally objective, definitive knowledge of humanity and the world is and remains inaccessible to us. We know the order of nature in its all-encompassing integrity only by way of familiarity and participation. That is, we know it interpretatively, as we let ourselves be guided by the patterns of convergence that strike us and the perspectives we construe.

This has consequences. The task of interpretation faces human understanding with redoubtable standards of excellence, not in the last place because the standards will recede forever: interpretation, like tradition, is never done. If no individual person and no human community can know humanity and the world conclusively and definitively, then no individual, no group can ever claim exemption from interpretation; none can claim knowledge that is neither perspectival nor based on convergence.

[§64]   AGAIN: THE CHRISTIAN DIALOGUE WITH THE WORLD RELIGIONS

[1]   This is the moment to return to our principal thesis: the Christian respect for the universal order of nature must naturally extend to the ways in which other religions have acknowledged and interpreted that natural order. The lengthy analysis just conducted leads to a conclusion: in today's global world community no individual and no community—not even the Christian Church with its divinely authorized, universalist missionary commitment—can propose their understanding of the natural order of humanity and the world as definitive and, in that sense, exclusive; none can afford to dismiss alternative interpretations of the world and humanity as ultimately irrelevant, dated, or unworthy of consideration [k].

---

[k] This point has special relevance in Christianity's encounter with Judaism. The fact that the Christian profession of faith involves the fulfillment of Israel's faith-journey (§40, 3) does not in the least entail the profession that Judaism is dated, or, for that matter, that Christianity represents the fulfillment attained. Cf. F. J. van Beeck, *Loving the Torah More than God?*, pp. 3-4, 66-82. Norbert Lohfink, in *Der niemals gekündigte Bund* (ET *The Covenant Never Revoked*), has convincingly argued that Christianity and Judaism are embraced by *one and the same* Covenant, namely the *New* Covenant. Both, too, are short of the fulfillment of God's promises; both travel on their several ways of salvation, which are not separate, but "dramatically" related to one another; that is, both need one another's instruction and correction if both are to attain to the perfection of the Torah.

This can be put differently. We—non-Christians and Christians alike—profess positive faiths that also imply a fundamental understanding of the natural order of the world and humanity. Not surprisingly, our positive statements of faith differ a great deal, but then, it is in the nature of positive religious traditions to be very different. Our understandings of the world and humanity are different, too, but it is clearly the same world and the same humanity we are referring to, even though we do not comprehend just *how* they are the same—that is, we agree they are the same even though we interpret them differently.

Where do we get the idea that it is the same world and the same humanity we are referring to? What makes us think we can get past our interpretations of them? The answer must be: the *implications of the act of interpretation itself* (cf. §102, 4, a).

[a] Let us start with a parallel. We know from experience that simply hearing someone speak a different language conveys, in and of itself, the present situation's potential, both for continued incomprehension (with the likelihood of hostility) and for mutual understanding (with the possibility of peace). This is so because it is obvious to us that we both speak *languages*, and we know that languages, no matter how foreign-sounding they may be, are—must be—*interpretable*, at least to an appreciable extent. Thus *the speech-situation in and of itself lays bare the fact that we are meant to communicate even if we do not understand each other's language*. But this experience of communication *below* the level of language faces us with a choice: we can either decide not to pursue the process, or we can decide to learn how to cross the linguistic boundary and to communicate with each other by particular linguistic means—that is, by linguistic interpretation. There is something else that speech-situation conveys as well, at least unthematically: neither communication nor interpretation has anything to gain from the assertion, on the part of either party, that its particular language is superior to the other's.

Positive faith-professions, as George Lindbeck has rightly argued, have basic characteristics in common with languages; chief among these is that languages are cultural in nature; they must—and can—be *learned* (§13, 1, [*f*]; §22, 2, a; §51, 4, d; §58, 1, c, [*c*]).[16] Just as we must both resolve to communicate across linguistic divides and develop the interpretative skills to do it, so it takes willingness as well as interpretative skill to communicate across the divides laid bare by the encounter between the great religions. Both the willingness and the skills to deal with the particulars are a matter of learning. To those open to learning, the simple encounter with a different world-view, like the simple encounter with a speaker of a foreign language, involves the realization that the stated convictions we both live by are *interpretations*—our particular interpretations of humanity and the world. It also make them realize that these interpretations harbor, in and of themselves, the potential for mutual understanding and enrichment, simply because they are *interpretable*, at least to a large extent, to others—that is, others can learn about them.

[2] This recognition has implications. Most of all, in our very attempts at interpreting our various interpretations of the natural order to each other there is implicit a twofold *fundamental* affirmation—one on which we find ourselves in practical agreement: the world and humanity are basically intelligible, and we humans are one at least in the sense that we recognize each other as essentially equipped for the kind of intelligent, interpretative communication that can lead to growth in shared, participative understanding of truth, of the kind that may endure [*l*].

[3] This final affirmation, which is *implicit in the persistent practice of interpretative communication* must guide the dialogue among the great religions, rather than any *explicit* profession of a single, common, overarching, *systematic* philosophical or religious faith. It is only by participation—that is, by interpretation—that all of us know humanity and the world in their natural integrity. Does it not stand to reason, then, that it is by the patient sharing of our several perspectival understandings of humanity and the world that we are

---

[*l*] This is as good a moment as any to make a brief statement of philosophical principle, partly inspired by Johann Baptist Metz' insistence, in recent years, that transcendental neo-Thomism has insufficiently confronted the individualism inherent in the Enlightenment and Idealism, and thus suffers from a lack of affinity with history and society as primary realities. The thesis developed in the present paragraph is one that is implicit in many of the discussions developed in *God Encountered*; it is, I think, insufficiently developed in the work of, say, Karl Rahner and Bernard Lonergan. It is this. The subsistence of any creature is rooted in its being unconditionally related to God; relatedness is integral to its ontological constitution. No wonder relatedness also constitutes an area of basic, ontological affinity among creatures; interrelatedness is part of the originality of any creature. Specifically, therefore, the human person's dynamic, transcendental attunement to God encompasses, as an integral element, an orientation to *interpersonalness*. In developing this conviction, Martin Buber and Hans-Georg Gadamer have been my principal mentors.

likely to come to a better—if never definitive—understanding of the world and the humanity we share? And could it even be that such a persistent practice of hermeneutics will also help reveal two fundamental implicit truths about the natural order we appear to have in common: the essential intelligibility of humanity and the world, and the fundamental unity of humanity in virtue of its capacity to find and appreciate truth—that is, our native resemblance to the transcendent One (cf. §2, 1)? Could it be, too, that in this way we will also best succeed in conveying that as believers we profess faith-commitments that we find endlessly enlightening and of which we expect that they will provide us with guidance to the end? That as believers we are not living by the affirmation and imposition of totalitarian ideologies that brook no questioning? And thus, could the interpretative dialogue reveal, by implication, that our faith-commitments do indeed aspire beyond the furthest imaginable horizon—to the One that many of us—Jews, Christians, and Muslims—worshipfully call God?

[4] Despite some appearances to the contrary, the proposal just advanced is not an attempt to trade in the mistaken Christian triumphalism of the past for an equally mistaken relativist pluralism,[17] for several reasons.

[a] First of all, the proposal, which is fundamentally indebted to Hans-Georg Gadamer's work, understands tradition as a process of ongoing interpretation, which keeps alive a continuous adjustment of perspectives—in Gadamer's term, a "fusion of horizons"— across times and places (§56, 11, b; cf. §23, 5; §51, 2, [o]).[18] In interpreting the judgments of the past, we try to reconstruct the historic concerns that prompted, inspired, and thus prejudiced the judgments, in such a way that they were able to serve as appropriate (or at least understandable) responses to them. But what happens in this process of interpretation is that the past puts *us* on the line. Under the impact of our own questioning, judgments made in the past turn out to be able to challenge *us*; the judgments of the past lay bare the concerns that prompt, inspire, and thus prejudice the judgments *we* live by. Thus the examined and interpreted past reveals us to ourselves.

Implicit in Gadamer's hermeneutical theory is the affirmation of absolute truth as a living *reality*, ultimately transcendent, yet endlessly fascinating in the present. Those truly devoted to the process of interpretation will find themselves continually chastened as well as delighted by the discovery that knowledge of this ultimate reality is available only by participation, in perspectival fashion, even asymptotically, and not in a form that will ever be exhaustive or definitive [m].

[b]   Secondly, it is true that the Christian Church professes its faith in an overarching divine design, namely, that it is in Jesus Christ risen that God has definitively welcomed humanity and the world into the divine life [n].   Still, "the Church has re-

---

[m] This last formulation is inspired by Pius XII's *Humani generis* of 1950. This encyclical rejects (albeit mostly by caricature) the contention, allegedly held by "the more insolent" [*audaciores*] among contemporary Catholic theologians, that "the mysteries of the faith can never be signified by means of adequately true notions [*numquam notionibus adaequate veris significari posse*], but only by means of, as they put it, 'approximative' and ever-changeable notions, by means of which the truth is to some extent suggested [*indicetur*], but also necessarily distorted [*deformetur*]" (DS 3882; cf. CF 147).   The passage is correct, of course, in affirming that the mysteries of the faith can be expressed conceptually; however, it overlooks the fact that such conceptual expressions always proceed to become part of a living Tradition.   In this light, as L. Loosen has aptly observed, "behind all ecclesiastical pronouncements, even the most venerable, there is never a period, always a comma" ("Geen christendom zonder joodse Jezus," p. 264).   Consequently, as time goes by, not only does it take interpretation to determine just what a dogma meant to say when it was first formulated; under pressure of new times and places, the dogma itself may come to invite further reflection, and hence, possible development.

[n] Here it is of the utmost importance to realize once more that the central theme of the Christian faith is the glory of God and God's commitment to share the divine nature with humanity and the world (cf. §20, 2); it is *not* the question "Who is saved?" (cf. Lk 13, 23-24!).   Thus I cannot agree with Paul F. Knitter's decision to seek for a firmer foothold for pluralism in "soteriocentrism" (*The Myth of Christian Uniqueness*, p. 187).   If the salvation issue is allowed to become Christianity's dominant preoccupation (as it has in many ways since the sixteenth century), Christians are likely, by an exercise known to psychologists as projection, to interpret other religions far too narrowly.   This undiscerning approach turns other religions into *competing systems of salvation* (and eventually, under the influence of rationalist tolerance, into alternative ones, even though a liberalized version of Christianity usually continues to be presented as a philosophically superior salvation system).   In the long run, great, original figures like Gautama Buddha then get ignorantly lumped together under the rubric of "Savior figures" or even "Christ figures"; whether this alien characterization is imposed on them in admiration or in disqualification is irrelevant.   The great Tradition of the undivided Church has been less prejudiced.   It has viewed, with far deeper discernment, the great souls in the history of religions as revelations of the eternal *Logos* in creation (cf. §23, 3, a) and the religions themselves as expressions of humanity's natural desire for God, and thus as worthy of careful, appreciative (if critical) understanding (cf. NA 2-3).   It has also been prepared to recognize them as potentially misleading manifestations of human depravity, which makes them worthy of careful, compassionate understanding.   And when it comes to the question who is saved, a pilgrim Church that can commit some of its own sinful members to God's judgment by excommu-

ceived this truth, not in its fulfilled shape, but in the witness of Jesus Christ. He came 'to bear witness to the truth' (Jn 18, 37). The faith, while eschatologically unconditional, is a transitory, finite shape of the Truth."[19] That is, the fulfillment of this divine commitment remains a matter of hope; consequently, *the Christian profession of faith remains true only to the extent that it is interpreted perspectivally* (cf. §59, 5; cf. also §40, 1; §42, 1).[20] Present faith does not give the Christian Church any present grasp of the *shape* of the eschatological fulfillment of humanity and the world; what access to the fulfillment the Church does have must operate on discernment—that is, on *interpretation* [o].

This leads to a further point. Later on in this volume, it will be argued that the catholic tradition holds that the natural order is fully revealed only in the act of being divinely exceeded (§82, 4; cf. §69, 4). This proposition already has a consequence for our present argument: in not claiming to grasp the shape of the *fulfillment* of humanity and the world to come, the Christian faith implies that it has no definitive understanding of them *in their natural integrity* either [p]. For all the eschatological assurance inherent in the Christian profession of faith, it is in the nature of Christianity, and hence of its universalism, to be *transitional*—a proposition we will argue later on, too (§76, 1). Consequently, the Christian Church need not— and indeed must not—think it incumbent upon itself, simply by virtue of its definitive profession of Christ's sovereignty and uniqueness, to sit in judgment on other religions or to assign definitive places to them, either in God's kingdom to come or in God's world as we know it already. Just *how* Christ is Lord, already in the present moment, of all the dead and all the living (cf. Rom 14, 9) is a mystery of eschatological faith and hope, not a matter of present comprehension. This mystery, in other words, is inaccessible to Christians except by way of perspective—the kind of perspective that is designed to foster in the Church the attitude of the pilgrim, not the arbiter.

---

nicating them with a view to their salvation (1 Cor 5, 4-5), can surely entrust to God's merciful judgment those who, as a matter of simple fact, seek God with an upright heart along other pilgrim paths.

[o] This raises, of course, the difficult issue of the hermeneutics of eschatological language—to be discussed later, in its appropriate context.

[p] At this point it should have become clear why the term "universalist *perspectives*" was used when it was explained, in §58, that the Creed mediates between, on the one hand, humanity and the world, and on the other hand, their graced fulfillment in God.

[c] What, then, are we to make of Karl Rahner's proposal to call
the countless people who live well and nobly outside the Christian community, by the light available to them, "anonymous
Christians"? The expression, unfortunately, has elicited as least
as much misunderstanding as genuine Christian openness. It is
clear that it must not be understood as an expansionist gesture
by which countless admirable non-Christians, unbeknownst to
themselves, are captured by a totalitarian church that brooks no
goodness in the world outside itself. It is clear, too, that it is
one way to express the Christian marvel at the free revelation of
God and the *Logos* in the world (cf. §23, 3, a); hence, it also conveys the Christian commitment to respectful missionary effort.

Unfortunately, however, it must also be said that Rahner's insight has encouraged a whole generation of systematic theologians to content themselves with a generous wave of the hand in
the direction of the great non-Christian religions, and to think
of themselves as dispensed from all attempts at a detailed understanding. This amounts to turning the phrase "anonymous
Christians" into pure theory. To be credible, marvel at the manifestation of the *Logos* at work in the world must inspire encounter at close quarters. For that reason, too, it has been argued
that the interreligious dialogue must concern itself with the
religions' positive elements (§62, 1, c).

[5] The mention of close quarters calls to mind the figure of the
historical Jesus. The imitation of Christ would seem to commend
truly Christlike approaches to other religions (not to mention Judaism) to the pilgrim Church. This is not to imply, of course, that the
historical Jesus, or the early communities in imitation of him, showed
appreciation for religious *systems* not their own. But time and again,
Jesus did make Israel's universalist tradition (cf., for example, Is 66,
18-21!) his own, and found and admired true faith outside Israel, and
glorified the Father for it. The Gospel of Luke goes so far as to have
Jesus address the Christian community with an eschatological threat
based on that same Jewish universalism (Lk 13, 24-29).

The memory of that threat, it is true, does not come naturally to
a triumphalist Christianity still residually accustomed to the attractive (and often quite constructive) privileges of the Constantinian
establishment and its aftermath. But now that the Christian faith
no longer defines the prevalent cultural climate, it is easier to see
that those privileges had a dark side to them, too. They caused the
Church to lose its pre-Constantinian ability to give an account of its

faith from a position of equality and even subordination, amidst a variety of non-Christian religions and philosophies and often before the tribunal of the powers that be (cf. §74).[21] The second-century apologists had still been ready to do that; so had Origen (§27, 4, a-c). In accepting establishment, the Church lost touch with some of the patience and neighborliness that the early communities, in imitation of the historical Jesus, had shown vis-à-vis outsiders (cf. §32, 2). In the process, it also lost, in all likelihood, some of its original sense of Jesus' God, as Gerd Theißen pointedly (if somewhat testily) reminds us (cf. §106, 2):

Christian faith in God has often been fundamentally compromised by its entanglement with power and domination. A persecuted minority for centuries, Jews have more credibly testified that the God of the Bible is not on the side of the powerful and the dominating.[22]

[6] Recent years have seen a vigorous discussion of fresh proposals—fresh indeed but some of them also strongly reminiscent of questionable eighteenth-century precedent [q]—aimed at understanding all the great religions, as a matter of stated principle, in a pluralist perspective, by means of a universalism that thoroughly relativizes particular religions by "placing" them in an all-encompassing framework. In this setting, all the religions' allegedly universalist intentions tend to be viewed as equally right, and all their allegedly particularist claims as equally mistaken (cf. §28, 4, a, [d]). While allegedly promoting dialogue among the religions, this approach in reality favors "a new monologue containing them instead."[23]

[a] The more general theological writings of the learned islamicist Wilfred Cantwell Smith are a good example of this very unsatisfactory approach [r]. The problem is that Smith offers,

---

[q] For a competent discussion of no less than 14 recent books related to this issue, cf. the twin review essays by Francis X. Clooney ("Christianity and World Religions: Religion, Reason, and Pluralism") and Paul F. Knitter ("Making Sense of the Many") in *Religious Studies Review* 15(1989): 197-204.204-07.

[r] While I must strongly disagree with Professor Smith, I wish to recognize expressly that his approach to religious pluralism bears the marks of his lifelong struggle to understand a different religion in all its particularity, Islam. This spells the difference between Professor Smith and an author like John Hick, who has also treated the issue of religious pluralism with great frequency, but always in almost entirely general terms and in reliance on secondary materials (cf., most recently, *An Interpretation of Religion*, p. xiii). Professor Hick's oft-repeated rejection of the absoluteness of Christianity would seem to be the principal source of the energy with which he has committed himself to very firm judgments about

under cover of an exhortation to dialogue, what is in reality a hierarchical classification of all positive religions. As long as he simply discerns a "vision of world brotherhood" as a development that "we *believe* to be *a step towards* God's vision," there is still a welcome note of perspective and provisionality, even though Smith's reference to God's vision as the (known?) point of perspective raises doubt [s].[24] But there is good reason to enter firm reservations when Smith proposes that it is the task of theology "to formulate *not a view of others seen through Christian eyes*, but rather a view, in global perspective, of humankind, ... *a God's-eye view*, one might *almost* wish to say, of *all the human family.*" Are divine eyes—eyes other than Christian ones—available to Christians? Are they available to anyone? Finally, reservation should turn into firm rejection when the "almost" is dropped and the ruling is handed down in all its undisguised immodesty: "... in God's eyes there is genuine pluralism" [t].[25] This is the kind of illegitimate theological language that cries out for the realization that when it comes to the knowledge of ourselves, other persons, and humanity and the world—not to mention God—there are, in the final analysis, no judges and arbiters, only participators, discerners, and interpreters.

The curiously highhanded, even authoritarian overtones of this new, enlightened orthodoxy are due to the fact that its advo-

---

other religions. But the problem with those judgments is that they would appear to have exempted the author, in advance, from the conscientious, detailed study of any of the religions themselves.

[s] The doubt is reinforced by the anthropological reduction of religion implicit in the title of the essay from which the quotation is taken: "Mankind's Religiously Divided History Approaches Self-Consciousness." Is human self-consciousness the essence of religion? Even more pertinently, is the "God" whose vision Smith wishes to approximate simply human self-consciousness writ large (cf. §25, 4, d; §35, 2-3)?

[t] Smith can write, with an astonishing lack of awareness of the relativity of his own position: "I am ready to argue with a Christian theologian, on Christian premises, that the modern comparative religionist's vision of the religious history of mankind provides a truer vision of that *total history*—that is, a vision closer to *God's way of seeing it*, a more authentic *Heilsgeschichte*—than is *any interpretation of this wideranging matter formulated within the Church* before the present information, *or indeed any serious historical information*, was available. It is significant to add this: that I would argue the corresponding point with Muslim theologians, on Islamic premises. I write that sentence not glibly, but in full seriousness, realizing that *the radically new vision* that it implies *would have to be* defended before and ultimately *assimilable by Muslims themselves.* ... [T]his religious reconceptualization is not simply my wish but is *necessitated by the advance of modern knowledge*" (*Religious Diversity*, p. 112; italics added for emphasis).

cacy of tolerance comes mainly from above. Those who profess it tend to claim, whether implicitly or explicitly, that they occupy the higher ground—that theirs is the viewpoint from which all religions, not to mention humanity and the world as a whole, can be *placed*—that is, *judged*. The principal problem with such a principled pluralism is that it fails to realize that *its* understanding of the world and humanity, too, is *participative*, not comprehensive. What is unacceptable, therefore, is the definitiveness of its claim—or, in other words, *its deficient awareness of the relativity of its own perspective.*

Curiously but not really surprisingly, blindness to the relativity of all understanding is precisely what this new approach would seem to have inherited from the very orthodoxies it regards —often with reason—as dated because they are out of step with the temper of the present, allegedly tolerant age. Under cover of the fine-sounding, tolerant slogan of "pluralism," therefore, this approach invites all religions to submit to the new universalism by giving up whatever is incompatible with it, just as the old orthodoxies—supposedly—had demanded that all other faiths give up whatever was incompatible with themselves. But why would anyone wish to trade in an old, sturdy (if theocratic) orthodoxy for an almost entirely theoretical, pan-humanitarian ideology that looks so blatantly like a benign form of post-Christian, rationalist, Western imperialism?

Very sensibly, therefore, in a world torn apart by patently unjustifiable differences and inequalities that beggar description, this brave, suspiciously *painless* type of liberal universalism of Western origin has been accused of "view[ing] the whole world as like unto itself, and [of keeping] its distance, even if it be a sympathetic distance, from the wretched of the earth" [*u*].[26]

[7] This can also be put in the straightforward, uncompromising language of Christian doctrine. The original unity of all of humanity, along with the whole world, is protological: it is of God's fashioning, and it is in the nature of a first instalment on a magnificent promise. The ultimate unity of all of humanity, along with the whole world, is eschatological: again, it is of God's making—however and whenever God may fulfill creation's native potential beyond

---

[*u*] For recent Catholic attempts to avoid the liberal universalism widely associated with the name of John Hick, cf. Francis X. Clooney, "The Study of Non-Christian Religions in the Post-Vatican II Roman Catholic Church."

anyone's wildest dreams ever, by virtue of the full sharing in the divine life.

For the here and the now, however, as the remaining chapters in this first part of our second volume will make clear, we will have to argue a somewhat paradoxical proposition. While we will uphold the virtual finality of the Creed we profess [v], we will invoke that finality to argue that *our Christian commitment must be to the in-between*—that is, to the ongoing pursuit of justice and truth in the present. This will partly consist in the respectful cherishing of all that truly distinguishes all of us and in the painstaking overcoming of all that estranges us in the distinguishing. This conception of truth and justice will forever show signs of the here and the now; it will have to submit to the dynamics of provisionality; it will have to combine modesty with hope. The modesty will consist in reckoning with the possibility that at any time and in any situation any of us *may*, by absolute standards, be thoroughly misguided in what we think or do, even in our best moments and our surest judgments. The hope will consist in the trust that humanity and the world will truly come into their own by a design not conceived by human reason nor made by human hand—an incomprehensible, hidden design that is as holy as it is loving, and that comes to do justice to us from beyond us. In view of the accomplishment of that hoped-for design, neither truth nor justice is accomplished by claiming that it is in the nature of Christianity (or, for that matter, of any other faith or philosophy) to give us a commanding bird's-eye over-view of humanity and the world—a view claimed to be a "God's eye-view." Only the Lamb who was slain, the Lion who has conquered, is worthy to open the scroll that has the mysteries of the fulfillment sealed up in it (Rev 5, 1-5. 12). Final, absolute justice and final, absolute truth are ours to anticipate, not grasp.

And in any case, we know from the Gospel just how God means to direct our gaze as we view humanity and the world. We are to view them not from any height, but, so to speak, "from below"—that is, from the traveling Samaritan's patient, neighborly viewpoint. For the pilgrim Church to try to define, in the name of God, the final unity of humanity and the world while it stills finds people lying by the

---

[v] This terminology is borrowed from Bernard Lonergan. The affirmations of the Creed are not absolute in the sense of "formally unconditioned"; rather, they are judgments of the "virtually unconditioned" kind. Cf. *Insight*, pp. 280-81, 377-78, and esp. 670 and 707-13.

roadside with no one to understand or serve them would be the equivalent of walking to Jerusalem with blinders on. Or, to change the metaphor, to dream up a common language this side of the eschatological Halleluyah amounts to compounding the already existing confusion of tongues with yet another vociferous idcological jargon; in that sense, it would only help shore up the tower of Babel.[27]

[8] It is time to round off our initial explorations of the subject-matter of these first two chapters: the implications of the fact that the Creed offers itself, to the Church as well as to all of humanity and the whole world, for *interpretation.* This is not to imply that the next chapter will now be able to rush into commentary on the text of the Creed itself; that will be mainly the task of the third part of the second volume of *God Encountered.*

For the moment, we must continue to remember that the text of the Creed is properly understood only in the light of its univer-salist perspectives. While intelligible, these perspectives are yet in-comprehensible, because, taken together, in their proportion to each other, they form an *absolute* knowable only by participation: the height of grace held out by God, and the depth of nature up-held by God and open to God (§57, 4).

This is the kind of challenge capable of giving rise to further fundamental theological thought. Hence, after an opening section designed to summarize the state of the question, the next chapter will continue our exploration of these two horizons, so forbidding yet so irresistible. It will do so by reflecting on the former this time—that is, on the height of grace held out by God.

CHAPTER 3

Gateway to Contemplation

RETROSPECT AND OUTLOOK

[§65] TWO COORDINATED UNIVERSALISMS

[1] Before embarking on our interpretation of the Creed as it points to God, let us take some time to sum up. The Creed is a structure with windows. It places the Christian faith, *and hence itself,* between two perspectives. It is in virtue of *two coordinated universalisms* that the Creed elicits and mediates the absolute faith-abandon that is beyond any articulation, let alone comprehension. For the two universalisms involve God's all-encompassing, radically transcendent mystery and the corresponding mystery of humanity, which is utterly dependent on it (§9, 1-2; cf. also §35, 4, a).

On the one hand, and known mainly from the point of view of *retrospect,* there is the universalism that is based on the depth of God-given *nature.* On the other hand, and knowable principally from the point of view of *prospect,* this nature is meant, in God's inscrutable design for all-encompassing salvation, to be encountered, embraced, cleansed, and filled to overflowing by God, in a culmination of self-communicating grace (cf. §57, 2, c). The two universalisms find their common center in the person of Jesus Christ risen—"the same yesterday, today, and forever" (Heb 13, 8). In his presence to the Church in the Spirit, he is the eternal root, the enduring embodiment, and the everlasting promise of the "admirable exchange" between God and humanity.

[a] Taken together and personified in Jesus Christ, these two transcendent, universalist perspectives—the depth of God-given nature being encountered by the height of God-given grace—comprise the *doxological essence* of the Christian faith (§36, 1-2), in virtue of which humanity and world are being drawn, by participation, into the worship of the living God.

It is in place and time that this essence is being played out, in
response to the person of Jesus Christ revealed as the Way. This
is where the *content* of the Creed is set, between the universalist
perspective of the first creation and the universalist perspective
of the new creation. There it functions, like a bridge, between
eternity and eternity. The Creed's content, therefore, also
known as "the articles of the faith," firmly belongs to the sphere
of the *history of salvation* which—not surprisingly—has produced
the text of the Creed and which the Creed in its turn continues
to help shape. But just as the history of salvation must be interpreted in the light of the doxological essence which it plays out,
so the content of the Creed must be interpreted in the entranc-
ing perspective of the two universalisms between which it is set—
that is to say, *symbolically* (cf. §78). No wonder it is often *sung*
(§52, 6).

[2] From what has just been explained, two intimately related conclusions must be drawn—both of them relevant to the practice of
theology. First of all, the Creed must be understood and interpreted in the perspective of *an understanding of God as utterly and transcendently gracious*—that is to say, as the God who holds out the fulfillment of the promises professed by the Creed beyond all laws and
regularities that human reason can establish (§36, 2). Secondly, the
integral interpretation of the Creed involves the recognition of *God
as the mystery in and below the natural order,* that order, therefore, invites *fundamental theological reflection.*

In this way, the great Tradition—a tradition, it sometimes (sadly)
seems, as often sinned against by dint of pusillanimity as enjoyed in
the assurance of faith—cherishes the Creed on two fundamentally
related counts. First of all, it cherishes it in the light of Christ's resurrection, as *an invitation to universal ecstasy inspired by the grace prompted by faith in Christ risen.* But, secondly, in that light the Tradition
also cherishes it as *an invitation to human authenticity in believing, inspired by universal humanity's God-given capacity for God*—a capacity definitively revealed in the resurrection of Jesus Christ.

Today, therefore, in the midst of a culture excessively involved
with the present moment and accustomed to reading both literally
and hastily, the catholic tradition must insist that the Creed should
be neither accepted nor rejected at face value. Rather, it should be
read in a way that is as civilized as it is prayerful and contemplative.
That is to say, it should be *interpreted* in the light of its perspectives,
to enable us both to meet the culture and to encounter God. For

the Creed is not *ad hoc*; it does not deliver its goods instantly. If it did, it would be either an attempt to confine God (or faith in God) to a formula, or an instrument of bondage to confine the faithful to sectarianism. Instead, it is neither. As Flannery O'Connor wrote to an inquiring friend:

Dogma can in no way limit a limitless God. The person outside the Church attaches a different meaning to it than the person in. For me a dogma is only a gateway to contemplation and is an instrument of freedom and not of restriction. It preserves mystery for the human mind. Henry James said the young woman of the future would know nothing of mystery or manners. He had no business to limit it to one sex.[1]

[3] Of the two conclusions just drawn, the first concerns the consequences which the Creed's eschatological universalism imposes on the theological interpretation of it. Put differently, it concerns the consequences of the fact that the Creed must be interpreted in the perspective of *Christian worship*—the worship that is prompted by the risen Christ. This chapter will elaborate this theme.

The second conclusion is that the Creed invites theological reflection, in a universalist perspective, on the natural order, so as to meet human nature's native need for intellectual integrity and to do justice to the world to which the Christian profession of faith addresses itself. This can be put differently, too. The Creed needs to be interpreted in the perspective of Christian *witness*; the Christian Church owes the world a sign that it understands and loves it in a fundamental fashion—even more fundamentally, in the light of faith, than the world understands and loves itself. This second conclusion will be the subject of detailed discussion in the sixth and seventh chapters.

In the light of the two perspectives just elaborated, it was said, the content of the Creed is to be understood symbolically. This recognition will lead, in the fifth chapter, to important conclusions regarding the nature of Christianity, but not till after we have entered, in the fourth, into the painful debate that the issue of the nature of Christianity has raised, at least in the past five centuries.

PROFESSING THE CREED BEFORE GOD

[§66] THE MYSTERY BEYOND THE CREED

[1] At the root of the Church's profession of faith, it was explained in the first volume, lies the awareness of God's condescension. This

condescension is and must remain a transcendent mystery of glory
and love—a mystery that inspires an awe and an intimacy never to
be captured in thoughts or words, and to be approached and cherished mostly, as well as most appropriately, in worship. Far from
keeping the worshiping community at a distance from God,
Christian worship is the act by which it most closely participates in
the divine nature. This participation, however, is provisional; it is
wholly oriented to a fulfillment that remains entirely God's to bestow: the eschatological inheritance that consists in the final forgiveness of sins and the full participation in Christ's resurrection (§23,
4, c; cf. §34, 2; 6; §36, 2; §38, 5). Any present ecstasy of participation, therefore, must be tempered by a keen awareness of incompleteness. The Church's present union with God in the risen
Christ only serves to stir up its yearning for the total fulfillment of
humanity and the world; and the yearning in turn inspires a constant prayer for holiness of life in anticipation of the fulfillment (cf.
§36, 3; §40, 1; §46, 1; §47, 1).

[2] The Creed primarily reflects the Christian community's worship
and the eschatological aspirations implied in it (§59, 5; cf. §38, 2-4;
§52, 2). In keeping with this, the universalism first and foremost
professed by the Creed concerns the order of grace: the community
believes in God's universal salvific design as revealed in Jesus Christ
risen from the dead. That is to say, as a piece of positive religion,
the Creed professes that divine grace, freely and sovereignly bestowed
in and through Jesus Christ, is now taking shape in place and
time (§57, 2, d and [b]). Consequently, the Creed must be principally interpreted in the perspective of an understanding of God as
utterly and transcendently gracious. God is professed as the One
who holds out the fulfillment of the promises professed by the
Creed beyond all laws and regularities that human reason can establish as measures of reality (cf. §58, 9; cf. §36, 2) [a]. Any reliable interpretation of the Creed, therefore, must place it in the perspective of Christ's resurrection—the eschatological mystery that has
prompted it and which it seeks to profess. That is to say, theolo-

---

[a] The Creed professes that Jesus Christ is, in person, both the revelation and
the fulfillment of those gracious promises. Thus Jesus Christ is the only measure
(a measure incommensurate with any human measure) that is adequate to God's
graciousness. In him, by God's decree, the divine fullness resides embodied (Col
1, 19; 2, 9); he is the only one to whom God gives the Spirit *ouk ek metrou:* "without
measure" (Jn 3, 34).

gians must demonstrate the reasons why and the ways in which the Creed, properly understood, will in the last resort defy complete intellectualization [b].

[3] The Christian Tradition, therefore, has conclusive, *positively theological and christological* reasons of its own to insist, in endorsement of the main philosophical traditions of the West since Philo,[2] that God transcends human knowledge, and hence, that God is more adequately known by way of ignorance than by dint of affirmation. Paradoxically, therefore, in proportion as Christians have more emphatically professed that in Christ risen they truly know the God they worship, they have also felt more, not less, deeply compelled to profess God's utter transcendence. This profession preferably takes the form, not of forceful affirmations (whose rashness would belie the ignorance professed), but of speechless awe. Thus Gregory of Nyssa can take his cue from Qoheleth (Eccles 3, 7), and write, in a classic passage:

... no created thing can get outside itself by means of comprehensive contemplation; it stays within itself and whatever it may contemplate, it keeps itself in view; and if it should think it was contemplating something above itself, it does not have the nature [that would enable it] to contemplate what is outside itself. ... Still, the Good, which we have been taught to seek and to treasure, and which we have been counseled to grasp and hold on to, is above all created reality, and hence above comprehension. ... Now [the mind], busy as it is, runs through all that is known; still, it does not discover any means to run through the understanding of eternity—a way, let us say, to place itself on the outside, so as to pass beyond the above-mentioned world of [created] things.

But it is like someone who finds himself on a mountain ridge. Let us imagine a rock-face, flush and sheer. Seen from down below, it reaches up, with its straight, smoothed-down contours, up to an immeasurable height; and seen from above, up high, it is crowned by this summit, which plunges, from the precipice of its brow, down into a bottomless abyss. Now imagine the likely experience of anyone who would touch, with the tip of the toe, the rocky edge where it goes down into the abyss: one would find

---

[b] Using the terminology I used in *Christ Proclaimed* (pp. 249-53; cf. pp. 191-202), it would be possible to say that *the act of professing the Creed* adequately conveys its meaning, rather than the articles professed. This is so because the former conveys the *totality of the commitment elicited by the risen Christ*, whereas the latter convey the Christian discernments—partial by their very nature—about what is involved in believing in Christ's resurrection.

no place any more to put one's foot nor anything for one's hand to hold
on to.

This, I think, is also what the soul experiences when it passes beyond
its foothold in measurable thoughts, in its quest for that which exists from
all eternity and is immeasurable. It has nothing it can grasp a hold of, no
place, no time, no measure, nothing else of the kind—whatever is accessible to our understanding. Rather, as, from every side, it fails to catch on
to the ungraspable, it gets dizzy and does not know what to do, so once
again it turns to what is like itself in kind, happy now to know this much
about the Transcendent: it is persuaded that it is different in kind from the
things that it knows.

Thus, when reason touches on the things that are beyond reason, that
is the 'time to keep silence.' ... Thus in the understanding of God, when
the inquiry is about God's essence, then is the 'time to keep silence.'[3]

[a] If the mind's willing abandon to ignorance takes the shape
of negative theology, it is not surprising that there should arise
in the believer a matching willingness to settle for a sense of
mystery in the areas of anthropology and cosmology as well.
Gregory himself is not slow to point this out: "For at least in my
view, the creature has not yet come to know itself; it does not
understand what is the nature of the soul, what is the nature of
the body, whence are the things that are, how things arise out
of one another, how non-being comes into being, how what is
gets dissolved into what is not, what kind of harmony arises out
of opposites to result in this world. Now if the creature does not
know itself, how will it ever explain the things that are beyond
it? Thus about such things it is 'time to keep silence', for silence
is better in these matters."[4]

[4] This, Baron von Hügel insists, is the "legitimate agnosticism"
that "grows large in direct proportion to God's gift of himself to
man."[5] That is, in the closeness of God's self-revelation in Jesus
Christ, God has become proportionately more, not less, adorable
and ungraspable (Gk. *akataléptos*) for being so intimately known (cf.
§34, 2).

The great John Richardson Illingworth (1848-1915), therefore,
is right in pointing out that the language about God's total incomprehensibility, found in the patristic tradition from Clement of
Alexandria to John Damascene, serves the purpose

not ... of intellectual agnosticism, but of religious awe—*awe intensified* not
by the thought of God's remoteness, but *by the conviction and experience of his
intimate nearness to men.* It is thus much more akin to the reverential absti-

nence from the use of God's name, which characterised later Judaism, than to any sympathy with the Neo-Platonic exaggeration of his transcendence—his aloofness from the world.[6]

[a] Something else could have been added to this. The Christian affirmation of God's incomprehensibility has even less in common with René Descartes' resolve to prescind from the Christian faith in order to attempt, by dint of sole reason methodically applied *more mathematico*, to place God outside the reach of all skeptical and atheistic doubt and denial. The result of his reasoning was an abstract God, whose transcendence in relation to the universe was shorn of all immanence, and thus became a matter of mere remoteness. No wonder that this God was to turn out, ultimately, to be nonessential to the world (cf. §29, 1, [h]). What makes all of this doubly disquieting is the fact that Descartes' personal intentions in undertaking this line of argument were entirely pious, and that the spiritual director who encouraged him to pursue it, Cardinal Pierre de Bérulle, had a reputation for saintliness.[7]

[§67] EDUCATED IGNORANCE

[1] In its Western form, the Tradition has expressed its conviction about God's total incomprehensibility by affirming, in an idiom coined by Augustine of Hippo, that God is ultimately known in *docta ignorantia*—"educated ignorance." Significantly, for Augustine as for many other fathers, this conviction arises, not from rational argument—that is, as a necessary conclusion deduced from, say, a *philosophic concept* of *divine* infinity—but from the acknowledgment of a *human desire*.

In Augustine, the wellspring of this desire is twofold. Proximately, it stems from *eschatological anticipation*. Augustine finds it in Paul's letters, where thankfulness prompts aspiration, and aspiration a constant prayer for fulfillment. But only slightly more remotely, just below Augustine's explicitly Christian feeling of hope and anticipation, we can detect his indebtedness to the neo-Platonist sources of the broader patristic tradition, and to Plotinus in particular. All religious language is ultimately inadequate to the divine, but the anguish of this intellectual *impasse* is more than counterbalanced, and thus made supportable, by that highest of all human activities: the practice of *theōria*, that is to say, *longing contemplation*. "It is yearning that makes the heart deep."[8]

Thus for the Christian neo-Platonist Augustine, the ascent of the mind to God occurs as the person cultivates habits of prayerful aspiration to the fulfillment of God's promises. It is in the form of prayer that we become most directly (if negatively, in experiencing our ignorance) aware of the limitlessness of our own inner desire for beatitude, which is our total consummation in God. In contemplative desire we realize, as Augustine explains in his letter on prayer addressed to Proba, that we are looking for something more than we can understand even in the most enlightened of our prayers, namely,

the peace that surpasses all understanding [Phil 4, 7]; hence, in the very act of asking for it in prayer we do not know how to pray for it as we should [Rom 8, 25-27]. For obviously, we are ignorant of something if we cannot be cognizant of it as it is. At the same time, we will reject, repudiate, and find fault with all the prayers that do come to mind; we know they are not what we are looking for, even though we do not yet know what the thing that we *are* looking for is like. This shows that there is in us, so to speak, an educated ignorance of some sort—an ignorance educated by the Spirit of God, who comes to the aid of our weakness [Rom 8, 26].[9]

The Christian's self-abandon to the Spirit of God in the present moment, in the darkness of faith, so Augustine implies, is the anticipation of the beatitude that lasts forever.

[2] Medieval Christian thought in the West is unimaginable without this notion of *docta ignorantia*; it is part of the bloodstream of medieval mysticism as much as of scholastic theology and philosophy. Still, it entered into that bloodstream only very partially through Augustine. Thus, for example, while *docta ignorantia* is an integral part of the treasury of Thomas Aquinas' lifelong convictions, his immediate authority is not Augustine, nor even Anselm of Canterbury (cf. §101), but the Eastern patristic tradition. For Aquinas, the vehicle of that tradition is an influential treatise entitled *On the Divine Names*, traditionally associated with the name of "Dionysius the Areopagite," who came to believe at Paul's preaching on the Areopagus (Acts 17, 34) [c].

---

[c] The treatise's real author, who remains unidentified, was active around A.D. 500, probably in Syria; he wrote a sizable and very authoritative *corpus* of theological writings; he is nowadays known to scholars by the elaborate name of pseudo-Dionysius the Areopagite.

Like Augustine, pseudo-Dionysius belongs to the neo-Platonist mystical tradition. Unlike Augustine, the pastor and preacher, he is a monk—a theologian as well as a master of contemplative prayer. Not surprisingly, he makes explicit a small but significant step left implicit by Augustine, at least in his explanation of the expression "educated ignorance" in the letter to Proba. *Docta ignorantia*, for the author of *On the Divine Names*, is not primarily what it is for Augustine: the soul of our desire for *our total fulfillment in God*—the dark, unthematic anticipation, implicit in our every prayer for God's blessings, of the full beatitude that is to come. It is also, and more radically, *the actualization of our native capacity to enter into a direct, unmediated understanding of God's very being.* This capacity darkly and silently undergirds our every explicit thought about God as well as our minds' self-awareness; the practice of contemplative prayer can bring it to conscious, if totally obscure, awareness.

In a crucial passage in *On the Divine Names*, pseudo-Dionysius begins by accepting that God is appropriately worshiped by being addressed and named *affirmatively* (or, as the technical term goes, "*cataphatically*"), that is, by a variety of positive metaphorical names derived from created beings:

... we rightly say all these things about God, and [God] is [rightly] praised by means of names derived from all things that exist, inasmuch as all things whose cause he is are proportionate to him.

But after this, breathtakingly, he at once plunges into the ineffable:

But then again, the *most divine knowledge of God* is that which comes about *by ignorance, by way of a union that surpasses the mind,* when the mind, *taking its distance from all beings, and then also letting go of itself,* is united [with God] by splendors more than dazzling, out of which and in which it draws enlightenment, by the inscrutable depth of [divine] wisdom [d].

---

[d] Chap. 7, §3 (*PG* 3, coll. 871-2 AB; italics added for emphasis). For the most radical expression of this, cf. Evagrius Ponticus, *De Oratione*, 70 (*PG* 79, 1181C): "Prayer is the removing of thoughts" (*proseuchē gar estin apothesis noēmatōn*). Aquinas' commentary on the passage from Dionysius runs as follows (*In Librum Beati Dionysii De Divinis Nominibus, Cap.* 7, *Lect.* 4 [42]; Marietti n˚ 732): "[God] is known and praised on the basis of all things, inasmuch as they are proportioned to him as to their cause. But then again, there is another, most perfect knowledge of God, namely, one that works by removal, by which we know God by means of ignorance, by means of a kind of union with things divine that surpasses the nature of the mind." Another relevant passage in ps.-Dionysius is *Epist.* 5 (*Ad Dorotheum*, *PG* 3, coll. 1073-6). A most important passage is found in what became, arguably, ps.-Dionysius' single most influential work in medieval spirituality, the short treatise *De Mystica Theologia* (esp. chapter I, §§1-3; *PG* 3, coll. 997-1002). In English mysti-

The Areopagite makes no secret of his conviction that the uncovering of the human person's underlying capacity to enter into a direct understanding of God's being has an immediate consequence. If the highest, unifying knowledge of God is attained in the ignorance of self-abandon, then *this ignorance deserves to be, not only accepted, but actively cultivated.* This is done by positive "un-saying," or, in technical terminology, "*apophatically.*" Many centuries later, Baron von Hügel was to point in the same direction by recognizing the human capacity for a "dim, deep experience" of the transcendent God, which "causes our reflex knowledge of God to appear as no knowledge at all."[10] Hence, by pointedly removing from our conceptions of God all that God is not, we begin to make room in ourselves for the ignorance that unites with God.

Aquinas is following the Areopagite when he pays tribute to this ignorance that looms at the end of the mind's long road of *remotio* —the "removal" of all that is not God (cf. §107, 1; 4; §109, 4; 6; 10-11). There, in acts of awareness both luminous and obscure, the contemplative person's search for God (cf. §36, 2) will take shape in acts of naked surrender, animated by an ignorance which, better than any thought, will unite a person with the God *Who Is*—the Unknown and Living One.

This is why [John] Damascene says that [the name "the One Who Is"] does not designate what God *is*; rather, it designates a kind of infinite ocean of substantial being—undetermined as it were. Hence, when we proceed towards God on the road of removal, we first deny everything corporeal of God. Then we go on to deny everything spiritual as it is found in creatures, such as goodness and wisdom. At that point, all that is left in our minds is that God *is*, and nothing else; thus God *is* in some kind of perplexing fashion, so to speak. Last of all, however, we remove from God even this very *being* according as it occurs in creatures. At that point, God is left to dwell in a kind of darkness of ignorance; yet *after the manner of this ignorance*—at least as long as we are on our present way—*we are best united with God*, as Dionysius says. This is a dark cloud of sorts, in which God is said to dwell.[11]

---

cism, the influence of this latter treatise is most obvious in the cluster of writings attributed to the anonymous author of *The Cloud of Unknowing*, who is very probably also the translator of the treatise itself, under the title *Deonise Hid Divinite*. Cf. *Deonise Hid Divinite* (ed. Hodgson), pp. xxxiv-lvii, 2-10; *The Cloud of Unknowing and the Book of Privy Counselling* (ed. Hodgson), esp. pp. lxxvii-lxxxvii. On the theme of educated ignorance, cf. also §54, 6, b.

In a much later work, he puts it more succinctly as well as more emphatically:

This is the uttermost limit and the pinnacle of our knowledge in this life, that ... *we are united with God as unknown.* Now this will happen to us provided we know about God *what God is not,* while it remains utterly unknown what God *is.* Hence also, to demonstrate the ignorance involved in this most sublime knowledge, we read of Moses that *he approached the darkness in which God dwells* [Ex 20, 21]."[12]

[3] In seeking to understand these passages, it is essential to begin by interpreting the text taken from the Areopagite, and to interpret it in careful accordance with the writer's intentions. From the entire tenor of the passage it is clear that what the Areopagite has in mind is that marriage of love and understanding which is the soul of *worship and prayer.* Contemplation animated by love lies at the root of whatever intellectual insights he may develop. The anonymous fourteenth-century author of *The Cloud of Unknowing* identifies it, in his *Epistle on Prayer,* as "reverent affection": the worshipful love with which God is loved "chastely"— that is, ultimately, for the sake of God alone.[13] In other words, if pseudo-Dionysius is discussing the *semantics* of worldly language as it refers to God, he is not doing so simply on account of the intrinsic logical interest of the matter. The theoretical discussion of the relationship between *humanity* (and world) and God, and of the knowledge involved in that relationship, is entirely subordinated to the discussion of the quality of the relationship between *worshiper* (and world) and God—the relationship experienced in established practices of liturgical worship and mental prayer.

[a] The Areopagite begins by justifying those forms of worship in which natural language positively mediates between the worshiper and God; he does so by appealing to the analogy that results from creation. After that he moves on to higher forms— that is, to forms of worship characterized by silence, in which worshipers abandon their dependence on world and self so as to attain to God, transcendent as well as quite simply present, in *immediacy* and *union.* This explains why his primary conclusion is not negative ("no language will do complete justice to God") but positive ("true union with God can be attained through total ignorance and by means of that self-abandon that involves the highest form of knowledge"). This shows that throughout, the writer's interest—a genuine interest —in the natural order (and

hence, in the natural semantics of religious language) is rooted in his experience of the order of grace [e]. The latter provides him with the setting in which the reflection on the order of nature (and culture) makes sense.

[4] Aquinas' commentaries on pseudo-Dionysius invariably stay close to the original texts, yet they show a characteristic lack of emphasis on one theme: *the worshiper's abandonment of self*—that essential gateway to mystical prayer explicitly mentioned by the Areopagite. Aquinas replaces it by the theme of *the mind exceeding its natural capacity*. The reason for this is obvious: Aquinas' agenda is not initiation to contemplative prayer but introduction to theological reflection. Integral to the agenda behind this reflection is the development of *a theological epistemology reliably guided by philosophical reason* operating to the full extent of its capacity.

Yet not even in this heady context is the reference to mysticism and worship totally absent. It is characteristic of Aquinas (as well as a clue to his deepest intentions in doing theology) that he continues to mention union with God, and especially that he alludes to Solomon's temple dedication prayer and Moses' entrance, at Mount Sinai, into the presence of God—the latter a *locus classicus* in the Greek fathers to symbolize the mystical union with God to which the Christian is called (cf. §54, 6, b, and note 24).

Like so many of his peers in that fascinating twelfth and thirteenth century surge of humane and intellectual daring, Aquinas the Christian believer finds the use of human intelligence to the full extent of its natural ability as intelligible as the acceptance of its limitations. Consequently, he can afford to enjoy all the natural attractiveness of the mind's intellectual ascent to God. Consequently, too, he is not unnerved at the thought that there is a point at which mind will reach its limits. In fact, his clearheadedness about "knowing what God is not" is precisely what lends the character of real knowledge to his admission of ignorance about "what God is." This is so because *faith* has guided his naturally inquiring mind on

---

[e] The *Book of Privy Counselling* subtly shows that the "leaving behind" of articulate prayer forms has nothing to do with contempt of them. The author allows the persons whom he encourages to ascend to "negative" forms of prayer to continue to engage in reading and vocal prayer, but advises them not to make them central to their awareness (*The Cloud of Unknowing and the Book of Privy Counselling*, p. 135/13-19). Negative theology, in other words, *subsumes* and *integrates* affirmative theology; it does not reject it any more than faith rejects reason or grace rejects nature.

its way up through the degrees of worldly being; Thomas knows that, at the point where faith takes his mind beyond the limits of the world and beyond its own natural capacity for understanding, he will find himself truly at home in the emptiness of his mind, because he can abandon himself to the transcendent order of grace properly professed by faith. For *faith respects and recognizes all natural limits in the very act of going beyond them.* After all, it was faith that set his mind on its way of natural inquiry in the first place. Aquinas knows that union with God is rooted in nature, but he considers it anything but natural; it takes progressive elevation by grace to encounter God, not regression to nature (as the Enlightenment and Romanticism thought). Yet he also knows that in the encounter, the person's natural originality is actualized to the full.

Thus for Aquinas as for pseudo-Dionysius (and for Anselm as well: cf. §101, 9), it is the experience of grace that encourages and warrants the understanding available to the mind by reason of its natural ability to know. If neither exhibits the slightest confessional nervousness about the ultimately agnostic nature of the human understanding of God, it is because autonomous human intelligence is not their tribunal of last resort. Faith seeking understanding is. As a result, neither is threatened by unknowing or, for that matter, fascinated by it; neither has a vested interest in subject-centered philosophic agnosticism [*f*].

[a] All of this helps explain why a fourteenth-century treatise like *The Cloud of Unknowing* can display such "insistence upon the need for grace at every stage of contemplative prayer" [*g*], and at the same time be so charmingly natural, universalist, and even "agnostic" in its account of unitive prayer (cf. §36, 2 for a

---

[*f*] It might be added that neither the Areopagite nor Aquinas shows any trace yet, in this largely pre-literalist age, of the nominalist's (or, for that matter, the deconstructionist's) preoccupation with *the ascertainable meaning of words and statements taken in isolation being the norm of "real" knowledge.* This is the preoccupation that has so often led to disillusionment with words and statements. When literalists realize that writable or printable words and statements cannot *capture* the total meaning, they find themselves disappointed and tempted to say, on the rebound, that words and statements are no more substantial than the air used to pronounce them—*flatus vocis.* Then it is time to remember that *of course* there are gaps and crevices between words and between statements, but ordinarily these suggest depth of understanding, not lack of it; for thank God, there is at least as much to be read between the lines as on them.

[*g*] Thus rightly Phyllis Hodgson in *The Cloud of Unknowing,* p. lxx. Miss Hodgson quotes passages from chapters 1, 2, 27, 29, 34 to prove her point.

telling sample). Far from being a merely incidental feature, this emphasis on grace places *The Cloud* (and comparable medieval writings) firmly and positively in the Christian tradition.   In these writings, it must be observed, that tradition is so much taken for granted that the references to the explicit terms of the Christian profession of faith can afford to be few and far between [*h*].   For that reason, *The Cloud* can even go so far as to encourage the reader to leave behind, *in this particular, advanced form of prayer*, all thought of doctrine and piety.   This seemingly agnostic naturalness is liable nowadays to appeal to those who find modern, post-Christian and non-Christian forms of universalist contemplation attractive.   Yet it would be a mistake to conclude that the teaching of *The Cloud* can be *exhaustively* interpreted as a form of unspecified, natural, subject-centered religiosity, in post-Enlightenment, Romantic fashion [*i*].

[*h*] There is good reason to assume that the difference between Christian mysticism of the *seemingly* "purely natural" variety and explicitly "christological" mysticism is far smaller than the difference in usage would seem to indicate. What looks like "purely natural" mysticism to post-Christian readers, often presupposes identification with Christ in the Spirit as a matter of course in the ascent to God. Hence also the phrase "*implicitly* christological ground rule" in §36, 2.

[*i*] Ira Progoff, therefore, is making the characteristically modern mistake of *reductive interpretation* when he proposes a purely *anthropological* reading of *The Cloud.* Today's reader, he writes, is free to prescind from the explicitly Christian elements in *The Cloud.* They are a feature of merely historical interest, attributable—he explains, astonishingly—to a "rudimentary stage" of development in Western culture. Progoff overlooks the fact that the reduction of mysticism to autonomous natural inwardness was well known in the Middle Ages. Ruusbroec, for instance, described it in detail, especially in *Die geestelike brulocht* (pp. 538-71), and in *Vanden gheesteliken tabernakel* ("The Spiritual Tabernacle": RW II, pp. 335-37; cf. §109, 9, e), while making pointed references to it in *Vanden seven sloten* (pp. 162-165) and in *Een spieghel der eeuwigher salicheit* (RW III, pp. 198-99; cf. 191-93; ET *A Mirror of Eternal Blessedness*, in *The Spiritual Espousals and Other Works*, pp. 235-36; cf. 229-31). He even wrote his *Boecsken der verclaringhe* with the express purpose of giving a *reasoned* account of the thesis that true mysticism is a matter of grace, not of the cultivation of natural inwardness (cf. esp. pp. 114-21, 156-57). Unaware of all this, Progoff can endorse, without much ado, the modern "turn to the subject" as final, and explain that *The Cloud* encourages prayer that is in reality "self-sustaining," and that it "works toward its spiritual experience on *psychologically neutral ground*, where the modern and medieval *individual* can meet and understand each other not in terms of their *historical differences*, but in terms of their *essential quest*," in which "the references to the Bible, to Jesus, and to the nature of God have *only a transitory significance*." And in a condescending display of modern Deist and individualist prejudice, Progoff concludes, with a confidence that is truly amazing: "The Author of *The Cloud of Unknowing* describes the discipline of the contemplative life within the *framework* of the Christian orthodoxy of the fourteenth century; but *it soon becomes apparent* that he does not consider the *formal observance of ritual* to be dominant. He cautions his young student not to relax his

[b] Aquinas is not alone in making consistent efforts to arrive at a harmonious combination of grace and nature, and of faith and philosophy. In fact, his efforts have deep roots in the philosophical and theological traditions that have arisen in *all three branches of Western monotheism,* all of which avow that "God lies beyond our ken." As a matter of fact, the search for a true understanding of God—a search, significantly, always conducted *in close association with the search for the ways in which we understand everything else there is to understand*—is one of the principal characteristics of the intellectual traditions of "Jews, Christians, and Muslims who share the burden ... of *the one God, creator of heaven and earth, and Lord of all.*"[14]

Thus—to mention only one example—the great twelfth-century Jewish philosopher Moses Maimonides, in his *Guide for the Perplexed,* can resolutely put philosophy at the service of genuine religious faith. He does so, for example, by pointing out how foolish it is to praise God in extravagant ways, and by commending the "Men of the Great Synagogue" for their moderation in prayer and in speech about God [*j*]. This enables him to explain how God is properly approached by negative language, and conclude by writing: "I do not merely declare that he who affirms attributes of God has not sufficient knowledge concerning the Creator, ... or conceives Him to be different from what He is; but *I say that he unconsciously loses his belief in God.*"[15]

[5] Any reflection on human language, in antiquity and in the high Middle Ages as well as in our own day, tends to stimulate interest in the signification of words and the structures of knowledge, and reflection on both. Whenever this kind of reflection is applied to religious language, the tone of awe and the experience of worship tend to recede into the background; reason rather than faith

---

obedience to the teachings of the Church, but that *seems* to be mainly a *precautionary* measure. He does not want the neophyte to lose his connection with the traditional practices and institutions *before he is ready to sustain himself by individual work.* In this we can see *a clear indication* of the role that the teachings of *The Cloud of Unknowing* are to play *in the individual's development.*" Cf. *The Cloud of Unknowing,* ed. Progoff; quotations pp. 21-24 (italics added for emphasis). Cf. also §109, 9, a-b and d, and esp. [*bb*].

[*j*] The expression "the Men of the Great Synagogue" (*'anšê hakkᵉneseth haggᵉdôlah*) refers to a legislative body of 120 men, established (according to a legend found in the third-century collection of rabbinical sayings known as *Pirqê 'Avôth* ["Chapters of the Fathers"]) in Jerusalem in the fifth century B.C., at the time of Ezra and Nehemiah, to verify the text of the Hebrew Scriptures.

becomes prominent. The central thesis that God is known in ignorance usually continues to be vigorously affirmed, but the reasons
for it tend to be increasingly drawn from philosophical and logical
reflection and analysis.

This *relative* secularization of the concept of *docta ignorantia* can
be well observed in an important fifteenth-century author like Nicholas of Cusa, the author of the famous treatise *De docta ignorantia*
(*Of Learned Ignorance*).[16] Both Cusanus' philosophy and his theology are deeply universalist, and his platonizing style shows the
depth of his commitment to this attractive and very ecumenical
orientation. It also causes him to place his Catholic faith consistently in the context of an encompassing philosophical world view
characterized by positive ignorance. He insists that God absolutely
transcends all differentiations and oppositions; still, since God also
accounts for and *encompasses* the whole variety of being, the divine
transcendence must be understood in paradoxical terms, as the "co-
incidence of opposites." Accordingly, the *human understanding of
God* must transcend all the differentiations and oppositions that are
the stuff both of created reality and of human knowledge. In knowing God in ignorance, therefore, human knowledge, which is always
imperfect, attains, so to speak, the culmination of its imperfection:
in *docta ignorantia*, human understanding attains God as well as its
own perfection. This, however, is also the very point where human
nature discovers its high affinity with God—so much so that it,
among all creatures, turns out to have the natural capacity for the
incarnation of the Word [k].[17]

[6] It is useful to pause here for a moment, to notice the distance
we have traveled between Augustine and Cusanus, who can fairly be
said to represent, respectively, the start of the Christian West's reflection on *docta ignorantia* and its philosophic high point.

In Augustine's letter to Proba, it is *the givenness of Christian prayer*
that raises the issue. On the one hand, we find ourselves praying; on
the other hand we must admit that in praying, we find ourselves naturally ignorant, since we clearly do not comprehend the one thing
we know we are asking for. Thus the very practice of prayer brings

---

[k] Rudolf Haubst has reliably shown that Cusanus' philosophical reflections on
the incarnation, especially those in *De docta ignorantia*, must be placed in the
context of his indebtedness to far wider biblical and patristic traditions, which he
philosophically enhances in a strongly universalist perspective. Cf. *Die Christologie
des Nikolaus von Kues*, conclusions, pp. 305-12.

home to us that prayer is puzzling: we recognize that our every prayer is inadequate, yet we keep on praying. In the face of this inherent
irresolution, we wonder why it is that human ignorance—which is
weakness—does not succeed in paralyzing our prayer. Augustine
breaks the impasse by inferring, in faith, that the Holy Spirit must be
inspiring and supporting us in praying. Our surprising perseverance
in prayer, in other words, teaches us that our ignorance is deeply *doc-*
ta, which must be due to *the Spirit of God*, who bestows on us a real,
if entirely implicit, knowledge of our anticipated, God-given beatitude. We can abandon ourselves to this "knowledge." *Augustine's*
analysis is explicitly theological from beginning to end, even if there is a
strong philosophical, neo-Platonist undertow to lend credibility to
the analysis.

For Nicholas of Cusa *docta ignorantia* can be entirely conveyed in
terms of reason. Human ignorance is only natural where God is
concerned, and the human person is naturally educable to an
awareness of it. This education occurs as the mind, in its ascent to
God, gathers an ever deeper insight into the inadequacy of *all* its
understanding, and thus, *a fortiori*, of its understanding of God. In
this way, it ultimately attains the high realization of its total ignorance.

Yet even for Cusanus, worship, not philosophy, remains the root
experience. Thus he can open his dialogue *De Deo abscondito* ("on
the hidden God") with the following terse interchange:

Pagan: I notice how *you are most devoutly prostrate*, and shedding
tears—and not insincere ones, but from the heart. Who are you, please?
Christian: I am a Christian.
Pagan: What do you adore?
Christian: God.
Pagan: Who is the God whom you adore?
Christian: I do not know.
Pagan: How can you so ardently adore what you do not know?
Christian: Precisely because I do not know, I adore.
Pagan: Amazing, watching someone experiencing the appeal of something
he does not know.
Christian: It is more astonishing for someone to experience the appeal of
something he thinks he knows.
Pagan: Why?
Christian: Because *we know what we think we know even less than what we know*
we do not know.[18]

A modern commentator on the dialogue explains:

Knowing ignorance becomes the gateway, as it were, into the land of faith and love—the bridge that arches, out of the solitude of the I, over into the encounter of this I with the You of God. But in all this it must not be forgotten that the human person does not attain the vision of God in virtue of its *own* power, but that it is entirely left to God to turn graciously to the person in love and mercy, so as to enable the person to 'behold' him. The 'vision' of God, in the act of faith in him, is predicated on grace as much as on the heart's voluntary preparedness for this grace. ... Cusanus' 'intuition' is born out of the humility of the believing Christian in the presence of God; the intuition of the vitalist philosophers is separate from this God and places the human person at the center of being. 'Only a soul full of humility apprehends, in virtue of its breadth and depth, God most exalted,' Nicholas himself acknowledges.[19]

Thus Cusanus brings us back to naked faith (§9, 1): his deep delight in the boundless dimensions of his inner self turns out to be rooted in an even deeper acceptance of his utter dependence on a God who transcends all bounds.

EDUCATED IGNORANCE TODAY: WHICH AGENDA?

[§68] A MODERN ISSUE IN THEOLOGICAL INTERPRETATION

[1] The brief survey just completed calls for a moment of reflection. It is not difficult to notice the great variety of ways in which diverse thinkers in the Judaeo-Christian tradition have combined elements of faith and reason, grace and nature, and positive and natural religion (cf. §30, 2). In this variety, the catholic tradition's fundamental aim has typically been the *integration* of the two: it views the order of grace both as rooted in the order of nature and as its perfection (§26, 2, a). To make this integration intelligible, the catholic tradition (like the Jewish) has characteristically allowed theologians a fair amount of latitude of construal (cf. §22, 1). Yet not every synthesis is equally satisfactory. In fact, many catholic thinkers show traces of irresolution, inconsistency, and even dereliction in the way they apportion the responsibilities (cf. §27, 1, a) [*l*].

[*l*] An example of a serious failure of Catholic theology has been capably explained by Michael J. Buckley (cf. §56, 3; §84, 2, a, [*u*]; §99, 3, a). The rise of atheism in the Christian West, he has shown, is substantially rooted in a theological failure. At the dawn of the modern era, the credibility of the Christian faith was seriously suffering from the debilitating doctrinal quarrels that came in the wake of the Reformation. In this situation, an otherwise competent theologian like the

[2] This raises serious problems of interpretation today. We tend to separate reason and faith more sharply, which makes us more demanding when we find them combined. Just what *are* the really fundamental commitments of such great religious thinkers like Philo, Augustine, Maimonides, Aquinas, Dante, Spinoza? How do they apportion the relative authorities of faith and reason? And specifically, in regard to God, is the ignorance they propose a matter, ultimately, of faith or of reason? Is their acknowledgment of God a matter of professed, "positive" religious *awe* leading to adoration, or a matter purely philosophic, *reflective self-awareness* leading, perhaps, to an almost purely theoretical, Deistic acknowledgment of the existence of God, or to principled agnosticism?

[a] No wonder that modern scholars often disagree in their interpretations of the great religious thinkers. Where some will find harmony, integration, and balance between faith and philosophy and admire it where it can be found,[20] many more will detect irresolution and even inconsistency. Some will find, say, in Maimonides, pure philosophy with a mere veneer of residual (or merely practical, or even simulated) orthodoxy (cf. §27, 1, a), and are eager to unmask this.[21] Others will cry foul when great theologians combine faith and reason; they will accuse them of hanging on (or so it would seem to them) to anxious or prejudiced orthodoxy while at the same time availing themselves of philosophical concepts according as they are serviceable, using them "(to borrow a metaphor from Schopenhauer) like a 'hired cab' which one dismisses when one has no further use for it."[22]

[b] This kind of interpretation, while understandable, should give us pause. *In the modern era*, and especially in North America, we should remember, the cultural prejudice is that reason is the tribunal of last resort, and a fundamentally unprejudiced one at that; hence, we must *choose between* positive religion and reason,

Jesuit Leonard Lessius (1554-1623) relegated the entire responsibility for the fundamental question of God's existence to *philosophy*. As a result of this move, not only did Christian theology lose its footing in the natural understanding of the created order; it also positively contributed to the development of a new, exclusively secular concept of god based on the emerging natural science and the new, critical philosophy. Over time, however, this "god" got attenuated to the point where it became, at best, a superfluous hypothesis. Christianity had produced its own alienation. Cf. *At the Origins of Modern Atheism*, pp. 42-55, 304-06, 341-45.

because reason is "as good as" (that is, better than) "organized religion." This should make us somewhat suspicious of the often-heard demand for consistency in dealing with fundamental issues in terms of *either* faith *or* reason, despite the nobility of its declared purpose. For the demand may in fact represent little more than the modern cultural bias against positive religion—a bias unknown, to the same extent at least, in antiquity and the Middle Ages (cf. §30, 2).

Nor surprisingly, this bias is unthematically shared, in a variety of degrees, by many modernist or modernizing Christians, including those of catholic persuasion. Many of them tend to express broad agreement with a variety of latitudinarian propositions on natural or civil religion. Thus they become in fact, if seldom in theory, crypto-rationalist Deists. They tend to distrust—vaguely and thus all the more effectively—positive professions of faith as instances of sectarian, fideistic prejudice; when pressed they will agree that natural religion is what unites humanity in a manner more tolerant and hence, far superior, than positive religion could ever succeed in doing. Accordingly, if they glorify *docta ignorantia*, they tend to do so not so much out of awe before God as because they share a culturally prevalent investment in universalist agnosticism [*m*].

[*m*] "Charismatics," with their characteristic preference for negative theology, are especially susceptible to this temptation (cf. §54, 4, c; 6, b.) Among Roman Catholics, especially in North America, this often takes the shape of a mistaken application of the principle of religious liberty. The Catholic Church has recognized and accepted, at the intelligent urging of thinkers like John Courtney Murray, the separation of Church and State and freedom of religion as positive goods (DH 6-7; cf. GS 76). This liberty allows, and indeed favors, the free exercise of humanity's natural religiosity, including the practice of that religiosity in the form of a variety of positive religions. In such an arrangement, all of these religions agree—on political grounds but also on very good theological ones—to abstain from the use of political and legal means to compel compliance to any one religion. In the *public arena*, therefore, the various positive faiths are *subsumed* under the common "civil religion" or its agnostic equivalent: toleration in the name of the constitution viewed as the embodiment of the common good. But this subsumption, no matter how acceptable or even desirable *politically*, does not thereby acquire the status of *an article of Christian faith*; while recognizing freedom of religion as a *theological* good, the Church has never agreed that the Christian faith is simply one among the many possible, *fundamentally equivalent* shapes natural human religiosity has taken. In fact, the second Vatican Council's declaration on religious freedom, *Dignitatis Humanæ*, avails itself of its endorsement of religious freedom to exhort all members of the Church to attend to the Church's positive teaching, and to avail themselves of religious freedom to bear witness to their faith in the public arena (DH 14). Commitment to religious freedom and genuine respect for other religions, therefore, does not commit the Christian to a diluted profession of faith, let

By contrast, and on the rebound, many Christians who lay claim to orthodoxy tend to suspect philosophical skepticism behind every reflective, universalist approach to religious faith. On the Catholic side, traditionalists and fideists will insist that "the tradition"—usually a reduced version of it (§19, 1, a-d)—is the only valid form of Christian faith. On the Evangelical side, fundamentalists make analogous claims on behalf of "the Gospel" or "Biblical faith"—usually a selective version of it (§20, 1-5). Such types of faith, however, are in reality forms of irrational authoritarianism. Orthodox Christians of this type tend to welcome the profession of human ignorance about God, but never in order to commend or glorify it; they usually interpret it as the sinful plight of those who refuse to believe, and proceed to take advantage of it as an occasion for more insistent indoctrination. Thus fundamentalism and traditionalism will emphasize the theme of ignorance about God, not because of God's transcendent mystery, but because they have a theological investment in an uncritical acceptance of authority. No wonder that both tend to favor authoritarian options in the political arena, too.

[c] All of this leads to a general observation—one that amounts to an encouragement to apply the "hermeneutics of suspicion" to the opinions of those modern authors who are the most ardent advocates of positive religion or most skeptical in its regard. Given the modern reluctance to hold faith and reason together in harmony, or at least in creative tension (cf. §§28-30), modern interpretations of the great masters of the past must be read as critically as the past masters themselves. Whenever, therefore, a modern interpreter spots irresolution, inconsistency, prejudice, or special pleading in a classical author's treatment of the relationship between faith and reason, or grace and nature, it is wise to return the favor and to entertain the possibility that the inconsistency or the prejudice is to be found, not so much in the author interpreted as in the interpreter's mind.

[§69] THE CATHOLIC TRADITION

[1] The catholic tradition of interpreting the Creed acknowledges both reason and faith. Consequently, it will encourage articulate,

---

alone to a principled, fundamental agnosticism.

affirmative, reasoned thought and speech about God. Yet it will also affirm, paradoxically, that what guarantees true thought and speech about God—*including the thought and the speech involved in the Creed and in theology*—is the fundamental recognition that God is and remains the absolute mystery, and in that sense, beyond the grasp of creed, theology, and philosophy (cf. §9, 2). It operates on a dynamic of "saying and unsaying to a positive result."[23]

The basic structure of christology bears out the synthetic relationship between cataphatic and apophatic approaches to God in exemplary fashion. The *act of speech* by which faith in Christ risen is professed—that is, articulately professed—is prompted by the Spirit of God alone (cf. §34, 5-7); no particular, articulate reason can account for it. Yet the many articulate professions do carry and convey the ineffable act by which Christians dedicate themselves to God in Christ risen.[24] Thus the Christian glorification of God (which ultimately "un-says" all words and ideas) integrates and sustains all particular christological affirmations, which, while inadequate in themselves, express something transcendent: the total abandon to God in Christ. Deism, by contrast, will typically *reject*, or at least disqualify, affirmative language as a way to God, and content itself with emphasizing that all speech about God is inadequate and immature. But then, Deism's affirmation of God as transcendent is in reality an affirmation of God as *separate*—that is, as *neither present nor immanent*; hence, there is nothing in creatures, whether naturally or by virtue of grace, that would empower them to seek union with God.

In the catholic tradition, the demanding road of the fullest possible exertion of the human capacity to understand the Christian faith is the road that starts at the sanctuary (where the Creed is at home: §52, 2), keeps the memory of the sanctuary alive on the way, and ultimately leads back to it. Only on that road will travelers avoid mistaking wayside shrines and hedge-row chapels for the Holy of Holies. Only on that road, too, will it become clear—even abundantly clear, if evermore darkly as well—that God is more, not less, adorable and ungraspable for being so intimately known even on the way (cf. §34, 2), and hence, so persistently sought after, and so insistently made into the "object" of theological reflection [n].

---

[n] Our treatment of the crucial significance of *docta ignorantia* and the apophatic theology connected with it cannot come to a close without at least a passing reference to a striking fact: not a trace of apophatic language marks the idiom of

[a] Since theology is a form of reasonable reflection fed by living faith in the living God, depth of theological understanding
is to some extent naturally verifiable, the criterion being *the
quality of the ignorance* the theologian ultimately succeeds in expressing and commending. That quality of ignorance, in turn,
is measured by the quality of the theologian's insistence on the
search for true understanding and on the fostering of it. For
not any kind of ignorance is authentic bliss. The mature, contented, self-abandoning ignorance that is the hallmark of a true
understanding of God is the fruit of consistent attempts to understand; it treasures the mind while it is operating and continues to treasure it when it finds itself empty. Truly theological
ignorance, in other words, is not predicated on any experience
of the inadequacy of the *mind* as such, but of the inadequacy of
the *concepts* the mind works with in the process of understanding. Thus it has nothing in common with merely fiducial capitu-
lation before God's mystery, whether of the lazy (anti-intellectual
or pietistic) or the authoritarian (fundamentalist or integralist)
kind [o].

Theologians, therefore, fail to acquit themselves of an essential task if, out of an alleged respect for the divine mystery, they
take shelter behind lazy or calculated pleas of humble ignorance. For if the affirmation of the human mind's true ability
to know God is eliminated from theology, theology itself tends
to be reduced to anthropology—a mere commentary on human
religious experience or on Christian doctrine insofar as it can be
domesticated and brought to heel and accounted for within the
compass of human self-consciousness (cf. §9, 2). Needless to
say, here lies a broad and easy path to modernism.

For similar reasons theologians cannot hold themselves excused from the intellectual issues raised by the Church's worship. For example, it is a *theological* mistake to claim that rever-

---

the historical Jesus as we know it. The New Testament contains no evidence that
Jesus spoke of God in any but the most affirmative terms. This issue will call for
reflection at the appropriate moment in this volume.

[o] I seem to have noticed that such self-serving pleas quite often take cover
behind the alleged sufficiency of soteriology (cf. §20, 2) or the Church's teaching
authority (cf. §19, 1, c), as when it is said that it should be enough for Christians
simply to accept the Gospel's assurance that they are saved, or the *magisterium's*
certainty about the content of revelation, and that it is dangerous and presumptu-
ous to seek to inquire any further into the mystery of God. On this profoundly
non-catholic approach to the understanding of the faith, cf. §3, 1.

ence with regard to God's mystery (or, at the opposite pole, the requirements of scholarly method) demand that what occurs in the sanctuary and the prayer-room be kept discreetly separate from the pursuits properly practiced in the study and the lecture hall. The tendency to overstate the characteristic differences between the language of the sanctuary ("imaginative," "symbolic," etc.) and the idioms of the study ("rigorous," "rational," etc.) is a symptom of the same disease. Again, unless the reality of God—which is indeed primarily conveyed and experienced in the act of worship (§34, 7; §35)—is in some central fashion the subject-matter of rigorous intellectual effort, *theo*-logy loses its connection with faith in its integrity, and hence, its own identity as a distinctive discipline.

In other words, the theologian is expected to show that the fundamental faith-abandon to God's incomprehensibility demanded by the call to Christian worship—the *sacrificium intellectus*—is *intellectually* meaningful [p]. The only plea of ignorance that is both legitimate and desirable in theology is the plea that is based on the ultimate realization that *the object* of one's efforts to understand is utterly transcendent. This is the *positive* ignorance that is at home with worship.

[b] At the risk of being repetitive, let us recall that, while both elements—affirmation and removal—are essential, both in worship and in theology, they do not enjoy equal status; their relationship is (again) asymmetrical. All theological understanding, it was argued, must be guided by the nature of the object to be understood (§8, 6). The partnership between God and humanity and the world in the orders of both creation and incarnation is entirely of *divine origin*. Consequently, theology must *more deeply respect the divine initiative* that prompts the Christian Creed

---

[p] The *sacrificium intellectus*, in other words, is to be understood, like all sacrifices, not as destruction but as offering to God. It consists, not in the liquidation of human intelligence before the mystery of God, but in the deployment of it to the full extent of its capacity *and beyond*, in acts of intellectual worship ultimately transcending its natural limits. This intellectual worship, of course, symbolically conveys the thinking person's self-abandon, in praise and thanksgiving. Incidentally, much as self-restraint in the expression of one's considered theological judgments in obedience to the holders of pastoral office in the Church may at times be a noble and Christ-like thing for a theologian to do, it cannot *in itself* be considered an act of *sacrificium intellectus*. The latter is offered only to God, not to ecclesiastical teaching authorities (though often at the latter's legitimate bidding).

than that Creed itself, which conveys the *human* response to that initiative.

It follows that *no intellectual verification* of theology's claims to be a credible witness to Christian truth is as *theologically* compelling as a cogent account of the incomprehensibility of God and the inscrutability of God's designs. It is possible, and indeed imperative, for Christian theology to entertain human thoughts about God and to speak human words about God, but this holds only on the basis of the deeper recognition of theology's inability to think and speak adequately at all—a recognition that must be thematically stated and elaborated. It is important to be clear and resolute about this, without giving in to "pastoral concern" or "catechetical nervousness." In the long run, educated ignorance, painful and unsettling as it may be, will prevent us from becoming the prisoners of a naively affirmative, excessively (and needlessly) "pistic" conception of God.

[c] One example of a compelling magisterial statement of the position developed in this chapter is found in a document promulgated at the Fourth Lateran Council in A.D. 1215. It is a classic formulation of the principle that founds both Christian worship and the catholic teaching on the analogy that prevails between creation and God. It reads: "It is impossible to note any likeness between the Creator and the creature without having to note, between the two, *an unlikeness that is greater*" (DS 806; cf. CF 320).[25]

[d] All of this is deeply consonant with the age-old tradition kept alive by the teachers of the spiritual life—a tradition born out of experience and tested by it. *Those who experience, in growing faith, a habitual desire for prayer yet, puzzlingly, find themselves consistently dissatisfied with both vocal and merely meditative mental prayer*, have reason to assume that they are being called to some of the higher, "contemplative," "agnostic," "unitive" forms of prayer [q]. There they are likely to come to the realization

---

[q] Modern treatments of contemplation, of the secular but also of the Christian variety, often seem unaware of these sobering preconditions, found in the writings of many teachers of the spiritual life, also in non-Christian traditions. Without previous purification and patient enlightenment, a soul will find nothing but itself in agnostic meditation and prayer; there is no quick inside track to the grace of the more direct forms of encounter with God in unitive prayer. Cf., for example, *The Book of Privy Counselling* (ed. Hodgson), pp. 164/15-167/7; (ed. Johnston),

that the living God is more adequately known in the blind desire for God and in the undifferentiated self-abandon to God (as well as in the humble yearning for fulfillment in God) than in the experience of God in vocal and meditative forms of prayer. The latter are of necessity partial and anticipatory in comparison with unitive prayer. Still, unitive prayer, once attained, tends not so much to eliminate vocal and mental forms of prayer as to give a new life and a deeper resonance to them.

[2] It is time to sum up. Our discussion opened, in the first chapter, with the declaration that the subject-matter of this volume would be the Church's central piece of witness: the profession of faith. This profession is the fruit of a worship whose source, soul, and term is a transcendent divine initiative. Hence, only an abiding reliance on the worship that inspires, sustains, and directs the affirmations of the Creed will enable us to come to a true understanding of the Christian faith, by enabling us to interpret the Creed in the perspective of the reality which alone authorizes it: God's transcendent self-communication, which is ultimately eschatological. As a result, we have discovered, a truly *theo*-logical understanding of the Creed requires the cultivation of *positive ignorance* as a foundation.

However, in the process of discovering that theology must foster educated ignorance in order to do justice to the transcendence of God and God's designs, a second, related set of *anthropological* perspectives spontaneously came into view, again and again. This took the shape of a variety of interconnected observations on the theme of the fulfillment of humanity's native potential.

Most importantly, we found that salvation history is inalterably oriented to the final transformation of humanity and the world; in other words, God's *exitus*, in self-effusion and self-communication, graciously does justice beyond mere justice to the deepest conceivable interests of humanity and the world. No wonder Christian worship is deeply human: in and of itself it actualizes humanity's native potential for union with God. Moreover, in prompting witness it also stimulates humanity's native potential for self-actualization and self-transcendence in dealing with the world.

In the practice of theology, a similar connection between the service of God and the service of humanity came to the surface: dog-

---

chaps. 18-19, pp. 180-83.

matic theology, in the final analysis, involves a response to God's sovereign self-communication, while being in itself a demanding exercise in human self-actualization. Far from excusing human intellectual effort, respect for God's transcendence requires the utmost expenditure of it; in fact, the caliber of human intellectual effort serves as a touchstone of the genuineness of that ignorance which is the highest form of truly human knowledge of God. In this way it was shown how educated ignorance in the intellectual service of the transcendent God radically promotes the development of humanity's native potential for understanding.

[3] In noticing the deep connections between this anthropological perspective and the theological one, we have recovered a number of observations made in a far more provisional fashion before—most of them long ago, in the first volume.

First of all, faith in God is ultimately naked and absolute. In essence, it occurs between two infinities: God's eternal Spirit and its mirror-image, the ever-longing human heart (§56, 14). Only total abandon will do justice to both the transcendent love of God and to the creature's unconditional dependence on God—a dependence that coincides with the creature's *nature* (cf. §9, 1). This account of faith is absolute. As such, it is characterized by *a twofold universalism*: just as the creature is originally dependent on God alone for the totality of its being, so the gracious God alone can ultimately be all in all—that is, the creature's total fulfillment.

Yet, secondly, human faith in God exists in proximate, concrete shapes (cf. §10, 1). It is practiced not only between the transcendent God and the nothingness out of which the creature emerges into existence, but also between religion and world, that is, in structured forms of positive religion. These forms must be recognized—at least in the case of the Christian faith [r]—as *the concrete shape of grace* as it is taking shape in place and time (§62, 1, c; cf. §26, 2; §57, 3, d and [b]). *The Creed is such a form.*

[4] In coming to this characterization of the Creed, *God Encountered* has touched upon an historic issue, namely, the discussion of *the nature of Christianity*. That issue, therefore, must be the subject-matter of the next two chapters.

---

[r] But again, by no means exclusively in the case of the Christian faith; cf. §35, 1, b.

CHAPTER 4

The Creed Torn Apart

THE NATURE OF CHRISTIANITY: THE ISSUE

[§70] HOLDING THE CREED AND ITS PERSPECTIVES TOGETHER

[1] In taking the content of the Creed for its theme, it was explained some time ago (and, it might be added, in a deceptively straightforward manner), the present volume commits itself to the development of a theological account of the *nature of Christianity*—that is, its *normative essence* (§57, 2, a). The complexity of this commitment, it is hoped, has become clearer in the previous chapters. On the one hand, the Creed must be interpreted, yet not interpreted out of existence (§58, 2, a); on the other hand, it can be rightly understood only in the twofold universalist perspective of the transcendent mystery of God's grace and the God-given depth of humanity and its world (§63, 1-2); between these two, the question of the normative essence of Christianity—that is to say, its "idea" (§44, 1)—can hardly be straightforward. Not surprisingly, therefore, raising it will put our understanding of the Christian faith to a severe test.

[2] In interpreting the Creed, it is important first of all to realize that the text of the Creed is not a freestanding theoretical structure. That means: it cannot be expected to deliver up its meaning without much ado. Like all Christian teaching, the Creed is idiomatic; and since idioms are linguistic usages shared by communities, the Creed necessarily comes with a community agenda. It is to a large extent the function of the Creed's idiomatic features to give shape to the Christian community's concern with *coherence and fidelity*, in teaching as well as in conduct and worship (§51, 2). In committing ourselves to the interpretation of the Creed so as to resolve the issue of the nature of Christianity, therefore, we are likely to have our fidelity to the very particular, historic teaching tradition of

the undivided Christian Church put to the test. This, as will become clear in this chapter, is the *catechetical* side of the issue.

[3] However, after what was explained in the first chapter, it will be
clear that there is another, twofold point to be taken into account.
It was argued that the profession of the Creed acknowledges two
universalist perspectives that are mutually related: Christians profess
their faith, ultimately, with a view to the transcendent mystery of
God's grace and of the God-given depth of humanity and its world.
If catechesis is marked by the Christian community's particularity,
the perspectives of God, humanity, and world are characterized by
universality. For if it is integral to the very nature of Christianity for
the Church to profess itself to be the Church of God, then it is as
integral to the nature of Christianity that the Church recognize
God's design for all people to be saved and come to acknowledge
the truth (1 Tim 2, 4; cf. §42, 1). For the God we worship here and
now is the same God who, in the end, is to be all in all (1 Cor 15,
28). Thus it is essential that present Christian faith in God, no matter how much it is still straining and struggling, should already acknowledge that all of humanity, along with the whole world, has
been meant, from the beginning, to have its deepest hopes for integrity and freedom done justice to, in virtue of its union with God.
Consequently, as we will see, the Creed's two universalist perspectives
sum up the *spiritual* element of the definition of the nature of Christianity.

[4] Tension between the particular and the universal is part of
regular human life, and awareness of this tension has been one of
the immemorial sources of philosophical reflection. The Christian
Creed provides no one with an exemption from this rule. Given
the tension between the catechetical and the spiritual, between the
particularity that is so obvious in the *text* and the universalism that
is obviously implied in the *perspectives* in which the Creed is professed, it is not surprising that the critical question should have
been raised, "Just what *is* Christianity?"

As a matter of fact, the history of Christian life and thought has
witnessed a great variety of ways in which the "essence" or "nature"
or "idea" or "genius" of Christianity (*das Wesen des Christentums, le
génie du christianisme*) has been made the object of intensive theological discussion. In the last three or four centuries, however, in
the post-Reformation, and even more especially, the post-Enlightenment era, the issue has adopted one specific, and—it must be add-

ed at once—very problematic form. In this form, it has moved ever closer to the very center of the public theological and philosophical discussion of the West, where it has left an indelible mark, to the point where no systematic theology that claims to be contemporary can responsibly ignore it.

[a] A startling measure of the explosive potential of this modern approach to the issue is Ludwig Feuerbach's *Das Wesen des Christentums*, which appeared in 1841 [a]. Feuerbach recognizes religion as a deeply human phenomenon, but he also argues that, put very simply, it contradicts the nature of humanity. Religion, therefore, is untrue—that is to say, it is *inauthentic*. At the core of this inauthenticity lies the fact that religion is *theological*: it has God for its object. This focus on God is not reasonable; it is purely emotional, and it is adequately accounted for by the human experience of *unhappiness*. Unhappiness causes people to lose touch with what is truly real—that is, with what is intrinsically divine: their own humanity and the world— both in their original greatness. In practicing religion, people are merely being the prisoners of their misguided subjectivity; under the dominance of that subjectivity, from which they also desire to escape, they invoke God. Consequently, God is in reality no more than the postulate of the human craving for happiness.

In Feuerbach's construction, therefore, the essence of *all* religion, but of Christianity in particular, is the self-alienation of humanity on the basis, not of reason, but of emotionality. The churches, he adds, support this alienation. By dint of having people concentrate on God, the churches teach them to accept human incompetence, unhappiness, and insufficiency as divinely endorsed and blessed. Thus people are encouraged to keep their attention and commitment away from what is most truly real: humanity and the world. The Christian faith does so in a particularly misleading fashion, by constructing a contradiction. It proclaims a God of Love, manifested in the unity of full divinity and full humanity in the person of Jesus Christ. This proclamation, however, masks the fact that in reality the religious

---

[a] The year 1854 saw the publication of an English translation of Feuerbach's book, under the title *The Essence of Christianity*, by the novelist George Eliot, whose translation of another highly controversial work, David Friedrich Strauss' *Life of Jesus*, had appeared eight years before.

exaltation of Christ amounts to a glorification of an illusory divinity *at the expense of true, autonomous, self-reliant humanity.*

[b]   Feuerbach's analysis is in many ways quite unsubtle and even perverse. But it is quite representative. It is not difficult to recognize in Feuerbach's proposal the basic features of modern *humanistic atheism* as a widespread cultural movement [b]. It has obvious affinities with, say, the atheisms proposed by Karl Marx ("faith in God and religion only serve to rationalize and reinforce the human tendency to resign oneself to exploitation and slavery"; but cf. §76, 4, a) and Siegmund Freud ("faith in God and religion are to be understood as an illusion, being nothing but the shape of a residual human need for dependence on both protection and authority") [c].

[c]   It will probably come as a surprise to no reader that the treatment of the essence of Christianity to be offered in this volume will situate itself at a critical distance from the modern, atheistic approach to the essence of religion. Still, there is a positive side to humanistic atheism. These systems serve to show to what extent, in the experience of modern Western culture,

---

[b] For a moving and learned treatment, cf. Henri de Lubac, *The Drama of Atheist Humanism.* It is, incidentally, not entirely fanciful to trace Feuerbach's atheistic interpretation of Christianity back, ultimately, to the reduction of Christianity to an anthropology with a doctrine of human salvation for its center-piece—that is, to the liberal-Evangelical version of the Reformation's choice of sin and salvation as the central theme of the Christian faith (cf. §20, 2-5). Emmanuel Lévinas, who can hardly be accused of atheism, has made a similar point. He contrasts Judaism's mature, morally responsible faith in the God of the Torah with what he sees as Christianity's immature, morally evasive reliance on an Incarnate Savior-God—a God of pure comfort and forgiveness. Such a God of unqualified indulgence, he argues, is no more than a "heavenly magician," and as such, a dangerous illusion. People who live by faith in such a God will either remain childishly immature, or they will grow up and discover that this God is wholly ineffectual, and so reject any God as unreal. This puts the seed of humanistic atheism right in the soil of the Christian faith. Cf. §99, 2; cf. also David Brown, *Invitation to Theology,* pp. 111-13; F. J. van Beeck, *Loving the Torah More than God?,* esp. pp. 41-53.

[c] Feuerbach, Marx, Freud, and Nietzsche are, of course, among the various precursors of the "death-of-God theology" (cf. §99, 4), a phenomenon of some importance in the nineteen-sixties, when the demise of the Judeo-Christian understanding of God and Creation (cf. §§97-98) as the cultural matrix of the West hit home once again in the form of the *secularization* theme. For some of the principal documents in the Anglo-Saxon world, cf. John A. T. Robinson's agenda-setting *Honest to God,* Harvey Cox's *The Secular City,* Gabriel Vahanian's *The Death of God, Wait Without Idols* and *No Other God,* Thomas J. Altizer's *The Gospel of Christian Atheism,* Paul van Buren's *The Secular Meaning of the Gospel,* and Leslie Dewart's *The Future of Belief.*

the two universalist themes of God and humanity remain at the center of humanity's aspiration to full authenticity. This of course implies that they are also integral to the question about the nature of authentic religion. As a result, any serious contemporary interpretation of the Creed as the embodiment of the essence of Christianity will have to deal constructively with the challenge of modern humanistic atheism. Thus it should come as a surprise no one that this "contemporary" systematic theology considers it a matter of the highest importance to understand and appreciate the intellectual pedigree of the modern discussion, and even more its continuing agenda.

[§71] THE NATURE OF CHRISTIANITY IN THE GREAT TRADITION

[1] Before we treat the issue of the nature of Christianity in a more reflective way, let us briefly review some approaches associated with the great Tradition. This tradition has insisted on casting the essence of Christianity in the form of baptismal and (in due course) conciliar creeds. It is characteristic of this tradition to remember that one of the original functions of rules of faith and creeds is catechetical: creeds express, in formulas at once manageable and authoritative, the essential teachings of the Christian faith. Saint Cyril of Jerusalem is one of the more eloquent witnesses to this tradition, as when he addresses, in the course of a series of Lenten instructions, the candidates for initiation at Easter as follows:

In both learning it and professing it, embrace and observe only the faith now being handed down to you by the Church—the one guaranteed by all of Scripture. Why? Not all are in a position to read the Scriptures: some are prevented from becoming knowledgeable by illiteracy, others by lack of leisure. Accordingly, we summarize the whole content of the faith in a matter of a few lines, lest the soul perish from ignorance. Now I want you to learn this by heart, word for word, and to recite it to yourselves with all eagerness— do not just reproduce it, as you would on paper, but engrave it in your hearts, as a lasting record. ... Now you are to hold on to this same faith as to supplies that will last you a lifetime, and you are to accept nothing different in addition to it, not even if we should reverse ourselves and start to contradict what we are now teaching you. ... For the moment, as you listen to its being recited, commit the faith to memory. As opportunities arise, you should get to know how each proposition is sustained, on the basis of Holy Scripture. For the summary of the faith was never composed just as it occurred to some people to put it; rather, the most pertinent passages, pulled together from all of Scripture, add up to one complete statement of the faith.[1]

Not surprisingly, this creedal tradition has remained the backbone of orthodox, confessional Christian theology, whether its lineage is Oriental, Roman Catholic, or classic-Reformed. Its principal characteristic is the emphasis on confessional *identity* and *integrity*: the determination of the essence of the Christian faith occurs *from inside* the community of faith. The Creed, after all, is fundamentally the product, not of theological or political discussion or negotiation, but of the worship and the proclamation shared among the initiated.

[2] At this point, however, the better to prepare ourselves for our discussion, and for the history of dissociation and disintegration about to be recounted, we must raise a crucial question only barely touched on so far. Just why does *God Encountered* propose to treat the integral nature of Christianity by developing a commentary on the *Creed* (cf. §57, 2), rather than the Scriptures? In the context of contemporary Christianity—post-Reformation and (especially) post-Enlightenment as it is—this question is bound to come up. In the post-conciliar Catholic Church, which is being revitalized by the biblical renewal, the question is no less appropriate. Is the Bible not the Word of God, and the pre-eminent norm of faith? Moreover, have the past two hundred years not proved that careful and loving (as well as academically rigorous) attention paid to the Scriptures can furnish us with an understanding of the Christian faith that is infinitely more salvation-historical and hence multifaceted, and hence more lifelike, complete, and persuasive, than the lapidary, jejune, time-worn, sectarian-sounding Creed? The reply to these serious questions must be explained at some length, under three headings.

[a] First of all, in opting for the profession of faith, *God Encountered* is deferring to a *historical* fact of great hermeneutical significance. The great Tradition has *de facto* cherished, not the Scriptures, but the classic creeds as the authoritative statements of the nature of Christianity [d], and it has done so, in the main,

---

[d] When Lessing (who was hardly an orthodox Christian) pointed this out to a sectarian Lutheran pastor, he was on solid *historical* ground, even though, of course, he very much had an agenda of his own in making the point. Still, in his own way he was *theologically* right as well; when he referred both Protestants and

without forcing the Scriptures into a subordinate position—quite the contrary. In opting for the creeds, it has positively opted for the documents that embody and keep alive the original unity of the three elements that make up the Christian faith-community *as it concretely exists*: worship, life, and teaching. This requires an explanation.

The strength of the classic creeds lies precisely in that they do *not primarily* (let alone exclusively) provide an inventory of *doctrines* (cf. §52, 6). Taken at face value, creeds *are*, of course, statements of doctrine; as such, they invite understanding, and hence, theological study, interpretation, and discussion, not unlike the Scriptures as they present themselves in their *written* form. However, the classic creeds are meant to be (and do) far more. They are, and continue to be, the ecclesial-liturgical symbols of the Christian community's encounter, *in undisputed actuality*, with the living God; they are the certificates, of continuing validity and actuality, of the Christian entitlement. This entitlement involves the worship of God in the Spirit, in the Body of Christ, most especially in the Eucharist; the self-commitment, in reliance on the grace of the Spirit, to the communal demands of the life of discipleship with Christ, in anticipation of God's judgment; and the acceptance, in the Spirit, of the knowledge of the One True God revealed as the Father of the Lord Jesus Christ, the Word Incarnate, in his life, death, and resurrection. In this way, the creeds symbolize the historic continuity of the Christian Church, which "in its teaching, life, and worship, perpetuates and hands on to all generations all that it is itself, all that it believes" (DV 8; cf. §24, 7).

In opting for the Creed, therefore, *God Encountered* means to commit itself to a theological understanding of the Christian faith in its integrity, *as a distinctive, concrete whole* (cf. §53, 1). This distinctive integrity of the Christian experience came to be discovered and authoritatively symbolized, in the course of long and painful debates, in the fourth century, by means of creeds, among which the Nicene-Constantinopolitan Creed came to hold pride of place.[2] In laying down the rule of faith in the form of normative creeds, the Church also discovered that its

---

Catholics to the ancient *symbola*, he was challenging them to get beyond their incessant, sectarian appeals to *authority*, whether textual or papal, so as to recover their original unity in *believing* (§73, 1).

central doctrines are *the normative hermeneutical key to the Scriptures.* Only on the strength of creedal integrity can the Scriptures be assured pride of place in the worship and the life of the Christian community.

[b] Consequently—and this is the second point—our choice of the classic creeds is partly *corrective* in nature. It was explained long ago that the development of theology as an instrument of a holistic understanding of the faith suffered when theological exposition came to rely on the non-liturgical, "trinitarian-christological" creeds. These creeds, with their inventorial propensities, wrongly give the impression that well-ordered doctrines adequately account for the integrity of the Christian faith. More importantly, however, in due course these creeds attracted doctrinal expansions (often of a secondary kind), simply presented as additional matter for belief; thus they came to obscure the hierarchy of truths (cf. §52, 7-8).

The classic creeds have the great advantage of resisting treatment as if they were mere inventories of doctrine. This means that they prevent theology from interpreting the Christian faith in terms of an undifferentiated accumulation of manifest doctrinal items; such an interpretation would fail to respect both the reference to the mystery of God and the hierarchy of truths (§19, 1 and a; §23, 4, c). In modeling systematic theology after the classic creeds, therefore, *God Encountered* commits itself to an account of Christianity that resists the slide into integralism.

[c] Thirdly, as the present chapter will serve to illustrate, our option in favor of the Creed also has firmly *fundamental-theological* grounds. Not unimportantly, this option has the advantage of preventing theology's slide into modernism as well. Both points require some careful explanation and analysis.

At the heart of the suggestion that it might be *preferable* to account for the nature of Christianity by reference to the Scriptures *rather than to the Creed* (the implication of preference is crucial here), lies the important theological issue of *Scripture and Tradition.*

At the time of the Reformation and its aftermath, the *inventorial* tendency inherent in the trinitarian-christological creeds gathered momentum to the point where it came to contribute fatefully to the disintegration of the profession of faith as a credible carrier of traditional Christian faith-understanding. Doctrinal texts were increasingly experienced as incapable of representing the integral nature of Christianity. Initially, therefore, the great Reformers turned to the Scriptures. It was on that principal, original, authoritative source, they felt, that the Church should exclusively depend for the retrieval of authentic Christian faith from the accretions caused by useless speculation and ecclesiastical abuse, and hence, for the renewal of the understanding of the central Christian teachings.

However, in the second half of the seventeenth century, as the Reformation was increasingly losing itself in a tangle of competing doctrines, a new wave of Christians rose to the surface, weary of the argumentative ecclesiastical establishments and disillusioned by the proliferation of doctrine. They once again appealed to the Scriptures, but with a decisive difference: *the appeal to Scripture was now directed, both against the Creed and against the whole idea of any normative doctrine at all* (§72, 4, b-c. e). The classical Reformers had restored the Bible as the prime authority *in* the visible Church, *over* the tangle of historical *traditions* that had held the Gospel captive. Now the Bible was being played off, as a matter of principle, against the visible Church and *against the Tradition as such.* In this way, in neo-Protestantism, a sovereignly authoritative Bible could become the warrant, neither for the *Tradition* of the Church, nor even for its *reform,* but for its *contemporary reconstruction.* This reconstruction was, as a matter of principle, up to whoever cared to associate themselves with the idea of Christianity without caring to be scandalized by its historical reality, for the terms of the association had become free.

Wholly unintentionally, the Reformers' insistence on the inspired authority of the *literal text* of the Bible, apart from any clutter of interpretation, had laid the groundwork for this development, which was to have consequences familiar to this day: it gave us the non-ecclesial, non-confessional, tolerant, individualized, often fervently biblical variety of Christianity now so widespread in North America. But the problems of the development are obvious, too. For one thing, a divinely authoritative Bible, decontextualized and sovereignly placed *over against* the Church and *outside* it, can retain its divine authority only as long as its inspired character continues to be a matter of vigorous faith-consensus; yet for lack of an ecclesiological basis, that consensus will have to take the shape of a sheerly dogmatic, fundamentalist postulate: "Whether you believe in it or not, the Bible simply *is* the Word of God." Not surprisingly, in the liberal, tolerant atmosphere of Evangelical Protestantism, it was not long before this claim was quietly as well as widely dropped, with the Scriptures becoming interpretable, as a matter of principle, just like any other public literary or religious document. That is, they could be interpreted by means of any unprejudiced, reasonable hermeneutical key, which (or so it was thought) needed no normative, communal tradition of interpretation to guide it.

This enabled exegesis to join forces with modernism. For all its great attainments over the past two centuries, today's style of Scriptural interpretation, especially in theological academies, is still to an appreciable extent the heir of the neo-Protestant prejudice against "dogmatism." This has given rise to the (largely implicit) claim that *independent exegesis is a more reliable guide to "real" Christianity than any doctrinal commitment.* The claim, of course, does not hold, not even from a literary point of view, let alone theologically. Most of all, it overlooks the fact that the Bible *as a whole* is the record of its own historic (re)interpretation at the hands of communities living by the very commitments they were struggling to reinterpret. In its every structure, therefore, the Bible is both the fruit of ongoing communal faith-traditions and the most decisive factor in the ongoing reformation and transformation of those traditions. Thus even a purely literary approach to scriptural hermeneutics should recognize that interpretation, to be reliable, must be both traditional and theological: it demands that the interpreter willingly suspend any personal disbelief, so as to be open to appreciating the distinctive life-experience and self-understanding of the historic faith-community. Thus the Christian Church cherishes the Scriptures, warts and all, as the core of its Tradition, just as it draws life from their ongoing (re)interpretation in light of present experience, warts and all (cf. §4, 1) [e].

---

[e] Unless we carefully scrutinize our exegetical methods in the light of our theological agenda, we are all liable to the temptation of thinking that a non-traditional, confessionally neutral hermeneutic of Scripture is capable of furnishing us with as reliable a way to establish the "original" essence of Christianity as the doctrinal Tradition—if not, in fact, with a more reliable one. On this road, paved with opinion as it is, all access to faith is eventually obstructed as a matter of principle; accordingly, it invariably leads to the conclusion that there really is no such thing as an original Christian faith-commitment. To illustrate the tendency just described by means of a recent example, one wonders if there is not a hidden bias behind the widespread eagerness, detailed by John P. Meier (*A Marginal Jew,*

[d] Thus, in opting for the Creed as the framework for its account of the nature of Christianity, *God Encountered* is not proposing to relegate Scripture to an inferior position, let alone to subjugate it to the requirements of sectarian doctrinal traditions. Rather, it proposes *to set up the theological situation* that will enable us to do justice to the full meaning of Scripture. That situation, summed up and symbolized by the Creed, is *confessional* [*f*]. It is the great Tradition of worship, life, and teaching, which first formed the Scriptures by accepting, reinterpreting, and adding on to the Jewish Scriptures and then proceeded to live off them [*g*].

---

vol. I, pp. 112-66), to read the *agrapha* attributed to Jesus and the apocryphal gospels as evidence *against* the canonical gospels, with their clear confessional bias. What remains true, of course, is the central insistence of modern exegesis that any authoritative interpretation of the Scriptures that means to be faithful to the Tradition respect the demands implicit in the Bible's literary forms and in the literary and cultural context in which the Bible is set. This enables the Church to recommend that Scripture be fearlessly and properly *studied* in the light of new scholarly evidence, with the unprejudiced rigor that befits the academy (cf. §4, 1). For a coherent, up-to-date statement of an integral biblical hermeneutic as faithful to the Bible and its setting as to contemporary experience, cf. Sandra M. Schneiders, *The Revelatory Text*.

[*f*] Again, Lessing was not holding any brief for Christian orthodoxy when he explained this, but he did see the issue with great clarity, as is clear from his *Necessary Answer*, cf. *Lessing's Theological Writings*, pp. 62-64.

[*g*] On this point—the relationship between Scripture and Tradition—there happily has been substantial ecumenical convergence between Roman Catholicism and classical Protestantism, made tangible by the Report of the World Conference on Faith and Order of 1963 and the Dogmatic Constitution on Divine Revelation *Dei Verbum*. The Second Vatican Council dropped the clumsy and overstated two-source theory, which held that Revelation is "contained" in Scripture as well as in "unwritten traditions," the latter thought of as *separate* from Scripture (DS 1501; CF 210). Instead, it recognized two things. First of all, there is a difference between the Tradition and traditions (cf. Y. Congar's celebrated book under that title). Secondly, the relationship is organic: the Scriptures are the prime product of the living Tradition of the Church, which in turn has come to recognize itself in them in the process of canon-formation, and which now acknowledges them as the unsurpassable guide of its own growth and development (cf. DV 2). On the Protestant side, the outright rejection of Tradition has yielded to the recognition that all traditions must be criticized in light of the Gospel Tradition. The subject is well treated in *Neues Glaubensbuch*, pp. 547-60 (ET *The Common Catechism*, pp. 553-67); cf. also the papers connected with the Montreal Faith and Order Conference, collected in *Schrift und Tradition*. On a note of caution, however, it must be observed that both the Montreal Faith and Order Conference and the Second Vatican Council dealt with the issue of Scripture and Tradition only as it presented itself *within* the ambit of the *confessionally committed* Churches and its professions of faith. Neither dealt with the issue as it has developed in the encounter between the catholic tradition and liberal Protestantism—which is what the present treatment endeavors to do, at least in outline.

[3] In choosing the Creed for its framework, therefore, *God Encountered* is not only acting on the historical precedent set by the undivided Church's Tradition or seeking the assurance of indisputable doctrine. It is also involving itself in a fundamentally *theological* commitment: it means to interpret Scripture within the purview of the norms set by the Tradition. Somewhat unexpectedly (unexpectedly, that is, in the eyes of many of our liberal contemporaries, especially in North America), this tradition, for all its confessional firmness, allows for and indeed creates ample room for *openness* [h]. This is due to the fact that communities with a sound sense of creedal identity, even at the pistic level, tend to be clear-headed about the effects of their profession of faith on humanity and the world and *vice versa*. This is especially, though certainly not exclusively, characteristic of the Roman Catholic tradition, even though its systemic propensity to close-minded integralism must be recognized (cf. §19, 1, e). It is also characteristic of the classical Reformers and of a modern Reformer like Karl Barth, who have insisted so strongly on the recovery of the substance of Christianity and on its resolute proclamation. Precisely because the human hunger for God is so intense, so this tradition has always rightly insisted, people are entitled to have the solid food of the Christian faith —"the meat of the Gospel"—offered to them. They must not be fobbed off with some convenient mixture of faith and fashion, no matter how reassuring or appealing to current taste [i].

[a] In the history of Christian thought, the tradition of rendering the essence of Christianity by commenting on the Creed has produced not only such Reformed classics as Calvin's *Institutes* and Karl Barth's massive *Church Dogmatics*, but also a long series of shorter theological commentaries on the text of the Creed. In the twentieth century, this movement is represented by such diverse theologians as Karl Barth (*Credo* [1935]; *The Faith of the Church* [1940]), Gerhard Ebeling (*The Nature of Faith*), Gustaf

---

[h] For the various ways in which identity and openness are related in the various types of faith (pistic, charismatic, and mystic), cf. §54, 3, b; 4-5. Cf. also F. J. van Beeck, *Catholic Identity After Vatican II*, esp. pp. 11-21, 71-78.

[i] One important additional identity feature of this strongly *confessional* orientation *ad extra* is that it continuously forces the Christian community to try and make fundamental distinctions between what is essential in its Christian faith and what is peripheral, derivative, or mainly culturally determined—no mean asset in an age of ecumenism, as, to mention just one example, Heinrich Fries and Karl Rahner have shown (§48, 3, b).

Wingren (*Credo*), and Joseph Ratzinger (*Introduction to Christiani-ty*).

Works like those just mentioned, however, while setting out to expound the common profession of faith, usually turn out, on closer inspection, to be *interpretations*. They take their bearings from a *guiding idea*, which serves to focus the Christian faith around a *core vision of radical importance*. Thus Karl Barth's treatments of the Creed are predicated on his insistence that *Christian theology's agenda is set by the sovereign Word of God, not the culture*; Gerhard Ebeling treats the articles of the Creed entirely from the point of view of *the essential act of faith*; the Swedish Lutheran Gustaf Wingren has surprised many in his Church by his insistence on the *theology of creation* as integral to christology, the doctrine of the atonement, and to pneumatology; Joseph Ratzinger emphasizes throughout that the Christian faith offers a *fundamental challenge to the modern assumption* that Christian truth—like all truth—cannot be truly known, but only experienced, approximated, or acted upon amidst the contingencies of history.

In this same tradition, and especially in its Catholic branch, we also find treatments that dispense with commentary on the articles of the Creed altogether, in order simply to interpret its structure in theological terms. A prominent Catholic example of this is Henri de Lubac's *Christian Faith*, which explains how the *doctrine of the Blessed Trinity* is the doctrinal core of the Christian profession of faith, while *the doctrine of the Church* provides that profession with a dynamic setting. The well-known Swedish Lutheran Anders Nygren, in his *Essence of Christianity*, places, in classical Lutheran fashion, the concept of *reconciliation* at the center of the Christian profession of faith, and indeed of all true religion, as its ordering principle.

[b] In all these examples, in which theological reflection on the Creed has resulted in the determination of a *guiding idea* (or basic option (*Grundoption*), or principle of coherence [*j*]),

---

[*j*] This is by no means a strictly modern procedure. Even in the New Testament we find comparable, if more spontaneous and less sophisticated, summary characterizations of the substance of the Christian faith. Examples are the apostolic *kerygma* (Gal 1, 6); the presence of Christ interceding in the heavenly sanctuary as the assurance of the community's perseverance in the faith (Heb 8, 1); the community's faith in the name of Jesus Christ as God's Son and the love of each other (1 Jn 3, 23). Several of the New Testament *pistoi logoi* (cf. §51, 3, a) can also be

this idea (or option, or principle) is subsequently used as a reliable interpretative key with the help of which it is possible to unlock the Creed along with its transcendent perspectives, and to show just how it succeeds in being the authoritative formulation of *the normative essence of the Christian faith.* Indirectly, such a guiding idea can also help determine, in a constructive way, the structure of the hierarchy of truths (cf. §21, 4; §22, 2; §23, 4, c).

[4] Thus it is characteristic of the great Tradition to insist that the Creed we rehearse and profess, and the mystical horizons from which we take our ultimate bearings are part of one and the same world view. In that world view, the Creed is *both* the explicit, articulate, contractual symbol of the Christian Church's ongoing unity in believing (cf. §51, 4, [*q*]) *and* the gateway to the transcendent doxological and soteriological horizons that animate the Church's dynamism. That is to say, the *catechetical* elements and the *spiritual* perspectives mutually sustain and interpret each other. Not surprisingly, a sensitive and reliable interpreter of the great Tradition like Blessed Jan van Ruusbroec (1293-1381; cf. §90, 1) can explain, in all simplicity, right in the middle of the fourteenth century, when symptoms of the dissociation between the catechetical and the spiritual are in evidence all over Europe, that faith must

... have, in advance, two free commitments [*vrie begripe*], on which it is established. ... The first free commitment, on which our faith is established, is this: with the grace of God, we shall commit ourselves to lifting ourselves up above all the heavens, with a single vision, in one God, in whom we believe. In this way faith is established in God. The other free commitment, in which we practice and possess our faith without going astray, is this: with a free will and mind we shall commit ourselves to believe, with discernment, all that Holy Church holds and believes. And in this we shall be so unassuming, and so single of motive, that neither our own senses nor our natural reason will be able to make us either doubtful or conceited. And also, that no creatures (no matter how holy they may appear to be, or whatever they may work in the way of wonders and miracles) will be able to impress upon us a different or novel way of faith. So these are two free commitments that make us believers and keep us in the faith, without going astray.[3]

In the twofold foundation of the faith, therefore, the catechetical elements keep alive the memory of the sacraments of initiation,

---

read as brief summaries of this kind.

by which Christians enter, once and for all, upon the *integrity* of the Christian faith (cf. §53, 1; §54, 6, a); they commit the Christian to the visible Church as the way of holiness by union with God through Jesus Christ in the Holy Spirit. The spiritual elements, summed up in the single-eyed commitment to God (note that Ruusbroec gives it pride of place!), keep alive the *dynamics* of this faith, by setting ever-receding standards of excellence (§§53-54).

What the dynamic combination of catechetical and spiritual elements drives home is that all Christians are indeed fully members of the Church, but that this does not mean that they are all at the same stage of development and maturity in their faith-commitment. Hans Urs von Balthasar, therefore, is entirely on the mark when he insists on both catechism and spirituality:

> We must keep the two aspects together in the same perspective and hold fast to both of them, namely, that the Church is a unity—unequivocally characterized as such on trinitarian, christological, and internal, structural grounds—and that this unity is analogically expressed in its members.

Yet at the same time he most characteristically insists that the genuine norm of Christianity remains the experience of "those who have responded to a divine call to conversion, transformation and holiness,"[4] not the banal experience of those who merely abide by the catechetical elements that guarantee the Church's unity:

> ... we would be ignoring the facts if we did not acknowledge that, for the fathers and even for the high Middle Ages, the Church «proper» is the Church of those with a living faith. True, this insight has been misused by the Montanists, the Novatians, the Donatists, the Messalians, the extreme Origenists, and later on by the Bogomils and the Cathari. *The Church itself has only very reluctantly accepted it.* Yet the original, fundamentally Christian idea that Church and Love, unity of church and unity of love belong inseparably together has persisted ineradicably.[5]

[5] The Creed's transcendent, spiritual perspectives, therefore, are the true sources of the Christian community's spiritual identity, on the strength of which the Church professes the Creed catechetically, in set formulas rehearsed, handed on, explained, and interpreted in place and time. In other words, catechesis and spirituality (that is, the *articulate profession* of the Christian faith and *the two mutually related universalist perspectives* in which that faith is professed) are related *asymmetrically:* the Church's profession of faith as it travels on its pilgrim way is *ultimately* dependent on its Spirit-inspired yearning for the gracious fulfillment, in Christ, of humanity's native thirst for

the living God. Again, theology must *more deeply respect the divine initiative* that prompts the Christian profession of faith than the formulas of the Creed, which expresses the *human response* to that initiative (cf. §69, 1, b).

[6] The combination of articulate Creed and universalist perspectives is a somewhat unstable compound. Basically, this instability has a positive orientation: it is designed to prevent the Church from becoming dulled and hardened in its pilgrim state, to keep it attuned to its eschatological vocation (a vocation in which humanity's native desire for God finds itself divinely endorsed), and to animate its ongoing reformation (cf. LG 48-51; UR 6). Seen in this light, von Balthasar's enumeration of sectarian movements in the passages quoted—an enumeration that could easily be complemented from the pages of Ronald Knox' *Enthusiasm* and Norman Cohn's *The Pursuit of the Millennium*—witnesses to the holy *restlessness* that must characterize the Church as it yearns for its fulfillment. Only to the extent that this restlessness is kept alive can the officers of the Church—along with the great Tradition—legitimately insist on the need for *patience* in professing the Creed in the tedious contingencies of time and space.

JUST WHAT IS CHRISTIANITY?

[§72] DISSOCIATION AND DISINTEGRATION

[1] Restlessness and patience do not make a natural pair. Unstable compounds, we know, have a tendency to strive for a lower energy-state. They will disintegrate—even explode. Given the instability inherent in the profession of the Creed, therefore, it is not surprising that the catholic Tradition has had to be very firm in its insistence that the Creed and its transcendent, mystical horizons be held together. It is not surprising, either, that the history of Christian life and thought should have shown, at least periodically, signs of strain in its affirmation of the integral "substance" of the Christian faith, and even, occasionally, symptoms of *dissociation*.

As a matter of historical fact, however, the definition of the substance of the Christian faith has fared far worse: in the modern history of Western Christianity, dissociation has increasingly (and disastrously) become *disintegration*. This disintegration was brought about by, and in its turn helped bring about, two very different, competing, progressively polarized movements—the one *authoritari-*

an-catechetical, the other *spiritualist*. The painful history of this rush into disintegration must be told at some length, if only to provide a negative argument for the thesis that the essence of the Christian faith can be reliably stated only if the synthesis is maintained: the Creed professed in light of its transcendent perspectives [k].

[2]   The strain is evident in such a mediating thinker—and one with such deeply catholic instincts—as Erasmus. His attempt at defining the nature of Christianity takes the shape of the formulation of its *substance*, conveyed by means of a *guiding idea*. The substance of Christianity, Erasmus feels, must be retrieved from under a thick crust of a corrupt, almost completely acculturated version of Christianity. That version is most forcefully sustained by an unscrupulous papacy, by a secularized episcopate, by a venal clergy, by a disputatious university establishment, and by the corrupt religious communities, all of which also share an interest in the prominence of secondary doctrines and devotional practices, to the detriment of the substance of the Christian faith. It is precisely that substance—the heart of the Gospel—that must be retrieved and become the heart of the reform of the Church. From that vital center it will illuminate, purify, and sustain everything else that belongs to the faith; most importantly, it will inspire a new, authentic *spiritual* life. To convey what he means, Erasmus proposes, in a letter to a kindred spirit, a brief creedal formula. He writes:

The Christian philosophy ... is summed up as follows. We are to understand that all our hope is in God, who freely grants us everything through Jesus his Son. We have been redeemed by his death; we have been grafted into his body by baptism, so that dead to the desires of this world we should live according to his teaching and example, and this not only so as to allow nothing in the way of evil but also so as to do good to all. And if any adversity should befall us, we are to endure it in fortitude, in hopes of the future reward, which doubtlessly awaits all the godly at the coming of Christ. Thus we will always go forward from virtue to virtue, yet in such a way as to claim nothing for ourselves, but ascribe to God all that is good.[6]

---

[k] The account that follows is also an exercise—a negative one, an exercise *ex contrario*—in *ecumenism*: it is an attempt to understand how disintegration of the Church community and disintegration of the shared understanding of the essence of Christianity condition one another. Positively, the account is intended to suggest that a sound theological understanding of the integral essence of Christianity goes to the heart of ecumenism.

Characteristically, Erasmus' formula is carefully balanced. It is both catechetical [*l*] and spiritual, and it blends the order of grace with the order of nature, by combining the sober-minded dedication to the *imitatio Christi*, typical of the *devotio moderna*, with the careful dedication to the true reading of the New Testament characteristic of the *new humanism*.

However, there is something ominous about the passage as well—a symptom, not just of strain but of dissociation. Unlike Luther, whose pastoral instincts led him to maintain the Creed as the centerpiece of popular catechesis,[7] Erasmus offers a formula that *lacks all reference to the Creed*—an indication of the extent to which learned medieval theology and the catechesis inspired by it had come to lose touch with their most authentic source: trinitarian worship (cf. §52, 7-8).

[a]   It is touching indeed to watch Erasmus retrieve the language of the Bible and of spirituality—of Christian asceticism and mysticism—in his attempt to renew the Church. But for all the earnestness of his proposal, what he offers is a purely *soteriological* (and only implicitly trinitarian) rendition of the essence of Christianity (cf. §20, 1-2). Along with the late-medieval Church that he is still part of, Erasmus has forgotten that it is primarily worship, especially in the sacraments of initiation, that integrates the Christian community into the Body of Christ, by dint of praising and giving thanks to God and praying to God. Only worship, in which the world and humanity meet the living God in the living sacrifice of praise and thanksgiving, can be counted on to hold the Creed and its transcendent perspectives together. Worship, therefore, must be the soul of any exhortation to conversion.

[3]   Unfortunately, the advocates of the more traditional *catechetical* agenda gave evidence of the same blindness to the worship tradition behind the Creed as Erasmus did, only far worse. They came to define the normative nature of Christianity in increasingly nar-

---

[*l*] Erasmus expressly says that the points he offers "should be drilled into people's minds [*animis hominum inculcanda*] so that they may become, as it were, part of their nature [*velut in naturam transeant*]." On a different note, notice the parallel between Erasmus' project and Rahner's proposal of a variety of *Kurzformel* or short statements of faith (*Grundkurs des Glaubens*, pp. 430-40; ET *Foundations of Christian Faith*, pp. 448-59). Both propose *guiding ideas* as a way to approximate the normative essence of Christianity.

row and specialized doctrinal, ritual, and especially authoritative
terms, dissociated from their transcendent perspectives.

[a] Early on, and stretching far into the Middle Ages, catechesis
had aimed at condensing, for the rehearsal of the simple faithful,
the substance of the Creed in elementary formulas reflecting the
principal teachings of the episcopate. By the end of the Middle
Ages, however, and increasingly from the late fifteenth century
onward, formal *catechisms* (cf. §7, 1, a) began to be developed.
They were designed to help cope with the need for statements of
the Christian faith at once essentially complete, authoritative, and
manageable.   They were also aimed at the rumble of protest
against the luxuriance of popular religious practices of dubious
authenticity, at the widespread ignorance among the faithful, at
the abuses prevalent in ecclesiastical bodies, and at the high incidence of social (and anti-clerical) unrest, heresy, and freethinking.   Ominously, they were sometimes used to take aim at the
mystics: Eckhart, Suso, Tauler, even Ruusbroec. It was the mystics, after all, who were suspected, in certain circles, of attempting
to redefine the nature of Christianity in completely universalist
terms—terms, it was assumed, most menacing to the details of
creed, doctrine, and ordinary practice. Mystics had indeed constantly taught (although they had done so with a variety of subtle
and discerning nuances) that the essence of the Christian faith
is most adequately actualized in the "superessential" union with
God that is nothing but the flower of the native divine presence
in essential human nature.[8]

[b] The Reformation and Counter-Reformation, preoccupied
with religious instruction as they were, produced a flood of catechisms. Unhappily, they were preoccupied with polemics as well.
By distrusting and resisting the legitimate demands of spirituality
and universalism, the narrowly catechetical traditions (which eventually became predominantly, but far from exclusively, Catholic)
gradually locked themselves into windowless doctrinal fortresses,
and thus came to discredit themselves as theologically fruitful options. Catechetical authors vainly continued their attempts at interpreting the great Tradition by means of polemical accumulation of articles of belief drawn from authoritative sources (cf. §7,
1, b; §28, 1; §52, 7, a). In this approach, needless to say, the essence of Christianity was in immediate danger of being reduced
to its *manifest elements* (cf. §15, 3; §18, 1), and thus defined in sec-

tarian fashion. For whenever creeds and articles of belief are shorn of their transcendent perspectives and enforced as authoritative tools of mere conformity-by-rehearsal, they are bound to cease to be the carriers of the genuine essence of Christianity. Eventually, they will turn into the instruments of *integralism* (cf. §19, 1).

[4]   If the quest for a definition of the essence of Christianity in catechetical and creedal terms turned increasingly doctrinaire and fruitless, this was in no small part in terrified and polemical response to developments on the other side of the issue, in what may be called the *spiritualist* camp. There, where the quest for the substance of Christianity continued the tradition of searching for guiding ideas, an alarming development took place: the interpretation of the Christian faith turned against its central creedal elements. *Catechism and spirituality became enemies.*

[a]   It is the merit of Hans Wagenhammer to have shown, in his Tübingen dissertation *Das Wesen des Christentums: Eine begriffsgeschichtliche Untersuchung,* that this spiritualism eventually generated the modern tendency to define the nature of Christianity in ever more gnostic, philosophical, *modernist* terms.

But what is also clear from Wagenhammer's treatment is *the original agenda behind the modern quest for the essence of Christianity.* Significantly, it is the very thing suggested by Hans Urs von Balthasar. *Dissatisfaction with the present, narrowly particular, impenitent state of Christianity* generated *a quest for living faith,* which involved *a demand for the reform of the Church in light of its true, universalist vocation.* The systematic treatment of the essence of Christianity offered in this volume must include at least a rough historical account of the campaign—a painfully unsettling one in the end—undertaken, under such buoyant colors, to attain these essentially spiritual goals.

[b]   In the late fifteenth and early sixteenth centuries, a fresh discussion on spiritual renewal had begun as the concern of the learned and the religiously motivated. Initially, it took the shape of a quest for a consensus on the substance of Christianity. That quest was stimulated by the desire for *reform*—a desire that was especially strong in the cities, in the circles of reform-minded merchants and humanists. The aim of the quest was: the recovery, *by means of learned, responsible retrieval,* of the essential Chris-

tian faith from the profusion of scholastic dispute, ecclesiastical abuse, and popular religiosity.

The Reformation developed its own distinctive approach to the issue of the jeopardized substance of the Christian faith: it attempted to *retrieve* it by *separating* it from its alleged accretions. Ulrich Zwingli trenchantly formulated the idea. It was wrong, he wrote in one of his letters, to despise and destroy the main points (*præcipua*) of Christianity for the sake of doctrines "ignorance of which does not exclude anybody from heaven." The task of separating the essential from the incidental, however, turned out to be as intractable as it had seemed simple; unfortunately, the dynamics of dissociation and disagreement proved to be far more captivating than the quest for deeper unity. In a letter to Zwingli, Martin Bucer worried that the substance (*substantia*) of Christianity, which did, after all, constitute the area of agreement among all Christians, was being discredited by dissensions about minor issues.[9]

Just what was this substance? Not surprisingly, those with a spiritualist orientation defined it by means of a variety of *guiding ideas*. But underneath the variations, one theme was unmistakable: bewildered by the confusing, alienating, impenitent busyness both in the Church and the society it had helped shape, Christians were experiencing the pull to authenticity, spirituality, eschatology. The most real concern of the moment—a pained yearning for a purified, renewed, and *deeply* unified Christian commonwealth—came to look more and more like the one thing necessary. Thus a partial concern—albeit one of the highest urgency—translated into the one acceptable definition of the substance of Christianity: reliance on the eschatological promises graciously held out to struggling humanity by a merciful God.

In this perspective, Luther and Bucer and the orthodoxies that took their cues from them came to agree, albeit with characteristic variations, on one common theme: the substance of Christianity was *the profession of Christ as the only Lord and Savior, and total trust in him for true assurance of salvation.* That definition, it was felt, conveyed the kind of true, essential, universalist Christianity that could be counted on to put the debilitating details of the catechisms in their places. But the dream did not come true. For one thing, right at the dawn of the Reformation, a man like Heinrich Bullinger was already mining for reform at a deeper, even more universalist level: what gives the Christian faith its consistency, he taught, is *God's faithfulness to the Covenants*, from Abel on.[10] He was not the only early Reformer to attempt wider perspectives. But in the process, the substance of Christianity dwindled according as theological opinion about it increased and multiplied.

[c] Thus, what tenuous consensus about the substance of the Christian faith had existed among the parties to the first stages of the Reformation began to suffer the constriction—and, in cases, the death—of a thousand confessional qualifications. The pull of the catechism won out over the unity of the Spirit. A tangle of polemical and particularist secondary doctrines, all designed to protect the allegedly shared substance of the Christian faith (cf. §23, 4, c), frustrated all attempts to agree on that very substance; unity proved all the more elusive according as the oversupply of unconvincing theological positions grew; as doctrine became increasingly synonymous with disagreement and fragmentation, neither creed nor doctrine succeeded in symbolizing and supporting the one, shared substance of the Christian faith any longer; historic Christendom (which was a *community*) was being turned into "Christianity"—a broad set of (controversial) *ideas* that served to separate human communities as much as it held them together;[11] the wood was being lost sight of for the thicket.

In the public desolation brought on by the elusiveness of the substance of the Christian faith, the center did not hold, and a fateful centrifugal dynamic set in. That dynamic is well illustrated, in the world of the English Reformation, by the proposals towards Christian unity offered by the moderate, very conciliatory Puritan minister Richard Baxter (1615-1691), in his elaborate *The True and Only Way of Concord* of 1680. Unfortunately, Baxter's proposals, offered at the end of the book, are so pale and slender as to be virtually eclipsed by the sheer mass of negative argument that leads up to them. For, intent on driving home the need for moderation, Baxter reviews, in chapter after detailed chapter, sixteen centuries of Church history East and West, only to show that there are hardly any items of doctrine and church order that qualify as necessary, and hence, can serve as a basis for unity. Baxter, who by the end of his life was to find himself rejected by all the ecclesiastical factions he had tried to win over, brings the preface of his book to a final flourish by quoting the programmatic maxim *In necessariis unitas, in non necessariis libertas, in utrisque caritas* ("unity in what is necessary, freedom in what is not necessary, charity in both"; cf. §21, 3, [*b*]); but in the end, the book itself adds up to a massive (if unintentional) demonstration of the failure of that very formula to create consensus and peace. The problem is, obviously, that the maxim, while true and attractive in itself, invites a minimalist account of the essentials of the faith. No wonder it failed in England; it had already turned out to be ineffectual in Germany half a century before, in the early years of the Thirty Years war (1618-1648) [*m*].[12]

[d] In this situation, immemorial, long-latent propensities towards neo-Platonism and gnosticism, which had stalked the Christian Church from the beginning, had fresh opportunities to gain ground [*n*]. In gestures of deep and often resentful disappointment, many Christians began to view the traditional declarations of orthodoxy and the familiar protestations of subjection to the church order as empty, insincere boasts. In reality, so they believed, ecclesially enforced orthodoxy hampered true spiritual regeneration as well as human authenticity to the point where it had to be anti-Christian. In the course of the sixteenth, seventeenth, and eighteenth centuries, anti-confessional *spiritualists—* belated followers of the medieval *spirituales* and *fraticelli*—took advantage of the disarray of the churches to make their point.

[*m*] There are good historical reasons to think that the maxim is indeed a product of the aftermath of the German Reformation; the most likely date is the late sixteen-twenties, and the most likely candidate for authorship the irenic pastor and theologian Rupertus Meldenius (± 1630), of Augsburg, the City of Concord (cf. *Realencyclopädie für protestantische Theologie und Kirche* [Leipzig: J. C. Hinrichs, 1896-1913], vol. 12, pp. 550-52). Baxter quotes the maxim at the end of his preface, as follows: *Si in Necessariis sit Unitas; in non-necessariis Libertas, In utrisq; Charitas, optimo certe loco essent res nostræ* ("If there should be unity in what is necessary, freedom in what is not necessary, [and] charity in both, our situation would certainly be settled to best advantage"). In the third part of his book, entitled "Of Schism," Baxter quotes the maxim once again (p. [25]), now explicitly attributing it to Rupertus Meldenius, and adding that he has found it "cited by Conradus Bergius" (1592-1642). This maxim, he says, "might end all Schisms if well understood and used"; in fact, "it would do all our work."

[*n*] These tendencies, it may be added, found strong support in the latent Platonism of the new scientific learning, with its tendency to separate sensible observation and mental contemplation, (purely matter-oriented) cosmology and (disembodied) anthropology. Descartes' separation between matter and mind had been practiced long before it was philosophically formalized. Cf. §96, 4; §103, 1-2. For further suggestions, cf. also F. J. van Beeck, *Christ Proclaimed*, pp. 44-47.

Some were angry enthusiasts like the Anabaptists or quiet theoso-
phists like Jakob Boehme; others were practical universalists like
the Quakers and the Philadelphians, philosophical theologians
like the Cambridge Platonists, or aggressive freethinkers like John
Toland (§28, 1, a). All of them claimed to have found the essence
of Christianity in the *inner enlightenment that leads to spiritual rebirth.* At only a slight distance from the spiritualists, the *pietists*
(cf. §103, 3), whose influence on British Methodism was to be
notable, found essential Christianity in the *inner feeling of blessedness.*[13] All of them, however, agreed that God was to be found
in Spirit and truth in a variety of places, and that the established
churches, with their militant orthodoxies and their oppressive
church orders were among the more unlikely ones, since they so
obviously failed to guarantee peace, unity, and a serene, upstand-
ing life.

[e] If the Roman Catholic Church, meanwhile, succeeded in remaining united under the papacy, its unity in believing was frequently a matter, not so much of experienced doctrinal harmony, as of political establishment and ecclesiastical discipline, by
dint of Roman compromise, conflict management, arbitration,
and fiat. This dominative exercise of papal authority was often
justified by appeals to the monarchical nature of the
Church—appeals all the more credible since they suited the philosophy prevalent in the absolute monarchies of the day, with
their high-minded conception of the divine right of kings. Authority simply *had* to succeed where real, felt consensus about
the faith was elusive, and in any case, widely unsupported by
lively practices of common sacramental worship.

It is not surprising, therefore, that Catholicism was experiencing, in its own way, the equivalent of the nervous doctrinal bat-
tles that were fracturing the Protestant world. On the positive
side, the catholic theological culture of the seventeenth century—both in Roman Catholicism and in *via media* Anglicanism
—was anxious to hold on to the central, "dogmatic" truths.
Wisely, it avoided speculative discussion; instead it vigorously
concentrated, in scholarly fashion, on historical, patristic warrants. Thus there arose, in the midst of the restlessness of the
century, a succession of learned positive theologians, mainly in
France and England: the monks of the newly-founded (1621)
Benedictine Abbey of Saint Maur; the classicist Isaac Casaubon,
the Jesuit Denis Pétau (Petavius), and the Oratorian Louis Tho-

massin d'Eynac (Thomassinus); bishop Lancelot Andrewes, archbishop William Laud, and the other "Caroline divines" in
England—all of them dedicated to moderation and the avoidance of contentiousness in the retrieval of the integrity of the
Christian faith.

Still, in the Catholic Church, the positive theologians' wari-
ness of speculative theological reflection and argument was more
than counterbalanced by the many who started a rather pointless
tradition of positively reveling in the exploration of "free" questions—that is, those that allowed for legitimate differences of
opinion. It often began to look as if theology was less a reflection on the faith than a largely agonistic exercise, designed to
provide its practitioners with an occasion to indulge in an appe-
tite for overstatement totally out of proportion with any desire
or need for understanding or with the importance of the matter
debated [o].

As the speculative parts of theology became increasingly identical with controversy, the disputatiousness of the age found an
outlet in waves of strident, mainly clerical disputes, with schools
of Catholic theology furiously taking sides on peripheral issues
treated as if they were decisive. Thus positive theologians and
baroque scholastics were forever engaged in mutual recrimina-
tion, with a bitterness equal to that prevailing between the Puri-
tans and the Anglican establishment in England; religious orders
and the diocesan clergy tended to be sharply at odds about local
jurisdiction and papal authority; in Catholic France, a seeker for
peaceful Christian reunion like Bossuet could get involved in an
ugly, nervous fight with a fellow-bishop, Fénélon, about quietism;
with an energy worthy of a better cause, and flying in the face of
solemn papal commands to discontinue the debate, Jesuits and
Dominicans kept on fruitlessly discrediting each other, in the
battle *de auxiliis*, about the nature of the relationship between
grace and freedom—devoted as they both were to in-house "orthodoxies" about purely speculative, marginal issues framed in

---

[o] The theology faculties in the universities, and even more, the newly reformed
Tridentine seminaries have been aptly compared with *gymnasia*, seemingly meant
to train the members of the clerical subculture in curious, disputatious brands of
doctrinal loyalty. One of the most widely read Italian journals aimed at the diocesan clergy in the field used to bear witness to this mentality in its very title: *La
palestra del clero*—"the clergy's wrestling school." Cf. Walter J. Ong, *Fighting for Life*,
pp. 51-59, 118-48.

a wrong-headed manner in the first place; and Franciscans and Jesuits were accusing each other of heresy in the matter of inculturation, in the fight over the Chinese rites.

Thus the fault-line that had begun to develop, centuries before, between the liturgical Creed and theological understanding (§52, 7, a) was finally causing fissures throughout the ecclesiastical landscape. Not surprisingly, in the Catholic countries, many of the Catholic educated laity found themselves painfully scandalized; they fled in the direction of Jansenist rigorism, pietism, or quiet agnosticism. Even less surprisingly, the unsettling tremors eventually drove large numbers of thinking Catholics, tired of overstatement, out to the margins of the Church and beyond. They adopted forms of anti-clerical Deism, or joined associations like freemasonry, where the atmosphere was humane and free, and less charged with clerical pretense (cf. §28).

[f] It was not long before the spirit of the Enlightenment capitalized on the weariness caused by interminable discussion. It began to formalize the deep rift that had opened, everywhere in the otherwise divided Christian world, between the catechisms of Christianity, with their profusion of secondary doctrines, and its spiritual meaning (that is—or so it was believed—its true, universalist essence). The German Neologians, like the Christian Deists in England, still tried to keep up appearances of doctrinal continuity by proposing a simple, straightforward, artlessly biblical Christianity (cf. §28, 1-3, esp. [c]). In doing so, they were building on earlier, more universalist Reformed traditions like Bullinger's and Arminius'; thus they ended up proposing that Christianity is simply the most recent, most enlightened form of the universal covenant initiated at creation [p].

---

[p] It may not be out of place here to insert an explicit comment on the subject of Christianity's alleged superiority over other religions (cf. also §62, 1, a, [f]). This theme is to be traced back, not (as John Hick and, lately, Paul Knitter have claimed) to orthodox Christianity, with its allegedly "exclusivist" affirmation of the divinity of Christ, but to rationalist Christian Deism, with its claim to philosophical superiority over all forms of organized religion. No less person than Gotthold Ephraim Lessing was well aware of this. His habit of "teasing" and "pestering" others with theological argument, he wrote to his brother Karl in 1777, was a matter of "interest in sound common sense [den gesunden Menschenverstand] rather than theology"; and precisely for that reason "I prefer the old-fashioned orthodox (basically tolerant) theology to the newer (basically intolerant) one, only because the former plainly gives ordinary human common sense an argument, while the latter prefers to bribe it" (Gesammelte Werke, vol. 9, p. 729).

Increasingly, however, consistent rationalism won out, and even the semblance of orthodoxy was dropped. The Creed, along with the whole array of doctrines that detailed it, became a matter of merely historical interest, as theologians first began to pare down the substance of Christianity to its philosophically essential, rational minimum. This minimum was to be equated with the essence of all religions; in the final analysis, the particularities of Christianity's doctrinal tradition could be better accounted for in purely traditionalist, historicist terms [q]. It had served its purpose in its day—now it was deadwood, ready, at last, for the pyre of history.[14] Finally, the true essence of Christianity was becoming available, without the alienating preconceptions and prejudices of the churches—stuff that had only served to encourage dogmatism and controversy. Simple, serene belief in the existence of an invisible, yes, even a provident God would heal the scars that kept alive the memory of the unnecessary wounds inflicted on humanity by an intolerant Christianity propped up by *anciens régimes.*

[§73] THE IMPASSE PERSONIFIED: LESSING AS A MODERN PROPHET

[1] In many ways, Gotthold Ephraim Lessing (cf. §28, 3-4) personifies the stalemate that had resulted from the complete dissociation of the Creed from its transcendent perspectives—that is, from the divorce between the Christian faith's catechetical elements and its spiritual import.[15] In a historic response to an aggressive Lutheran pastor who has challenged him to state how he understands Christianity, Lessing gets his chance. Not being a party to any debate among Christians, he can feign innocence, while at the same time being "as definite as anybody could ask of me." And what does he do? Infuriatingly, he formulates Christianity's essence in the terms of the great, historic Tradition of the undivided Church:

The Christian religion must be understood in terms of the doctrines contained in the *symbola* of the Church of the first four centuries.

Thus, with consummate irony, Lessing the agnostic directs divided Christianity back to its original profession of faith [r].

---

[q] In this context, note the parallel development in the interpretation of Judaism, in Moses Mendelssohn's *Jerusalem*: §28, 4, a, [d].

[r] Cf. "Nötige Antwort auf eine sehr unnötige Frage des Herrn Hauptpastor Goeze, in Hamburg" (*Gesammelte Werke*, vol. 8, pp. 417-23; quotation p. 418). In

[2] In Lessing's view, however, this traditional, historic Christianity is not a live option any more. It simply no longer exists, and if it were to exist, it would in all likelihood fail to convince a century in which "the proof of the spirit and of power" is no longer available, and in which miracles do not happen any more.[16] Instead, those who now profess the Christian faith as a positive religion have become fanatics crusading on behalf of either the Bible's authority or the Pope's. This proves not only that they fail to understand the true spiritual import of what they profess, but also that they misconstrue the letter of the profession of faith itself, by interpreting it in a crudely supernaturalist fashion unacceptable to any thinking person. Thus the churches are the clearest evidence of the bankruptcy of the catechetical approach.

Is spiritualism, then, the answer? Perhaps, Lessing suggests, but we have to be cautious as well as critical: it is unwise to trade in one type of credulousness for another. For example, the Neologians' attempt to solve the problem by lacing the Bible with rationality has proved to be futile. With the supernatural, revelatory bite taken out of Christianity, the rational, only residually Christian theology produced by the Neologians is neither flesh nor fowl—nothing but "a patchwork of bunglers and half-philosophers" (§28, 3, a).[17]

Thus, Lessing concludes, in the final analysis, those who wish to adopt a single-minded, consistently enlightened point of view have no choice but to cease being Christians and become principled rationalists. If they are still interested in the essence of Christianity, they are so only for purposes of debate: all they will ever want to do is explain that the Christian faith is nothing but one particular version of the one universal truth equally accessible to all by virtue of Reason.

[3] It is against this background that Lessing stakes out what he claims—though never quite believably—to be his own personal position. On the intolerant catechetical terms proposed to him by the Christianity he knows, he is in no sense a Christian, nor does he wish to be. Yet he cannot keep himself from being involved, if only

his response, Lessing also states that the Apostles' Creed and the Athanasian Symbol have comparable authority, as does the *regula fidei*, which is the true, original summary of the Christian profession of faith (cf. §23, 4, c). For that reason, if there is any rock on which the Church is built, it is the rule of faith, and certainly not Scripture or Peter and his current Successor. Cf. *Lessing's Theological Writings*, pp. 62-64. (Regrettably, H. Chadwick translates only Lessing's 20 propositions on the *regula fidei*, not the introduction and the epilogue of the *Necessary Answer*.)

because the Christians cannot get themselves to leave him alone (or so he says). Thus he can cast himself in the role of Paul in front of the Sanhedrin (Acts 23, 6ff.): as Lutherans and Catholics fanatically fight each other on his account, he stays in his own "fortress" without committing himself, leaving it to the combatants to defend him against one another's attacks.[18]

Lessing, however, does not adopt this irritatingly non-committal posture simply for effect. It is, he claims, the *principled* option; intellectual integrity forbids one to accept a compromise between prejudiced fanaticism and reasonable tolerance (since the latter, in effect, avoids any positive faith-commitment). Hence, when it comes to *believing with integrity*, Lessing sees no alternative except the straight dilemma between honest, classic, historic Christianity (which, however, is extinct) and pure Reason.

[4] This, however, is not the end of the story. The eighteenth century may have treated faith as irrational; it was far from unfeeling—pure Reason is cold comfort in any age. So, curiously (thank God for eighteenth-century *Sentiment!*), Lessing's fortress turns out to have a window after all—one that allows him to look out, even if it does not give others much of a chance to look in; one bridge leading from human reasonableness to Christianity as a positive religion remains. If he finds it impossible to *accept* Christianity as a matter of *belief*, Lessing does not find himself at all incapable of *understanding* it as a matter of true *religion*. Historic Christianity can be genuinely appreciated and even followed, provided it is interpreted as *a work of genius*. Like any work of art, the Christian religion delivers up its essence only in the act of drawing the beholder into the central experience it embodies. That experience must be twofold: towards God, it consists in the upright life in self-abandon to providence; towards humanity and the world it consists in loving all that is truly good. This is the essence of Christianity; not surprisingly, it is also the perfection of humanity. It is, admittedly, not the Christian religion found in the Christian churches. Rather, it is something entirely different from it, to the point of incompatibility: the religion of Christ himself.[19]

[5] Thus, in Lessing's aesthetic interpretation, truly Christian existence turns out to be the shape of the truly human existence before God, in imitation of Christ; and surprisingly, Lessing himself turns out to have been, all along, the advocate of a Christianity of the purest, most original kind. This enables him, from behind his

unbeliever's mask, to implore Christians not to read him entirely out of their company. After all, he muses in a letter to Elise Reimarus, who would expect a judge to send to the gallows a criminal who has insisted on remaining anonymous throughout the trial, yet who, at the moment of sentencing, is suddenly identified, by someone in the crowd, as the bastard son of the local lord?

Thus we find Lessing suggesting, with unparalleled irony, that, unbeknownst to all, he is a servant of God, too, albeit in the form of "the great Lord's dear bastard."[20] Far more of a rationalist yet far less of an anti-Christian than he usually sounds, Lessing ends up being a prophet—though safely outside the ecclesiastical camp, of course. In his own voice and, more importantly, entirely on his own terms, he is deploring the fact that the essence of Christianity has gotten lost because Christians have failed to live up to the spiritual, universalist dimensions of the faith they profess. Ironically, the quest for the essence of Christianity once more takes the form of a plea for the reform of the Church—one coming from a principled, if somewhat theatrical, outsider this time.

[a] Lessing's story of the hanging of the local lord's son may have been inspired by a passage in the Babylonian Talmud. "R. Meir said: ... To what is this matter comparable? To two twin brothers [who lived] in one city; one was appointed king, and the other took to highway robbery. At the king's command they hanged him. But all who saw him exclaimed, 'The king is hanged!' whereupon the king issued a command and he was taken down."[21]

Whether Lessing knew the story and used it or not, the difference in point between the two is enormous. In the Talmudic parable, mercy is shown to the king's brother's dead body out of *compassion for the king*, who has been embarrassed and saddened by his wayward brother's sorry fate. Lessing's parable, on the other hand, is entirely self-serving; he requests mercy *for himself*, reminding the Christians that although *he* is an infidel and a scoundrel, *they* are supposed to be kind to him, for the love of the God *they* believe in. Characteristically, not a word about the question as to whether Lessing himself has saddened God. What matters is the integrity of humanity; the integrity of God, Lessing obviously thinks, is God's business.

[6] Lessing is a landmark in two different though related landscapes. First of all, he sums up the *impasse* created by the fact that the *content*

of the Creed has gotten divorced from its transcendent, universalist *perspectives*. This divorce will give rise to two traditions nervously at war with each other for at least a century and a half. On the one hand, there will be a long string of *defensive, intolerant, fideistic, traditionalist accounts of orthodox Christianity*, on the other hand, we will see a whole series of *aggressive philosophical ideologies of liberation* (including some atheistic ones, like Feuerbach's, Marx' and Freud's) *to rival the Christian faith.* From his place in this landscape, Lessing continues to remind modern theology that if Christianity is to survive, it must do everything to encompass both the Creed and its universalist perspectives.

But Lessing also points to a new debate—again, on the essence of the Christian faith. The pale, rational Christianity of the Neologians and the other Christian Deists had ended up endorsing the Enlightenment's reduction of *Christian doctrine* to a set of general truths. In that doctrinal void, however, it could become clearer and clearer that the Christian faith does not really depend on abstract doctrine alone to stake out its identity; it has *historical* claims to make, too. And so the thought could arise, Is it possible to reconstruct *the true essence of Christianity on the basis of the historical Jesus?* Lessing stands at the cradle of this issue.

[a] Here too, however, the prospects for orthodox Christianity are dim. It was Lessing who, between 1774 and 1778, had published Reimarus' *Fragments.* One can see why. The Christian religion, he wrote in 1780, was something quite different from the religion of Christ himself. This, of course, opens yet another rift between reason and faith: one between the historical, exemplary Jesus who worships and proclaims God, and the transcendent, divinized Christ who is worshiped and proclaimed as God [s]. The former belongs to all of humanity; the latter is the sole property of the churches. Lessing claimed he could accept and understand the former; the latter could only be the source of perpetual, alienating dispute.

In this way, the Christian Church has been handed another radical challenge to its self-understanding. Not only is its essen-

---

[s] Thus Lessing becomes one of the first articulate representatives of the proposition that true Christianity was lost and must therefore be completely reconstructed, which requires that Scripture be interpreted afresh, in its historical purity, apart from any existing doctrinal commitments. Cf. §71, 2, c.

tial doctrine—the incarnation—indistinguishable from rational philosophy; it has also misinterpreted the historical Jesus.

However, the further analysis of that very questionable judgment and its resolution must await treatment elsewhere, in the context of christology, in the third part of this second volume of *God Encountered.*

[§74] CLOSING MEDITATION: ESTABLISHMENT AND IDENTITY

[1] The lengthy survey just completed must give us pause. During the period covered, serious Christians on all sides were determined to retrieve and pursue the substance of Christianity. They often found themselves having to do so in trying circumstances: they got to endure the condescending smiles of the many who, while remaining outside the Churches, claimed to have discovered a purer conception of Christianity, and especially a more universalist one.

[2] From a more strictly theological point of view, however, the life of the Church, East and West, during the period is characterized by deep ambiguity. On the one hand, there is lively and diverse movement in Christianity. This holds especially for spirituality and art; it holds even more noticeably if we recall the political—even geopolitical—developments associated with the spread of Christianity throughout the globe. On the other hand, however, there is a serious lack of theological reflection on the heart of Christianity—the Creed and the *regula fidei.* Instead, there is increasing theological conflict and division about secondary matters, of the kind that is about to break up Christendom altogether. Is this symptomatic of an underlying lapse in the Church's sense of identity?

[3] Asking this question raises further, unsettling retrospects. Underneath the faith, the virtue, the mysticism, the creativity and the intelligence of the early and high Middle Ages, could it be that the Christian Church's deeper sense of identity had been lapsing, both in the East and in the West? Could it be that Christianity's *primary* agenda since, say, the second Council of Nicaea in A. D. 787 (the last Council to deal with an affirmation in the Creed) had imperceptibly shifted—shifted from *theology* to *ecclesiology*, from being divinely identified to self-identification, from pilgrim people to sociopolitical establishment, from eschatology to history, from the simple depth of Christian faith—*fides divina*—to the intricate web of church doctrines—*fides ecclesiastica*—and canon law, from communi-

ty of faith in Christ to Christian civilization? As the Christian Church was settling down in the massive shape of Christendom, did sedentarization produce acculturation, and acculturation compromise, and compromise creeping idolatry, and creeping idolatry alienation and fragmentation, as it is bound to do—as it had done, long ago, in Israel? And in that perspective, was Luther, perhaps, even more on the mark than he could have realized himself, when he raised the specter of a new Babylonian captivity?

Or could it be, perhaps, that in all these deviations the Church was being sent, like Israel, into a *diaspora* more bewildering than any conventional sense of Christianity identity could handle? And could it be that this exile was in reality full of promise? That, in God's Providence—that is, in reality—this *diaspora* was a test of the Church, to prepare it for a mission to a new world? And was this test necessary because the mission was to demand of the Church a sense of Christian identity deep and varied and sophisticated enough to support a truly global universalism (cf. GS 93)? To the eye of faith, could this even be another instance of grace superabounding where sin had been plentiful (Rom 5, 20)?

[4] Asking these questions is also suggesting answers; asking them in such sweeping terms is suggesting answers so sweeping as to cry out for considerable qualification in the light of the specifics of both history and contemporary experience, in all their considerable variety. But at least three suggestions may be made, to guide the theological imagination.

[5] First of all, it is wise to recall that a lot of the history that has been recalled in this chapter (albeit in strokes too broad for completeness and real accuracy) has gone into what remains to this day the very fabric of the religious sensibility of North America, and of the United States in particular. To mention just one example, while the foundations of the Federation were roundly and explicitly religious, they were also roundly and explicitly anti-denominational, or at least denominationally indifferent. The normative religious culture of the United States does indeed hail the universalist themes of God, humanity, and the world; it also places a wall of separation between this universalism and all particular catechisms, which it regards as a matter of private conviction, or, at most, as the basis for purely voluntary association. This means that the religious freedom enjoyed in the United States by the Catholic Church—along with all other churches, denominations, and

faiths—is at least partly based on *a principle opposed by the entire catholic tradition: the separation between the spiritual and the catechetical.* While there prevails, in the air we breathe, an atmosphere of respect for the churches, there also prevails an inclination to interpret them all as sects. To countless serious Americans, including many Christians, the essential nature of *all* religion, including Christianity, lies in its human and cosmic universalism rather than in any Creed (cf. §30, 5, [*k*]). No wonder so many of our friends can sound positively religious when they profess that they are against "organized religion."

In this light it is not surprising that confessional Christianity in North America has such a strong tendency towards authoritarian, sectarian fundamentalism. This serves a double function. On the one hand, ironically, fundamentalism serves to confirm the national culture in that it accommodates civil religion's prejudice that confessional Christianity is liable to be more or less sectarian. On the other hand, it cultivates rugged loyalty to the Christian faith (as well as to the national virtues of independence and private initiative) by counteracting, in the name of the Gospel, the leveling, modernizing influence of the liberal latitudinarianism that surrounds it.

In this context, those dedicated to the great Tradition of the undivided catholic Church face a serious challenge. Faced with the wall of separation between universalist religiosity and particularist fundamentalism, between the tolerant breadth of American civil religion and the persistent, repetitious intolerance of the sects, they must profess their Creed—that is, establish their identity as Christians—by holding together Christianity's catechetical elements and its spiritual perspectives.

[6] Secondly, in this context, there is wisdom in looking to the great Tradition for cues. That is, there is theological and catholic, not just historical or political, wisdom in taking seriously the Oriental Orthodox Churches' self-identification as "the Church of the Seven Councils."[22] Not only do the first seven Ecumenical Councils *de facto* represent the consensus of the undivided Church; the entire teaching of these Councils is also a direct commentary on the Creed of Nicaea and Constantinople, in a way the teaching of all the later Councils and Synods and Convocations, East and West, is simply not. Respect for the hierarchy of truths should persuade catholic theologians of every tradition to develop their understanding of the Christian faith in accordance with this fact of radical theological—that is, ecumenical—significance.

[7] Thirdly, systematic theology, theoretical as it is, may not be able, in practice, to prevent the disintegration of the Christian Church. Still, it must at least attempt to develop the kind of basic theological understanding of the essence of Christianity that can support true unity and authentic diversity in the Church. It will be the principal task of the next chapter to develop such an understanding.

CHAPTER 5

The Portrayal of the Divine Nature

AGAIN: THE NATURE OF CHRISTIANITY

[§75] WHAT DOES THE CHRISTIAN'S PROFESSION MEAN?

[1] In the late fourth century, the Christian Church was at a watershed comparable, in many ways, to the Renaissance and its divisive aftermath in the Christian West eleven centuries later. It was a much smaller Church in a much smaller world, of course, but the challenge it was facing was still vastly out of proportion with its accumulated experience. It had accepted the imperial aegis and, along with it, its status as the Roman Empire's state religion; it had also experienced, under the emperorship of Julian the Apostate (A.D. 361-363), some of the more precarious effects of this privileged position. It had authoritatively (if not without a lot of conflict and secession) discovered and laid down the essential commitments that would guarantee its unity in believing, in the Council of Nicaea (A.D. 325) and its aftermath—commitments that the first Council of Constantinople (A.D. 381) had finalized. It was attracting a new generation of well-educated young intellectuals, often from prominent families, whose talent and sophistication were often matched by deep personal commitments. If it continued to be torn, understandably, between the peace that the new settlement had brought and the restless Christian hunger for a higher justice, it was also developing ways of cultivating both, in fresh combinations, especially in the form of monasticism and by means of sophisticated catechetical and theological education. That is, it was achieving "discretionary fit" with the culture that it inherited, both from the pagan past and from its own heroic past (cf. §14, 2), by making choices between half-Christian accommodation and the kind of Christian identity capable of certifying itself by openness to the world.[1]

A letter to a friend on the nature of the Christian faith, written, in the last decade of the fourth century, by one of the great theological minds of the period, Saint Gregory of Nyssa, is a fine instance of a radical reflection on this critical situation.

[2]   Known under the title *What Does the Christian's Profession Mean?*,[2] the letter is a notable piece if for no other reason than that Gregory expressly states that he means to give a definition of Christianity.[3] He begins by explaining to his friend Harmonius that the "profession" (*epaggelma*) of Christians—what they "profess to be"—must refer to something *essential*. A person does not become a Christian by merely adopting the label any more than an ape becomes a human being by being dressed up like one or even by acting like one, as is well illustrated by Lucian's story of the ape that had been taught how to dance. Gone was the illusion of humanity when, during a show, one spectator dropped a few sugared almonds in front of the beast: he tore off his mask and showed his essential simian nature by abandoning the dance for the delicacies.[4] Being named after Christ, therefore, must involve us, not just in aping him, by flaunting his name, but in *participating in what he is*.

What Christ *is* is indicated by his proper name. Without explicitly mentioning the root meaning ("anointed") of the word, Gregory explains that it means "King." This points to Christ's transcendent majesty. Participation in what Christ is, therefore, involves sharing in the transcendent, divine nature indicated by his name. But this in turn involves something directly connected with it. In the Christian idiom, Christ's divine nature, which remains inexpressible, is detailed and elaborated by means of a variety of *titles* ("justice," "wisdom and power," "truth," "life," "goodness," etc. [*a*]). However,

---

[*a*] Virginia Woods Callahan (*FC* 58, p. 84, n. 4) states that out of a total of nine titles enumerated by Gregory, six are biblical, while three are taken from the language of the philosophers. Callahan's references, identical to those listed in Jaeger's footnotes (vol. 8/1, p. 134), are unreliable. Here is a corrected list. Out of ten titles of Christ listed by Gregory, five are biblical: "justice" (1 Cor 1, 30), "wisdom" and "power" (1 Cor 1, 24), "truth" and "life" (Jn 11, 25; 14, 6; Col 3,4). "Salvation" is biblical, too, of course, though (unlike "Savior") it does not occur in the New Testament as a title of Christ. However, it does occur as a divine title in the Hebrew Scriptures (Ps 35, 3; 62, 2). Gregory mentions four titles that convey conceptions of the divine borrowed from philosophical authors: "goodness," "incorruptibility," "the unchangeable," and "the inalienable." Incidentally, the spontaneity with which Gregory combines biblical and secular titles is a good indication of the naturalness with which he integrates Christian faith and cultural wisdom.

addressing Christ by these titles has consequences: it commits the Christian to the practice of the virtues from which the titles are derived, that is, to *mimēsis*—true "imitation" [b]. Failure to commit oneself in this way would lead to a mere show of religion—that is, it would amount to aping and nothing else. Gregory explains:

We [Christians] bear the same name as [Christ], who surpasses all the names that explicate the incorruptible nature. This is so because by our faith in him we are joined together with him. It definitely follows that, accordingly, our sharing the name must also come to involve all the notions that we entertain about that incorruptible nature. For just as in virtue of participation in Christ we have received the title "Christian," so, accordingly, it is fitting that we should also take upon ourselves the sharing of all of those noble names. ...

Therefore, whoever clothe themselves in the name of Christ, yet fail to exhibit in their lives all the notions connected with the name, such persons belie the name; in the terms of the example we have used, such persons dress up the ape, in a soulless mask that merely resembles a human person. For just as it is impossible for Christ to be anything but justice and purity and truth and the rejection of all evil, so it is not possible to be a Christian (that is, truly a Christian) without exhibiting in oneself the sharing of those names. So, just as someone might want to explain the idea of Christianity by means of a definition, we will put it as follows: Christianity is the portraying of the divine nature [*christianismos esti tēs theias physeōs mimēsis*].

Now let no one quarrel with the definition as being immoderate and exceeding the low estate of our nature; for the definition does not go beyond that nature. For if we should call to mind the first condition of humanity, we will discover, through the teaching of Scripture, that the definition does not exceed the measure of our nature. For one thing, the making of the first human person took place in imitation of God's likeness; that is how Moses conceives of man, where he says: "God made man; in the

---

[b] Gregory's central proposition is a telling example of what Auerbach has explained in his classic study, entitled *Mimesis*, of "imitation" (that is, "the interpretation of reality through literary representation"). Auerbach comes to the conclusion that the Christian faith is the crucial factor in the development of *realism*, the "ruthless mixture" of the everyday and the sublime that characterizes Western culture, and hence, Western literature (*Mimesis*, pp. 554-57). The Christian claim that Jesus Christ, and the Christian Church in his wake, involve a true representation of the true God in the real world (cf. §23, 2, n. 36) amounts to a decisive shakeup of the classical world picture—a shakeup, it should be added, decisively inaugurated by Israel's monotheism and its cultivation of prophetic narrative. — For the relationship between faith-commitment, the naming of Christ by means of titles, and the interpretation of Christ's meaning, cf. F. J. van Beeck, *Christ Proclaimed*, pp. 88-93, 112-43, 510. Cf. also §34, 4; §42, 2; §43, 3.

image of God he made him" [Gen 1, 27]. For another, the profession of
Christianity involves that humanity is raised up again to its original happiness. Now if it is true that the human person is God's resemblance of old,
then we have not formulated an extravagant definition in declaring that
Christianity is the portraying of the divine nature. True, the undertaking
involved in this title is enormous, and it might not be out of place to think
that it is hazardous for a person to assume that name and not live in accordance with it ...[5]

Gregory goes on to elaborate that it is in human lives of freely
chosen purity and virtue that God is both faithfully and persuasively
portrayed. Very importantly, this portrayal of God's perfection is a
matter of *participation*, and hence *real*, not just a matter of appearance. This can be so because God, however transcendent, is not remote but near. Drawing on a broad familiarity with Stoicism (cf.
§27, 4, c and [*i*]),[6] Gregory explains to his friend:

... the divine is equally in all and it permeates the whole of creation in
the same way, and nothing could remain in being apart from the One
Who Is. Rather, the divine nature touches each being equally, encompassing all things within itself with the power of its embrace.[7]

The letter ends on a note of eschatological hope. It is true,
Gregory admits, our virtue in this world is always limited and uncertain; but, he reminds the reader, with an appeal to the Sermon
on the Mount (Mt 6, 19-21), what counts is not the money in hand,
but the prospect—the reward to come. That reward is assured by
the nature of the One to whose safe keeping we entrust our deposit:

In view of the nature of the one who receives the deposit, the return is
certainly bound to be a matter of great glory. For if what *we* have to offer
is poor, we are only operating in accordance with our nature—we are the
way we are. In the same way, it stands to reason that the One who is rich
in everything will graciously give to the depositors everything *he* has by
nature.
So let none be discouraged when they bring into the divine treasury
what is [only] in accordance with their own power, as if what they have
given were the measure of what they will come away with. Rather, let the
measure of their anticipation be the word of the One who says that he will
give great things for small ones; that he will trade earthly things for heavenly ones, transient ones for everlasting ones—such things as cannot, by
nature, be grasped by thought or come within the compass of verbal explanation. This is what the inspired Scripture means when it teaches that "eye

has not seen, nor has ear heard, nor has it occurred to the human heart—all that God has prepared for those who love him" [1 Cor 2, 9].[8]

[3] One feature of Gregory's letter deserves special attention. If we recall the Greek fondness for definition in terms of *ideal natures*, it is remarkable that Gregory defines the nature of Christianity in terms of *action* and *process* [c]. Bearing the name of Christ commits Christians to freely chosen conduct; the profession of Christianity remains a pretense and an illusion unless it is verified in a Christlike way of life (cf. §45, 3; §47, 2). What will come about in that way of life, however, is *the actualization of two "natures."* Both *true humanity*, created "of old" in the divine image and now restored in Christ, and *true divinity*, shared by virtue of faith in Christ, will be visibly taking shape in Christians, on the basis of the union with Christ that is initially bestowed on them. Thus *the explicit Christian profession of faith makes sense only if it serves as a bridge* on which persons are observed to walk from virtue to virtue, with Christ calling and guiding and attracting them, since he has already made them his own. And as they thus visibly walk here in the world, Christians go from one horizon to another: from immemorial human nature to humanity divinely fulfilled (cf. §67, 1, a). And at both horizons as well as beyond them, the invisible God and Jesus Christ the Eternal *Logos* abide.

[4] Gregory's definition is a good example of a *guiding idea*—a key concept by means of which the *normative nature* of the Christian profession of faith can be reliably interpreted (cf. §70, 3, a-b). However, what is crucial is the *agenda* behind the definition: it explains the Christian faith as a way of life, and hence, the profession

---

[c] Even Aristotle, like Plato, associates true knowledge with the eternal order of things, which is primarily symbolized by the past. In his *Metaphysics*, he explains that definitions formulate essences or natures; he conveys his idealist understanding of the notion of "essence" or "nature" by means of a "philosophic imperfect," conveying timelessness: "essence" is a being's *to ti ēn einai*—its "being what it (always) was" (*Met.* 5, 8 [1017^{b}22]; cf. Joseph Owens, *The Doctrine of Being in the Aristotelian* Metaphysics, pp. 180-88). Aristotle's philosophy, of course, differs from Plato's in its insistence that this definable nature has no actual existence in and of itself, but only in actual, particular subjects (*Categ.* 5 [2^{a}11-18, 33ff.]). Yet even in this way a subject's nature remains fixed, and thus continues to determine the course of that subject's existence. For example, it sets the pattern of its *changes*, by being its principle of growth (*Met.* 5, 4 [1014^{b}16]), and of motion and rest (*Phys.* 2, 1 [192^{b}21ff.]). Nowhere does it appear to occur to Aristotle any more than to Plato to propose that processes of change, such as motion and growth, are themselves fit objects for definition.

of faith as an act of "testimonial autobiography" (cf. §41, 2; §45, 2; §46, 2)—that is, as a deed of commitment (cf. §51, 4, [q]). Behind Gregory's definition, therefore, stands the Creed as an essentially *performative language act.*

Because of this, the Christian profession of faith resists complete reduction to an idea of universal validity. Only to the extent that the Creed is lived out, as part of the history of salvation, will it deliver its spiritual, universalist meaning [d].

> [a] Especially in this last regard Gregory's explanation of the nature of Christianity is clean contrary to the modern, spiritualist dynamic of late-medieval origin. There the search for guiding ideas turned into a quest for a *stable, identifiable substance.* That quest, unfortunately, produced interpretations of the Christian faith that increasingly quarreled with the Creed and with the orders of the Churches that continued to profess it. Eventually, such interpretations came to acknowledge the essence of Christianity merely as a religious-philosophical ideal, conceivably realized in the historical Jesus, and in him only in an exemplary way. In the process, much universalism had been gained, but continuity with the historic Christian community had become extremely tenuous. In that same process, the embattled Christian community—itself the scene of endless debate and fragmentation—had increasingly been edged out of the world of the learned and the polite. In that enlightened world, Christianity was treated as an assortment of particularist sects, or, in the case of an established church, as a largely political organization, in which reflection counted for little and expediency for a lot.

[§76] CHRISTIANITY AS TRANSITIONAL: TWO CONCLUSIONS

[1] Our discussion of Gregory of Nyssa's definition of Christianity yields a major insight. It is the following. *Real Christianity is in a*

---

[d] The Creed and Christian worship or prayer are not expressly mentioned, either in Gregory's letter or in the treatise *On Perfection,* which bears a close resemblance to it. Initiation and the catechesis connected with it are assumed rather than discussed, as are the heights of union with God to which the Christian has access in prayer. Gregory treats the former in works like the *Catechetical Oration,* a manual, at once catechetical and apologetical, for the use of those instructing candidates for initiation (cf. §51, 4, a and [r]); as for the latter, Gregory often touches on it in his writings on the mystical sense of Scripture, like *The Life of Moses.*

"state" of continual transition, from the order of nature to the order of grace. The nature of Christianity is intrinsically determined by its commitment to an eschatological fulfillment that is still in process of being actualized; the living Church is forever in dynamic tension between the "Not Yet" and the "Already" (cf. §110, 5) [e]. In Hans Urs von Balthasar's terms, it is in the very nature of Christianity to be unresolved and hence, "dramatic." This insight in turn yields two significant conclusions.

[2] The first is: while the Church of Christ and the truth of its positive teachings can be sufficiently identified in place and time by faithful, open-minded discernment guided by divine grace, the nature of Christianity cannot be grasped in a definitive way. This means that Christianity will defy all attempts at definition by means of conclusive, stabilizing, "arresting" concepts [f]. On the positive side, this feature opens Christianity to exploration and illumination with the help of guiding ideas.

---

[e] Hans Wagenhammer (*Das Wesen des Christentums*, p. 256) comes to the same conclusion, namely, "... that the nature of Christianity can never be grasped with absolute concreteness [*daß das Wesen des Christentums nie absolut konkret gefaßt werden kann*]." And he continues: "As long as Christianity claims to be *the* truth and *the* way of salvation, and as long as it holds on to the eschatological proviso, it cannot be definitively nailed down."

[f] Stephen Sykes, in his attractive monograph *The Identity of Christianity*, arrives at a comparable, though far from identical, conclusion. Christianity's normative essence ("idea"), which must also furnish it with unity and continuity, he successfully argues, is not establishable by a stable definition; rather, it is "an essentially contestable concept." This contestability is due to the fact that Christianity can find its identity only in the vicissitudes of theological controversy, in the dialectic between inward dispositions and outward profession of faith, and in the course of dealing with the power-struggles inherent in the Church as a historic institution. There is much to be admired in Sykes' book, especially in the way in which he shows the historic complexity of the issue as it has affected the theological world, in his analyses of Schleiermacher, Newman, von Harnack, Loisy, Troeltsch, and Barth. Still, the constructive parts of the book approach the issue of Christian identity on a basis, it would seem to me, that is too narrow—or perhaps, too narrowly Anglican. Consequently, in my view, the book suffers from systematic limitations. Let me suggest four, in the form of questions. Is *contest* (especially theological contest) an adequate avenue of exploration to deal with the ecclesiological fact that the Christian identity is a dynamic, developmental matter? Is the *dialectic between* (Evangelical?) *inwardness and* (High Church?) *outwardness* capable of providing a sufficiently *theocentric* analysis of that dynamic identity? If Jesus' resurrection identifies God as Lord over death and as Lord of *judgment*, can the identity of Christianity be discussed without any discussion of *holiness of life as an eschatological issue?* And even if the responsibility of learned theology in forming the sense of Christian identity is acknowledged, is it not a bit donnish to suggest that all the *body* of the Church has to go by is "popular religion"?

[a] The realization just formulated in a theoretical way takes us back to the dawn of the Christian community. The accounts, in Mark and Luke, of the formation of the community of disciples take the form of Jesus' journeying, first in Galilee, and then, decisively, from Galilee to Jerusalem. The Christian community depicted in the Acts of the Apostles is simply called "the way" (Acts 9, 2; 19, 9. 23; 24, 14. 22), and its message is that of "the way of salvation," and even "the Lord's way" and "God's way" (Acts 16, 17; 18, 25-26). Christians are a people in exile (1 Pet 1, 1; 2, 11), traveling to their true home after the pattern of the great believers remembered in Israel and especially after the pattern of Jesus (Heb 11, 13-16; 12, 1). Their true citizenship is where Christ is (2 Cor 5, 6-10; cf. Eph 2, 19-21).

[b] In light of the present discussion, the enormous significance of the choice, at the second Vatican Council, of the dynamic metaphor "People of God" to characterize the Church must be obvious. The Council uses the metaphor to bid a firm farewell to the closed Roman Catholic triumphalism of the past, and to emphasize the Church's present state of pilgrimage, its universalism, its eschatological orientation, its connections with other Christian communities and with humanity at large, and its vocation to a life of increasing holiness and unity (LG 9-17). The People of God, in other words, is a *people on its way*. Specifically, the Council points out that the Catholic Church's claim to be the complete actualization of the Church willed by Christ does not imply that all those incorporated into this Church are by that fact alone saved. Salvation remains eschatological—a matter of living in charity and persevering in it (LG 8; 14).

[c] Without using the image of the People of God, some of the great modern Catholic theologians (especially of the Tübingen school) had already proposed "definitions" of Catholicism in the form of guiding ideas strongly reminiscent of Gregory of Nyssa's, except that (unfortunately) they are usually less emphatic than Gregory about the *moral* dimension of the Christian life, that is, about the call to holiness implied in it (cf. §47) [g]. Their common characteristic tends to be a strong emphasis on sacramentality—on the ongoing presence of the divine life in humanity and

---

[g] This is best explained as an illustration of the fact that moral theology has long tended to drift apart from doctrine (cf. §54, 7).

the world through the mediation of the Church as the representative of Christ.

Our enumeration must start with Johann Adam Möhler's stirring *Die Einheit in der Kirche, oder das Prinzip des Katholizismus* ("Unity in the Church, or, The Principle of Catholicism") of 1825. Möhler sets the fundamental theme of the book in his summary of the first chapter: "Our assimilation of Christianity is conditional upon the communication of the Holy Spirit; he gathers all the faithful into a spiritual community, through which he communicates himself to those who do not yet believe [: <this is> the inner tradition]. Through the love that is generated in us as we assimilate, in the Church, the [higher spiritual] life that flows in it, Christ is concomitantly given to us; only in the community of believers do we become conscious of him" [*h*].[9]

In the twentieth century Karl Adam has continued this tradition in his classic *Das Wesen des Katholizismus* (translated into English under the title *The Spirit of Catholicism*). In his view, "the single basic thought," "the essential form that gives life to the great structure which we call Catholicism" is the *resolute affirmation, without any subtraction or selectivity, of all reality:* of the fullness of the living God, and of humanity and the world in their integrity. The warrant for this affirmation lies in *the ongoing presence of the living Christ in the historic Catholic Church.* Similarly, shortly after the war years, amid the continuing devastation of the city of Munich, Michael Schmaus reverted to the theme of the nature of Christianity in order to explain once again, in *Vom Wesen des Christentums* (*The Essence of Christianity*), that the heart of the Christian faith is neither truth, nor morality, nor even love, but *God's love entering history in the person of Christ, and transforming it through the Church.* Finally, in an equally explicit way, Henri de Lubac, in his book *Catholicism*, took advantage of Émile Mersch's marvelous historical and theological studies on the Church as the Body of Christ, in order to explain systematically that *Christian doctrine is nothing if not social.* As a result, he explains, *Catholic Christianity is essentially historic, universalist* [*i*], *and mission-*

[*h*] The pointedness with which Möhler identifies the Church as the community which *alone* can communicate Christ-consciousness is hard to miss, if it is remembered that he is writing in the period dominated by the authority of Schleiermacher, who views this issue as the distinctive difference of Catholicism. Cf. §24, 1, [*a*].

[*i*] The original theology of Christ's Mystical Body was universalist as well as

ary, and it is precisely in this fashion that *it represents the transcendent mystery of God.*

[3] In light of the surveys and discussions in this chapter as well as the previous one, it seems appropriate to go back for a moment to the issue of *modernism.* Conclusive, "arresting" conceptual definitions, by nature, tend to present themselves as *final;* for that reason, they tend to they aim at "the introduction of massive theological-systematic fixity where the faith exhibits an organic— that is to say, open—unity of structure" (§17, 1; cf. §15, 4; §21, 1). Rather than *interpreting* the ongoing Christian Tradition, arresting definitions would seem to want to *replace* it with something surer or more relevant. And so the question arises, Are the attempts to capture the nature of Christianity in definitions, perhaps, at least partly an effort to alleviate the craving for spiritual certainty and assurance—an effort that ends up misconstruing the Christian faith? In light of this question, is it surprising that the history of the Christian West shows a connection between the quest for adequate (which usually means minimal) definitions of the nature of Christianity and modernism (just as it shows a connection between catechetical literalism and integralism)? If this should be true, little wonder, then, that *guiding* ideas have proved more illuminating in bringing about an understanding of the Christian faith as a *way* than definitions, or for that matter, catechisms offering doctrinal propositions for literal rehearsal.

[4] Our second conclusion must start with a question. If the nature of Christianity cannot be definitively laid down, does it follow that it is pointless to raise it as an issue? The answer to this question must be a qualified one.

A first point. If there is no fixed definition of the stable essence of Christianity, then there is no fixed definition available to enable anyone to point to any concrete, particular Christian church or community as the full actualization of the nature of Christianity. Raising the issue of the essence of Christianity, therefore, is *pointless if its agenda, whether overt or covert, is the identification of the true*

---

spiritual: it consistently set the Church, viewed as the community intimately united in Christ, against the horizon of the unity of the human race. It is regrettable that the more recent theology of Christ's Mystical Body came to be encumbered, especially at the hands of Roman theologians, with such strongly hierarchical and institutional accretions that by the time Vatican II came together the image of the People of God had to be introduced by way of corrective.

Church. This realization must help put an end to all forms of triumphalism [*j*], sectarianism, and theocracy, whether of the institutional or the charismatic kind; it must also help place every Christian community in the sobering perspective of God's judgment (§42, 3).

> [a] It should, incidentally, also help put an end to all cheap, because mainly theoretical, purely noetic, self-justifying forms of atheistic triumphalism, of the kind exemplified by Feuerbach (cf. §70, 4, a). This criticism does not apply to Marx, whose agenda differs from Feuerbach's in that he emphasizes the need for corrective political action to remedy the social injustices that lie at the root of much of humanity's wretchedness.

[5] But—and this is the second point—there *is* a way in which raising the issue continues to be meaningful. To appreciate this, we must go back once again to the theme of the instability inherent in the Christian profession of faith: without holy restlessness, the Church will harden in its pilgrim state and cease to be the Church of *living faith* (§70, 5). The question about the nature of Christianity can still do for the Church what the Marcionites and the Montanists, in their sectarian zeal, tried to do for the Church of the second

---

[*j*] To clarify this important conclusion, a comparison of Gregory of Nyssa's letter with the concluding books of Eusebius' *Ecclesiastical History* is illuminating. Gregory begins his definition of Christianity in *pistic* terms: Christians have been marked by the name of Christ. He immediately goes on to view the faith in essentially *mystical* terms: Christians share Christ's ineffable nature. From these premises, he draws a *charismatic* conclusion: the true Christian life consists in a virtuous living-out, in the world, of Christ's many names, in expectation of the fulfillment. All of this safeguards the divine transcendence, yet brings the living God near by virtue of the Christians' participation in Christ. Eusebius shows no such theological subtlety. He conceives of the true Church in a far more simplistic, secular way, in terms of a triumphant empire directly and palpably endorsed by God; this ends up *confusing* God and the world. Without much ado, Eusebius identifies the Constantinian establishment as salvation history, and, by a piece of extraordinary rhetoric, turns the idea behind Gregory's definition on its head. Constantine and his son Crispus do not portray God the Father and Christ by the divine way they live; rather, the Father and Christ are made to look like Constantine and Crispus: "... because they had as *guides and comrades-in-arms God, the sovereign King and the Son of God, Savior of all,* the two of them, *father and son,* [...] gain an easy victory. ... The most great victor Constantine, excelling in every virtue connected with the service of God, together with his son, emperor most beloved by God and in all respects *resembling his father,* ... established the one unified empire of the Romans as of old" (*Hist. Eccl.,* X, 9, 4. 6 [*SC* 55, pp. 119-120]; cf. Glenn F. Chesnut, *The First Christian Histories,* p. 118, 153-162). The entire passage, incidentally, suggests a link between Eusebius' triumphalism and his clearly subordinationist christology.

and third centuries, and what the *pauperes Christi*, the mendicants, and the radical *spirituales* attempted to drive home in the Middle Ages, the Quakers in the seventeenth century, and so many Christian utopians in the nineteenth. They all served to remind the Christian establishment of the radical demands of the Gospel. The monks who took their lead from Anthony and made a city of the desert had done it for the increasingly comfortable, newly-established Church of the late third and early fourth century in Alexandria. Mystics and founders of religious communities of every stripe have done it for conventionalized, unduly acculturated Christianity everywhere ever since. In the wake of Vatican II's commitment to being the Church in the modern world, countless motivated, "charismatic" Catholics of all kinds (as well as other Christians) have been awakened to the cause of faith and justice in its profusion of forms; they are part of that same age-old spiritual movement [*k*].

[6] Thus there is no clear, unequivocal, conceptual answer to the question "What is the essence of Christianity?" But asking the question has an abiding *performative, rhetorical, prophetic* significance. Precisely because the issue is incapable of being resolved by means of conclusive, conceptually compelling answers, raising it can act as a salutary irritant, to help keep the Church's sense of provisionality alive, in a perspective that is eschatological—that is, *mystical.* Thus the question can also express *the charismatic Christian's dissatisfaction with dull, lifeless, pretentious, impenitent, or merely pistic Christian establishments.* In this light it is hardly surprising that disquiet about unfocused, ineffectual, mediocre, and even hypocritical Christianity is the very concern that has caused Gregory of Nyssa, Erasmus, the Reformers, and so many other ardent souls, including systematic theologians like Karl Barth and Hans Urs von Balthasar, to raise it as a theological issue [*l*].

[*k*] Johann Baptist Metz has given us a profound analysis of the connection between spiritual renewal and commitment to justice, in a visionary little book, *Zeit der Orden: Zur Mystik und Politik der Nachfolge* (ET *Followers of Christ: Perspectives on the Religious Life*). However, it could easily be overlooked that Metz' treatment fundamentally *applies to the membership of the Church as such,* and not only to the membership of religious communities and secular institutes. In this regard, the two opening chapters of *Lumen Gentium* (LG 1-17) are of the profoundest theological significance. Anterior to the differentiation of vocations, ministries, and degrees of holiness in the Body of Christ, the People of God in its entirety participates in Christ's mediatorship; the mystery of the Church is defined, as a matter of fundamental principle, by the unity of mysticism and humane universalism.

[*l*] Hans Wagenhammer, therefore, is right in concluding (*Das Wesen des Chris-*

[a] In this context, the issue of *patience* (§70, 5) regains its relevance.[10] To the extent that the question about the nature of Christianity springs from involvement in the Church, or from suffering love—even disappointed love—of the Church, it is truly charismatic [m] and can help keep alive the Church's essential restlessness. However, the situation changes when the question begins to be inspired by impatience and disaffection—the main symptom of which is that the questioner begins to insist on definite answers. For every definition of Christianity is by definition unsatisfactory; moreover, every Christian Church, when challenged, will have to admit to its failure to live up in practice to the essence of Christianity, however well it professes it in worship or formulates it in words.

Raised in an impatient fashion, therefore, the question about the nature of Christianity is little more than an alienating irritant. Raised in the spirit of meekness and long-suffering, it might have rallied the Church, in a common hunger and thirst for perfect justice; now it turns mainly critical, divisive, and even punitive. It becomes a summons, delivered at the Church's door, harshly demanding reform; but those who deliver it have justified themselves in advance, by becoming the judges of the faith of others. Thus they have placed themselves at a safe distance from the only real Church—the one that so deeply appreciates its sense of Christian identity that it is prepared to pay for it—by the patient realization that it is not living up to it.

[§77] INTERPRETING THE CREED: RETROSPECT AND OUTLOOK

[1] It is time to take stock and to prepare, at least remotely, for the sixth and seventh chapters. *God Encountered*, it was pointed out long ago (§23, 3), is committed to an interpretation of the Christian faith in terms of *grace and nature*. God's gracious encounter with humanity and the world, so the great Tradition has thought, builds upon (and in so doing graciously exceeds) the simply given; it is undergirded by a prior self-commitment on the part of God: crea-

---

tentums, p. 256) that the unavailability of a conclusive definition of Christianity "makes it necessary again and again to work against the absolutizing of current conceptions and to look for more appropriate ones."

[m] Note the emphasis Maximus Confessor places on long-suffering and patience, in his characterization of what we have called the charismatic type of faith: §53, 2, c.

tion, of which humanity is the culmination. In the event, however, that encounter also turns out to make the most of the simply given, patiently laying bare the depth of its capacity for the encounter with the gracious God. Not surprisingly, the great Tradition has consistently maintained that the "admirable exchange" between God and humanity in Christ involves the promise of the full flowering of *the order of created nature*, whose latent potential must, therefore, ultimately be interpreted as *capacity for actual sharing in God's nature, by grace.*

[2] Broaching the interpretation of the Creed has spontaneously led us to elaborate and orchestrate this fundamental issue in catholic theology. The Creed is indeed the echo of Christian worship (§43, 1). It is also part of the Christian community's traveling equipment; specifically, it is that part of the core tradition around which the ongoing teaching tradition—the test of the community's fidelity to the authoritative past—takes shape (§43, 2; §51, 2; 4, a). Not surprisingly, therefore, the Creed prompts doctrinal development as well as theological reflection.

[3] But rather more importantly, as we have seen, the content of the Creed is reliably understood as *traveling equipment* only if it is both treasured as the Church's profession of faith, and patiently interpreted as a wayfarers' charter—that is, in the perspective of that professed faith's two universalist horizons. These horizons are integral to the full meaning of the Creed, yet they are not so much expressed as *represented*. They are represented, first of all, by the Christian community itself, in its commitment to the imitation of Christ by a life of virtue, ultimately in the service of an encompassing love. They are also represented by the Church's insistence the Creed must be interpreted as a *symbol*—that is, in light of the transcendent realities it can only *symbolize* (cf. §10, 1, [k]).

First of all, therefore, all theological interpretations of the Creed must ultimately respect and treasure the central mystery it symbolizes. This is the one mystery that grounds, enfolds, and brings to fulfillment both the Christian faith and the virtuous life it inspires, and most of all, the worship which alone is fully commensurate with that mystery (cf. §34, 7, a): God present and worshiped in hope, in the Spirit, in and through Jesus Christ risen. The Creed, therefore, is a gateway to longing contemplation; it is professed before God (§§66-69).

But, secondly, worship is the core of the "admirable exchange" between God and *humanity*. In worship, therefore, and in the life and the wisdom drawn from it, ever-longing humanity is being called (and in the Church, both being called and already being led) to the portrayal of the divine nature—that is, to its native perfection as God's mirror-image, shaped by God alone, and to be fulfilled by God alone. The Creed, professed by the Christian Church, but addressed to all of humanity, represents and symbolizes this longing, too (§59, 2-6). It is, therefore, not alienating (§10, 1, a; cf. §61, 3, a, [d]; §84, 1), but an instrument of humanity's perfect freedom. The next chapter will set out to explore some of the fundamental theological dimensions of this.

[4] Before this task is broached, however, two conclusions remain to be drawn from our discussions about the nature of Christianity. Both of them are vital to the worship, the life, and the teaching of the undivided Christian Church.

The first conclusion is connected with the insight that the Creed is to be interpreted symbolically. That insight is only one element in an intuition that is both far more comprehensive and far more pervasive: Christian existence in *all* its particularities—in all the details of its worship, its life, and its teaching—is radically symbolic, that is, sacramental. As it travels from creation to fulfillment, from nature to grace, the Church cannot but interpret its entire self as the sacrament of the presence of the living God in the world, and hence also as the sacrament of humanity's and the world's presence to God. And consequently, it cannot but interpret humanity and the world (that is, the stuff of which the Church is made) as the stuff of sacrament—that is, as radically charged with God's presence and thus as naturally fit to symbolize God.

The second conclusion immediately follows from this. If such is the natural capacity of humanity and the world in which it participates, then God is not—God cannot be—the adversary or opponent of the natural order; consequently, as Piet Schoonenberg has phrased it, in a classic essay, "God or Man" is "A False Dilemma."[11] The next two sections must elaborate these two conclusions.

CATHOLICITY: SYMBOLISM AND SACRAMENTALITY

[§78] A WORLD OF SYMBOLS

[1]   At a critical juncture in the first volume of *God Encountered* (§36, 3), it was observed that

Christian worship is set in space and time; like all worship, it reaches out, from space and time, to heaven and to eternity. But there is a difference. Space and time are not just the *setting* of Christian worship; they are part of its *substance.* ...   The Church's worshipful participation in the life of God is not only a reaching-out from space and time into heaven and eternity ...; it is also an ongoing activity whereby space and time are *drawn into worship.* Realities in space and time, in other words, are also the very stuff Christian worship is made of. ...   While seeking timelessness, therefore, the Church ... makes and re-makes salvation history in the very act of its access to the throne of grace; while seeking to reach the heavenly City, the Church travels and re-travels a world [that is] being made holy by its very act of pilgrimage. And that pilgrimage is itself recalled, too. The Church's praise of God in the Name of Christ, sung *in* the sanctuary, takes the shape of a wayfarers' song sung *on the way to* the sanctuary—a song that recalls the way-stations.

In other words, as the order of grace is taking shape in place and time (§57, 3, d and [*b*]; §66, 2), divine life is seeking to *integrate and transform,* right in the life of the Christian community [*n*], the order of nature itself. *It is not disdaining it*—either by covering it over in blind, undiscriminating indulgence, or by forcibly replacing it, out of disappointment, with a wholly new creation (cf. §87, 3). For far from canceling nature, grace builds on it and perfects it (§26, 2, a); God has truly "loved the world," sinful as it is, and Jesus Christ is the proof of that love (cf. Rom 5, 6-8; Jn 3, 16).

On the authority of God as revealed in Christ, therefore, the great Tradition holds that the world is and remains intrinsically good and lovable, and specifically that, by virtue of an eternal divine design,

this flesh is capable of such a wonderful share of life and immortality, if the Holy Spirit is joined to it, nor can anyone express or utter "the things the Lord has readied" [1 Cor 2, 9] for his chosen ones.[12]

[*n*] Though, again, it does not do so exclusively in the life of the Church, and within the life of the Church, it does not always and everywhere succeed in doing so (cf. §76, 2, b).

In the Christian view of the world, therefore, all that is natural, without exception or qualification, is being revealed as the very stuff of grace [o]. Wherever grace is operative, it is laying bare the created foundations of all that is: how the world is radically related to God and symbolizes God, and even more deeply, how God is sovereignly related to the world and freely reveals the divine glory in it.

[2] Few passages in the patristic literature bear such eloquent witness to the Christian faith's loving and reverent acceptance of the universe in its original, *natural* reality as the opening chapters of the fifth book of Saint Irenaeus of Lyons' great work *Against All Heresies*, written in the last quarter of the second century.

[a] The occasion is *Marcionism* (cf. §40, 3, d). This ardent, austere, zealous, and hence, very successful and widespread form of second and early third century Christianity saw in Christ the revelation, at long last, of the One True God. This God is wholly transcendent and uncontaminated—the God of pure Love, who had from time immemorial elected to be completely hidden. This God is not to be confused with the inferior, unreliable "Maker-God" (or "Demiurge," from Gk. *Dēmiourgos*: "skilled craftsman") of the universe—an inferior deity, inconstant to the point of cruelty. This lower god is identical with the tyrannical Giver of the Law, whom the Jews had acknowledged in their blindness. For this reason, Christ, the purely spiritual emissary

---

[o] Here lies the root of the problem the catholic tradition has had with the gloomy interpretation of natural love associated with a variety of sixteenth and seventeenth century *pietistic* movements, now usually lumped together (in Catholic circles) under the rubric of *Jansenism* (for examples, cf. DS 1934, 1938, 2444-47; CF 1988/34. 38, 1991/44-47). Pessimistic pietism of the Lutheran variety also underlies Anders Nygren's otherwise classic study *Agape and Eros*. Nygren is rightly eager to affirm, with the entire Tradition, that God's love is freely given, and hence, that it is not determined by the worthiness of the object of that love. But in his eagerness, Nygren construes a complete *opposition* between the dynamics of created love (which he characterizes as ultimately self-regarding) and divine love. The catholic tradition has insisted on *integrating* the two. The gracious love of God, while indeed overcoming the sinful self-centeredness of humanity, penetrates to the original core of all creation and all humanity, created "good" and indeed "very good" (Gen 1, 12. 18. 21. 25. 31), and in so doing restores to them the native ability to love God and others in a manner that is both thoroughly natural and free from self-regard. For these reasons, Max Scheler's analysis of the sensibility of the Christian West in terms of its acceptance of "the sense of unity with the cosmos" (*kosmische Einsfühlung*) is closer to the mark than Nygren's (*Wesen und Formen der Sympathie*, pp. 87-104; ET *The Nature of Sympathy*, pp. 77-99).

of the true God, could not possibly have come to fulfill the Jewish Scriptures, or to restore humanity and the world to any allegedly prior dignity (nor, of course, could he have been born of a human mother, not even of one who was a virgin). Quite the contrary: he had come to overthrow the Demiurge, to abolish everything Jewish and impure, and to create, for the first time ever, Spirit and Love where formerly there had been only Matter and Law. Evil people, associated with the Demiurge, had indeed succeeded in killing him, but ultimately they had been unable to touch him. Now at last, in the churches of the truly pure, the strife of the perishing world had ceased and the New Age had dawned; the true structure of world history had been revealed; direct and truly spiritual access to the divine mystery had finally become available. In the Marcionite communities, the living Christ, whom only Paul had fully understood, was wresting humanity and the world from the stifling grasp of the lower god, who was still holding the catholic churches in thrall, through their continued veneration of the utterly carnal Jewish Scriptures and the residually carnal Gospels [p].

[3] With the sure touch of synthetic genius that characterizes his writings, Irenaeus explains that acceptance of the Christian faith in its integrity must imply the acceptance of the integrity of the natural order. Taking his text from the prologue of the fourth Gospel ("he came into what was his own": Jn 1, 11), he rejects Marcion's sectarian supernaturalism. Gradually, however, argument yields to rapture. In the liveliest of strokes, Irenaeus ends up painting the Christian vision of the world, in all its catholic comprehensiveness: how Christ, the Church, and especially the Eucharist are the embodiment of the *fundamental harmony* that prevails between the natural, created order and the divine life that God graciously bestows on it.

---

[p] Cf. Peter Brown, *The Body and Society*, p. 90: "Rather than building outward slowly from a core of established Old Christian families, the Marcionite churches deliberately wrenched the individual out of the familiar structures of society. Tertullian warned his readers: Marcion's view of Christ's coming into the world, to 'snatch' His own away from the established rule of the Creator God, threatened to 'snatch' sons from their fathers, pupils from their teachers, slaves from their masters [*Adv. Marc.* 1.23.8]. Small though such groups might have been, they spread with unusual rapidity. Marcionite churches competed as equals with the other Christian communities in Asia Minor and Syria. Beyond the Roman frontiers, in Iraq and in the foothills of Iran, the Marcionites successfully monopolized the term 'Christian' up to the end of the sixth century."

Those also are senseless who say that the Lord entered a home that belonged to someone else, like one who is after things that are not his own [cf. Jn 1, 11], and that he did so in order to offer to God a humanity made by another. God [they say] neither made nor created humanity; rather, from the beginning [they say] God kept himself at a distance from the creation of humanity.

But surely, there is no justice in [Christ's] coming to a place that belongs to others, against their will? And he did not really redeem us with his blood if he did not really become man, and if he did not restore to the work of his hands that humanity which, we read, was made in the beginning, in the image and likeness of God [cf. Gen 1, 26]? But no, he did not deceitfully steal what belonged to another; rather, he regained what was his own, [and he did so] both justly and generously. He acted justly with regard to the Apostasy, for he redeemed us from it at the cost of his blood [cf. Col 1, 14. 20] [q]. He acted generously with regard to us, the redeemed: for we did not give him anything in advance [cf. Rom 11, 35], and it was not as if he needed something from us—in fact, it is us that need communion with him. Hence it was out of generosity that he poured himself out, so that he might gather us in the bosom of the Father.

Completely senseless, then, are those who reject the whole of God's dispensation [*pasan oikonomian ... tou Theou*]: they deny the salvation of the flesh and repudiate its rebirth, and maintain that it has no capacity for incorruption. But if there is no salvation for the flesh, then surely neither did the Lord redeem us with his blood, nor is the cup of the thanksgiving the sharing of his blood, nor is the bread that we break the sharing of his body [cf. 1 Cor 10, 16]. For there exists no blood other than that which springs from veins and flesh and the rest of the constitution proper to humanity, which is exactly what the Word of God truly became so as to redeem us. That is why the Apostle says: "In whom we have the redemption by his blood, the forgiveness of sins" [cf. Col 1, 14. 20]. And because we are his members [cf. 1 Cor 6, 15; Eph 5, 30] and receive nourishment through creation—and that creation is furnished to us by him, who makes his sun rise and causes it to rain as he pleases—he declared that the cup, taken from creation, is his own blood [Lk 22, 20; 1 Cor 11, 25], from

---

[q] Here lies the root of the concept, which was to be elaborated in all its legal precision by Origen and especially by Tertullian, that, as a result of Adam's sin, humanity belonged, *by right*, to the *devil*, and that thus it was a matter of justice that God, in redeeming humanity, should give the devil the payment due to him, by allowing him to seek the death of Christ. Needless to say, the present passage does not require this dubious construal. All Irenaeus is saying is this. In sending Christ as redeemer, God took the Fall (by which humanity had been *unjustly* destined for the great Apostasy) seriously. God did so by dealing with it, not by the exercise of raw power, but by "counsel," thus doing justice to *humanity*'s reasonableness (*Adv. Hær.* 5, 11 [*SC* 153, pp. 18-21]. Cf. Raymund Schwager, *Der wunderbare Tausch*, pp. 36-7).

which our blood draws growth, and he confirmed that the bread, taken from creation, is his own body [Lk 22, 19; 1 Cor 11, 24], from which our bodies draw growth.

Thus the cup mixed and the bread prepared open themselves to the Word of God and become the Eucharist—Christ's Body and Blood—and from those, the substance of our flesh acquires growth and consistency. How, then, can they say that the flesh has no capacity for God's gift (that is, life eternal), if that flesh is nourished by Christ's Blood and Body and is a member of his? That is why the blessed Apostle, in the Letter to the Ephesians, says: "We are members of his body, made of his flesh and of his bones" [cf. Eph 5, 30; Gen 2, 23]. And he is not talking about some kind of spiritual, invisible humanity, "for a spirit has neither bones nor flesh" [cf. Lk 24, 39], but about the structure that is proper to humanity as it really exists [*peri tēs kata ton alēthinon anthrōpon oikonomias*]: it consists of flesh and sinews and bones, and as such it draws nourishment from the cup which is his Blood and growth from the bread which is his Body.

The wood of the vine, withering in the earth, bears fruit in its own good time, and "the grain of wheat, fallen in the earth" [cf. Jn 12, 24] and decayed, is raised up multiplied through the Spirit of God who holds all together [cf. Wisd 1, 7]. Then, thanks to [human] ingenuity, they are turned to human use; then they assimilate the Word of God; thus they become the Eucharist, which is Christ's Body and Blood. Just so it is with our bodies, too: nourished by [the Eucharist], and withering in the earth and decayed in it, they will arise in their own good time, when the Word of God will graciously bestow the resurrection on them, "to the glory of the Father" [cf. Phil 2, 11]. He clothes with immortality what is mortal, and freely bestows incorruptibility on what is corruptible [cf. 1 Cor 15, 53], for God's power comes to perfection in weakness [cf. 2 Cor 12, 9].

All this is to prevent us from ever becoming inflated, as if we had life out of ourselves, and from rising against God, with minds turned back to ungraciousness. We know from experience that it is from God's majesty, not from our nature, that we have the steadfastness that endures forever. Thus we will never stray from the true understanding of God, nor misjudge our own nature; rather, we will know what God is able to accomplish and what humanity receives in the way of kindness, and we will never slide away from the true understanding of how things really stand—that is, with God and humanity. And could it even be that this is the reason for what we mentioned earlier—could it be that God has permitted our decay in the earth so that we, taught and trained in every way, might henceforth become [people that are] responsible in everything, being heedless neither of God nor of ourselves?[13]

If humanity and the world are not accepted in their natural, mater- ial, carnal integrity, Irenaeus says, Christianity itself disintegrates; none of it survives. There is *concordance* between the divine life and the natural order; God's saving plan *intrinsically fits* the humanity and the world that are to be saved [r]. If the natural world is rejected as irrelevant to salvation or if its natural capacity for the divine life is denied, then there is no divine creation either, no incarnation, no redemption by the shedding of Christ's blood, no restoration of humanity to the divine likeness, no Eucharist, no membership in the Body of Christ, no resurrection, no life eternal, no responsible Christian life now [s].

Is this naturalism? Of course not, says Irenaeus. God accomplishes everything, and humanity receives everything. Nothing comes from our nature; everything is from God. As we eat and drink Christ's Body and Blood in the Eucharist, we absorb the life-giving lesson of Christ's passion, death, and resurrection. That lesson, however, turns out to be nothing but the culmination of the lesson we might have absorbed naturally, in the process of our living off the created cosmos: we, like every creature, are natively dependent on God for the totality of life and existence, witness God's kindness shown in the gifts of sun and rain. In the same way, we, along with everything, are natively oriented towards God, again with the totality of our being, witness God's faithfulness shown in the chain of transformations through which the medicine of immortality—the Blood and the Body of Christ—is drawn from the dead vine and the dying seed. Thus it is truly in virtue of its original affinity

---

[r] Significantly, Ignatius uses the same word (*oikonomia*; cf. §43, 5, [z]) to refer both to the "design" of God's saving dispensation and to the "design" of humanity as it exists in reality, rooted in the world: the former fits the latter as a key fits its lock. This is such a central theme of the great Tradition that I cannot resist making a related point. Needless to say, a lot has happened to our understanding and experience of the cosmos between the end of the second century and the mid-twentieth century. Yet it is not too far-fetched to note at this point, without further elaboration, the deep affinity between the cosmic theologies of Irenaeus and Pierre Teilhard de Chardin. Cf. §9, 1, [i]; §20, 2.

[s] Not surprisingly, Irenaeus can view the world marked by the resurrection as the very world made by God in the first place. The just will drink the cup of life with Christ, not "on high," in an unworldly "place above the heavens" (*anō en hyperouraniōi topōi*: Adv. Hær. 5, 33, 1; SC 153, p. 407), but in the new Eden—the Garden teeming with Life Superabounding. Thus the new creation is simply the present world "restored to its former state" (*apokatastatheisan eis to proteron*), except that it is "without let or hindrance at the service of the just" (*Adv. Hær.* 5, 32, 1; SC 153, p. 399). It is by virtue of only the slightest touch of interpreter's licence that Peter Brown (*The Body and Society*, p. 73) can write that "the new body ... would live in a fully material world that was as heavy with goodness as the intoxicating breath of a field in full flower."

with God that the whole of creation, without exception, now lends itself, in Christ, to the glorification of God.

[4] Here we stand at the cradle of one of the undivided Christian Church's fundamental convictions. To the eye of faith (a faith, incidentally, challenged in an unprecedented fashion in our own day, by the scientific discovery of the fantastic improbabilities and risks inherent in any form of natural order in the cosmos; cf. §115), the entire world is theophoric; it is destined to be drawn into God's kingdom; it must be natively equipped for its task of guiding humanity from nature to grace. Hence it cannot but be essentially good as well as symbolic, charged with the potential to be the sacrament of God's life-giving presence. That potential is fully actualized in Christ the *Logos* who is truly Incarnate; that actualization is being continued, in palpable sign and symbol, in Christ's Body, the one Church spread throughout the world (cf. §43, 5); it is continued especially in the Eucharist, which sums up and embodies the present world's aspiration to the resurrection of the dead and life eternal.

[a] Not surprisingly, the Christian affirmation of the incarnation of the Word has been the crucial factor in the formation of the great Tradition's appreciation of *humanity* in its full carnal, cosmic reality (cf. §10, 1, a).

One characteristic example from the christological tradition of the Latin church may serve to convey this. In the fourth book of the *Summa contra Gentiles*, Aquinas responds to a large number of contemporary philosophical objections to catholic faith in the incarnation raised in an earlier chapter. Aquinas' explanations are, as always, both very efficient and highly technical, but what is really telling is his *non-technical imagery*. He consistently uses verbs that imply *acceptance* and *intimacy*: the Word of God "has taken on" (*assumpsit*) humanity; it "draws" humanity unto itself (*trahit ad se*); in this way, humanity "is united" (*unitur*) with the Word [t]. He also implies that human na-

---

[t] It is not unimportant to note at this point that the great Tradition does not favor the language of divine *intervention* or *interference*, let alone of divine *intrusion* to express the incarnation of the Word (cf. §79, 2; §94). These latter idioms, often heard today, connote that the *Logos* acts like an alien power, which in intervening offends the integrity of humanity and the world and puts them down. No wonder this language is often used to cast doubts on the very concept of incarnation.

ture is something natively *noble*. Thus he can write: "The soul and body of Christ are drawn unto the person of the Word, yet without constituting a person apart from the person of the Word. Far from diminishing their standing, ... this confers a greater dignity on them. For when united with something nobler than themselves, things enjoy a higher form of being than when existing [simply] by themselves. For example, the animal soul enjoys a nobler form of being in the human person than in other animals; in the latter it is the principal determinant of how they exist, which is not the case in the human person."[14]

Thus the acknowledgment that humanity has been "assumed" or "taken on" by the Word of God affirms that Christ is more, not less of a human individual than we; but it also implicitly affirms the natural dignity and power of signification of humanity. Human nature, in its full cosmic, carnal integrity, is created in God's image and likeness. Hence, it includes not only the native longing for salvation and union with God but also the native capacity to represent and portray God [u], not only by means of a life lived religiously and virtuously, but also by means of the whole gamut of humane and artistic endeavor, both in and outside the liturgy, and by the myriad applications of science and technology.

[b] This has further, cosmic ramifications. Specifically, the Christian appreciation of humanity as continuous with the world in which it is rooted grounds the catholic tradition's appreciation of the organic coherence of the cosmos as a carrier of transcendent meaning and value. Thus the cosmos is the medium through which persons and communities "seek the unknown God in shadows and images" (LG 16; possibly an allusion to the epitaph John Henry Newman wrote for himself[15]), and the living God encounters humanity in sacramental sign and symbol [v]. It also accounts for the firmness with which the

---

[u] Here lies the point of departure of Karl Rahner's "transcendental" christology (cf. §31, 1, b), as well as the fundamental theological importance of the affirmation of the human person as the unity of *body and soul*. On this latter subject, cf. especially Francis Peter Fiorenza and Johann Baptist Metz, "Der Mensch als Einheit von Leib und Seele."

[v] Karl Rahner's profound essay "Zur Theologie des Symbols" ("The Theology of the Symbol") remains a classic exploration of the fundamental dimensions of this theme. Here also lie fruitful avenues of exploration of the relationships between the great religions and Christianity. For an illuminating example, cf.

great Tradition has recognized (at least before both the Reformation and the Counter-Reformation became doctrinally nervous about just exactly which rites were sacraments and which not) not only a variety of "sacraments of the Old Law" [w], but also *natural sacraments*—both of them, in Otto Semmelroth's phrase, "embodiments of God's universal will for salvation."[16] Finally, it accounts for the catholic tradition's reluctance to having the Christian faith reduced to a plan of purely *human* (as opposed to fully cosmic) salvation, for its broad interest in Christian humanism in its many forms, and even more broadly, for its civilizing bent (cf. §14, 1; §19, 1, e; §20, 2).

[c] In its own distinctive way, and despite its neo-Kantian tendencies, Paul Tillich's philosophical theology clearly reflects his commitment to this central theme of the great Tradition: the Christian affirmation of the natural world as transparent toward God. No wonder he can write that "the concept of symbol" is "the center of my theological doctrine of knowledge"[17]—an affirmation borne out by a variety of treatments of symbolism in all his important works. In one characteristic passage, Tillich explains: "... *religious symbols take their material from all realms of life, from all experience—natural, personal, historical.* ... This is how we should understand a religious symbol. It is material taken out of the world of finite things, *to point beyond itself to the ground of being and of meaning, to being itself and meaning itself.* As a symbol *it participates in the power of the ultimate to which it points;* or, to use a word which we commonly use when we speak of the power of ultimate being, it participates in the 'holy.' ... *The religious symbol participates in the holiness of that to which it points, that is, to the holy itself.* Religious symbols are not holy in and of themselves,

---

Francis X. Clooney's analyses of the symbolic ways in which one particular non-Christian tradition has dealt with the interrelationships of God, the believing community, and believers among themselves: "In Joyful Recognition," and "Liturgical Theology in a Comparative Context." For a good summary, cf. John McKenna, "Symbol and Reality: Some Anthropological Considerations."

[w] Against Manichaean dualism, Augustine emphatically insists that the sacraments of the Old Law refer to the same divine realities as those of the New Law, despite both verbal and ritual differences; this is so because the former are related to the latter as promise is related to fulfillment (*Contra Faustum* XIX, 16-18; *CSEL* 25, pp. 512-18; ET Dods, vol. 5, pp. 338-42). Aquinas remembers this passage as authoritative: *S. Th.* III, 60, 5 and 6; 61, 3 and 4. The later tradition in the West will continue to affirm this, though with a greater emphasis on the essential difference in *efficacy* (cf. DS 1310; 1347-48; 1602; CF 1305; 1003; 1312).

but *they are holy by their participation in that which is holy in itself,* the ground of all holiness. This participation gives them meaning, but at the same time sets limits to their meaning. ... *They are more than signs.* They not only point beyond themselves to something else; they also participate in the power of that to which they point. ... Religious symbols open up the mystery of the holy and they open up the mind for the mystery of the holy to which it can respond" [x].[18]

[5] A most important point must at least be touched on in this connection. In regard to its devotion to the natural world order, the Christian tradition is the heir of *Israel's* thoroughly cosmic faith-tradition. At least two basic Christian convictions are inconceivable apart from their roots in the Bible: the Christian recognition that the living Word of God is heard and read in fully human words [y], and the Christian understanding of Jesus Christ as the obedient, suffering Servant, as the *Logos* made flesh,[19] and as

---

[x] Curiously, despite his catholic emphasis on participation in the ultimate reality as characteristic of religious symbols, Tillich follows the Protestant tradition of "againstness" in construing the theological relationship between existence and revelation in an adversary (if correlative) fashion (cf. F. J. van Beeck, *Christ Proclaimed,* pp. 49-50, 202-20), and in his emphatic skepticism with regard to sacraments, depicted as possible temptations to idolatry. Could it be that Tillich had the traditional Protestant reservation vis-à-vis the natural order of *reality* in mind when he stated that the concept of symbol was the center of his theological doctrine of *knowledge?* Did he mean to view the world, not as intrinsically symbolic, but as the neutral provider of mere "materials" to the symbol-making mind, thus regarding symbolism solely in terms of conscious self-transcendence (cf. William J. Hill, *The Three-Personed God,* p. 98)?

[y] This fundamental recognition, to which we will have to return, is the core of Pope Pius XII's encyclical *Divino Afflante* of 1943 (cf. DS 3825-31, esp. 3829-30; CF 232-36, esp. 236). This important document finally marked the reversal of the Roman Catholic Church's purely magisterial (and hence often authoritarian) approach to the interpretation of Scripture. It also opened the way to a less fanciful theological account of the inspired character of Scripture, and to the resolution, in Vatican II's Constitution on Divine Revelation *Dei Verbum,* of the Catholic Church's neuralgic debate with the Reformation about the relationship between Scripture and Tradition. The older approach, developed especially by Cardinal Johann Franzelin after the first Vatican Council, was in reality far more rationalist and historicist than many Catholic theologians recognized. In the final analysis, it failed to understand the full theological significance of the traditional scholastic thesis that the scriptural authors were true "instrumental causes." For a good account of this history as it affected the Catholic study of the Bible in North America, cf. Gerald Fogarty's *American Catholic Biblical Scholarship,* esp. pp. 35-198; for a pioneering explanation of scriptural inspiration as immediately connected with the Incarnation, cf. Jean Levie, *La Bible, parole humaine et message de Dieu* (ET *The Bible, Word of God in Words of Men*). For a profound discussion of the whole theme, cf. Hans Urs von Balthasar, "God redet als Mensch," in *Verbum Caro,* pp. 73-99.

the key to the whole universe. Israel's prophetic interpretation of its history proclaims that the God who chose and delivered it is also the God who made it and who gave it as well as all the nations their places in the world. The opening page of the completed Hebrew Scriptures sums up Israel's conviction that the original, natural harmony and reliability of that world manifests the faithfulness of the God whom it had come to trust as its Deliverer in history. Late Judaism's cultivation of wisdom, in which faith and worldly experience meet so naturally, confirms those convictions. Divine Wisdom had been God's own agent in creation (Prov 3, 19-20; 8, 22-31), the Word by which God had created the world (Sir 24, 3-4). In that capacity, Wisdom was present everywhere, at home "in every people and nation" (Sir 24, 7), even though it had come to dwell pre-eminently in Israel, in the form of the Torah.[20]

[a] In this way, Israel's religious worldliness, continued in diaspora Judaism down to this day, also accounts for what is easily the most fundamental characteristic of the intellectual traditions of the entire religious culture of the West. Jews, Christians, and Muslims share the privilege of believing in the one God, who is the creator of heaven and earth, and the Lord of all. This means they share the burden of having to explain how God is to be found in the world and beyond it, but never apart from it [z], and that the world cannot be understood apart from God (cf. §67, 4, b). The history of philosophy amply illustrates how Israel's monotheism has determined a large part of the philosophical agenda of Judaism, Christianity, and Islam. We will have to come back to this later on (§95).

[b] This also leads to a related point of some importance in recent theological debate. The sixteenth-century humanists (especially those who opted for the Reformation) and, to a far greater extent, the mid-nineteenth century romantics and their disciples (especially those who opted, with von Harnack and Loofs, against the church-

---

[z] Nicholas Lash's splendid book *Easter in Ordinary* is, in my opinion, the best, most sustained recent argument to illuminate this central Judaeo-Christian thesis. Lash very efficiently unmasks the critical weaknesses of the analyses provided by that most overrated of modern thinkers, William James. In James' theological anthropology, "religious experience" is a totally separable, privileged inner event. Lash's energetic reconstruction of an adequate theological anthropology by means of a judicious reading of Schleiermacher, Newman, von Hügel, and Buber is most enlightening.

es, and for the historical Jesus as an attractive spiritual ideal) have tended to criticize the tradition's (especially the Catholic tradition's) enslavement to Hellenistic nature-philosophy and its abstract, universal, static thought-patterns. There, they have said, in the adoption of a philosophical style that froze the warm dynamism of biblical faith into the cumbersome deposit of cold dogmatic ideas, lies the source of Catholicism's alienation from the Christian faith in its simplicity, purity, and directness. By dint of a mistaken, naturalist reliance on nature and reason as the conditions for the possibility of grace and faith, they have alleged, Catholicism has moved biblical, living, existential faith into the background [aa].

The charge is not wholly groundless. It has been especially to the point whenever it has taken aim at the kind of medieval-nominalist and Enlightenment-rationalist scholasticism that had lost all sense of history, and of salvation history in particular (cf. §86, 3, c).[21] Still, it oversimplifies a complex issue by overlooking at least two related things.

First of all, we have to wonder if the agenda behind the charge is not the dubious contention, of liberal Protestant origin, that "true Christianity" can only be reconstructed on a purely biblical basis—that is, apart from such hermeneutical keys as doctrine (cf. §71, 2, c).

Secondly, it must be recalled that it was Jerusalem, not Athens, that taught the Christian Church to develop a healthy natural interest in a thoroughly worldly humanity naturally known and loved by God, and in an intrinsically good world naturally entrusted to humanity by divine design. The Bible depicts the universe as fundamentally stable and reliable by divine design, even if continuous change is part of its definition. It also implies that it is by virtue of their very stability and reliability that such a humanity and such a world offer themselves to human understanding and ingenuity and love, no matter how intractable they may be, and more importantly, no matter how keenly humanity may be aware of its waywardness and its dogged resistance to God.

Thirdly, this is exactly the point where Jerusalem has given Athens substantial food for fresh thought. For it was Jerusalem

---

[aa] Incidentally, it is a measure of the neo-Protestant unfamiliarity with Judaism that analogous charges of Hellenism were never brought against the philosophical traditions within Judaism.

rather than Athens that determined the *agenda* for the Church's theological and philosophical reflection. The Christian Church professed a reliable knowledge of, and the promise of permanent union with, the faithful God who is the Creator of humanity and the world. Athens had thought differently about that. Wisdom, it had taught by and large, unites human reason with the divine, which alone is free and eternal. This left two choices. Either the divine is all-pervasively present but *impersonal* (as the Stoics taught; cf. §27, 4, a-c; cf. §30, 5; §77, 2). Or it is *wholly elsewhere*, which makes the present world, subject to change to the point of being habitually deceptive, into an inappropriate object of philosophy, since it encumbers and inhibits wisdom, which is characterized by stability [*bb*].

The (Jewish and) Christian understanding of humanity and the world in their divinely established stability made it an urgent priority to find correspondingly reliable ways of understanding them and of doing justice to their natural integrity. Much as Christianity went to school in Athens, where it acquired new, and largely reliable, tools of rational understanding, it was Israel, not Hellenism, that taught it its basic lesson of love and reverent acceptance, for the sake of a *loving, personal* God, of the universe in its *original, natural, reliable* reality. In the Church—the Cappadocian fathers and Augustine and even Aquinas come especially to mind—the lucid Greek mind acquired a habit unknown in ancient Greece: that of *cherishing* this world. That is, it came to understand it, not against the background of a world order whose intelligibility was ultimately a matter of dark, faceless necessity (*heimarmenē*), but in light of its understanding of the transcendent God who, far from being remote, embraces the world

---

[*bb*] Thus Plato could have Socrates teach that becoming like (*homoiōsis*) the divine is a matter of *fleeing* the world with all possible speed (*hoti tachista*): "We should speed from over here to over there; taking flight means becoming like the divine so far as we can; and that likeness is a matter of holy purity by means of wisdom" (*Theaet.* 176^{b}1-4; cf. *Republic* 613^{b}1; cf. the close parallel in Aristotle's concept of the contemplative life: *Eth. Nic.* 10, 7-8; 1177^{a}10-1178^{b}23). When he defined the search for true righteousness in this world as an effort to distance oneself from this world as much as possible, was Socrates—residually and philosophically, of course—still the heir of the popular belief that the gods lived in a carefree, immaterial, irrelevant world of their own? That they ventured out of that world only to interfere, by means of a variety of disconcerting metamorphoses, in the world and human affairs as it suited *themselves*, thus making of the world an unreliable place, by divine agency? And hence, that they were best recognized from a respectful distance and otherwise left alone?

and loves it in person. Thus Christian thought put *conceptual stability and lucidity* of Greek origin *at the service of the profession of God's fidelity* it had inherited from Israel.

This thesis has implications of the highest importance.

[§79] "IF GOD IS FOR US...." (ROM 8, 31)

[1] In Irenaeus' vision, the order of grace reveals a fundamental feature of God. Irenaeus affirms that the dispensation of salvation lovingly and deeply accommodates the natural order; that is to say, *it reveals a wholly transcendent God who nevertheless is in no sense creation's adversary or opponent.* In particular, *matter* in all its forms is not natively alien to God, not even where it takes the shape of that strangest yet most intimate partner of the soul, *the human body.* However recalcitrant or mulish matter and corporealness may often be, however much we may experience them as intractable and resistant to human intelligence and mastery, and however much they may both awaken and frustrate the human drive to try to achieve superiority over them by the use of force, they are of God's own making, and thus, capable of transformation by the divine embrace.

Consequently, if God redeems the world, God does so neither from a distance, nor by resorting to some intermediary agency (so as to protect the divine transcendence from contamination), nor by force applied to the world from outside. The second-century *Letter to Diognetus* is at pains to set the Christian faith off against such mythological constructions. Instead, the anonymous apologist explains, God patiently reveals the divine Truth and Love in the world *without mediation*, in the person of

the designer and maker of the universe himself. ... But surely (or so a human person might figure) God would send him in sovereignty, and fear, and terror? Nothing of the kind! Rather, in gentleness and meekness, as a king might send his royal son—that is how God sent him. God sent him as God; God sent him as a human being to human beings; God sent him as one who saves, as one who persuades, not as one who forces, for the wielding of force is no attribute of God [cc]; God sent him as one who

---

[cc] Gk. *bia gar ou prosesti tōi Theōi.* In the cosmology of the hellenistic world, *bia* denotes the kind of *physical* force that can be wielded *against* opposing forces. For this reason, it belongs in the lowest, sublunary regions of the universe. In those realms, inertia prevails; bodies are naturally dull and resistant. Motion, therefore, will occur only if inertia is overcome by force applied *from the outside.* This, the author of the *Letter to Diognetus* explains, is not a way of operating that is attributable

calls, not as one who gives chase; God sent him as one who loves, not as one who judges.[22]

[2] If God so relates to humanity and the world as their Savior, it is inconceivable that God should be any different as Creator. In creating the world, God has had no adverse primal forces to wrestle down. And in dealing with the world in the present, God has no contrary forces of inertia to surmount, no thresholds to pass, no hindrances to conquer, no enemies to subdue (cf. §98, 4, a); God need not break to enter. And since God need not enter by force, no worldly force can keep God out; hence, God does not save a hostile, resistant world by eminent domain, nor does God correct (that is, by implication, reject) the natural world by putting a new face on it. God, in other words, does not save the world by superimposing on it a new, additional, "supernatural" or "spiritual" world. For God can work from the innermost inside. God Most High is also God Most Nigh;[23] God's majesty and God's intimacy coincide; far from making God remote, the divine transcendence is the guarantee of God's closeness to every created being, as Gregory of Nyssa well saw (cf. §72, 3).

[a] If God can work out of the innermost intimacy of the person, and if the relationship between nature and grace is characterized by fundamental harmony, then the actual presence of the Spirit of God can be verified, in principle, by the *experience of inner harmony*. Here lies the anthropologico-theological basis for many of the "Rules for the Discernment of Spirits," developed in the *Spiritual Exercises* of Saint Ignatius of Loyola. Persons can come to a sense of assurance that they are being guided by God, even in the ambiguous particulars of their lives; this assurance can be drawn from a careful interpretation (usually in regular conversation with a spiritual director) of a variety of inner experiences of harmony known as *felt consolation*. (This interpretation, incidentally, most often occurs when the experience of consolation is compared with the experience of its opposite, desolation.) Ignatius is both following and refining the long tradition that goes back to the first origins of monasticism when he points out that consolation encourages beginners who make progress in the Spirit; that consolation that comes entirely unanticipated, unannounced, and unoccasioned is a sure sign of

---

to God.

God's presence; that an undeviating, sustained series of inner experiences, without distraction from good purpose or confusion
about one's resolve, is characteristic of God's inner guidance;
and that authentic consolation can be recognized by its naturalness—it touches the spiritual person "softly, lightly, and gently,
like a drop of water making its way into a sponge." God's grace,
in other words, can be reliably discerned by the proper interpretation of its harmonious, enhancing effects on a person's naturally accessible self-experience.[24]

[3] Few texts in the patristic literature convey this insight so profoundly and at the same time with such impeccable logic as a memorable passage from the exposition of the Creed presented by Saint
Augustine at the General Council of the North African Churches
held at Hippo Regius, in the year 393.

[a] Augustine's mind had been newly sharpened for the occasion. He had been debating the wide-spread movement whose
meetings he had attended for a period of nine years much earlier in life, as an auditor: the Manichaeans.[25] The Manichaeans
interpreted the fundamental structure of the universe as they
experienced the human self: as *torn*. That is to say, they interpreted it *dualistically*—as the precarious product of a continuous
standoff between God and Satan, light and darkness, spirit and
matter. In this cosmic struggle, the salvation of the world could
occur only if those on the side of light did their utmost to re-
lease that light from the enveloping darkness, by means of a
whole array of ascetical practices.

[4] Now, at the age of 39 and a catholic presbyter, Augustine was
bringing both the experience of his conversion and his Christian intelligence to bear on the issue of God's relatedness to all that is not
God. That relatedness is supremely manifested in the one who is
Light from Light, God from God, and the Word Incarnate. Augustine explains:

I am confident that those who understand things spiritually will recognize
that nothing can be the opposite of God. God is the One who *is*, and only
of God can this verb be properly predicated. (For what truly *is* remains
without change, since what is subject to change *was* at one time what it no
longer is, and *will be* some time what it is not yet.) But if this is so, then
God has nothing opposite to him. If we should be asked what is opposite
to white, we would answer, black. If we should be asked what is opposite
to hot, we would answer, cold. If we should be asked what is opposite to

quick, we would answer, slow, and thus we could go on and on. However, when it is asked what is opposite to what *is*, the right answer is that it is not.[26]

This is where logic meets mysticism. Ultimately, the integrity of humanity and the world is guaranteed and enhanced, not threatened and diminished, by the God who creates and assumes it. This can be so because God's majesty has nothing to fear from the work of the divine hands. God is immeasurably great, *beyond compare*, hence the creature can rest assured: God is no tyrant who needs to be humored by serfs. The divine greatness need not be shored up; hence, no diminishment or self-abasement is required of humanity and the world in the service of God.

[a] Again, this interpretation of the relationship between God and creation has solid roots in the tradition of Israel's faith, concretized in the *Covenant*. The relationship of mutual fidelity established in the Covenant between God and Israel is characterized by a *congruence* and an *equality* that seems, at first blush, purely anthropomorphic. However, this covenantal partnership is possible because it is *rooted in the mystery of the order of nature* that undergirds it—that is, in the fact that God, as creator, has nothing to fear from creation, but is sovereignly free and independent of it. Hence, God can invite Israel to partnership without ever compromising the divine transcendence or, for that matter, without ever having to *force* Israel's acceptance or faithfulness.

[b] The contemporary Jewish philosopher Emmanuel Lévinas has sharply reformulated this shared conviction of Jews, Christians and Muslims. He takes on the kind of liberal Christianity that diminishes both the divine transcendence and human responsibility; it does so, Lévinas explains, by considering God as a mere provider of inner religious comfort, and by thinking of humanity as mainly dependent on divine indulgence. Thus he protests: "... to have created a humanity capable of *responding*, of turning to its God in the attitude of a creditor and not all the time in the attitude of a debtor: *that* is truly divine majesty! ... How vigorous the dialectic by which the equal partnership between God and humanity is established right at the heart of their incommensurability!"[27] Again, we will come back to this crucial theme (§98, 6).

[c] The order of grace does not defeat the natural world but integrates it. What is more, it integrates it *as such*—that is, in its proper, integral, natural being, and hence, radically and comprehensively, and not selectively. In doing so, the order of grace is bringing to the surface another important fact: *sin*, no matter how evil, *does not defeat God's transcendence or influence God's design.* Hence, *sin does not enjoy the same ontological— and hence, theological—status as created reality as such.* Sin, therefore, no matter how pervasive, is neither radical nor final. This theme, however, must await treatment at a later point in this volume (cf. §113, 3-4 and 5, [s]]) [*dd*].

[5] At the same time, a reservation remains to be made. Precisely because it takes its inspiration from God, the Christian community's embrace of the world of matter and corporealness is not unconditional; Christians embrace the world *as what it is*—that is, *as finite*, and even as touched by sin; the embrace remains as provisional as it is genuine. This has consequences. The fundamental one springs from the fact that everything desirable that is not God inherently arouses *tension* in the one that cherishes it. That tension is, first and foremost, a matter of restlessness; those who live by anticipation and eschatological desire are unsettled in their very embraces (1 Cor 7, 25-35; cf. §75, 5; 6, a). But the tension has deep roots in the natural order, too, where it takes the shape of *ambiguity*. For on the one hand, we sense that the world and humanity naturally participate in the mystery of God, on whom they are absolutely dependent (cf. §65, 1; 2); thus there is an invitation to awe involved in any encounter with created reality; this inhibits any facile embrace. But by the same token, the world and humanity also declare a transience that sometimes borders on futility; this introduces an element of radical hesitancy into the abandon with which the world and humanity are embraced. The Christian aware-

---

[*dd*] As we stated long ago (§12, 1, b), we will then also have to repeat, in a different way, that our positive, entirely supralapsarian construal of the relationship between grace and nature (and hence between faith and understanding) is not a matter of light-hearted naturalism, of the kind that fails to take sin seriously (cf. §84, 3-4). In fact, it will be argued that our construal ultimately offers a sounder, because more *theological* (rather than merely existential-anthropological interpretation) of sin; hence, we will claim that this interpretation does more, not less, justice to the deep depravity involved in sin and to the effects of sin on the human mind's ability to know God.

ness of the God-given goodness of the cosmic order, therefore, is
laced with tension, and on more than one score.

Not surprisingly, this is played out institutionally, in the shape
of the Church itself. From its earliest days, the Christian community has embraced the world yet also cultivated that particular form
of restraint with regard to the world known as *religious life* (cf. §54,
5, c).

[a] By the end of the third century, Christianity has accepted
and integrated *two distinctive ways of Christian living*, which have
become part and parcel of the catholic tradition ever since. A
settled majority, solidly committed to Christian virtue, and associated, initially, with ordinary households but increasingly with the
developing urban churches around their bishops, is quietly transforming a pagan civilization into a Christian one (cf. §14, 1; §19,
1, e). But the late fourth century wave of conversions to Christianity also created a new, unprecedented uncertainty among
Christians. Not surprisingly, this first took place in the East,
where a wave of monasticism swept through the Christian
world—a story attractively told in Derwas J. Chitty's *The Desert a
City*, but soon the Christian West followed suit. Thus, in those
heady days, inspired and inspiring minorities were arising everywhere, sometimes by the majority's side, sometimes in apparent
opposition to it. In this situation, both the juxtaposition and
the opposition saw to it that the motivated minority was never
wholly unchallenged, much to its own benefit.[28] And as "the
vanishing of the lines which marked out Christians in their society helped to reinforce the ancient appeal of monastic withdraw-
al and ascetic self-denial," the asceticism of these minorities began to look, at least occasionally, "like the mark of authentic
Christianity in a society in which to be a Christian no longer
needed to make any very visible difference" in a person's life (cf.
§109, 12, b).[29] Augustine provides us with a characteristic instance of the predicament fervent Christians in the West were
liable to find themselves in. When recalling the days immediately prior to his retreat to Cassiciacum in the late summer of
386, to prepare for baptism the following Easter, he can remember, with feeling, the predicament of his friend Verecundus, un-
baptized like himself. Being married to a baptized wife, and
hence, unable to become the kind of Christian he would like to
be, Verecundus finds himself unable to become a Christian at
all; but Augustine can proceed to recall, with a thankfulness that

is somewhat lurid, his friend's deathbed baptism less than two years later.[30] Augustine was more fortunate in this regard; he never married, and his own conversion consisted precisely in finding himself empowered to take the once-impossible jump into the ascetical form of life. Accordingly, Augustine can characterize the vital relationship of the ascetical minorities to the majority of the faithful in the admiring phrase *anima viva fidelium*[31]: whether by virtue of prophetic provocation, mediating prayer,[32] service to the poor, or example of community life, the ascetics are the soul that helps keep the community of the ordinary faithful alive in the Spirit.

Institutionally committed to an ascetical life, at a noticeable distance from "the present age," these early minority movements within the Church saw that "age" variously concretized [*ee*]. To the second and third century Encratites in Syria (where the idiom of the Hebrew Scriptures was still very much alive), the present age was simply identical with "the flesh"; to the Egyptian desert monks and to John Cassian in Marseille in the early fifth century, it was the comfortable Christianity of the city churches. But such divergent, sophisticated men as Cyprian, Chrysostom, and the Cappadocians could think of it in far more differentiated ways, often against the background of the public careers they themselves had left behind: the "social expectations associated with success, with status, with comfort and security";[33] Ambrose saw the present age in the powerful world of contaminating spiritual influences at work everywhere; ominously, Gregory of Nyssa saw the dead hand of the present age in the slavish subjection of human persons, and of women especially, to the harsh requirements of procreation, in a world where death, always impending, cast the terrifying shadow of possible extinction on every human community.[34]

As, living in the world, ascetical Christians reached out beyond the natural world, they lived by contemplative visions of the restoration of Adam's stable state in Paradise or by aspirations to the freedom of everlasting life in the Resurrection. Most ascetics devoted themselves to some form of common life, which naturally tended to include elements of obedience to the elders and

---

[*ee*] Cf. Henry Chadwick, "The Ascetic Ideal in the History of the Church." Cf. also Peter Brown's brilliant monograph *The Body and Society*, to which the present section is deeply indebted.

voluntary abdication of private property. Without exception, however, the ascetical vocation demanded the practice of principled, or at least post-marital, sexual renunciation—that peculiar boast of the Christian Church, well-documented from Justin Martyr on.[35]

[6] This raises the fundamental issue of the Christian interpretation of the body, and specifically of sexuality. The contemporary wave of what is often called sexual liberation has a tendency to suspect, behind institutionalized sexual renunciation, a deep-seated, inauthentic refusal to accept the body and sexuality and the charms and excitements connected with them, ultimately resulting in a variety of neurotic patterns of individual and social behavior. It must be granted that deviations in matters sexual are not uncommon anywhere at any time; yet it is important to understand that the sexual continence of the early Christians (in possible continuity with a few precedents in Judaism, but far more probably in imitation of Jesus himself, of the self-made "eunuchs" in the Matthaean community, and of the Apostle Paul[36]) was primarily inspired by eschatological urgency; typically it did not spring from dualistic preoccupations or preconceptions; it was not a form of contempt of either marriage, or the body; if the unmarried life was glorified (as it often was), this did not spring from an isolated anxiety about the body and sexuality [ff]. Rather, elected celibacy (or "virginity")

[ff] Peter Brown argues this point against, for example, A. J. Festugière's charge that the spirituality of the desert is "deeply dualistic": *The Body and Society*, esp. pp. 235-40; cf. pp. 160-77. Incidentally but not unimportantly, Brown also convincingly shows that it is a mistake to attribute any form of sexual puritanism to Augustine. Augustine derided the vulgar notion that "the only sins you could commit were those in which you use your genitals" (*Augustine of Hippo*, p. 172). He also enjoyed the sexually active life enough to be faithful to his concubine for fifteen years, and to find the prospect of foregoing marriage daunting enough to become engaged for a brief period shortly before his final resolve to embrace celibacy. It is true, of course, that Augustine did come to have, as through a telescope, a direct intuition of the deep-seatedness of concupiscence—the effect of Adam's sin—in the uncontrollable spontaneity of the organs that initiate human life. But this was not an isolated preoccupation, since the equally uncontrollable forces that terminate life afforded him the same vision. "Like death," Brown writes, "the onset and culmination of sexual sensation mocked the will. ... Like two iron clamps, they delineated inexorably mankind's loss of the primal harmony of body and soul." It was the repressed mentality of a later day that was to project on to Augustine its own dualistic, anti-sexual preoccupations. Only a residually Victorian modern sensibility could venture the hypothesis that Augustine's well-known reservations about sexual intercourse in marriage sprang from an unhealthy revulsion at his own past life; this also gave rise to the *simpliste* notion that Augustine was an unrepentant

was seen as a comprehensive dedication to the life with God—a dedication wisely shaped by a measured distance from a whole host of absorbing human concerns. Accordingly, its counterpart, sexual involvement in marriage and childbearing, was invariably set within the wider context of a whole array of other, equally consuming and (in the light of the Resurrection) equally transitory pursuits. A passage from Chrysostom's treatise *On Virginity* bears out this wider context. Whatever the risen, everlasting life may be like, Chrysostom explains, its concerns are

not marriage and the pangs of labor any longer, not sensual pleasure and sexual joining, neither wealth aplenty nor the care of estates, neither food nor clothing, not the labor of the farm and the sailing of the seas, not arts and crafts and not building projects, neither cities nor households, but a different state and conduct of life. All those other things will perish in a little while.[37]

[a] As if to support this refusal to isolate sexuality, *pursuits other than sexual continence have always linked the ascetical and the continent firmly with the communities of "ordinary" Christians*, who have opted for the life that includes marriage as a matter of course. In the ancient Church, such pursuits already covered a wide range of possibilities. At one extreme, there were the critical challenges sharply proffered to the comfortable Christian homesteads and the sedentary urban churches: the prophetic severities of the Encratites' "apostolic" vagabondage, and, in the next few centuries, the long prayers and the demanding austerities undertaken in the service of the abnegation of self-will in the monastic communities in Egypt, Syria, and Palestine. But at the other end of the spectrum, there were the monastic communities at Lérins and Marseille, where, under the influence of John Cassian's writings, contemplation was quietly turned into the study of Scripture, with a view to enabling the monks (increasingly recruited as bishops) to teach the uncouth local churches of fifth and sixth century Gaul;[38] there were the contented

---

Platonist after all, who thought sexuality was tainted and the body bad (cf. *The Body and Society*, pp. 387-447; quotations pp. 408, 416; cf. also Henry Chadwick's polished remarks on the same subject in the Introduction to his translation of the *Confessions*, pp. xvi-xix, and Robert Markus' observation that Augustine's distrust of sensual delights "springs, not from loathing, but from a sharp sensitiveness to their beauty and their power, combined with a no less sharp concern not to allow them to run away with reason and judgement" (*The End of Ancient Christianity*, p. 49; cf. *Confessiones*, X, VI, 8-10 for a telling example).

communities of prayer and study of Augustinian inspiration around the bishop in many cities—a form of regulated ("canonical") community life of devotion that was to carry over, in the West, into the medieval cathedral schools. There was also, at Annesi in Cappadocia in the late fourth century, the quiet charm of matronal households such as the farmhouse community of ascetics led by Macrina, the sister of Gregory of Nyssa; there were church-supported sisterhoods devoted to the contemplative delights of virginity, like those idealized by Methodios of Olympos in the East, or, a century later, by a worried Ambrose in Milan [gg].[39] On a larger scale, there were the sizable and influential late fourth century communities of consecrated virgins, such as the one led by Olympias right next door to the patriarchal compound at Constantinople, or the sophisticated convent of expatriate women from the West led by the matronly Melania in Jerusalem, on the slopes of the Mount of Olives.[40]

[7] All this is beginning to suggest a *pattern*. The catholic tradition sees humanity's natural goodness *endorsed* in the very act of being assumed by the Word, but also *transformed* by it, by being raised to heights naturally inaccessible to humanity (cf. §87, 4, a). Analogously, it has cherished the practice of acknowledging God by means of names intelligently derived from material things, but also it has also transformed that practice. It has done so by placing the names of God on the threshold of the sanctuary in which the removal of all names introduces the worshiper to the most divine knowledge of God, by way of an understanding of through union —one that surpasses the naturally intelligent mind (§67, 2). Analogously again, the Tradition has taught that the virtuous life consists in the full deployment of natural freedom, but it has transformed the appreciation of that freedom by placing it on the threshold of the doctrine that all virtuous life is exhaustively a matter of divine

---

[gg] Without saying so in explicit terms, Peter Brown's treatment suggests that the obvious idealization of women's virginity (as against men's) in the ancient Church must be partly interpreted by contrasting the freedom of a life of virginity with the enormous ecological pressures placed on married women, who bore the heavy burden of pregnancy and childbirth in situations where only the highest birth rates could ensure the community's survival. For the idea that Paul's preference for the unmarried state had already fundamentally liberated the Christian women from the duty of finding identity and status in belonging to a man, cf. Elisabeth Schüssler Fiorenza, *In Memory of Her*, pp. 222-26.

grace (cf. §49, 2, a) [*hh*].   Similarly, the catholic tradition has insisted, paradoxically, that human nature, and all created nature along with it, is fully revealed only in the act of being divinely exceeded (§82, 4), just as it has taught that faith respects and acknowledges the natural limits of reason in the very act of going beyond them (§67, 4).

The Christian practice of sexual continence follows the same pattern of acceptance and transformation.   It experiences and views the body as "this body, that God has afforded me, as a field to cultivate, where I might work and become rich."[41]   Peter Brown has masterfully summed up the reflections on virginity of that most original and elusive of Church Fathers, whose depth and daring, both as a Christian and as a theologian, are best measured by the contradictory ways in which he has been interpreted: Origen.

Looking at the body at close quarters [Brown writes], as a source of temptation and frustration, Origen offered little comfort to his readers: *You have coals of fire, you will sit upon them, and they will be of help to you.* Yet in the eyes of God, each particular human spirit had been allotted a particular physical constitution as its appropriate sparring partner. Each person's *flesh and blood* was particular to that person, and had been exquisitely calibrated by God, "who alone is the searcher of hearts," to challenge the potentially mighty spirit of each to stretch beyond itself. Thus, far from regarding the body as a prison of the soul, Origen arrived at an unexpected familiarity with the body. It always seemed to him that each person's spirit must be as vividly distinctive as were the features of his or her face. The gentle precision of God's mercy ensured that each body was adjusted to the peculiar needs of its soul down to the finest details, much as the lines of each person's handwriting remained unmistakably their own. ... Confronted with their own, irreducibly particular *flesh and blood*, all believers struggled to maintain, in themselves, the huge momentum of their spirit's longing for God.[42]

This leads to an important conclusion, which Peter Brown, guided by the seventh-century monk, Saint John Climacus, puts as follows:

... the body, in which sexuality lurked with such baffling tenacity, had come to be viewed in the searching light of a new, high hope: "What is this mystery in me? What is the purpose of this mixture of body and soul? How can I be my own friend and my own enemy?" Yet everyone, John

---

[*hh*] Donald M. Baillie's treatment of this paradox, in the fifth chapter of *God was in Christ*, remains a classic.

insists, "should struggle to raise this clay, so to speak, to a place on the throne of God."[43]

The Christian practice of voluntary virginity, therefore, turns out to be, not a suppression of sexual experience, but a paradoxical exercise of it; thus it is part of "an asceticism with a human face."[44] But by the same token, it is also an exercise in mysticism: it builds on the acknowledgment of the measureless desire that is felt to underlie the thirst for physical intimacy and offspring, and which struggles to anticipate the fulfillment of that desire to be received at the hands of God, who has raised Jesus Christ to life.

In this way, the life of sexual continence sums up the life of the Church, by embodying it, if not in the full extent of its cosmic expansiveness, then at least in the intensity of the aspiration which the Christian senses at the heart of the cosmos. It follows the pattern set by the Incarnation of the Word: the Christian faith cherishes the natural order in the very act of seeking to have it transformed. Realities in space and time are drawn into worship, to become part of its very substance (cf. §36, 3; §78, 1).

[8] It is time to sum up. The great Tradition, from Irenaeus on, has discerned, at the heart of the natural reality of humanity and the world, the touch of the Creator-God whose graciousness it acknowledges in explicit faith—a touch as natural and unobtrusive as it is mysterious. The Tradition has done so with reason illuminated by faith, which has guided its interpretation of Christianity as the transition from the natural order to the order of grace.

This realization must bring this lengthy chapter to an end, and prepare the ground for the next three chapters. The third chapter explored the proposition that the living, unknowable God is the ultimate term of faith's journey, and hence, the ultimate perspective of the Creed that mandates the journey. The fourth and fifth chapters have explored the basic interpretation of the Creed—that is, the nature of the journey itself: how it is possible to lose the way, how the way is to be traveled, and what the natural world looks like to those who are on the right way. What remains to be further explored in the final three chapters of this first part is the journey's point of departure: humanity and the world as they harbor—in their natural (if fallen) state—the promise of the Gospel. For it is in the very act of addressing itself to humanity and the world that the Creed acknowledges at once their natural integrity and their natural openness to God (cf. §58, 2). We must, therefore, go back once again to themes discussed in the first chapter.

CHAPTER 6

"Charity Perfects Nature"

AGAIN: THE FAITH PROFESSED BEFORE HUMANITY AND THE WORLD

[§80] INTRODUCTION: AQUINAS ON NATURAL TENDENCY

[1] Saint Thomas Aquinas died of a serious head injury at the age of forty-eight or forty-nine, at the Cistercian monastery of Fossanova, not far south of Rome, on March 7, 1274, while on his way to the Council of Lyons. He had set out on his journey a changed man. Four months previously, on December 6, 1273, while he was celebrating the Eucharist, he had been struck by a sudden numbness, which had left him totally incapacitated for intellectual work. He had accepted his affliction and even embraced it, even though up to that point (ever since, in September, 1272, he had arrived in Naples to open yet another house of studies for the Order of Preachers) he had been feverishly working on various writing projects, especially the *Summa Theologiæ*. And just before that fierce final fourteen-month period of teaching and writing, he had, with unbelievable intensity, worked on the *Summa* in Paris, during his brief, restless second stint at the university, from 1269 until early 1272.

In the years 1266-1268, however, with Thomas in his early forties and at the peak of his intellectual powers, work on the *Summa* was still in a first (though only slightly less intense) phase. He was back in Italy, having been recalled from Paris by the Master General of the Order, to the region of his birth. Long ago, he had left it to pursue his vocation. He had been nineteen when he first tried to make his way to Paris, in May of 1244. However, one of his elder brothers had intercepted him; and after unsuccessfully attempting to break his resolve by slipping an attractive young girl into his bedroom, he had taken him to Roccasecca, the home of his widowed mother Donna Theodora. This formidable lady, whose plans

for the family did not include her favorite son's taking the white
habit and black mantle of the Dominican mendicants, had forced
a fifteen-month house-arrest on him. He had waited it out. In the
late summer of 1245, he had at last been set free and gone to Paris.

Now, well over twenty years later, he was back, having opened a
new house of studies in Rome; within four months he had decided
to replace his commentary on Peter Lombard's *Sentences* by a new,
ambitious work for classroom use: the *Summa* (cf. §56, 3). Before
long, too, he was to find himself preaching and teaching around
the papal court at Viterbo.

Right from the start, the *Summa* was meeting the needs of a
thriving undertaking. In the brand-new Roman *studium*, a new generation of junior members of Aquinas' religious family, the Dominicans, now about half a century old and vigorously growing, was eager to be educated in the new theology, far away from the contentiousness of faction-ridden and anti-mendicant Paris.[1]

[2] At no point does the *Summa* shirk the far-flung venture. By now
well into the first part, Thomas has already treated of God—God
One and Triune, God the Creator. He is about to move on to the
treatment of Creation itself, in the orderly fashion suggested by the
first chapter of the Book of Genesis. At this juncture, however,
Aquinas first deals with the unseen world that mediates between
God and the world of space and time: the powers of the universe,
angels and demons, their nature and their activity. Not surprisingly
in the course of such a treatment, he engages his students (as well
as himself) in a discussion about just how what angels *do* is related
to what they *are*. And so the *quæstio* arises whether angelic beings
are *naturally* capable of *love*.

Aquinas is writing almost eleven centuries after Irenaeus. A
world of differences separates the heady excitements of a scholastic
classroom disputation in the high Middle Ages from an immigrant
bishop's struggle against the sectarian tendencies prevalent in the
Christian communities of second-century Gaul. Yet there *are* parallels. As he is carefully picking his speculative way through the
world of the *invisibilia* professed by the Nicene Creed, Aquinas suddenly lets himself be carried away, not unlike Irenaeus in the fire
of his debate with Marcionism (§78, 3). And the result is one of
those splendid moments that must occasionally relieve the routine
of any theology classroom: the teacher takes his distance from the
immediate subject-matter and evokes a vision of the divine dispensation in its entirety. In this case, of course, the vision is conveyed ra-

tionally; *frater Thomas'* disciplined scholastic idiom is worlds apart
from Irenaeus' impassioned diatribe. Characteristically, too, Aquinas takes for its point of departure a philosophical idea rather than
a theological one. But the vision itself is substantially the same, and
as thoroughly catholic; what comes into view once again is the harmony between the order of grace and the natural order.

The natural tendency [Aquinas writes] *that we find in beings not endowed with*
reason is evidence for the natural tendency that exists in the will of beings endowed
with intellect. Everything in nature naturally, by virtue of the very thing it
is, belongs to something else; hence, everything tends to move first and
foremost in the direction of that to which it belongs, rather than toward
itself. This natural tendency is evidenced by actions that come naturally,
since 'the way everything is naturally moved, so it is liable to be moved to
act,' as we read in the second book of *Physics*.[2] Thus we see how a part
will naturally put itself at risk, to preserve the whole; for example, a hand
will put itself at risk, without premeditation, to ward off a blow, to preserve
the whole body. Now *since reason is patterned after nature*, we find this kind
of pattern in the political virtues. Thus it is characteristic of good citizens
to expose themselves to danger of death, so as to preserve the whole commonwealth; in fact, if human persons were naturally part of this society,
this would be a natural tendency for them. Let us conclude. The universal good is Godself, and this good encompasses the angels, human persons, and every creature, for *every creature naturally, by virtue of the very thing*
it is, belongs to God. It follows that angels and human persons also love God
first and foremost, with a natural love, rather than themselves. Otherwise,
if *it were true that they naturally love themselves more than God, it would follow*
that natural love is perverse, and that it is not perfected by charity, but destroyed.[3]

Two elements are integral to this very characteristic passage, one
dominant, the other recessive. Reasoned reflection on the natural
order of things is the first and dominant element. The argument's
operative principle is drawn from Aristotle's nature-philosophy; its
principal data are drawn from the observation of natural phenomena; finally, the whole reasoning brims with the enjoyment of natural
intelligence and assurance. Here we have a characteristic sample of
the beginnings of the modern Western curiosity about the world,
combined with confidence in impartial rationality [*a*].

[*a*] Here lies one justification of the often-heard claim that the Christian faith-
tradition, viewed as a cultural force, continues to be, even in our "post-Christian"
world, the deepest single source of the West's permanence as a civilization built
on rational appreciation of the cosmic order in its natural integrity.

There is a second element. That element is faith—Christian faith reflecting on the order of grace as well as nature. That element, however, is recessive. Not until the very last clause do we find a strictly theological argument: charity does not destroy the natural order, but perfects it.

Yet it is precisely in that final, *theological* clause that Aquinas shows his hand. The order of charity, he knows, has not defeated or slighted nature; it has liberated and enhanced it. God does not hate the work of the divine hands; the God of Love is not set against the natural universe. Christians know the features of the God of Love—that is to say, the God who gave Jesus Christ up for the good of the whole universe and who is now bringing the world home by pouring out divine Love into human hearts by the gift of the Spirit (cf. Rom 8, 32; 5, 5).

Those who thus believe can interpret the whole world, and the features of God as the natural world suggests them are unmistakable: they are the features of no God other than the God of Love revealed in the Scriptures. All things naturally—that is, instinctively—gravitate toward whatever it is they depend on; cosmic love recognizes indebtedness, and thus points away from self. Selfless love, therefore, is so natural that it can show its appealing face even in an instinctive gesture; or rather, the very instinctiveness of such a gesture is evidence for the thesis that selfless love naturally governs and directs all of creation, no matter how unobtrusively. Consequently, it would be nothing short of unreasonable to think that beings endowed with spirit and mind and will—human persons, angels—are naturally less generous in their spiritual desires than infrahuman beings are in their natural instincts. Infrahuman nature, humanity, and the invisible powers of the universe —can they not be expected, *all of them*, naturally to show the features of the God of Love revealed to the Church in faith? Is the whole universe not made by God, and hence, of a piece (cf. §102, 10, [*t*])?

[3] Aquinas had argued a similar point about fifteen years earlier, when he was first teaching at the university of Paris—a youthful *sententiarius*, barely thirty years old. It had been his task to provide classroom commentary on the *Sentences*, Peter Lombard's systematic anthology of authoritative patristic texts (cf. §52, 7, a).

The younger Thomas' argument, however, had been quite different. Specifically, it had been more Augustinian and very much less Aristotelian: not the instinctive dynamics of infrahuman nature, but the human heart's desire for absolute goodness had been his point of departure. He had commented:

What is good in us is perfectly good in God—God being the universal, first, and perfect cause of everything good. For that reason we are natural-ly more pleased at the existence of goodness in God than in ourselves. And for that reason it is natural for human persons to love God more than themselves, *and with a love such as exists among friends.* And *since charity per-fects nature, it is in accordance with charity, too, for human persons to love God above themselves as well as above all other particular goods.*[4]

The differences between this early argument and the later one are as interesting and revealing as the correspondences. By the time he is writing the *Summa,* Aquinas' ability to develop an encompass-ing—that is, an ever more fully Christian—vision of the world has deepened and expanded immensely. Gone is any residual Plato-nism he might have held over from Augustine. Along with a greater familiarity with Aristotle, what has come to him is a freer, more dar-ing, more intellectual appreciation of the yearning resident in the natural order even apart from charity. Moreover, that natural order has come to include the infrahuman realms of reality; the analogical imagination has organically connected them with the human world [b].

Here, then, lies the difference between the later argument and the earlier. Our comparison shows how, in the words of a contem-porary commentator, "the growing Western mind ... needed to be liberated by theology into an unimpeded exploration of the natural world."[5] Guided by faith, Aquinas' theology has gained in appreci-ation of the natural, created order; this is especially symbolized by the fact that his anthropology has come to include, besides religion and ethics, cosmology as well [c].

---

[b] Aquinas' encompassing world picture is not his alone, of course. To be appreciated in its fullness, his thought has to be set against the background of thirteenth-century culture as a whole, with its waves of increasing refinement in every reach of life. For an enchanting account, cf. Hélène Nolthenius' *Duecento: Zwerftocht door Italië's late middeleeuwen* (ET *Duecento: The Late Middle Ages in Italy*).

[c] Here lies the principal difference between the classic world picture of the great Tradition, here represented by Aquinas, and the modern world picture, represented by René Descartes and Immanuel Kant, to mention its two most semi-nal thinkers. For the latter two, anthropology and cosmology are separate; the uni-verse is *not* of a piece; they draw a sharp distinction between the world of matter and objectivity ("nature") and the world of spirit and subjectivity ("freedom"). Fortunately, modern developments in scientific cosmology have driven us back to the unitary view (even if this unitary view now includes the awareness that the

Still, the two arguments continue to be carried along on a strong undertow of continuity. The essential theme has remained the same throughout: *grace perfects nature without destroying it*, hence *nature can be trusted and hence, freely explored*. The supreme gift of grace, which is the selfless love of everything, and of God above everything, is not alien to our native human selves. We have a *natural* tendency to love God first, and not just in a way that is merely self-serving, but *amore amicitiæ*—with the kind of love that characterizes relationships between friends. That tendency towards unselfish love has the deepest conceivable moorings: it is anchored in *nature*—it reveals God's act of creation. No wonder that infrahuman instinct, too, in following *its* nature, shows the signs of unselfish love, like human intelligence and freedom. And so finally, why exclude the angels from this most intimate, most encompassing law of nature?

In faith, we have received God's grace, of course; but if we, along with all of creation, were not *naturally* apt to reach out beyond ourselves, not even divine grace would ever succeed in getting us to do it—unless, of course, we were to think of the gracious love of God as a force that compels us to do something wholly unnatural, something alien to us, something forced upon us from the outside (cf. §79, 1-2).

[4] It would be a mistake, therefore, to suggest that faith is incidental to Aquinas' arguments from nature or merely adventitious to them [*d*]. In fact, the opposite is true: positive Christian faith suffuses them and accounts for their vigor. Faith, it would seem, especially accounts for the fact that Aquinas' arguments, by modern standards, seem to be blind to any available evidence to the contrary, not only in nature, but also, and especially, in human persons [*e*]. Aquinas' reasoning implies that *fundamental* theologi-

---

cosmos and humanity are beset by random violence to an incomparably larger extent than was ever imagined: cf. §115). Cf., for example, the "anthropic principle," formulated, in its "hard" form, by Stephen M. Hawking as follows: "We see the universe the way it is because if it were different, we would not be here to observe it" (*A Brief History of Time*, p. 183; cf. pp. 124-25; cf. also Christopher F. Mooney, "The Anthropic Principle in Cosmology and Theology." Cf. §87, 2, d, [*gg*]; §94, 6, a; §104, 1. It is obvious that all of this has enormous consequences for the theological understanding of God and of faith in God. Cf., e.g., §9, 1, [*i*].

[*d*] Here lies the root of our contention that it is a hermeneutical mistake to construe Aquinas' natural theology in Deistic terms (cf. §31, 2; §84, 2, a).

[*e*] Notice, though, how carefully Aquinas implies, in the passage from the *Summa*, that it takes *virtue guided by reason* (cf. §50, 1, b) to achieve what, in fact, does

cal reflection can safely discount such negative evidence, as *ultimately* irrelevant to nature, and thus to reason. Nature is fundamentally stable, and in this way it shows the features of the God of faithful Love. Hence, reason can safely *imitari naturam*— "follow the pattern set by nature."

All of this shows that faith has inspired and guided and shaped the philosophical understanding of the natural order that Aquinas has found so delightfully furnished, first (as was to be expected) by Augustine, but then also (far more surprisingly as well as decisively) by Aristotle. Christian faith has *sponsored* and *enabled* natural reason, with all its newly accumulated sophistication, to trace the natural structures of all reality, and trace them back even further than Augustine or, for that matter, Aristotle had done. With the courage of a mind freed from preoccupations, Aquinas traces those structures down to their deepest roots, to the creative will of God, *to whom all creatures belong even more deeply than they belong to themselves.*

[§81] NATURAL THEOLOGY: TWO APPLICATIONS

[1] In teaching, not only that created nature remains integral to the order of grace, but also that grace reveals created nature to best advantage, Aquinas is a characteristic representative of the constant catholic tradition. He is an equally typical representative of that same tradition in implying a second proposition, which is the natural foil to the one just formulated. That proposition is: not only do humanity's natural capacity and desire for understanding remain integral to Christian faith, but Christian faith positively guides human reason to the perfection of understanding (cf. §67, 5).

[2] Traditional Catholic theology has drawn a fundamental conclusion from all of this: rational reflection on the order of nature, precisely inasmuch as it is predisposed to welcome grace, is integral to Christian theology. In the present context, this conclusion has two closely related applications.

---

not come naturally. Only a *good* citizen, he observes, will give his life for the commonwealth, even though this kind of sacrifice looks deeply appropriate and in accordance with nature when it occurs. Aquinas may be an optimist about natural tendency; he is under no illusion about the need for virtue. Unlike some of the middle and late nineteenth century Romantics, he gives us no grounds for thinking that human indifference and nastiness in the Middle Ages were any less in evidence than natural calamity, or that both were less common then than they are today.

First of all, if nature is predisposed to grace, then *humanity and the world are naturally waiting for the call of the Gospel.* Moreover, if the features of faith can be discerned as consonant with the structures of reason, then there are bound to be *reasonable grounds for Christian faith.* Consequently, it is possible to discover essential grounds for Christian faith in the natural order, and to explain these grounds modestly and reasonably. As a result, the Christian profession of faith is, and can be shown to be, naturally attractive. Hence, too, the Creed is not only authoritatively proposed by the Church for acceptance; it is also inherently *credible.* Far from being a sectarian, doctrinal straitjacket that persons have to be forced into, Christian doctrine is (in Flannery O'Connor's words) an instrument of freedom:[6] it liberates the native, universal human longing for faith by giving shape to it (§65; §77, 3). To put this in technical theological language, *humanity and the world provide reason, illuminated by faith, with the material for a pertinent apologetic in favor of Christianity.*

The second application is even broader. If nature is predisposed to welcome grace, then the natural order itself must be broadly evidential *even apart from any explicit reference to the Christian faith.* Nature, in other words, provides pointers to God: it inspires and carries natural worship; it activates the natural desire for such natural justice as opens out into naturally attractive holiness; it directs the mind to the hidden truth that can be naturally surmised in and beyond the truths of nature. In technical terminology: *humanity and the world have an affinity with God that is rooted in the very thing they are*—that is, they naturally reveal themselves to human understanding as *God's Creation* (cf. Is 40, 12-28; Rom 1, 20; Acts 17, 24-28). Thus, on a more reflective note, *created beings provide natural human reason with the material for natural theology.*

[3] The present, first part of this second volume of *God Encountered* is specifically devoted to the thematic exploration of the relationship between grace and nature, and between faith and reason. In the context of this theme, it was promised, the final chapters of this first part would deal with humanity and the world insofar as they harbor the promise of the Christian profession of faith (§79, 6). Hence, the next two chapters will discuss the basic structures of Christian apologetics: the seventh by exploring its anthropological foundations and the eighth by raising three fundamental contemporary themes.

For now, however, let us gather up and somewhat further elaborate, in three sections, some of the themes and insights that have surfaced, in the course of the previous five chapters, in relation to the great Tradition's fundamental-theological appreciation of the natural order and of human reason's natural capacity to understand it in a divine perspective.

GRACED NATURE AND REASON ENLIGHTENED BY FAITH

[§82] NATURE RATIONALLY DISCERNED IN FAITH, NOT AUTONOMY

[1] Precisely as a document of explicitly Christian faith, we have argued, the Creed warrants a natural theology with a universalist appeal (§59, 2-6). Positive Christian faith acknowledges the abiding integrity of the natural order, and thus graciously enlightens and encourages natural reason to attain an understanding of it ("reason illumined by faith": DS 3016; CF 132). Thus faith encourages reason to follow its native urge to understand humanity and the world. In doing so, it also encourages reason to discover—which, given the reality of sin, always also means: to recover—its own native yearning to understand them as natively oriented to God, and thus, as naturally equipped for integration into the Christian faith-abandon to God.

> [a] The catholic tradition's passionate pursuit of the theological questions implicit in the nature of humanity and the world is reflected in the conviction, undeveloped by the Creed but implicit in it, that grace mandates reflection on the fundamental integrity of nature. The Christian faith respects the positive elements of religion as superior to the natural ones (§31), but that superiority is from God: far from disgracing and putting down what it finds, it enhances it. Thus, far from canceling the order of nature, grace—that is, the historic order of grace thematically and primarily professed by the Creed (§59, 5)—presupposes and indeed perfects it (cf. §26, 2, a; §14, 4, [j]).
>
> Ultimately, this conviction is predicated on a christological doctrine. God is not set against creation (§79, 2-4); in being united with the divine *Logos*, Christ's human nature is not diminished but dignified (§78, 4, a); it is "not taken away by being divinized, but preserved all the better" (DS 556; cf. 302; CF 635; cf. 615).[7]

[2]   This constructive harmony between grace and the order of nature gives legitimacy to *the term "supernatural,"* first used as a regu-

lar term by Theodore of Mopsuestia,[8] and so frequently employed in Christian (and especially Catholic) theology to designate the order of grace. The history of both the term and the concept has been tortuous and beset by ambiguity,[9] and neither the concept nor the term can be said to be absolutely indispensable in theology of the catholic kind. The principal problem is that the term has continued, to this day, to carry the unsettling overtones of nervous controversy—overtones it acquired long ago, when it was treated as an absolutely indispensable counterpart of "nature" (cf. DS 1921, 1923, 3891; CF 1984/21. 23). Misunderstanding, misinterpretation, and caricature have remained the lot of both concepts. Still, the continued frequent use of the term "supernatural" in the Catholic tradition makes it imperative that it be carefully treated, so that it may at least be accurately understood [f].

[3] The basic misconception suggested by "supernatural" is that grace is a reality extrinsically *superimposed* (often with connotations of forceful intervention) on pure nature (cf. §78, 4, a, [t]; and again, §79, 1-2), thus *leaving nature, and especially human nature intrinsically untouched* [g].

---

[f] And since "supernatural" is not a natural-language word but a *term*, its meaning cannot be established by reference to ordinary usage; even less can it be read off from the shape of the term itself. Terms are technical; they are part of the idiom of a trained profession, which has established their meaning by *definition*. Hence, both the meaning and the appropriate use of a term have to be learned from those who understand its meaning and know how to use it, in the interest of scholarly understanding (which, in the case of "supernatural," is professional-theological understanding). On this subject, also cf. F. J. van Beeck, *Christ Proclaimed*, pp. 64-93. Bernard Lonergan makes a similar point when he explains that the "supernatural" as it occurs in Albert the Great and Aquinas is a "theorem" (*Grace and Freedom*, p. 13): it is not the natural name of a particular entity, but a tool to understand grace theoretically. On this precise issue, cf. also Sebastian Moore's essay "Ratzinger's 'Nature' Isn't Natural."

[g] It is the abiding merit of Henri de Lubac (*The Mystery of the Supernatural*, esp. pp. 154-216) to have traced the history of this error to Cajetan's misinterpretation of Aquinas' understanding of the term "nature" *as it applies to humanity*. Cajetan wrongly explains that Aquinas borrows his definition from Aristotle's *nature*-philosophy. This move—typical of the mid-sixteenth century's passion for narrowly circumscriptive, objectivist definition (§7, 1, a)—turns human nature into a reality essentially closed in on itself and deprives it of its openness to grace as integral to its constitution. The misinterpretation had dreadful consequences for the traditional catholic understanding of the harmony between grace and nature. On the one hand, the Reformation was losing touch with the great Tradition by emphasizing the depravity of nature and hence, the non-existence of any natural good; thus it went back, with a vengeance, to the Augustinian tradition, and upheld the unconditional necessity of grace *over against* nature. Catholicism, on the other hand, reaffirmed the traditional teaching on the total gratuitousness of grace as

[a]   This misconception also suggests, rather more insidiously, that God's sovereign grace is *comparable* with, and hence *measurable* by, the natural order, as if the givenness of the creature were capable of setting limits to the Creator's free gift—as if the creature were capable of conditioning the Creator's free and sovereign graciousness.   There *is*, of course, a sense in which this is true, for the concept "nature" does represent a *reality*: it denotes the finite creature's *measured capacity* for union with God.   In the catholic tradition, however, this measure does not become *fully* recognizable until the divine graciousness that fills it to capacity *and beyond capacity* is revealed.

[b]   Thus, within the context of Christian theology, the concept "nature" serves two crucial *philosophical* purposes.   First, it safeguards the radical difference between the infinite Creator and the creature.   The creature is finite in virtue of *what it is*—that is, in virtue of its *nature* the fact that it is *this* and not *that* [h].

But secondly, and most importantly, the concept "nature" implies, not just radical difference, but also radical relatedness. *The creature's limits*, which account for its infinite qualitative difference from God, *have their origin in God, who set them.*   That is to say, its relationship with God is *asymmetrical*: the creature does not account for itself in its natural integrity— God wholly accounts for it.   A very important conclusion follows from this. The creature's natural limits—which define its finitude—do indeed constitute real boundaries *from the point of view of the creature,* for in virtue of its natural limits, the creature is set apart, not only from other creatures, but also, and far more radically, from God.   But *from the point of view* (so to speak) *of God, the creature's limits are not a limitation; they do not set God apart from the creature.*   In virtue of its very nature, the finite creature's access

---

well as the traditional, positive appreciation of nature.   However, in doing so, it began to treat grace, in its relationship to nature, in purely adventitious terms, *in juxtaposition* to "pure" nature.   This "extrinsecist" understanding of grace opened catholic thought only too readily to the Protestant accusation of "naturalism" (§83, 1, a).

[h]   This, incidentally, makes it necessary to handle the concept of "divine nature" with great care.   What must be avoided is the implication that God is "something"—*this* and not *that.*   Hence, when the question is asked, "What is God?" the answer must simply be, "God *is*."   Put technically, it is God's nature simply *to be.* Cf. §79, 4.

to God is as limited as it is real; yet that same nature limits neither God's transcendent sovereignty, nor God's access to the creature, which remains as immediate and intimate as it is unconditioned and free [i].

[c] The point just made is an articulation of the insight that underlies Irenaeus' affirmation that there is, not only "generosity," but also "justice" in the Incarnation. The Incarnate Son of God went where he had a *right* to go in the first place—that is, he came into what was his own (§78, 3); God need not break to enter (§79, 1-2).

[4] The catholic theological tradition, therefore, uses the concepts of nature and the supernatural in the service of a *paradox*—a paradox as unknown to Aristotle as it is to common sense. *Human nature* (and all created nature along with it) *is fully revealed only in the act of being divinely exceeded.* Put differently, *nature is fully revealed only in the light of the supernatural, for which it has a natural aptitude* [j].

---

[i] Aquinas explains this by distinguishing between two kinds of relationships. Between two distinct subjects (that is, two subjects neither of which depends on the other for existence) a relationship is real (*realis*); in other cases it is a matter only of understanding (*rationis tantum*). Thus creatures are related to God by way of a "real" relation [*realiter*], whereas God is related to creatures by way, not of a "real" relation, but "only according to reason, inasmuch as creatures are [really] related to [God]" [*secundum rationem tantum, in quantum creaturæ referuntur ad ipsum*] (*S. Th.* 1, 13, 7. *in c.*; cf. also *S. c. G.* 2, 11-14). This has been misinterpreted to mean that creatures have no choice but to be concerned with God, whereas God, being absolutely transcendent, is not "really" concerned about creatures or affected by them, but only "thought" to be so concerned and affected. Aquinas means no such thing. His distinction serves to convey what we have labeled the *asymmetry* inherent in the order, both of creation and of grace (§23, 4, b; §57, 3, a): creatures are dependent, God remains free. But our awareness of this divine freedom must serve, not to imagine God as being "above it all," but rather to enhance our sense of the incomprehensible mystery of God's faithful love, and hence to appreciate its unfathomable depth (cf. §34, 2).

[j] This proposition runs parallel to the thesis explained above: faith respects and acknowledges the natural limits of reason in the very act of going beyond them (§67, 4). Aelred Squire has well expressed the paradox, as follows (*Asking the Fathers*, p. 15): "... a kind of creative recognition of what is already somehow obscurely known. It may seem a somewhat startling leap to make, but to the great spiritual masters of the undivided Church, the revealed doctrine of man as having been made in the image of God universally inspires this feeling of glad recognition. They go on, in fact, to take it seriously for what it claims to be, a long lost memory of their true selves, and from that all the rest they have to say follows. Their doctrine is concerned to arouse in their disciples a sense of the implications of a memory they believe could not have been initially reawakened without a divine intervention."

To the extent, therefore, that the term "nature" (and even the confusing term "pure nature") is the bearer of the conviction that *the integrity of created reality remains inviolate in the act of being filled to overflowing by God*, it is an essential theological concept. It enables the theologian to do justice to the full reality of the created order, while at the same time maintaining its radical openness to God [k].

[a] Consequently, since created reality *as it actually exists* is both affected by sin and being healed and enhanced to the very core of its being (and thus called to full perfection) by the existing order of grace, the concept "pure nature" is like an auxiliary line in a geometrical figure: it clarifies the figure without being part of the argument. The reason for this is obvious. "Pure nature" is an abstract concept; "nature" *as such* is not available to human experience apart from the concrete order of sin (which distorts nature) and grace (which heals it by elevating it) any more than purely natural religiosity is available to human experience apart from any positive form (cf. §25, 3, a). *De facto*, human nature exists in a world in which grace is already taking shape in place and time, not only in the form of Christianity as a positive religion (§57, 3, d; §78, 1), but also in the form of a whole variety of positive human responses, both social and individual, to the experienced promptings of the divine presence.

For this reason, Karl Rahner, making use of a metaphor from arithmetic, has rightly insisted on calling *the concept of "pure nature"* a "remainder concept" (*Restbegriff*), as follows. "A *precise* demarcation between nature and grace (if this should be feasible at all), and thus, a really pure concept of pure nature, could in any case be attempted only with the help of Revelation. The latter tells us what about us is grace, and thus provides us with the means of subtracting this grace from the whole body of our exis-

---

[k] Here lie solid theological grounds for the principled claim, often heard nowadays among Christian ethicists, that not even the most sensitive, compelling arguments drawn from the natural law are ever definitive and final (cf. §50, 1, c). To the extent that the natural order is appreciated and understood, in any place and at any time, in its integrity, it demands that justice be done to it, in moral behavior that respects that integrity. But the theological fact of the natural order's enhancement by divine grace forbids that the natural law be construed in a tyrannical fashion, as the final say. Cf. Karl Rahner, "Zur Enzyklika «Humanae Vitae»" (ET "On the Encyclical 'Humanae Vitae'") and "Theologische Bemerkungen zum Zeitbegriff" (ET "Theological Observations on the Concept of Time").

tential experience of what it is to be human, and thus of arriving at pure nature (in its *totality*) as a 'remainder'."[10]

[5] A very important conclusion follows. In the Christian construal of reality, the *nature* that is the object of natural theological reflection is *intrinsically situated in the context of the order of grace and participating in it,* just as the *rational reflection* upon it is *intrinsically situated in the context of Christian faith and participating in it.* The catholic tradition properly acknowledges the relative autonomy of both nature and human reason, but the agenda behind this acknowledgment, ultimately, is the thankful recognition of their elevation by grace—an elevation grounded in their native openness to it. *The agenda of natural theology is never the restriction of the primacy of grace and of faith,* let alone their rejection.

From this, an important contention immediately follows. The catholic theological tradition's habit of engaging in reasoned reflection on the natural order is not, *in and of itself,* an act of human arrogance and hence, a symptom of humanity's alienation from God. Catholic natural theology is not, *in and of itself,* the full deployment of human self-sufficiency in understanding; it is not an act of self-enlightened human autonomy that is unholy, let alone rebellious. Nor is it necessarily a display of willful, sinful, ungrateful human self-assertion over against the God of grace. In fact, *in the catholic tradition,* which understands nature as perfected by grace and reason as enlightened by faith, it is the opposite of all this. This contention has faced challenges from two sides: the mentalities associated with, respectively, the classical Reformation and modern humanism. This calls for elaboration, in two consecutive sections.

[§83] THE CATHOLIC TRADITION AND THE REFORMATION

[1] The contention just formulated has long put catholic theology seriously at odds with the classical Reformation, traditionally distrustful of the catholic tradition in this regard. The Reformed tradition has tended to suspect that the catholic interest in the natural order is maintained principally in the interest of downplaying the essential Christian awareness of the all-pervasive power of sin [*l*].

_____

[*l*] This suspicion is in keeping with the Protestant tendency to restrict the core of the Christian faith to the twin themes of sin and salvation (§20, 1-2). But the roots of the problem go deeper. The theological traditions of Western Christiani-

[a] This classical Protestant objection to the "naturalism" of the catholic (and especially the Roman Catholic) tradition is by now (thank God) largely dated. This holds especially in the New World, where large segments of Protestantism have come to treat the austere Reformed doctrine of human nature's total depravity as a stirring doctrinal affirmation rather than as a guide to the lived Christian life, which is spontaneously far more upbeat in tone. Still, a long history of mutual accusations and some lingering suspicions make it important for catholic theology to keep emphasizing the twin points just made: it is grace that perfects nature, it is faith that enlightens reason. What also needs to be repeated, on the Catholic side, is that prominent currents in late-medieval and post-Reformation Catholic thought were, in fact, guilty of naturalism, not only in theory (cf. §82, 3, [g]), but also in practice, by uncritically embracing dubious natural and cultural values and thus discrediting the very Christian humanism it was intent on promoting.

[b] Ecumenically-minded catholic theology, therefore, in harmony with the great Tradition of the undivided Church, must hold that it is in virtue of the existing order of grace, and *in virtue of that order alone* that the Creed addresses itself, *as a matter of actual fact*, to all of humanity. To this, however, it adds that the Creed is *capable* of so addressing humanity *only in virtue of the underlying order of nature* (cf. §59, 6). Consequently, if our proposal to engage in fundamental theological reflection on the natural order is to be called "naturalism," that naturalism emphatically views the natural order as embraced by the reality of grace, and never as independent of grace. Specifically, our understanding of the natural order is not of the autonomous kind, nor does it overlook or disregard the reality of sin—that pervasive corruption of the natural order and of the human ability to understand it in the perspective of the living God (cf. §79, 4, b and [dd]; §12, 1, b).

---

ty, especially those associated with Bonaventure and, later on, with the Reformation, have continued to cherish Augustine's interpretation of grace in counterposition, not to *nature*, but to *sin*. This has immense consequences for the conception, say, of "natural law." On this subject, cf. Bernard Lonergan's *Grace and Freedom*; cf. also Sebastian Moore's provocative essay "Ratzinger's 'Nature' Isn't Natural."

[2]   For purposes of further clarification, the position just stated can be profitably compared and contrasted with the distinctive positions that two important modern Protestant theologians, Paul Tillich and Dietrich Bonhoeffer, have adopted vis-à-vis the relationship between what the catholic tradition has called "nature" and "grace" (cf. §78, 4, c; §22, 3, d).

[3] Tillich begins by pointing out, rightly, that both humanity and God are the proper themes of fundamental theological reflection. He goes on to explain that theology must construe the relationship between humanity and God as a dynamic, mutually complementary correlation, between a strictly questioning humanity (cf. §102, 4) and a strictly responsive God:

Theology formulates the questions implied in human existence, and theology formulates the answers implied in divine self-manifestation under the guidance of the questions implied in human existence. ... The answers implied in the event of revelation are meaningful only in so far as they are in correlation with questions concerning the whole of our existence, with existential questions. ... Being human means asking the questions of one's own being and living under the impact of the answers given to this question. And conversely, being human means receiving answers to the question of one's own being and asking questions under the impact of the answers.[11]

Tillich is here attempting to reconcile the concerns of the Reformation with those of the Enlightenment, and in doing so, he shows himself to be a characteristic exponent of neo-Protestantism. His indebtedness to the Enlightenment makes him very much aware that theology cannot avoid involving itself, first and foremost, in *anthropology*—that is, in reflection on the *recipient* of the divine self-manifestation. On the other hand, his Reformed heritage prevents him from construing that recipient in merely "natural" terms.

[a] As a result, his proposal has two features in common with the tradition of the Reformation. Firstly, it treats "essential human nature" not as an inner "moment" of the concrete order of grace, but only as a logical necessity—a mere *idea* [m]. For

---

[m] In this way, Tillich agrees with Rahner in his rejection of "nature" as an actually existing reality. Rahner, however, does not consider "human nature" a mere idea; he maintains it as an integral, real component ("moment") of humanity and the world as they exist in actuality—the component that continues both to spell out their utter dependency on God and to distinguish them from God. As

Tillich, essential human nature is not positively accessible to human experience or understanding in any degree of actuality, since the only humanity accessible to us is human nature as it actually exists—that is, humanity existing under the conditions of the estrangement inherent in our existential predicament. Secondly, no less than the classical Reformers and the great Tradition (though in far more philosophic a vein), Tillich is at pains to affirm the sovereign transcendence of God, by placing the true God radically beyond any possible human conceptions of God.

Still, there is a serious problem with the correlation as he proposes it. For all his emphasis on the sovereignty of God, his account of the Christian faith *de facto* ends up limiting the divine self-revelation. The reason for this is that the latter must remain strictly adjusted to humanity's existential predicament. That predicament, in other words, acts as a Kantian *a priori* that determines the scope of humanity's possible union with the sovereign God, and hence, the possible scope of God's revelation.[12]

In this construal of the relationship between God and humanity in exclusively soteriological terms, as a correlation between human estrangement and divine restoration, Tillich is the heir of a deep-seated tendency of the Reformation: that of making the correlation between sin and redemption the core of the Christian faith (cf. §20, 1-2). But on the other hand, where he interprets the correlation as ultimately governed, not by the gracious God, but by the human predicament, Tillich parts company with the Reformation, by factually denying the primacy and sovereignty of divine grace. This is where Tillich joins the Enlightenment, in its emphasis on the human subject as the measure of authentic religion.

As a result, Tillich's interpretation of the Christian profession of faith suffers from a double loss of perspective. *Protological*

---

a result, Rahner's analysis of the relationship between nature and grace recognizes three elements: (1) "pure" nature (the "remainder-concept"—in Tillich's construal, nature as the purely logical idea); (2) the concrete order of fallen but graced nature; and (3) divine grace. Tillich, on the other hand, recognizes only two elements: the divine self-revelation and "fallen nature." Consequently, he construes the actual divine-human relationship wholly in terms of contrariety; fallen humanity and self-revealing God. In so doing he forfeits the possibility of interpreting Christian eschatology in correlation with a theology of creation, that is to say, in terms of God freely and graciously fulfilling as well as exceeding the natural limits of humanity and the world.

human nature, along with its Creator, disappears in the darkness of
the present human predicament; *humanity's eschatological fulfillment in virtue of its actual union with the gracious God* is attenuated
to a purely asymptotic concept.

[4] A brief account of the theological development of another important twentieth-century Protestant theologian, Dietrich Bonhoeffer, must serve as the conclusion to our discussion of the encounter
between the catholic tradition and the Reformation on the subject
of nature and grace.[13]

Bonhoeffer's theological position is deeply characterized by his
incessant cautions against naturalism, and a great esteem for the
positive, confessional elements of the Christian faith. This puts
Bonhoeffer very much in the main tradition of the Reformation,
which took its distance from late-medieval theology's excessive reliance on late-scholastic philosophical speculation, mainly of the
nominalist kind. It also makes of him one of the chief defenders
of live Christian faith against all attempts at domesticating it—in
this case, the National Socialist attempts at promoting "German
Christianity." At the same time, however, there is a deeply humanistic side to Bonhoeffer: he remains deeply indebted to, and appreciative of, his cultured, agnostic family background. This latter
trait, along with his own lifelong interest in public, "secular" issues,
prevented him from ever fully embracing the traditionally Protestant, narrow distrust of nature and culture, and viewing them as
unreliable ways to the living God on account of their inherent sin-
fulness [*n*].

Still, in his theological approach to the natural order, Bonhoeffer does follow the mood of the Reformation; Luther's characterization of the human heart as "bent upon itself"—*cor curvum in se*—
has left deep marks on his theological vision of the world. Not surprisingly, therefore, he follows the Reformation's lead in rejecting
the theological authority of *reflection on the potentialities of the natural
order.* In his view, all reflection on the *humanum* as such runs the
risk of *self-absorption.* Theology, being a form of reflection, is not ex-
empt from this hazard; it always runs the risk of *replacing* the actual,
direct experience of the encounter with the living God by some

---

[*n*] Bonhoeffer's doctoral dissertation *Akt und Sein* ("Act and Being") is in many
ways the record of his struggle with these two conflicting loyalties, which he found
embodied in the polarity between the "confessionalism" of Karl Barth and the
"naturalism" of the Roman Catholic church.

form of reflection, first on the encounter itself, and eventually on the natural human capacity for it.

Hence Bonhoeffer's insistence that

... it is not in self-reflection, but in the actual relationship [*im Aktbezug*] to God that human persons understand themselves, that is, only where they really stand in the presence of God. Not where they find potentialities in themselves by virtue of which they can stand before God.[14]

If he regards reflection on human *nature* as theologically unpromising, Bonhoeffer is even less sanguine about modern Christianity's readiness to defend itself by defending its relevance to contemporary *naturalistic culture*. Self-definition and self-cultivation in the interest of currying the favor of the powers that be, after all, will all too easily turn into just another exercise in self-absorption, enabling secular powers to use the Church for its purposes. No wonder that, in a different though ultimately related context, Bonhoeffer sharply objects to the tendency in modern theology to view Christianity's *relevance* as the measure of its *truth*. Christians who commend Christianity as relevant to the modern world usually do so in the interest of making collaboration with the forces of contemporary culture attractive; this puts them habitually on the brink of compromise and betrayal. Thus Bonhoeffer can write:

... wherever the issue of present relevance becomes the *theme of theology* we can be certain that the reality [of the Christian message] is already betrayed and sold.[15]

Slowly but surely, Bonhoeffer came to take his distance from too confessional a form of Christianity. He found Barth's narrow reliance on the codified data of revelation ("*Offenbahrungspositivismus*") too confining to deal with the real world, just as he found the Confessing Church itself too self-centered in its conservatism and self-absorption, and too reluctant to take its share of Christian responsibility for the world. In this way, he more and more moved over to a balanced position. Deep down, he eventually found, the world and the Christian faith were not at odds; the Church can be free enough to meet the world without feeling obliged to either assail it or apologize to it. According as he came to understand the true maturity of the modern world ("the world come of age"), Bonhoeffer also came to cherish it more deeply; in the process, he found himself cherishing Christ's Gospel even more, as the source of his ability to embrace the world precisely in its maturity. That combination of faith and deep appreciation, he discovered, was deep

and radical enough to stand the test of imprisonment and martyrdom.

Bonhoeffer's mature conviction is best expressed in the extraordinary survey of modern theology he wrote down in prison, on June
6, 1944. It culminates in a new, courageous re-definition of the relationship between the world and the Gospel, the natural order and
the order of grace:

... the maturity of the world is no longer an occasion for polemics and
apologetics; rather, it is now really understood, and better understood than
it understands itself, namely on the basis of the Gospel, of Christ.[16]

Here Bonhoeffer has abandoned the principled "againstness" so
characteristic of the tradition of the Reformation.[17] He has redis-
covered the great Tradition of the undivided Church. Mature Christian faith has once again become the setting in which there can
develop a mature understanding and appreciation of the world,
both in its promise and in its waywardness. In the confinement of
prison, Bonhoeffer the believer and the theologian has found and
forged a new, liberating form of unity between faith and culture (cf.
§14, 2)— that is, between grace and nature, and between faith and
reason.

[a] In view of this later development, there are good reasons to
think that the earlier Bonhoeffer had been unnecessarily skeptical with regard to the hazards involved in theological reflection
on the order of nature. Such theological reflectiveness, in other
words, need not necessarily lose touch with faith in the living
God; theology appropriately cultivates an appreciative awareness
of the potentialities of nature or culture.

Yet despite this imbalance, even the younger Bonhoeffer remains a sound teacher of Christian realism. As he matured, Bonhoeffer seems to have lost some of the confessional nervousness
that was the dark side of his determination not to compromise
the integrity of his Christian faith. Thus he could come, eventually, to the realization that the responsible practice of systematic
theology involves the search for a balance between the authoritative demands, *both* of the Christian faith *and* of human nature
shaped by the surrounding culture. The search of this balance,
it was argued long ago, is an essential theological task, and it involves *discretionary judgments*—judgments no theologian can be
excused from making (§14, 3-4). The younger Bonhoeffer's only
problem was that he made a theological principle out of what was

a sound (and even heroic) discretionary judgment of Christian faith. Thus his warnings against compliance with the world on easy terms deserve to be taken seriously even today, also in the catholic tradition; Christians should be wary of *the agenda behind all fundamental theological reflection,* lest they involve themselves in too uncritical an identification with what passes for *normative* on either purely natural or purely cultural grounds.

[b] Two modern theologians have developed notable fundamental theologies that attempt to mediate between the Catholic emphasis on "nature" and the Protestant insistence on "confession." For both, the idea of "word-event" plays a decisive role. The Protestant Gerhard Ebeling has developed this idea both at the fundamental-theological level, in *Einführung in theologische Sprachlehre* (ET *Introduction to a Theological Theory of Language*) and *Wort und Glaube,* and at the strictly dogmatic level, in *Das Wesen des christlichen Glaubens* and *Dogmatik des Christlichen Glaubens.* Ebeling's Catholic admirer Peter Knauer has offered a treatment both fundamental-theological and ecumenical, in *Der Glauben kommt von Hören.* It would seem that one of the real merits of both authors' approaches lies in their having developed an idea that was very dear to Bonhoeffer (as well as linguistically sound), namely, that the word is primary address and only secondarily idea. Only in responding to a word of *address* that comes to us from outside does it become clear, both to ourselves and to others, just who we are and what we really think. Fundamentally, in other words, it takes *encounter* to lay bare what is authentically natural. This, of course, will require further elaboration (§95, esp. 1; 1, [gg]; 7).

[5] It is precisely on this score that Bonhoeffer would appear to be an especially reliable guide even today. In present-day North America, it would seem arguable that catholic theology, especially as it is practiced in the university, has sound *discretionary* reasons to be aware of the risks involved in overconcentration on that cherished topic of academic conversation: the intellectual preliminaries to the Christian faith. Instead, it might be well advised to find a *positive starting-point* (cf. §31, 3-5) [o].

---

[o] To be explicit, let me suggest that today's catholic theologians in North America might wonder about the extent to which loyalty to the prevailing academic culture, so strongly marked by the ideals embodied in American civil religion, takes pride of place in their practice of catholic theology. Could it be that our

[§84] THE CATHOLIC TRADITION AND ENLIGHTENED HUMANISM

[1] We have seen how the catholic theological tradition's habit of engaging in reasoned reflection on the natural order entails a decision to distance itself from the Reformation's tendency to discredit the natural order as simply depraved, and hence as inaccessible to us in its integrity, and consequently, as an unreliable way to God, in theology as in the lived life. Our account of Bonhoeffer's theological development, however, has already served to introduce us to the other side of the story: catholic theology must firmly take its distance from the opposite position, too.

In the Western world, that position is *naturalism*, and it comes to us, historically speaking, as the legacy of the Enlightenment. It holds that the *autonomy* of the truly emancipated human individual is the privileged (if not, indeed, the sole) norm of authentic religion. That autonomy is found by a *return to nature in its purity*: to be authentic, people must recover their native innocence—that source of indomitable energy. Humanity is to shake off the restrictive yoke that it has too long agreed to bear by dint of submission to tradition, including religious (that is, ecclesiastical) tradition. True religion, in other words, shows no signs of *heteronomy*; it is independent of communal practices of worship, mandatory standards of living, traditional canons of teaching. For religious structures presented as the privileged (if not, indeed, the sole) vehicles of God's presence are suspect: they cannot be more than incidental to true religion, and they may be downright alienating.

---

deference to matters of *method* and our devotion to the *conditions for the possibility* of faith-*cum*-integrity owes more to the expectation of tolerance in the academy than to the catholic faith in its full scope? Has our fundamental theology, perhaps, become a symptom of suspense of intellectual commitment? Or are we, in the face of doctrinal specifics, suffering from the syndrome known to psychotherapists as failure of will? Could lack of confessional resolve account for our sweeping (and often quite blandly universalist) approach to comparative religion, and for our apparent reluctance to concentrate on the appreciation, not only of the positive elements in the Christian and catholic faith, but also of their functional equivalents in other religions (cf. Francis X. Clooney, "Liturgical Theology in a Comparative Context")? Or are catholic theologians, perhaps, lingering at the door of the house of doctrine because they are afraid of (again?) getting caught inside a prison? Or could the pressure be roundly ecclesiastical—are we afraid to find ourselves associated (again) with incompetent colleagues, or with pressure-groups with conservative or integralist ecclesiastico-political agendas, or (worst of all) caught in an ecclesiastical establishment that takes anti-intellectualism for faith and loyalty?

Religion, in this world-view, simply consists in the mature person's natural, immediate, self-authenticating knowledge of, and access to, God. All forms of shared, positive, "organized" religion are, at best, purely instrumental: they serve tradition, not truth. At worst, however, they are the instruments of continued slavery, and hence, alienating (cf. §10, 1, a; §61, 3, a, [d]; §77, 3) [p]. The norm of authentic religion, therefore, is *immanent*: it is found in those enlightened persons who have the courage to avail themselves of their own intelligence; in those responsible people who live by their own inner sense of duty; in those truly self-identified people who have discovered the god-consciousness at the center of their self-awareness (cf. §25, 4, b-d).

[a] Paul Tillich, who has faced the claims of the Enlightenment as few other modern Christian theologians have, has given us a classic critique of this claim.[18] The upbeat assertion of human autonomy overlooks the fact that human life, and human religiosity in particular, is in fact characterized by deep *ambiguity*. Thus the human quest for autonomy is, in fact, only one of two elements in a dynamic situation marked by *inner conflict*. That situation is the human existential predicament, torn as it is *between autonomy and heteronomy*. In Tillich's view, only the revelation of God can overcome the conflict, by enabling human reason to both integrate and transcend the conflicting biases of autonomy and heteronomy [q], and thus to redefine its new,

---

[p] Here also lies the root of the modern identification, so widespread in North America, of faith in God with "religious experience." This experience tends to be viewed as a completely inner event—that is, an event to be interpreted entirely on its own terms. Thus religion (and presumably, faith in God) is turned into an individual claim, whose sole verification is the authenticity of the individual who makes it. (Needless to say, this idea has profoundly affected the discipline usually referred to as "psychology of religion.") In this construction, faith in God, along with whatever interpretative knowledge of God goes with it, is radically divorced, in Cartesian fashion, from the shared human understanding of humanity and the world. Nicholas Lash, in his brilliant book *Easter in Ordinary*, has demonstrated how untenable this proposition really is.

[q] The word "overcoming" (*Systematic Theology*, I, p. 147) is an instance of the agonistic, masculine bias that governs Tillich's theological idiom. Consistent with it, Tillich views faith in terms of valor ("courage") and revelation in terms of victory; the same bias also causes him to cast the relationship between God and humanity in terms of non-acceptance and judgment (cf. F. J. van Beeck, *Christ Proclaimed*, pp. 202-17). There are good theological reasons, some of which can be drawn from Tillich's own treatment of the subject in the third volume of his *Systematic Theology*, to view theonomy as bringing about the "resolution" (rather than the "overcoming") of the ambiguity inherent in autonomy and heteronomy.

regenerate, and authentic self in terms of *theonomy* [r].

[b] Tillich's enlightening analysis of the human religious predicament in terms of the dialectic between human autonomy and heteronomy—a dialectic that will find its balance only in the acceptance of theonomy—deserves a wider application [s]. Thus it can be turned to good use as a way to illuminate the dynamics of growth and development inherent in the Christian life itself (§§53-54), inasmuch as it is a transition from nature to grace (cf. §76, 1).

Pistics are right to receive the Christian faith as a gift, in dependence on ecclesial assurance, which they accepted on the authority of God. Still, in doing so they are tempted to do an injustice to the inalienable demands for autonomy inherent in their own natural, God-given humanity. Charismatics are in a different position. In seeking to appropriate their Christian faith as an immediate, actual concern and take it seriously, they are right to claim their responsibility, and in that sense, their autonomy. Yet by the same token they find themselves tempted to do an injustice to the full compass of the Christian faith, which, as the gift of the Spirit, remains the transcendent measure of all individual Christians and associations of Christians, and even of the Christian Church as a whole.

Only in the mystical form of faith do nature and grace meet in perfect harmony, as humanity truly comes into its own, on the

---

[r] Tillich is less successful in the way he *applies* his insight to actual persons and movements in the history of Christian life and thought. To mention one instance, while it is easy to see why he should classify Bonaventure's contribution as theonomous, it is hard to understand why Aquinas should find his work mentioned as an example of heteronomous thought (*Systematic Theology*, I, p. 85).

[s] Thus David Novak (*Jewish-Christian Dialogue*, p. 149) has applied Tillich's conception to morality, by taking on Kant's contention that moral commandments are autonomously established: "... if morality is the person's hearkening to a voice—which is the only way to maintain the centrality of personhood and future—then it is preferable to hearken to the voice of God than to the voice of any other creature, even one's own self. For what autonomy gains in terms of its independent will, it loses in terms of its connection with a world already there; and what heteronomy (the voice of some other creature) gains in terms of this connection, it loses in terms of the significance of personal action per se. Only theonomy (hearkening to the voice of God) can overcome this antinomy by a prior transcendence of its two disjuncts. The human response to God's voice can be only from freedom, which mediates between a heteronomy that would eliminate personal response and an autonomy that would reduce each person to an individual, unconnected to either history or nature. Autonomy is silent; heteronomy is deafening."

strength of total dependence on God. This occurs as, stirred by
God's sovereign grace, human persons engage themselves in acts
of unconditional faith-abandon. Thus they do justice to God,
according to the measure available to them, in the selfless silence of prayer of naked intent on God [*t*], of self-sacrificing
love of others, of naked ignorance in the search for understanding (cf. §36, 2; §49, 1, e; §67, 2-3). And in thus abandoning
themselves to God, or even to others for the sake of God, what
they also find is a new relational self; their deepest identity,
filled to overflowing, turns out to have an ability they barely, if
at all, suspected: the capacity for total abandon of self. That
capacity is the ability to obey God (*potentia oboedientialis*) that
coincides with a person's deepest identity. The *actual* experience of theonomy, in other words, is mysticism.

[2] In encouraging natural theology, therefore, the catholic tradition is not encouraging a proud humanity to claim its autonomy.
Even less is it replacing redemption by emancipation, by inspiring
a long-oppressed humanity, finally conscious of its maturity, to
claim its legitimate destiny, by wresting its native right to understand and control itself and the world from the grip of a jealous
heaven bent on mind-control and domination. Here lies the profound difference of *agenda* between catholic theology's devotion to
the natural order and some of the great modern Western human-
isms, both rational and romantic, whether of the Deist or atheist
variety (cf. §25, 4, d).

[a] The Deist tradition, which is so much part of the cultural
sensibilities of North America, tends to overlook this essential
difference. Its interest in natural theology, it must be remembered, is not rooted in medieval scholasticism's assurance about
the harmony between grace and nature, and between faith and
reason. Rather, it is the fruit of a late-seventeenth century mentality that was convinced of the exact opposite: the expectation
that scientific reasonableness and biblical simplicity were the
guarantee of truth and harmony, while the certainty of division
and controversy lay with allegedly revealed, dogmatic Christian

---

[*t*] Cf., for example, the expression in *The Book of Privy Counselling* (*The Cloud of
Unknowing and the Book of Privy Counselling*, ed. Hodgson, p. 135/19-21): "... and
see to it that nothing remain in your active mind, except a naked intent reaching
out to God."

faith, especially where the doctrine of divine grace was concerned [u]. As a result, Deism came to insist that the purely
natural and the purely reasonable coincide with the true, the
substantive, and the divine (cf. §28, 1-2).

In keeping with this, Deism has consistently tended to expose
any particular, "positive" order of grace (or "revelation") as, at
worst, a leftover from an unenlightened, unreasonable, "dogmatic," sectarian age, and at best, a provisional, non-essential, logically unnecessary, debatable, opinionated interpretation of what
is in reality one single, all-inclusively *natural* order (cf. §30, 2;
§23, 3, b). In practicing natural theology today, therefore, catholic theology, especially in North America, must be sensibly distrustful of too much acceptance or applause from the side of
modern Deism (§80, 4, [d]) [v]. This is all the more urgent
if it is remembered that some Roman Catholic theology remains

---

[u] Michael J. Buckley has shown (*At the Origins of Modern Atheism*, pp. 42-67) that
Catholic theologians very much helped prepare the ground for this dubious development, by abdicating, as early as the beginning of the seventeenth century, their
responsibility for the fundamental question of God's existence. As a result, not
Christian theology in its integrity, but the emerging natural science and the new,
critical philosophy became the exclusive, authoritative warrants for God's existence. Typical examples of the tendency are the Jesuit Leonard Lessius and the
Minim Marin Mersenne, both of whom resolutely made the god-question a matter
of, respectively, philosophy and modern science (cf. §56, 3; §68, 1, [l]; §99, 3, a).
Thus it was partly under Catholic auspices that a new concept of God, both purely
natural and radically Deist, was made pivotal, on the one hand, to the astounding
discoveries of the mechanics of the solar system, and on the other hand, to the
analysis of the human mind's operation on the physical world. On this issue, cf.
§96, 2, [a]; cf. also §66, 3, a.

[v] An important contemporary example. The eagerness with which much of
Karl Rahner's transcendental theological anthropology (and especially his concept
of "anonymous Christianity") has been hailed in modernist and almost-modernist
circles should make us skeptical (cf. §22, 3, d). This is all the more urgent because the applause is also anything but justified: Rahner unfailingly insists, against
Deism, that the transcendental is not available apart from the historical, the categorical, and the truly revelatory (cf., for example, *Grundkurs*, pp. 157-65; ET *Foundations of Faith*, pp. 153-61). In fact, the agenda behind his concept of "anonymous Christianity" is the opposite of Deism. Rahner developed it in the interest
of a *confessional*, thoroughly *Christian, theological* interpretation of the plight of the
upright non-Christian; consequently, far from creating a presumption against the
necessity of the explicitly Christian proclamation, it positively warrants it (cf. §64,
4, c; cf. also F. J. van Beeck, *Christ Proclaimed*, p. 450). Any Deist reduction of Rahner's transcendentalism, therefore, amounts to a misinterpretation. It remains
true, of course, that the misinterpretation can point to real affinities, on Rahner's
part, with the concerns of the Enlightenment (§22, 3, a); in fact, some of the
systemic weaknesses in Rahner's work are not unconnected with this (cf. §56, 5).

itself to be purged from a residual indebtedness to rationalism—a subject to which we must revert (cf. §55, 3, a, [s]).

[3] If the catholic interpretation of the universe, therefore, sees no
irremediable depravity in Adam and Eve deciding to eat from the
tree of the knowledge of good and evil, or, for that matter, in Prometheus stealing the heavenly fire, this is not because it interprets
them as symbols of an authentic humanism. Nor does the catholic
tradition view Adam and Eve and Prometheus as timeless exemplifi-
cations of a purely *developmental* naturalism. That naturalism holds
that moral failure and rebellion against established values are only
natural, and even desirable, in human beings, as long as they struggle to find themselves. Naturalism tends to think that, while failure
and rebellion are usually inconsiderate, and sometimes tragic, they
are essentially innocent; they simply are a necessary and thus a-mor-
al developmental phase—the price to be paid for any growth toward
authenticity, whether individual or social: "You have to do what you
have to do."

The catholic tradition is a little more reflective about what is
natural. What happens frequently, as a matter of naked fact, is not
necessarily what is truly natural and thus normative. Hence the
catholic tradition is not so sanguine about what is merely normal or
habitual in practice. In the light of past conversion and present
faith, it interprets Adam and Eve, as well as Prometheus, as the
embodiments of humanity's turn against God in sinful pride. It
recognizes this pride as contrary to the very dynamics of natural
existence, and hence, as essentially sense-less and incomprehensible. Consequently, the catholic tradition views the human claim
to total autonomy as directed against the nature of humanity itself,
and thus as self-defeating—as a gesture of self-defeat that is, ultimately, self-punishing. Thus the catholic tradition proposes Adam
and Eve, and Prometheus, neither for rejection nor for admiration,
but for acknowledgment and acceptance, in enlightened repentance, as exemplary companions in humanity's *immemorial, misguided
insistence on total autonomy.*

In the light of *present faith in the God of grace,* therefore, the catholic tradition, true to its Jewish roots, professes that there never has
been, in the natural order, any genuine *need* to rebel—to steal the
fire or to eat of the fruit—so as to be like God.

[4] In accordance with this, *the catholic tradition tends not to dignify
sin by magnifying it by an excess of righteous indignation.* True catholi-

cism, in other words, need not prove to itself, to its own moral satisfaction, how firmly it rejects sin. It considers Adam and Eve and Prometheus not so much perverse as blinded, not so much dead as wounded, not objects of wrath so much as compassion. For sin is as contradictory, and hence as futile and senseless, as it is perverse. It consists in humanity's attempt to steal from God's hand, by force and once and for all, the very treasure that God's hand has forever been seeking to entrust to humanity as its very own, from the very beginning. Humanity's native spark of intelligence and its native aptitude for creation—the natural gifts that forever identify human persons as made in the image of the unseen God—have always warranted trust in God, never protest against God.

For that very reason, too, the great Tradition has continued to discern, even in the state of humanity's self-induced slavery, the enduring signs of its original affinity with God: the continued (if ineffectual) desire to understand truth and the persistent urge to create goodness. Even as, chained to the rock face, Prometheus is suffering while his vitals are eaten out, and even as, driven from Paradise, Adam and Eve are living in a world of toil and violence, they continue to appeal to the empathy of common humanity—a sign that the original blessings are not entirely cancelled. Exiled humanity continues to give evidence of the dear, native things that mark human persons forever, through thick and thin, as born for citizenship in a world marked by the divine presence. Human persons are still motivated, if ever so unreliably in their fallen state, to have visions for the earth and to forge the implements of culture, as the living God's representatives and as fiduciaries of the world.

[5] It has often been proposed, especially by theologians dedicated to the Reformed tradition, that catholicism cultivates naturalism. The present chapter has argued that such naturalism as the mainstream catholic tradition has espoused is, in the last analysis, sponsored by Christian faith and in the service of Christian faith.

This interpretation of the catholic tradition must guide contemporary catholic fundamental theology as well. Three issues present themselves for special treatment under this rubric. What are the possibilities and standards for fundamental theology in today's culture? What must be the nature and the scope of Christian apologetics today? And finally and most importantly: If the great Tradition insists that the order of grace is the fruit of God's *special* revelation, is this compatible with the world picture of contemporary science and philosophy (or indeed with any coherent world picture), and if so, how? These issues remain to be explored in the eighth and final chapter of this first part of the second volume of *God Encountered*.

However, the philosophical and theological groundwork for this exploration must be laid first, in the next chapter.

Humanity's Natural Desire for God

THE CATHOLIC TRADITION AND THE MODERN STRUGGLE FOR AUTHENTICITY

[§85] BLONDEL: CATHOLIC FAITH SPONSORING FREEDOM OF THOUGHT

[1] In 1896, over a period of more than six months, a lengthy essay appeared in six installments, in the respected Catholic French journal *Annales de Philosophie chrétienne.* Its author was Maurice Blondel, a young professor of philosophy at Aix-en-Provence. The piece has become known, not by the unwieldy title under which it was published, but by the designation of "Blondel's Letter on Apologetics."

Less than three years before, on June 7, 1893, at the age of thirty-two, Blondel had defended his doctoral dissertation in philosophy at the Sorbonne—that is to say, in an academic environment devoted to principled *laïcisme,* firmly outside the sphere of influence of the Ultramontanist Catholicism that held the day. The work, a trailblazing phenomenology of the dynamics of the human spirit, under the title *L'Action,* took an appreciable segment of France's intelligentsia by storm. There were those, in fact, who thought, right from the start, that the project was striking enough to invite comparisons with what the young Hegel had first undertaken in his *Phenomenology of Mind,* almost a century before. Respectable Catholic journals had expressed their admiration, as a thankful Blondel was to recall many years later.

However, there had been other reactions as well. One of them was a cautious review-article in the September, 1895 issue of the *Annales de Philosophie chrétienne,* by its newly appointed editor, the Reverend Charles Denis. Denis had extended a carefully measured welcome to *L'Action.* He recognized, as others had done, that Blondel had placed himself in the company of the foremost Catholic French thinkers of the day, but he was unhappy with the fact that he had abandoned the proven method of apologetics. Catholic apologists had long (and, Denis implied, rightly) insisted on grounding the Christian faith on solid proofs of *metaphysical* import. In that way, apologetics had succeeded in showing that a true, fundamental understanding of *objective reality* led to the conclusion that truth was on the side of the Catholic faith. This in turn had enabled Catholic thinkers to insist, against all the fashionable claims of the modern age, that it was impossible to claim intellectual integrity while at the same time persisting in unbelief. No wonder the editor had been disappointed to find that Blondel had—dangerously—attempted "to disengage apologetics from its ancient forms of argument, and to move it to the area [that was] properly and exclusively psychological."[1]

The polite criticism formulated by the editor of the *Annales* may have been a bit worried; it was also genuinely probing. The same could not be said of some other, far less tentative, responses from less congenial quarters. In one of them, the idealist philosopher Léon Brunschvicg, while acknowledging "the sincerity, the breadth of conception, the dialectical subtlety of M. Blondel," had frankly (if anonymously) advised him to drop his illusions: he was likely to find, among his rationalist and laicist friends and associates, "courteous, but resolute opponents" of what he had to say, in *L'Action*, about the human spirit's fundamental openness to faith. Blondel had found out: the reservations expressed at the Sorbonne had become tangible, as for two years he had vainly looked for a teaching position in the state-sponsored higher education system, which kept turning him down under the pretext that he was doing, not philosophy, but apologetics.[2]

[2] While appreciating the honor implicit in being taken seriously, Blondel had found himself in this way a solitary target in the no man's land created and anxiously maintained by two opposing dogmatisms: anticlerical, Deist laicism and defensive, clericalized Catholicism. He had protested at once, and in the direction of the side that mattered most to him—the world of Catholic learning. At a much later date, the serenity of hindsight enabled him to recall how he had found himself caught, on that side, in a quagmire he had wanted no part of:

These various interpretations were a precious source of encouragement to me. However, they also made me realize, by their very praise as well as by their hesitations and reservations, to how severe a danger my thought was exposed, if the strictly rational conception that I had thought out was moved out of the domain of philosophy, *to which it should be restricted.* In a doctoral thesis defended at the Sorbonne, it had not been my wish to venture, nor did I in fact venture, out on to the slippery slopes of apologetics [*les pentes glissantes de l'apologétique*]. I absolutely did not claim, as people were apparently afraid I was doing, that I was drawing anything in the way of the truths of revelation from nature and reason, or postulating the existence of the order of grace.[3]

[3] Back in 1895, his immediate reaction had been less reflective and a bit more direct. In a letter to the editor, published in the *Annales* of November, 1895, he had pointed out that *L'Action* was being misunderstood. Appealing to his right of rejoinder, he had requested that the editor allow him to explain himself at length, in the foremost journal of Catholic philosophy in France, the *Annales.* And with an honesty as ominous as it was elegant, he had served notice of the challenge he meant to offer. He had done so by implying that the arguments for Christianity traditionally advanced by Catholic apologetics were far too convenient and serviceable, and especially, far too much out of touch with the temper of the times, to qualify as genuine philosophy [*a*]. For that reason, he had roundly forewarned the editor, he wanted to be heard, not as a traditional apologist for the Catholic faith, but as an advocate of *the integrity of philosophical method.* However, he had suggested— surprisingly for a man educated at the *École Normale Supérieure*—a *theological* concern as well: he would be writing as one who did consider the Catholic faith too important to have its credibility damaged by spurious argument and special pleading. Thus he had written:

In the area of the certainties of reason, [this question of philosophical method] is of the highest importance. I would envision explaining why apologetical philosophy, *precisely for the sake of the conclusions for which it prepares the ground or which it makes allowable,* may not become a philosophical apologetic. To put this bluntly, *there is nothing philosophical to something that is simply a tool or a means to an end.*[4]

[*a*] Blondel was to explain, in the *Letter* itself (*Les premiers écrits de Maurice Blondel,* p. 8; ET in *The Letter on Apologetics* and *History and Dogma,* p. 130), that in his opinion the principal problem with philosophical apologetics as practiced by Catholic theologians was not that it was wrong (*une philosophie fausse*), but that it was phony (*une fausse philosophie*).

The gauntlet thrown down, Blondel set to work. His detailed rejoinder appeared between January and July of the next year. It was entitled "Letter on the Requirements of Contemporary Thought in the Matter of Apologetics, and on Philosophical Method in the Study of the Problem of Religion."[5] Cumbersome as it was, the title served to keep the piece's *twofold agenda* in focus: Catholic thinkers had to take *modern thought* seriously, and they had to prove their own integrity by adopting *a philosophical method* that contemporary scholars would have to respect as truly philosophical—that is, as genuinely inquiring, and thus, as free and unprejudiced.

[4] Blondel's plea in favor of genuinely philosophical method was straightforwardly philosophical, and in that sense also academic, in nature. If philosophical thought was to convince it must be free even from the suspicion of dutifulness and ulterior motive; if philosophy was to serve theology in the role of a handmaiden, he obviously felt, it had to be free: *non ancilla nisi libera*. Minimally, therefore, philosophical reflection practiced in the service of religion must be seen to be studiously unprejudiced and impartial. There is never any doubt, therefore, that Blondel meant to speak as a philosopher, *and only as a philosopher*, even where his theme was religion, and the Catholic religion in particular. Still, in all of this he meant in no way to prescind from the fact that he was a Christian and a Catholic. For deep down, Blondel's plea for freedom of thought in philosophical apologetics was inspired by an agenda of far broader significance: he was aiming at the reversal of the siege-mentality prevalent in the contemporary Catholic Church.

Blondel elaborates this latter, cultural-theological part of his purpose in writing only when he has almost finished reviewing the various systems of Catholic apologetics current at the time and explaining the philosophical problems connected with them. Significantly, he places his call for catholic openness in the context of his critique of the last system he has reviewed—that is, the one prevailing in the Catholic Church: seminary theology of the neo-Thomistic variety (§86, 3) [b]. *There*, he obviously thinks, lies the principal

---

[b] Blondel quotes a newspaper report to identify this variety of apologetics (*Les premiers écrits de Maurice Blondel*, p. 26; ET in *The Letter on Apologetics* and *History and Dogma*, p. 145): it is the whole complex of arguments that "is precisely «what is taught at the start of theology as a whole, in the treatise on religion»" ("celle même «qu'on donne au commencement de toute théologie dans le traité de la religion»"). This was, of course, the well-known seminary treatise in fundamental theology, *De vera religione*.

problem; *there* Catholic thought stands most in need of having its intellectual integrity challenged by honest philosophy.

The Thomistic system of apologetics, Blondel explains, is far too *static* to inspire and support truly dynamic flights of thought—it provides "an inventory without inventiveness."[6] Such an apologetics may very well add up to an imposing fortress of triumphant coherence, but it fails to convince anyone who is not already inside the fortress. More importantly, it misreads the cultural situation we are in, and in doing so, it is making a *theological* mistake:

> Let us not waste our energy rehearsing the well-known arguments, and presenting [for acceptance] an *object*, whereas [the problem is that] the *subject* is not disposed [to listen]. The fault is never on the side of divine truth; it is on the side of human disposition, and it is there that the endeavor to offer arguments must be brought to bear. And this is not just a matter of adaptation, or of a merely temporary expedient; for this task of predisposing the subject is of the first importance, it goes to the essence and it is permanent, if it is true that human activity cooperates across the board with God's activity.[7]

[5] Blondel plainly shows that he recognizes that the modern "turn to the subject" (*die Wende zum Subjekt*) is a cultural *fait accompli*, and one of historic proportions. Modern culture, especially since the Enlightenment, has discovered the theme of *human authenticity*, and it is not about to surrender what it has struggled so painfully to find. Serious modern thinkers, therefore, rightly refuse to associate with the authority of (allegedly) the faith of the past if the price of the association is the forfeiture of *human integrity* in the present. Thus it is pointless for the Church and its theologians to keep on rehearsing (allegedly) eternal philosophical and theological truths. The only result this accomplishes is for the Church and its thinkers *to date themselves*: the very way they speak shows that they belong to the past—to that period of history that used to be unconscious of *the power of human subjectivity* so recently discovered, *and thus of historicity itself* (cf. §22, 3, c) [c].

---

[c] Blondel met this latter subject head on in *Histoire et dogme*, published in 1904 (*Les premiers écrits de Maurice Blondel*, pp. 149-228; ET *The Letter on Apologetics* and *History and Dogma*, pp. 221-87). Note the essential link between the theme of native human integrity dynamically understood (in Blondel's idiom, "immanence") and historical consciousness. Karl Rahner, too, has consistently insisted on this link, by pointing out that the transcendental point of departure of his theology, far from being a timeless truth, is predicated on the acknowledgment of an *historic* development: humanity's entering upon a new phase of consciousness of self (cf.

Now this, Blondel suggests, is the kind of situation where the Catholic Church must draw on its rich experience of Tradition. This is where it must show that it understands the dynamics of historical process; this is where it must also make a choice of historic import. Will it settle for unhistorical stagnation and siege, and keep rushing into judgment, seeing nothing but "deviations, «perverted minds», or «diseases of reason»" out there, in the surrounding culture? Will it continue to denounce the mistakes of the present in the name of an allegedly authoritative past? Or will it discern that "little by little, God's design in the conduct of humanity emerges from individual errors, fragmentary vistas, and the failures characteristic of one mind or another"?[8] Will it go out of its way and offer genuine understanding to the struggling present, so as to open the way to a future that will bear fresh fruits of *both* faith *and* reason?

Blondel has no hesitation about the direction that is to be taken. With an unmistakable appeal to the Christian conscience formed by the Scriptures, he urges, prophetically, that

... we attempt to discern the stress of travail that unceasingly shakes humanity [cf. Rom 8, 19-22], and we do everything to profit from this immense struggle, to illuminate it, to help bring it to fruition, to light the wick that is already smoking [cf. Mt 12, 20; Is 42, 3], not to be quick to believe that there is nothing beneficial to ourselves in those teachings that are most opposed to our own, to get used to others so as to get them used to us [cf. Mt 7, 12]. And thus we will find the source of intellectual fecundity.[9]

[6] We must recall that Blondel is writing in the middle of the period marked by the Catholic fortress-mentality—the period that was yet to culminate in a blind, undiscerning, integralist war on even the suspicion of modernism (cf. §20, 4, a). When this is realized, Blondel's Letter appears in its proper light—that is, as one of the original calls for an end to Catholic triumphalism. That

---

§9, 1, a). (This consciousness, it might be added in passing, is also manifested in the modern acceptance of the dignity of the person as the basis of human rights.) Like his fellow "transcendental neo-Thomists," from Pierre Rousselot and Joseph Maréchal on, Rahner reread and reinterpreted Aquinas in the light of this modern consciousness, looking for possible warrants, in the great Tradition and specifically in Aquinas, for his transcendental method. The first fruits of that search were *Hörer des Wortes* (ET *Hearers of the Word*) and *Geist in Welt* (ET *Spirit in the World*). On the whole subject, cf. Otto Muck, *Die transzendentale Methode in der scholastischen Philosophie der Gegenwart* (ET *The Transcendental Method*).

triumphalism, of course, was in reality a painful, anxious, deeply rooted defensiveness (§29, 4-5). Blondel is indeed one of the first to sound the theme that—decades later—was to put an end to the intellectual and cultural exile of the Catholic establishment—the theme that Pope John XXIII was to intone and the Second Vatican Council was to play fully orchestrated, in the Pastoral Constitution on the Church in the Modern World, *Gaudium et Spes*: the Word of God impels the Church to serve humanity and the world, not to dominate or condemn them, and the Church can do so only if, at bottom, it recognizes and cherishes both of them in their natural integrity. That is, the Church must encourage, not denounce, humanity in its natural struggle for wisdom and harmony, no matter how misguided it may often turn out to be. It must trust, not only that authenticity will lead to God, but also that genuine wisdom and harmony, *both natural and supernatural*, in the Church itself are the fruit of catholic openness to the world as it searches, not of dogmatic defensiveness against the world as it fails to find.

[7] It is against this background of Catholic faith-conviction that Blondel develops his case for "threshold apologetics" (*l'apologétique du seuil*): a bold, genuine—that is to say, a free and independent—*philosophical anthropology*, practiced right on the doorstep of the house of Christian faith. Such a philosophy, devoted to the exploration of fundamental human integrity, will discover that the native dynamism from which all human activity springs also harbors a native "human predisposition" to faith. In doing so, it will act on the ancient Christian assurance that God's generosity is never problematic, and that far from imprisoning and controlling the authentic dynamism of human persons, faith is meant to set it free, so that human activity can genuinely be shown to "cooperate across the board with God's activity."

In this way, one of Blondel's first writings has provided us with yet another instance of *the age-old Christian faith recovering its own native, authentic vitality by opening itself to the world*. And the proof of the authenticity of this revival is as old as the faith itself: faith will turn out to embrace and cherish the natural order; it will demonstrate that it is no threat to nature; it invariably intends to sponsor natural reason, and to encourage it to go to the very limits of its natural capacity. In this way the catholic faith conveys that it trusts human reason to rediscover for itself that it is an *intellectus quærens fidem*: a mind marked by a native capacity for dynamic self-transcendence towards God (cf. §12, 1, a; §67, 5; §81, 1).

[a] In opting for this strongly philosophical approach to the problem of the Christian faith's relationship with modern culture in the years, roughly, between 1890 and 1950, Blondel places himself squarely in the Roman Catholic theological tradition, always devoted to philosophy as a distinct discipline. In the long run, the approach inaugurated by Blondel proved to be very fruitful, as the present chapter will show. Still, it is only fair to note that alternative approaches were successfully attempted in other catholic traditions. To mention one illuminating instance, the Anglo-Catholic theology of the period, while dealing with the same fundamental cultural-theological issues, succeeded in framing them in far more positive-theological terms, with distinctive results. In his book *From Gore to Temple*, Archbishop Arthur Michael Ramsey has left us a wise and lucid account of an extraordinarily fruitful half-century (1889-1939) in Anglican theology, during which period Catholic theology was not a little stunted by anti-Modernist rationalism of a very authoritarian kind.

[8] We can now turn to the other part of Blondel's agenda: his plea for an acceptable philosophical approach to religion—that is, for an apologetics that will be able to stand the modern test of human authenticity. To appreciate this, we must first seek to understand the type of Catholic apologetics that Blondel found in his way.

[§86] THE FAILURE OF RATIONALIST-HISTORICIST APOLOGETICS

[1] In the first part of the Letter on Apologetics, Blondel reviews five different types of apologetics currently, or at least recently, in use in late nineteenth-century Catholicism. All of them, he explains, are unsatisfactory.

In the first place, Blondel explains, the view that the findings of *natural science* can furnish the human mind with an acceptable philosophical apologetic for the Christian faith has been abandoned [d]. Believers will have to learn that it is a pre-critical

---

[d] Michael J. Buckley has shown (*At the Origins of Modern Atheism*, pp. 194-321) that the warrants for certainty about God as the initiator of the universe, based on Cartesian philosophy and associated with thinkers like Marin Mersenne and Isaac Newton, gave way, in the eighteenth century, to an overwhelming sense of the chaotic irrationality of the dynamics of physical reality (§84, 2, a, [u]; §99, 3, a). Thus the theologian's former reliance on the discoveries of science proved to be

category mistake to appeal to God as the direct explanation of any natural realities as observed and understood by means of scientific method (cf. §103, 1) [e].

Secondly, Blondel reviews three kinds of apologetical arguments associated, broadly, with various nineteenth-century forms of traditionalism and fideism especially favored in France (§12, 1, a; §25, 4, a). All of these types of arguments are based on the observation that Christianity, as a matter of historical fact, has proved strikingly suitable and beneficial to humanity. In other words, the *practical* experience of the blessings of Christian life and civilization has many honorable people persuaded of Christianity's *truth* as well. It is not surprising, therefore, that attempts should have been made to turn the experience of historic Christianity into a coherent *theoretical* apologetics in its favor.

However, it is not difficult to see why Blondel should have considered this kind of apologetics a mistake. After all, the historic benefits reaped from the Christian faith may just be incidental to it. In other words, the appeal to the blessings of the historic Christian tradition gives no reliable insight into the *fundamental* relation between humanity and Christian revelation. In fact, it may do the opposite, for insisting on this argument may end up confusing humanity and God. First of all, it casts doubt on the natural order by suggesting that human nature is *essentially* unfinished and human reason *essentially* unreliable, and that we have the historical record to prove that humanity stands in *essential* need of positive revelation to attain to the truth. But if this is true, then, secondly, it makes no sense for the Church to continue to claim that faith is God's

---

a double-edged sword: it ended up disproving the existence of God as much as it had once served to prove it. This supported the later, more theoretical realization— Kant's philosophy is a prime example—that there is a gap between, on the one hand, the scientific understanding of the natural order in terms of establishable chains of causes and effects, and, on the other hand, the philosophical and theological understanding of causality in terms of a Creator-God attained as both transcendent and immanent. The two belong in two different categories. Though living in the pre-scientific age, Aquinas had already suggested this when he distinguished between *causa prima* and *causæ secundæ* (cf., e.g., *S. Th.* I, 19, 8, *in c.*; I-II, 19, 4, *in c.*). Cf. §66, 3, a; §68, 1.

[e] The end of this development is marked, as is well known, by a thinker like Dietrich Bonhoeffer, who rightly welcomes modern secularization, because it unmasks as irrelevant the "god" that serves only as the ultimate explanation of scientifically treatable phenomena. Such a god is nothing but a "working-hypothesis" god, and indeed, a "stopgap" god, to be called on, by way of relief, only in emergency situations. Cf. *Widerstand und Ergebung* (ET *Letters and Papers from Prison*), under July 16 and August 3, 1944.

free, supernatural gift; from the point of view of Christian theology, a divine revelation *intrinsically required by human nature* cannot be called either supernatural or wholly transcendent in origin and nature. For all these reasons, the various arguments in favor of the Christian faith current among the traditionalists and fideists do not amount to a valid apologetics. Finally, from a strictly philosophical point of view, these arguments are especially unacceptable: they build the faith on a foundation of human incompetence treated as integral to humanity. It is only right that they should fail to find a hearing among modern, humanistic unbelievers.[10]

[2] Lastly, Blondel mentions, though without much elaboration, a fifth system of apologetics—one, however, that he appears to regard as critically important: the philosophical apologetics associated with the neo-scholasticism of, ultimately, Thomistic extraction (cf. §85, 4). Along with its background and its content, this fifth system calls for our special attention, if we are to appreciate the full significance of Blondel's retrieval of the great Tradition's approach to apologetics.

[a] Let us open our lengthy treatment of this fifth system of apologetics—that is, the (neo-)scholastic one—on a note of prospect. At the end of the present discussion (cf. §86, 6, b-d), this scholastic system will turn out to combine the principal features of the four types already rejected by Blondel. For on the one hand it is based on a definition of miracle that is scientifically dated as well as theologically inept (cf. §86, 6, f); on the other hand it will prove to rely, in the last resort, on an all-encompassing fideistic-traditionalistic premise.

[b] Three interrelated themes must concern us in our attempt to understand the system: (1) the characteristics of nineteenth-century *Thomism*, (2) the teaching of the *First Vatican Council* on faith and reason, and (3) the basic structures of *the accepted rationalist-historicist Catholic apologetics*—the system of apologetics from which Blondel felt he had to take his distance, even though it appealed to both Thomism and the First Vatican Council as authorities.

[c] Understanding this complex of issues and influences is essential if we wish to appreciate Blondel's achievement in proposing a more adequate apologetics; more importantly, however, it is integral to an adequate interpretation of Vatican II, which is

part of the stated agenda of *God Encountered* (§23, 5). This can be made clear, again, on three counts. First of all, the Catholic apologetics that regarded itself as legitimately and authoritatively Thomistic remained an influence to be reckoned with for well over half a century after Blondel first called for its demise; in fact, it was a decisive (if ultimately ineffectual) influence in the preparation of the agenda of the Second Vatican Council. Secondly, both the agenda and the teaching of Vatican II were decisively influenced by the achievement of Vatican I. Thirdly, while Vatican II did not discredit scholasticism, it took its distance from its disproportionate dominance in ecclesiastical studies; moreover, it ended up accepting a radically recast variety of it— one that had taken to heart Blondel's call for "immanence" and openness to the culture (cf. §86, 6, e).

[3]   Contrary to currently prevailing stereotypes, late nineteenth and early twentieth century Catholic seminary philosophy and theology of the (broadly) Thomistic variety (cf. §85, 4) was *not* a completely uniform, standardized system. It was, rather, a sprawling aggregate of various schools of neo-scholastic thought [*f*]. Each of the schools had somewhat of a distinctive style of its own in providing systematic expositions, in scholastic fashion, of all of Catholic philosophy and theology. What these expository systems—many of them available in the form of Latin manuals, some of them even offering *cursus completi* of philosophy and theology [*g*]—did have in common was devotion to orthodoxy in all matters connected with Roman Catholic dogma. At the same time, however, they kept up at least a semblance of intellectual freedom by cultivating a fairly significant area of free questions (cf. §72, 4, d), vigorously—and by

---

[*f*] The principal schools were the Thomists (mostly associated with the Dominicans), the Scotists (mostly Franciscans loyal to the heritage of Blessed Johannes Duns Scotus, and further back, of Saint Bonaventure), and the Suarezians (mainly Jesuits, after the Spaniard Francisco Suarez, whose baroque synthesis showed features of both).

[*g*] For a characteristic example, cf. the tripartite series, in ten robust volumes, published in Spain in the nineteen-fifties under Jesuit sponsorship, and designed to carry out the Apostolic Constitution *Deus Scientiarum Dominus* promulgated by Pope Pius XI in 1931: *Philosophiæ scholasticæ summa ad mentem Constitutionis Apostolicæ "Deus Scientiarum Dominus"* (3 volumes), *Theologiæ moralis summa* (3 volumes, by Marcelino Zalba), and *Sacræ theologiæ summa: iuxta Constitutionem Apostolicam "Deus Scientiarum Dominus"* (4 volumes).

no means always charitably—debated among the various schools [h].

This whole array of scholasticism claimed the intellectual pedigree of Aquinas. In reality, however, its hegemony owed as much (if not indeed far more) to the reform of ecclesiastical studies along Thomistic lines mandated by Pope Leo XIII, in his very influential encyclical *Æterni Patris* of 1879 (DS 3135-3140).[11]

[a] The true agenda of this nineteenth and early twentieth century scholasticism, which continued to appeal to the authority of Thomas Aquinas, was the fight against rationalism. One of its prominent characteristics was a dogged inability to think of itself as one, and only one, approach to Roman Catholic theology; hence, it consistently failed to distinguish between itself and the great Tradition.[12] Not surprisingly, therefore, it taught conformity rather than a thoughtful reading of the Tradition. Thus neo-Thomism became a textbook example of *systematization in the service of exposition and control at least as much as understanding* (cf. §7). Previous developments had prepared it for this questionable role.

[b] In the sixteenth century, Thomism (pushed into the background and weakened by fourteenth and fifteenth century nominalism) experienced a major revival, at the hands of capable (if not always entirely reliable) commentators like John of Saint Thomas and Thomas de Vio—the latter better known as Cajetan. However, the revival also involved a critical transformation. Aquinas' original method had consisted in *raising questions, exploring arguments on both sides of every issue, and proposing responses* in the service of *new, shared understanding in dialogue with the great Tradition*. This method was now abandoned in the interest of *the stabilization of content*; Aquinas' work was rearranged so as to form a coherent *system of doctrine*; that is, it was made to look far more

---

[h] "Orthodoxy" in the *philosophical* area was imposed in 1914, by a *Motu proprio* of Pope Saint Pius X; it prescribed that the principles and the essential theses taught in philosophy should be those of Thomas Aquinas. In 1916, the Roman Congregation of Seminaries and Universities adopted the famous "24 Thomistic theses"; Pope Benedict XV confirmed the decision, which became law in 1917 (*Codex Iuris Canonici*, can. 1366, §2). Cf. Édouard Hugon, *Principes de philosophie: Les vint-quatre thèses thomistes*. Cf. also P. B. Grenet, *Les vint-quatre thèses thomistes (De l'évolution à l'existence)*. For a rather more inspired neo-scholastic rendition of the core theses of Thomist thought, cf. A. G. Sertillanges, *Les grandes thèses de la philosophie thomiste*.

consistent than it was. This, of course, also substantially transformed the *uses* to which Aquinas was put. Thomism (and scholasticism generally) was turned into a method, not of questioning and inquiry, but of *exposition and polemical argumentation*, in the service of drawing assured, *propositional conclusions from authoritative premises, natural or revealed.* This was done preferably by syllogistic means ("*Konklusionstheologie*"). One of the features of this system deserves special attention: in keeping with the temper of the age, it delighted in delimitation, distinction, and especially definition (cf. §7, 1, a-b). At this point, however, method decisively influenced substance, as firm lines of division were drawn everywhere, especially between the orders of nature and grace, at the expense of their organic unity, as proposed by, say, Aquinas (cf. §82, 3, [g]).

[c] A second transformation of Thomism had enhanced the more dubious features of the first. In mid and late eighteenth century Germany, Thomism additionally appropriated much of the rationalism of such important Protestant system-builders as Christian Wolff. That is to say, it tacitly accepted the contemporary axiom that Revelation had to be interpreted as completely separate from—and in that sense opposed to—Reason (cf. §94, 6, a). On the one hand, this move dispensed Reason from the task of understanding Revelation; this suited the mood of the prevailing pietism. On the other hand, it made it incumbent on Reason alone to demonstrate that accepting Revelation was the rational thing to do [i]. Accordingly, scholasticism developed a habit of proposing *compelling rational proofs for the credibility of the truly positive parts of the Christian faith*—that is to say, the parts that had to be accepted by faith alone, as entirely owed to divine Revelation, and hence, as inaccessible to genuine understanding. Consequently, it was widely assumed that such proofs had best be *entirely extrinsic to the order of Revelation*; that is, they had best be *objectively conclusive as well as wholly accessible to natural reason* [j]. There was, of course, a fateful implication in all of

---

[i] For an illuminating account, cf. Charles H. Talbert's introduction to *Reimarus: Fragments* in the *Lives of Jesus Series*, pp. 1-43. Cf. also §94, 3, a, [aa].

[j] Cf. Gerald A. McCool, *Catholic Theology in the Nineteenth Century*, pp. 28-29 and bibliography; M.-D. Chenu, "Vérité évangélique et métaphysique wolffiennne à Vatican II." For a brief, candid summary of the methods and the doctrines that distinguish late nineteenth and early twentieth century Thomism from the procedures and teachings of Thomas Aquinas himself, cf. *LThK* 10, coll. 161-65.

this. In the eighteenth-century mind, Reason increasingly came to stand for human authenticity, in the form of sincerity, tolerance, and brotherly love (cf. §28, 4, a, [d]); on the rebound, Revelation came to be associated with its opposite: inauthenticity, in the form of hypocrisy, dogmatism, and strife.

[d] It has already been pointed out that one fateful feature of late nineteenth and early twentieth century Thomism was its lack of openness to the surrounding culture; it largely stayed in the Ultramontane ghetto, where it was also protected against the emergence of historical consciousness (§85, 5; cf. §22, 3, c). It is precisely this lack of historical perspective that became fateful to scholasticism. The neo-scholastics treated their teaching as timeless truth; it seldom seemed to occur to them to question their own earnest protestations of fidelity to Aquinas [k], who—to mention one crucial example—had never driven the distinction between Reason and Revelation to such an extreme. In this way, the methods of latter-day scholasticism no more guaranteed fidelity to Aquinas' thought than the late nineteenth century neo-Gothic style guaranteed faithfulness to the spirit embodied in the great medieval cathedrals. For the late-Romantic illusion was pervasive. The Catholic veneration of the Middle Ages (which was such a powerful expedient to ensure the Catholic "feel," not only in Catholicism, but also among the later English Tractarians) was a child of its age. Unbeknownst to itself, the scholasticism that appealed to the golden past was largely unhistorical: it was part of the concerted Ultramontanist effort to bring about a radical administrative and educational reform of the nineteenth-century Catholic Church, by means of a mythical reconstruction of the Middle Ages designed to promote a unified Catholic culture against the errors and liberties of the times.[13] But dangerously, underneath its medievalism, late nineteenth-century Thomism remained profoundly beholden to the two movements that had combined to produce such neuralgic conflicts in the divided eighteenth-century soul: rationalist naturalism and sentimentalist pietism.

---

[k] The encyclical *Humani generis* of 1950 contains an eloquent instance of this undiscerning "fidelity": DS 3894 (*HG*, pp. 32-35). Not surprisingly, it indignantly rejects the charge that the scholasticism it upholds is infected by rationalism.

[4] There was an important second source on which rationalist-historicist apologetics relied for its authority: the alleged teaching of Vatican I on the nature of the Christian faith.

In the third chapter of the Dogmatic Constitution *Dei Filius*, entitled *De fide* ("On Faith"), the Council had begun by emphasizing, with the great Tradition and against the rationalists, that faith is a spiritual, wholly supernatural gift: the inner witness of the Holy Spirit (DS 3008; CF 118). After that, the Council had proceeded, against the fideists, to treat of external testimonies:

Nevertheless, in order that "the obedience" of our faith might be "in harmony with reason" [cf. Rom 12, 1], God has willed that the internal assistance of the Holy Spirit be joined by external testimonies [*argumenta*] of his revelation: that is, divine doings [*facta divina*], and most of all, miracles and prophecies. Since these help clearly demonstrate [*luculenter commonstrent*] God's omnipotence and infinite knowledge, they are signs of divine revelation—signs most certain and suited to the understanding of all.[14]

The Council had further confirmed this teaching by citing, as examples of the teaching just proposed, Moses and the Prophets, and most of all, Christ the Lord. Finally, it had added a reference to signs performed by the Apostles, clinched by a New Testament quotation on prophecy (DS 3009; CF 119; cf. DS 3033-34; CF 127-28).

> [a] This text requires careful interpretation. Much as defensiveness was a prominent feature of Vatican I, and much as some of its most important theologians were representatives of a questionable nineteenth-century scholasticism, the Council carefully avoided committing the Catholic Church to any particular school of thought. Consequently, its affirmation of the probative force of external signs of credibility accessible to natural reason, especially miracles and prophecies, had never become an isolated proposition; it had been *one theme* in a whole complex of balanced, evenhanded theological affirmations on the faith—its supernaturalness as well as its reasonableness. In other words, unlike the rationalist-historicist apologetics that came to appeal to it, *Vatican I had never declared that unaided natural reason was necessary, let alone sufficient, to establish, beyond a reasonable or respectable doubt, the credibility of the Catholic faith on miracles and prophecies.*

[5] In interpreting the teaching of Vatican I, late nineteenth-century Catholic theologians and their disciples were not very careful.

Relying on a scholastic tradition infected by rationalism, they ended up constructing, on the basis of *one* of the Council's affirmations, a purely rationalist-historicist apologetics. This apologetics was presented as a purely natural preamble to the whole edifice of Catholic faith and theology, and claimed to be both necessary and sufficient. In doing so, they suggested that the Catholic faith as a whole is something that it most certainly is not: *a closed system* capable of compelling all reasonable persons' assent—that is, a system capable of demanding that they accept the Catholic faith as credible *without appealing to anything in themselves other than the discursive intellect devoted to universally valid truths.*

Blondel sums up this approach to apologetics by quoting from a newspaper report on a recent conference on the situation of modern apologetics. The quotation could not provide a more accurate thumbnail sketch of the central contentions of the strictly rational-historical apologetics in defense of the Catholic faith current in the Catholic seminary theology of the day. It reads:

Reason demonstrates the existence of God. This God was able to reveal himself. History proves the fact of revelation; it also proves the authenticity of the Sacred Books and the authority of the Church. Thus catholicism can think of itself as established on a rational basis that is genuinely scholarly.[15]

[6] Thus the fundamental feature of accepted Catholic apologetics had become: the cocksure contention that the credibility of the Christian faith rested on a basis that was as rational and reliable (or so it was thought) as it was narrow: the purely philosophical arguments for the existence of an omnipotent God (cf. §84, 2, a, [*u*]), and the public and objective verification, by *miracle* and *prophecy*, of Catholic Christianity as divinely revealed [*l*]. A summary review

---

[*l*] In this type of apologetics, understanding was confused both with *the need for certainty* and with *the requirements of the classroom drill* (§21, 4, a; §7, 1, a). It is broadly, but fairly, characterized by A. Dulles, in his account of the Roman theologian Giovanni Perrone (*A History of Apologetics*, p. 183). Perrone's "apologetic [Dulles writes] lacks nothing by way of clarity and logic, but it rests on narrow and uncriticized assumptions. His step-by-step movement from natural theology to Christian revelation, while highly suitable to classroom presentation, fails to correspond to the actual process by which the mind progresses toward religious truth. Like other apologists of the time Perrone falls into a type of supernatural rationalism that grew out of a combination of medieval Scholasticism and Cartesian mathematicism. Bautain and Newman, whose work he corrected, would have had much to teach him."

of the structure of this type of Catholic apologetics must serve to detail and clarify this [m].

[a] Natural reason, it was taught, is readily capable of identifying both miracles and prophetic announcements of future events. The reason for this is that the former are departures from the laws of nature, whereas the latter are a challenge to the unknowability of specific future events. Since the laws of nature are naturally knowable by natural reason, miracles are naturally identifiable, precisely *as* departures from those laws; and since only God establishes the laws of nature (shades of Newton!), only God can suspend them in individual cases; thus the actual occurrence of miracles is accounted for only by recognizing direct divine interventions in the natural order. Prophecies, too, are naturally identifiable. Only God has knowledge of *futura contingentia* (contingent events that have not happened yet); hence only direct divine inspirations accorded to particular human persons can account for correct predictions. Now the Bible contains passages which the Magisterium has consistently interpreted as prophetic predictions; if it should turn out that the actual course of history has certified such prophecies as correct predictions, then such predictions would be naturally identifiable as due to divine intervention.

Hence, while the obviously *supernatural origin* behind both miracles and prophecies involves the strongest conceivable inducement to accept their *import* by *faith, reason itself* can *naturally identify* miracles and prophecies, as well as *know them with perfect certainty.* Whenever they occur, they *can* be recognized; once recognized, they naturally present themselves as observable ("external") *signs,* accommodated to natural human reason. As signs, they are indications of divine endorsement, and hence, "credibility motives" (*motiva credibilitatis*)—that is, grounds for faith. But that is not all. Nature and history being what they are, miracles and prophecies naturally *demand* to be identified and accepted for what they are: *hard, universally observable facts.* As such, they constitute *proof positive* of divine endorsement, and

---

[m] For examples of once-respected theological treatises in English along these lines, cf. Franz Hettinger, *Revealed Religion,* or Walter Devivier, *Christian Apologetics: A Rational Exposition and Defense of the Catholic Religion.* For a typical Latin seminary manual along these lines, cf. A. C. Cotter, *Theologia Fundamentalis,* or the apologetics in the first volume of the theological manual cited above (§86, 3, [g]).

hence, "motives that involve the obligation to believe" (*motiva credenditatis*)—grounds for faith that can be disregarded only by dint of positive error, excusable only in the case of simple people in good faith [*n*].

These allegedly philosophical premises are developed in the abstract, but their application comes as no surprise [*o*]. The Scriptures of Christianity and its Mosaic substrate attest to the actual occurrence of both miracles and prophecies, and the veracity of Scripture guarantees its historical reliability [*p*]. Consequently, the Mosaic religion and even more its fulfillment, the Church of Christ, present themselves to natural reason as divinely authorized. That is, they are *naturally* certifiable as revealed. Not only does natural reason commend them as *acceptable by faith*; by virtue of reason, they *compel the assent of faith*.

Once established on these rationalist-historicist premises, the system was in a position to allege other, less compelling arguments, by way of corroboration. Thus the established credibility of the Catholic faith was held to be corroborated by the tradi-

---

[*n*] Within the framework of the apologetics under consideration, the particular miracles envisaged here are sometimes called "apologetical" miracles, since they are considered essential to apologetics. They are to be distinguished from the merely "intellectual" and "moral" miracles—extraordinary forms of insight and heroic forms of virtue. Astonishingly in the context of a Christian theology, these latter "miracles" do not pass muster; they are useful rather than indispensable in apologetics; this is so because, while certainly possible, they can only rarely be identified as incontrovertible miracles. True "apologetical" miracles suffer from no such disadvantage. Not only are they possible; they can also be identified as miracles with perfect certainty; in that capacity they also are an incontrovertible criterium of true divine revelation. Cf. A. C. Cotter, *Theologia Fundamentalis*, pp. 63-82. All of this, incidentally, vividly shows how, in the theology of a bygone age, *certainty* was at least as pressing a concern as both faith and understanding (cf. §16, 6; §17).

[*o*] This is why Blondel protests (§85, 3) that there is nothing genuinely philosophical to these arguments. They are a setup, in support of foregone conclusions; they mere tools, means to an end.

[*p*] Here lies the connection between the *doctrinal* rationalism of the apologetics under discussion and its *biblical* rationalism—that is, its purely dogmatic, historicist conception of scriptural inspiration and inerrancy, apart from any literary study of the biblical text. A historic illustration of this connection is Joseph Clifford Fenton's fanatical essay "The Case for Traditional Apologetics" of 1959, which, incidentally, also illustrates (pp. 414-15) the prevailing habit of appealing, in a one-sided fashion, to the text from Vatican I quoted above (§86, 4). Gerald P. Fogarty's *American Catholic Biblical Scholarship*, which treats Fenton's article in the context of the development of the Catholic Biblical Association on the eve of Vatican II (pp. 282-84), competently chronicles the entire history of the struggle between integralist rationalism and alleged modernism in biblical studies as it affected the Catholic Church in North America in the twentieth century.

tionalist experience: Catholic Christianity is certified, even humanly speaking, by the attractiveness of holiness. That appealing holiness is found in transcendent form in the person of Jesus Christ, who can be demonstrated to have been divinely certified (especially by the historic miracle of the Resurrection) as God's divine emissary. Not surprisingly, holiness can also be shown to have been consistently found, along with unity and spiritual fruitfulness, in the one Church founded by Jesus Christ— that is, the Roman Catholic Church.

[b] If this type of scholasticism had been more reliably formed by the dynamics of the great Tradition, its adherents might have discerned that such a completely closed rational system *had* to be incompatible with catholicity (cf. §17). In particular, what does this whole system have to do with faith and salvation? And what are we to say of a theology in which conclusions drawn by pure reason have become stronger arguments for the Christian faith than the holiness of its founder?

Unfortunately, however, defensiveness won out over discernment. In fact, the system fell victim to a tendency towards even deeper entrenchment. Like any theory that suffers from being both entirely coherent and utterly implausible, rationalist-historicist apologetics (and the philosophical-theological system it was part of) got itself backed, eventually, on to a last line of defense. Only there was it to become evident how clearly it favored integralism (cf. §19), and how little it had to do with the catholic tradition of openness in professing the Christian faith.

This last line of defense consisted of two positions—the former indebted to rationalism, the latter to traditionalism. For a compelling illustration of these two positions, let us turn to the encyclical *Humani generis* of 1950.

[c] The first position was the emphatic affirmation of an (allegedly) most fundamental scholastic thesis—one (it was asserted) wholly unacceptable to each and every form of modern philosophy, frivolous as it will always be. That thesis is the *purely philosophical* proposition that the human mind is naturally capable of knowing unchangeable truth fully and certainly, and not just by approximation (cf. DS 3892) [q].[16] This first propo-

---

[q] It is characteristic of this type of scholasticism to caricature knowledge by convergence as mere "approximation"; this amounts to ridiculing all non-definitive

sition was needed for two purposes. In dogmatic theology, it had to uphold once and for all the possibility of dogma defined with certainty, against the assaults of relativistic modernism; in apologetics, it had to back up the natural human ability to identify miracles and prophecies with certainty.

The *objective* warrant for the mind's ability to know the truth in this definitive way, it was maintained, lay in scholastic philosophy's *realism*: its "principles and concepts [were] derived from a true knowledge of created realities" (DS 3883).[17] The former were the "unshakable" metaphysical principles that are "self-evident to the human mind": the principles of sufficient reason, causality, and finality (DS 3892-93);[18] the latter were the "terms and concepts current among scholastic theologians"—capable of refinement perhaps, but certainly not impugnable or subvertible, let alone disposable (DS 3883; CF 148; cf. DS 3893).[19] Together, and to the exclusion of all other philosophies, these fundamental principles and concepts, taught and understood *ad mentem Sancti Thomæ*, represent the one reliable, ageless, and thus "perennial" philosophy (*philosophia perennis*; cf. DS 3892-94)[20]—the only philosophy that is transcultural and hence, universally intelligible and applicable [*r*].

---

knowledge as imprecise and hence *uncertain* (cf. DS 3882; CF 147; *HG*, pp. 14-15; §64, 4, a, [*m*]). Fairness requires that it be recognized that *Humani generis* expressly mentions "knowledge by connaturality"—that is, *interpretative* or "participative" knowledge (cf. §63)—as valuable in matters of moral practice. Still, it regards this form of knowledge, in a fashion redolent of rationalism, as merely supplementary; it has a low opinion of its ability to *compel the mind*. And after all, it is axiomatic that in matters of doctrine the functions of the will must never be confused with those of the intellect (*HG*, pp. 36-39). Not surprisingly, Newman's distinction, explained in the *Grammar of Assent*, between notional assent and real assent is foreign to the encyclical's way of thinking.

[*r*] This latter thesis is the overstated form of a proposition, well-known in the former scholasticism, that served to oppose the claims of skepticism and fideism (cf. DS 2767; CF 103). It is implied, though not expressly stated, in *Humani generis*. Oddly, however, it found its way into Pope Paul VI's encyclical on the Eucharist, *Mysterium Fidei*, of 1965. In this encyclical, after appealing to Augustine's explanation of the Church's need for rules of speech (cf. §51, 4, d), the Pope points out, sensibly, that hallowed formulas must not be too eagerly *replaced* by new and allegedly more up-to-date ones, and concludes: "Similarly, none must be allowed to impugn, of their own accord, the formulas which the Council of Trent has used to propose the Mystery of the Eucharist as a matter of faith." But then the encyclical goes on, astonishingly as well as unnecessarily, to wildly overstate its case: "For those formulas, just like other ones that the Church uses to propose the dogmas of faith, express concepts that are not beholden to any particular form of human culture, to any particular [state of] scholarly progress, [or] to one or another school of theological thought. Rather, they convey what the human mind

In this way, the truth of the Christian faith has come to depend, unconditionally and exclusively, and as a matter of rational principle, on one single, (allegedly!) purely philosophical system, (allegedly!) based on one single thesis that (allegedly!) grounds the whole Tradition: scholasticism is the only philosophy enabling the human mind to exercise its natural capacity to fully and certainly know the unchangeable truths that are the roots of all true knowledge.

[d] So massive (and hence, so improbable) a claim is bound to be desperate for vindications, and peremptory ones at that. But since the system, totalitarian as it already is, has run out of possible intellectual tribunals to appeal to, it will have to cast about for vindications elsewhere: they will *have* to be "extrinsecist." In this way, rationalism produces *the second position* of the system's last line of defense: it is forced, by the extremism of its own logic, to take refuge *outside* the rational system, in *a fideistic traditionalism of the most authoritarian kind.*

Thus it could come to be taught that the scholastic system was privileged and unimpeachable because it had become inseparable from one of the two authoritative sources of Revelation: the Tradition (cf. §71, 2, c, [g]). *Humani generis*, for example, could point out that the system had become the sacred vehicle of revealed truth; ecumenical councils had sanctioned it; the Magisterium had weighed it in the balance of divine revelation and found it true (DS 3883; CF 148; DS 3892).[21] Consequently, it was *theologically* inconceivable that the fundamental scholastic concepts and principles could be anything but right; hence, it would be mindless as well as theologically irresponsible to trade them in for something that *had* to be less assured, if not downright erroneous.

[7] Firmly relying on this tradition of immobilism, the preparatory theological commission of Vatican II formulated two draft decrees (*schemata*), for adoption by the Council: *De fontibus revelationis* ("On the Sources of Revelation") and *De deposito fidei pure custodiendo* ("On Inviolately Preserving the Deposit of Faith").[22] As it turned out,

---

apprehends about reality on the basis of universal and necessary experience, and expresses by means of appropriate and semantically stable words, borrowed from either ordinary or educated speech. For this reason they suit people of all times and all places." Cf. *Mysterium Fidei*, p. 758; ET p. 6.

they were to represent the last hurrah of this entire system, which the Council was to reduce to the status of "preconciliar" theology (even though it has continued to be advocated by traditionalist alliances, including scholarly ones, to this day).

[a] Rumblings of conciliar thunders to come could be heard at the meetings of the Central Preparatory Commission in January, 1962, when the latter *schema* ran into especially heavy weather. After noting that "our faith has no foundation other than the Word of God," Cardinal Achille Liénart denounced the *schema's* reliance "on rational arguments from theology and even on mere philosophy"; he was supported by Cardinal Joseph Frings.[23] Mercifully, the *schema* never reached the Council floor.

The *schema* on the sources of revelation had been firmly criticized in the same Commission, on November 10, 1961, especially by Cardinals Augustine Bea and Bernard Alfrink, the former of whom found much support among the Commission's members.[24] Cardinals Liénart and Frings led the charge against it on the Council floor, in unmistakable terms, on November 14, 1962.[25] In the end it was completely reworked and adopted as the Dogmatic Constitution on Divine Revelation *Dei Verbum.*[26]

[8] This is not the moment to elaborate the sea-change in theology unleashed by the Second Vatican Council. Still, it is appropriate to interrupt our account of the structure of traditionalist theology for a moment, in order to recall briefly some of the most pertinent reasons why the traditional reliance of Catholic apologetics on miracles and prophecies has been mercifully laid to rest.

[a] First of all, the notion that prediction is the core of *prophecy* has been abandoned. The literary study of Scripture has taught us again that prophecy (and apocalyptic) primarily deal, not with future events as such, but with faith-interpretation of *present* experience with a view to God's judgment, understood in terms of past promise and fulfillment to come. Consequently, the interpretation of prophetic texts no longer postulate that they contain a deeper, hidden, *completely foreordained* "fuller sense" (*sensus plenior*), reposited, by *direct divine intervention*, in the prophets' utterances, unbeknownst to the prophets themselves—a sense made manifest only in the historic fulfillment. The relationship between Scripture and Tradition is now much better understood.[27] The Scriptures as we have them, we have come to un-

derstand, bear witness, in and of themselves, to the living faith-Tradition that has prophetically reread and reinterpreted them (cf. §40, 3, b, [s]). And any deeper and fuller understanding of the Scriptures that might come to us today occurs, again, by virtue of the *present* experience of the Spirit at work in the Christian community (§4, 1; §17, 1, a, [b]).

[b]   The volatile topic of *miracles* [s] has been similarly modified, especially since L. Monden published his cautious, yet pioneering monograph *Signs and Wonders.* First of all, cosmological ("apologetic") miracles do not play a major role in the Bible. Biblical views of the natural order stress, not miracles, but their opposite: the *reliability and harmony of the world,* which convey God's faithfulness and majesty (for example, Gen 1; Wisd 9; Rom 1, 19-20); in this way, Israel's hidden, faithful God sharply differs from the gods of the ancient pantheons, who are always liable to meddle, capriciously, with the world and human affairs, whether to entertain themselves or to flaunt their power. Miracles, signs, and wonders, *are,* of course, found in the Bible. But more pertinently, they are not presented as rationally incontrovertible, compelling, entirely self-sufficient arguments for faith. They typically appeal to faith already established (for example, Mk 5, 34; 10, 52); they also help call doubters to faith (Jn 3, 1-3). And finally, *seeking* the miraculous is antithetical to faith, as Jesus suggests in the gospels (Mk 13, 22 parr.; Jn 4, 48).

Gregory of Nyssa echoes these biblical views when he remarks, in passing, that the performance of miracles is not meant to perplex chance bystanders, but to benefit those being saved[28]—that is, those who believe or seek to believe. That is to say, the Judaeo-Christian tradition holds that there is *an essential connection between miracles and human testimonies about them.* Now Christian rationalists have this in common with non-Christian ones that they fail to distinguish between *testimonies* (which are interpretative and discretionary) and *reports* (which are factual). Consequently, they agree that both are inconclusive, and want to replace them by compelling *proof,* based on the laws of

---

[s] Blondel experienced just how volatile a topic this was: cf. A. Dulles, *A History of Apologetics,* pp. 206-07.

nature, that the events themselves, all testimonies and reports aside, are incontrovertible miracles [t].

Of late, philosophical reflection on the nature of science has decisively modified the (rationalist) concept of "law of nature" that underlies this reasoning. From a scientific point of view, miracles are events that defy known regularities and hence, established expectations; they invite, not rejection or attribution to divine agency, but suspense of judgment and critical inquiry. From a theological point of view, too, miracles invite critical scientific inquiry, to test allegedly miraculous occurrences, in the interest of discouraging credulousness and unmasking fraud; more especially, however, they invite *discernment*—that is, *interpretation* in a faith-perspective, *by participative knowledge* (§63). *Neither* science *nor* theology requires (though on different grounds) that any particular miracles be attributed to unmediated divine causality; but in general, miracles—in the sense of occurrences that defy known laws and regularities of nature—do remind both scientists and believers to recognize that the world is and remains mysterious [u].

---

[t] Again, Lessing poignantly exemplifies the rationalist attitude. In his debate with Celsus (cf. §27, 4), he explains, Origen had relied on "the proof of the Spirit and of Power" (1 Cor 2, 4) to show the truth of the Christian faith. But the situation has changed: "... if even now miracles were done by believing Christians which I had to recognize as true miracles," he would be prevented from accepting them; the spirit of the age would force him to look for other explanations—that is, explanations *independent of human testimony*. Thus he writes, "I am no longer in Origen's position; I live in the eighteenth century, in which miracles no longer happen. If I even now hesitate to believe anything on the proof of the spirit and of power, *which I can believe on other arguments more appropriate to my age*: what is the problem? The problem is that this proof of the spirit and of power ... has sunk to the level of human testimonies of spirit and power. The problem is that *reports of fulfilled prophecies are not fulfilled prophecies; that reports of miracles are not miracles*." (*Gesammelte Werke*, 8, pp. 10-11; ET *Lessing's Theological Writings*, p. 52; italics added.)

[u] I have met scientists who appeal to the scientific insight that natural laws have a statistical basis. They do so in order to argue that, from a scientific point of view, unusual phenomena remain theoretically conceivable. Lately, however, this reasonable position seems occasionally to take the shape of the claim that science involves no real knowledge of nature's regularities at all (cf. §63, 2; 4, a)—an obvious overstatement. Not surprisingly, however, I have heard this overstatement made by natural scientists with a fideist or fundamentalist agenda. Such people will argue, implausibly, that miracles pose no intellectual problem for scientists at all, because they themselves view the world as wide open to direct divine intervention.

[9] More than sixty years before the Second Vatican Council, in the Letter on Apologetics, Blondel had suggested, without much e-laboration, that the whole scholastic system called for a healthy dose of cultural and theological realism. Thinking outsiders simply do not accept the neo-scholastic premises taken for granted in the seminaries; they view the whole reasoning as nothing but a preju-diced attempt to force human reason into an exile of its own mak-ing. For though these arguments draw their force from natural hu-man intelligence, they are designed to turn that intelligence against itself, by making it unreasonable, on purely rational grounds, not to accept the revealed teachings of the Church. But in what sense can a realm of revealed truths whose credibility is so dependent on concepts and principles established with such certainty by natural reason still be considered revealed and supernatural? How can it be saving [v]? And how can a philosophy whose survival de-pends on enforcement by a traditionalist ecclesiastical authority extrinsic to itself be an exercise in human intellectual integrity and a true search for truth? And how can such a "philosophy" possibly commend the free acceptance of the Christian faith as a freely be-stowed divine blessing that truly fits humanity and the world, even though it goes beyond humanity's wildest dreams?

The problem is, of course, that this tightly closed system is har-monious only in appearance. For all its tightness, it harbors deep *conflict*; or rather, its very tightness is the principal symptom of the hidden conflict. A faith claimed to be both supernatural and ut-terly dependent on one single, impregnable set of allegedly purely rational arguments is conflicted; in any case, it is neither supernatu-ral nor a faith. Conversely, a system of natural, rational philosophy claimed to be solely in possession of the truth yet dependent on the sanction of a supernatural faith-tradition is conflicted; in any case, it is neither natural nor rational, nor is it a genuine philosophy. If Faith and Reason, and grace and nature, must be so forcibly held together by authority, this betrays that they are secretly thought of as essentially unrelated.

[10] In his book *The Mystery of the Supernatural*, Henri de Lubac has shown how true this is, and how one of the roots of this modern

---

[v] Avery Dulles' elaboration of this point, in his short monograph *Apologetics and the Biblical Christ*, first published in 1963, remains a cogent exposition of the inade-quacies of the rationalist-historicist approach to the credibility of the central af-firmations of Christianity.

problem was the tendency, among some authoritative sixteenth-century Catholic interpreters of Aquinas, to separate, and in that sense oppose, nature and grace (§82, 3, [g]). In the Letter on Apologetics, Blondel had made a similar suggestion, only he had pointed, in a few broad strokes, to the difference between the Middle Ages and the Reformation (cf. §83, 1, a) [w]:

At the outset, that is, for scholasticism, the natural order and the supernatural order, set one above the other in an ascending hierarchy, are *superimposed yet in touch with each other*, there are, as it were, three storeyed zones: on the lowest, ... reason is entirely at home with itself ... ; on the highest, ... faith alone reveals to us the mysteries of the divine life and of human life invited to the banquet of the divine life ... ; between the two [lies] an area of understanding or mutual encounter, where reason discovers in an incomplete way what faith illuminates and confirms in the area of the more important natural truths. And this is where, thanks to their recognition of the *objects* they have in common, the confluence occurs of two streams that flow from different though related sources, *mingling their waters without confusing them.* ...

Soon, however, this dual arrangement was to come across less as a solution than as the statement of a problem—of *the* philosophical and religious problem *par excellence.* In a spirit of violent reaction against the intellectualism of ... scholasticism, Protestantism ... suppresses the middle zone, as if it were liable to become the field of conflicts and war, instead of being the area of concord. The orders that had been *superimposed* began to be *juxtaposed* without any possible communication or intelligible link between them—united solely, it was claimed, in the mysterious intimacy of individual faith. As a result, from the day when reason, left sole mistress of the knowable world, claims to find immanent in itself all the truths needed for life, it radically excludes this [inner] world of faith; there prevails, no more juxtaposition, but *opposition*, and indeed, incompatibility.[29]

[11] A system of apologetics predicated on inner conflict cannot but arouse the "hermeneutics of suspicion." A system that settles on purely objective proofs of God's existence (cf. §68, 1, [l]) and objectively identifiable miracles and prophecies as the indispensable rational preliminaries to Catholic faith and theology cannot possibly be inspired by any desire to *understand* the relationship between *faith* and *reason.* There has got to be a hidden agenda behind this choice of preambles. What else can that agenda be but the blind, undiscerning *debate* between dogged *Catholic dogmatism* and free-

---

[w] For a far more broadly based analysis of the problem, cf. Louis Dupré, "The Dissolution of the Union of Nature and Grace at the Dawn of the Modern Age."

thinking *Deistic rationalism*—a debate inspired, on the Catholic side, by an unacknowledged *fear of losing the faith?* In a culture marked by increasingly aggressive anti-Christian prejudice, official nineteenth and early twentieth century Catholicism was indeed mortally afraid that it would lose its grip, both on the Christian faith and on its reasonableness, *if it lost that debate.* Hence its final, self-defeating recourse to a fideistic traditionalism unwilling to consider alternative philosophies; hence its ultimately misguided anti-modernism (cf. §20, 4, a); hence its dogged resolve to beat the surrounding rationalism at its own game; hence, finally, its lack of critical and historical self-awareness—its blindness to the unhistorical rationalism in its own bosom. For in trying to beat the rationalism that besieged it, official Catholicism had long, if unwittingly, joined it, with a vengeance. Even worse, it had mistaken it for the great Tradition.

REASON AND NATURE ASPIRING TO FAITH AND GRACE

[§87] "IMMANENCE": A NATIVE PREPAREDNESS FOR THE SUPERNATURAL

[1] Blondel opens the second part of the Letter on Apologetics with a clarion call for radical *philosophical* renewal (§85, 8). He does so with a courage that is the unmistakable sign of a deep and whole-hearted conviction. That conviction is also the one that is integral to the great Tradition of Christian faith and theology: *both nature and reason can be trusted* (cf. §80, 3; §81, 2).

For Blondel, this conviction must take the shape of a bold gesture of reconciliation. The Catholic Church must acknowledge, in a forthright and appreciative manner, the single most distinctive feature of the modern mentality—the very feature that accounts for the prevailing hostility and indifference to the Christian faith:

The well-worn forms of so-called philosophical apologetics no longer make any impression upon reason marked by unbelief these days, and the general drift of [modern] thought holds that this is only right and just. As we have seen, this is not happening without a deep-seated cause. ... I have felt obliged to undertake a stern critique; I could not have done so, ... if I were not convinced that the crisis I am referring to, though painful to some, will be salutary for all, by reason of what it demands in the way of fresh understanding and what it holds out in the way of future benefit.

...

No good comes from acting halfheartedly, by making painful and burdensome concessions, by accepting accommodations forced upon us, as if we had to settle for losses rather than standing to gain on every score. Perhaps, once we come to the end of this investigation, we shall judge that the heightened demands of modern thought are legitimate; that they are profitable; that they are consonant with the spirit of philosophy as much as with the spirit of Catholicism itself.

. . .

Summed up in a phrase (which must be explained, but which conveys at once the seriousness of the conflict), modern thought, jealously sensitive [about its autonomy], regards the notion of *immanence* as the very precondition of philosophy. I mean this. If there is one accomplishment, among all the ideas prevalent today, to which it is committed as to a definite advance, it is the idea—a very true one at bottom—that nothing can enter into a person that does not come out of the person, and which does not in some fashion correspond to a desire for development. Whether it be in the area of historical fact, or of traditional teaching, or of obligation imposed from outside, there is nothing that a person will view as a truth that counts and as an acceptable precept, unless it is in some sort autonomous and autochthonous. On the other hand, it is also true that there is nothing Christian, nothing Catholic unless is it *supernatural.* (I do not mean transcendent, in the simple metaphysical sense of the word; after all, we can think of truths or existences superior to ourselves about which, on the basis of our own resources, we make affirmations that in and of themselves would have to be called immanent.) [No, what I mean is the] properly supernatural; that is to say, what human persons cannot produce out of themselves, yet what they will profess has a claim on their minds and on their wills.[30]

Right here, in Blondel's forthright insistence both on authentic immanence and on the truly supernatural, and on humanity as the decisive locus of their encounter, we catch the great Tradition of catholic faith and theology astir once again, in the act of renewing itself (cf. §55, 4). There are two integral elements to this renewal, the former mainly philosophical, the latter primarily theological. Blondel emphasizes both, but orchestrates only one of them—the philosophical. The present section will do the same, by elaborating the former and only briefly stating the latter.

[2] In the first place, then, the great Tradition acknowledges and cherishes *the created order*, and it acknowledges it as essentially *dynamic*—that is, as a blend of constancy and variableness. In doing so, *the great Tradition also creates room for its own renewal*, for the acknowledgment of the dynamism resident in the created order is vital to the continued life of the Tradition. It is by embracing, again and again, humanity and the world, so as to rediscover the splendid, dynamic variety that is integral to them, that the Tradition must overcome temporary spells of rigidity and integralist conserva-

tism. Equally invariably, however, though especially in times of epochal crisis, the Tradition must recover the sense that humanity and the world are to be understood in terms of *stability and order* (cf. Gen 1; Wisd 8, 1); it must overcome the temptation to become undiscriminating and diffuse, and thus to lose itself in a modernistic world of change. Thus the great Tradition interprets the world and humanity as marked, in their native integrity, by both stability and change; in this way, they intimate a unified, immemorial, comprehensive undertaking of the divine wisdom, dynamically carried out with an undeviating resolve, of the kind that suggests a power so immeasurable that it can afford to be patient (cf. §79, 1):

> It mightily stretches from extremity to extremity,
>   and gently arranges all things.
>
> (Wisd 8, 1)

In interpreting humanity and the world in the perspective of a vigorous, yet never violent, divine faithfulness, twentieth-century catholic thought has developed (or in cases, recovered) some important insights.

[a] In acknowledging the dynamism that lies at the heart of nature in the making, catholic theology has renewed its sense of creation's native *finality:* creation's native attunement to God is not quiescent, but consists in an immanent *quest for transcendence* (cf. §80, 1-2; §81, 2; §102, 9). In the infrahuman universe, this natural quest for God remains implicit; in humanity, however, the native quest for God provides the impulse for the desire, on the part of human individuals and societies, to know and love God explicitly, not only by faith (*intellectus quærens fidem*), but also beyond that, in fullness of actuality.

In developing these insights, Neo-Thomism of the "transcendental" kind has in its own way endorsed Blondel's plea for the renewal of both Christian naturalness and Christian faith. It has recognized that *both* Christian philosophy and Christian theology are rooted in a dynamic that is native to the created order itself—*an ontological dynamism* towards the supernatural. In fact, neo-Thomism has convincingly shown that this conception is integral to the mature thought of Thomas Aquinas himself.[31]

However, the distinctive feature of the twentieth-century reinterpretation of these very traditional insights is its *anthropological*

point of departure [x].   This, after all, is the age, not only of
positivism, but also of personalism; for the twentieth century, the
recognition of the ontological dynamism inherent in creation
has been, first of all, a matter of *human self-experience*, both indi-
vidually and socially.   Not surprisingly, therefore, the transcendental   approaches   of   neo-Thomists   like   Pierre   Rousselot [y],[32]   Joseph   Maréchal,[33]   Bernard   Lonergan,[34]   and   especially   with   Karl   Rahner's   "theological   anthropology"   [z]
have characteristic features in common with Blondel's "philosophy of action" and his "catholic philosophy."

   All these philosophical-theological strategies are the products,
ultimately, of the sweeping movement begun in the Renaissance
and the Reformation, and culminating in the Enlightenment
and the modern period.   Humanity has come to occupy the central position in the Western universe of meaning; accordingly,

---

   [x] The traditional approach (rooted in Aquinas, badly isolated by thinkers like
Lessius and Mersenne, and finally rendered problematic by Kant's first *Critique*)
had been primarily cosmological (cf. §80, 3; §84, 2, a, [u]; §86, 1, [d]).   Charles
Denis had noted Blondel's abandonment of this approach, by pointing out that
the author of *L'Action* had moved apologetics away from "ontology," into the area
of "psychology" (cf. §85, 1).   The potentially dangerous element in this anthropological point of departure is its (post-Kantian) tendency to separate the personal
and the subjective from the natural and the objective.   This might lead to a theological endorsement of the situation science so dramatically described by C. P.
Snow, in his *The Two Cultures*: science and the thought-forms it has produced are
part of a culture irreducibly different from the culture governed by the humani-
ties, including theology.   Joseph Maréchal, a natural scientist by training, was more
acutely aware of this problem than any of the other transcendental Thomists.   Cf.
§9, 1, [i]; §80, 3, [c].
   [y] Cf. Blondel's *Le problème de la philosophie catholique* of 1932, which, by the way,
bears eloquent witness to the liveliness of the discussion on the topic among
French Catholic thinkers in the period between the two World Wars.   Incidentally,
the differences between Blondel and the neo-scholastics remained; Henri de Lubac
explains that Blondel's response to Rousselot's *L'intellectualisme de Saint Thomas* was
one of "'mixed feelings' of pleasure and irritation" (cf. Pierre Teilhard de Chardin
and Maurice Blondel, *Correspondence*, p. 11).
   [z] Cf. §85, 5, [c].   The opening chapters of *Grundkurs des Glaubens* (ET *Foundations of Christian Faith*) state Rahner's mature convictions in this area; but the
theme is already integral to his early writings, *Hörer des Wortes* (ET *Hearers of the
Word*) and *Geist in Welt* (ET *Spirit in the World*).   For the specific issues of the
natural desire for God and the relationship between nature and the supernatural
by way of the "supernatural existential," cf. "Über das Verhältnis von Natur und
Gnade" (ET "Concerning the Relationship Between Nature and Grace").   Rahner's
initial hesitations on the subject, under the pressure of Pius XII's encyclical *Humani generis* of 1950, can still be gathered from the original version of this essay: "Ein
Weg zur Bestimmung des Verhältnisses von Natur und Gnade" (cf. Joseph Sudbrack, "Die »Anwendung der Sinne« als Angelpunkt der Exerzitien," p. 111, n.
43).

human authenticity, integrity, and autonomy have become the principal arena in which the issues of both God and the world are to be tackled and resolved. In the course of the nineteenth century, however, it had become clear that modern humanism of the non-Christian, rationalist kind, for all its sincerity, had become the prisoner of a facile, close-minded optimism. This realization is what enabled both Blondel and the transcendental Thomists (as well as the early existentialists) to point out two things. First of all, thanks to the human spirit, human nature is a naturally open system, not a closed one; human authenticity, therefore, is not a mere matter of autonomous self-assertion—in the form, say, of an affirmation of the absolute primacy of the individual conscience. Moreover, human nature's openness is not a merely impassive quiescence; hence, human authenticity is not an assured, automatic, once-and-for-all given; rather, it must be actualized, by yielding to the elemental prompting of the human heart towards *action*. In other words, *it is in the nature of authentic humanity to take steps to stay authentic*, and *to have its authenticity tested in the process*. This applies even to the human pursuit of the truth. Far from being either a mere processor of objective data, or a self-assured repository of clear and distinct ideas, the human mind *works* to know the truth; it relies, for the judgments which it freely decides to affirm and propose *as true, both to itself and to objective reality*, on a spontaneous, innate (and in that sense "subjective") *dynamism toward affirmation*. Aquinas identified this innate dynamism as the human soul's innate potential to become "in a sense" all things (§2, 1). It is also the "immanence" that Blondel wished to explain as the very precondition of philosophy. In virtue of that dynamism, he saw, it could be truly said "that nothing can enter into a person that does not come out of the person, and which does not in some fashion correspond to a desire for development" (§87, 1) [*aa*].

Human nature is indeed marked by a native, dynamic luminosity that betrays an affinity with God [*bb*]. An inner light

----

[*aa*] This accounts for the mind's ability to come to real assent on the basis of *interpretation* of "objectively insufficient" data (cf. §63, 4, b, [*i*]; 4, c; 5), and thus for Newman's distinction between real assent and merely national assent (§86, 6, c, [*q*]).

[*bb*] Readers familiar with Aristotle will notice the parallel with his conception of the "agent intellect"; cf. *De Anima*, III, 4-5, 429ª10-430ª25. Cf. §8, 3, [*b*]; cf. also

equips every human person for an understanding of all things, at least in principle; this deep capacity for understanding accounts for the fact that particular experiences of understanding can feel so real and so delightfully genuine and authentic that they seem innate rather than acquired (cf. §8, 8). Yet we realize that it is *only in the venture* (and the test) of active, outgoing, committed living that genuine understanding will actually occur. Barely twenty-two years old, Blondel wrote in his diary, "Is it not true that action alone can define the idea?"[35]

[b] It is, incidentally, of some importance to be clear about the *kind* of action envisioned here, for not just any kind of activity proceeds from human authenticity in such a way as to enhance it [cc]. In other words, recognizing that human authenticity is dependent on action is no encouragement to the Ego to exert and assert itself without regard to either self or the other. There is indeed no authenticity apart from action, but this holds true only to the extent that a particular action is subjectively rooted in nature (that is, in the agent's native, self-authenticating spontaneity [dd]) and objectively respectful of nature (that is, the integrity of the other). Only genuinely self-regarding and other-regarding action, therefore, is so deeply natural that it does not require any *grim* effort of the will. In the present context, in other words, "to act" is not synonymous with "to take action," that is, forcefully to move *against* nature, as if it were a resistant or opposing force to be overpowered or defeated. Authentic action, rather, is deeply constructive and hence, growth-promoting. It is only in (as today's idiom goes) "flowing with" the deepest dynamisms of the human person (not by forcing issues) that the inauthentic drive toward fixation (and hence, to worry, control, and

---

§8, 8.

[cc] This realization is equally relevant to a modern, fully anthropological retrieval of the Catholic tradition's classical dedication to the natural law as the basic norm for moral behavior; cf. §50, 1, a-d.

[dd] Blondel's *L'Action* deals with this issue by offering an exploration of the basic, *ontological* dimensions of human activity. Concepts and ideas fail to capture the essence of humanity; it is only in committed action that human persons discover and recover their true selves. Pope John Paul II's dissertation, *The Acting Person*, deals with the same issue, but from a characteristically phenomenological and *moral* point of view: it is only in ethical action that persons reveal themselves and find their integrity.

belligerence) will yield to the taste of authentic freedom (and hence to carefreeness, trust, and disarmament) [ee].

Thus both nature and grace agree in suggesting that defensiveness is always self-defeating as well as destructive, and that only the disarmed disarm. Time and again, and in one place after another, human persons and societies must give up that inauthentic, deadly yearning for timelessness that consists in defeating opponents for good, and which is embodied in principles like monuments cast in bronze in memory of "moral" victories whose victims are dead and buried forever. They must give up their defensive posture vis-à-vis the powers that be, and in the act of laying down their arms also recover their native integrity; and in doing so, they will also regain fresh access to their native openness to God, and hence also, become susceptible to every renewed self-unveiling of God in history.

[c] In recovering its traditional awareness of the created order as essentially *dynamic*, contemporary catholic theology has also recovered the conviction, integral to the living Tradition, that true understanding, both of the Christian faith and of the world and humanity, is a matter of *ongoing intellectual accommodation and interpretation* ("an appreciative hermeneutic across space and time": §21, 3; §55, 4). Neither the great Tradition nor genuine human understanding depend on a dogged adherence to one single perpetually valid, comprehensive set of ideas. For the soul of understanding is not grasp but desire and delight (cf. §8, 14); forever wary of the threat of undiscerning prejudice, authentic persons and communities characteristically long for intellectual conversion; they desire to have their understanding informed and tested, again and again, by the matter to be understood (cf. §8, 6-7).

[d] Thus it is from the dynamic structures of created reality itself that the great Tradition draws an intellectual attitude that dynamically encompasses both devotion to constancy and taste for variety. This is important enough to invite some further re-

---

[ee] The story of David's defeat of Goliath may serve to make this point. David can move only after he is freed from the dead weight of aggression inspired by anxiety, symbolized by Saul's armor; once disarmed, he overcomes both Israel's fear of the giant and the giant himself, and he does so with only that most natural *and* gracious of combinations to assure him: native resourcefulness and the Name of the Lord (1 Sam 17, 31-47).

flection on the natural order and its relatedness to the order of grace.

To start with the variety, *the created order turns out to be fundamentally historical* [*ff*], in the sense that its stability is only apparent: it is forever in the making. If it remains reasonably constant and true to what looks like an "original" self of its own, it does so only by forever aspiring to rearrange and in that sense renew itself, in acts of both shaping and absorbing the inexorable movements of both human and universal history [*gg*]. And from the point of view of constancy, *history is guided by nature.* The flux of history will indeed keep drawing nearer to the stable truth it seeks, but it will do so only to the extent that it keeps on measuring itself by the standards of the natural order's inherent potential for ordered arrangement and development. History will overcome chaos, by drawing, time and again, on the deep knack for stability resident in natural process [*hh*].

[*ff*] For two ground-breaking monographs on the implications of an evolutionary understanding of the world for the theological understanding of creation and grace, cf. *God's World in the Making*, by Pict Schoonenberg, and *God in Creation and Evolution*, by A. Hulsbosch.

[*gg*] This brief reflection on nature and history is predicated on a philosophical premise—one explored, with characteristic incisiveness, by Hans-Georg Gadamer, in his "Geschichte des Universums und Geschichtlichkeit des Menschen" ("History of the Universe and Human Historicity"). The recent, consistently evolutionary understanding of the world has (somewhat surprisingly) generated the notion of "history of the universe" as a philosophical concept acceptable to scientists. (Who would have thought, even less than a century ago, that natural scientists would ever start using the word "history" again?) At the philosophical level, this application of the concept of history to nature helps put an end to that most cherished prejudice of the modern period—a prejudice most dramatically instanced in Kant's philosophy: the claim that there is an irreducible chasm between history and nature, freedom and determinism, humanity and world, subjectivity and objectivity, spirit and matter, anthropology and cosmology (cf. §9, 1, [*i*]; §94, 6, a; §104, 1). History *is*, of course, characteristically *human*; its essential features are freedom and self-consciousness; it operates—that is, it should operate, at least to an appreciable extent—in what Pierre Teilhard de Chardin calls the "noosphere." But humanity is also ineradicably rooted in the natural world, and hence, part of its inexorable dynamics. Thus the concept of "universal history" allows us to view the process of nature in one perspective with history understood as characteristically and specifically human. Here also lies the importance of Teilhard de Chardin's contribution to Christian philosophical thought. He views the non-human and the human as linked by evolutionary process, and interprets the dynamism that animates the sweep of universal evolution in terms of God's sovereign, yet creative and redemptive involvement. Needless to say, all of this has major consequences in ecology. In the second half of the second volume, we will revert to this theme, in the context of the theology of evil (cf. esp. §115).

[*hh*] This paragraph, and indeed this whole section, are substantially indebted

[3] All these realizations, finally, lead to the second element integral to the renewal of the tradition of catholic faith and theology. In the very act of cultivating the sense that God's creation is essentially, aboriginally, and immemorially in dynamic process toward God, we have also recovered *a fresh appreciation of the supernatural order.* That is, we have touched anew upon the paradox of nature and grace. Human nature is defined, not by fullness, but by the quest of it; hence total actualization of the human potential can only be *given.* That is, only God can bestow it, graciously. Natively moved towards the living God for whom we most deeply yearn we find that this God is forever beyond us, so that it is only by God's favor that we are effectively moved towards God; only to the extent that we freely abandon ourselves to God's enabling invitation (DS 1526; CF 1930) will we find our native selves actualized—find our selves freely restored to ourselves, as gift. In the final analysis, our true identity is responsive; it is acquired in the act of encountering God (§35, 1; 4).

[a] The human subject, we have thus come to realize, is naturally and radically "de-centered": the mature person's true center does not repose in the person. Authentic persons live on the strength of unfulfillable desire, which determines them rather than the other way round. A native thirst for ecstasy animates persons before they ever commit themselves to any particular choices. Thus we learn *from the natural order itself* to view the order of grace not as an opaque, impenetrable, indisputable realm of divine mystery descending upon an impassive natural order that imprisons every single being within the confines of its unalterably defined essence. Rather, grace comes to us as the divine endorsement *and* fulfillment of the dynamic aspiration that is integral to the native constitution of every creature. In fact, if the order of nature were an order of inexorable fixity, no order of grace could ever elevate it into transcendence; the most it could do would be either to cover it over or to change it by forcible intervention (cf. §78, 1).

---

to Rahner's examination of the mutuality of transcendence and history, under the title "Geschichte als Ereignis der Transzendenz" ("History as the Event of Transcendence"), in *Grundkurs des Glaubens,* pp. 145-47 (ET *Foundations of Christian Faith,* pp. 140-42).

[§88] SUMMARY: GRACE AND NATURE INTERTWINED

[1] We are ready to sum up, with the help of two witnesses. The evolving order of nature is, at root, not unlike the Christian life itself: in its own way, it is one holy desire (cf. §49, 1). Accordingly, the order of grace is the living, superabounding actualization of aspirations resident in creation. Grace graciously enables human persons, along with their world, to do that most natural, yet most divine of all things: freely to move toward God in total faith and abandon [ii]. In doing so, they will come to participate in the divine nature, and in the process, they will come to find and accept by way of pure gift their very own true, original, given selves—except that these selves are now coming true beyond their wildest dreams. Nature remains what it is, namely nature, and grace is nothing if not utterly gracious. In the divine plan, the order of nature is most deeply characterized by its *erōs*: never to be satisfied, nature will forever aspire, harmoniously, to the order of grace. And similarly, never to be disgusted, grace will forever offer the divine embrace to the order of nature, to transform it and draw it beyond itself; yet in doing so grace will never ravish nature—it will forever respect its native integrity.

[2] Piet Schoonenberg has formulated this dynamic relationship with the simplicity that betrays the master:

But what are we to say of the distinction between nature and grace? Is it not equivalently canceled, if the world and humanity turn out to be part of a creation that is evolutionary? For what is left of a nature that is clearly delimited—one against which it is possible to mark off grace as a supernatural reality? Viewed from a greater distance, the nature of all living things is always in process of development to higher forms; this even applies to the lifeless world, which for that reason is more appropriately termed "pre-vital." Human nature has been entrusted to the hands of human persons; yesterday's culture is today's nature. Could something similar, perhaps, be said of grace? What we were initially enabled to do by grace alone can, if accepted, become part of our own makeup; in the terminology of the treatise on the virtues, we might say that the *habitus infusus* turns into a *habitus acquisitus*: infused virtue gets personally integrated. In social life we

---

[ii] Cf. Trent's Decree on Justification (DS 1526; cf. CF 1930): "They are disposed for this very justice when, prompted and assisted by divine grace, they receive faith "from hearing" [Rom 10, 17] and freely move to God [*libere moventur in Deum*], believing the truth of whatever has been divinely revealed and promised."

can clearly observe how services rendered out of charity—that is, out of benevolence or compassion—in yesteryear's world are everybody's legal right
today. Yesterday's grace, too, would appear to have become today's nature.
This amounts to repeating what was said before: it is impossible to draw
precise limits between nature and the gifts of grace. But this is not to deny
that grace remains a gift.[36]

[3] If this is so, then it is not surprising that the great Tradition
should have distinguished the two orders of nature and grace (cf.
§23, 3), but also recognized them as tightly interwoven, and hence,
as not adequately distinguishable, except as a matter of abstract
principle. And not surprisingly either (despite the occasional
lapse), the Tradition has recognized this by both reason and faith,
operating in concert while mutually respecting their several compe-
tencies.

[4] The Catholic novelist Flannery O'Connor, with her uncanny
flair for the catholic tradition, has made this same point, but with
the artist's keener sense of the range of forms which the integration
of nature and grace can take. She is very much part of the literary
traditions of the Christian West, so it comes as no surprise that she
writes realistic narrative (§75, 2, [b]). She is also a traditional Catholic—that is, she instinctively believes in the unity of nature and
grace; hence, it is understandable that she finds it a mistake to
separate "fact" and "mystery." But when, in her fiction, she insists
on exercising her own indomitable talent, by casting nature in the
form of the *grotesque*, she is pressing the catholic point to the limit:
if grace is suited to natural reality and not an escape from it, then
the concrete natural order is to be embraced unconditionally, and
the test of the truth of the embrace is the acceptance of the mon-
strous. Thus she can write:

... in the dealings of Catholics with fiction you usually find a good deal of
what is basically un-Catholic.
   Or perhaps what you find is a misunderstanding of what the operation
of grace *can* look like in fiction. The reader wants his grace warm and
binding, not dark and disruptive. ... The word that occurs again and
again in his demands of the novel is the word "positive." ...
   Not long ago I received a letter from an old lady in California who
informed me that when the reader comes home at night, he wishes to read
something that will "lift up his heart." And it seems that her heart had not
been lifted up by anything of mine she had read. I wrote her back that if
her heart had been in the right place, it would have been lifted up. ...

I don't believe that you can impose orthodoxy on fiction. I do believe that you can deepen your own orthodoxy by reading if you are not afraid of strange visions. *Our sense of what is contained in our faith is deepened less by abstractions than by an encounter with mystery in what is human and often perverse.* We Catholics are much given to the instant answer. Fiction doesn't have any. Saint Gregory wrote that *every time the sacred text describes a fact, it reveals a mystery.* And this is what the fiction writer, on his lower level, attempts to do also.

The danger for the writer who is spurred by the religious view of the world is *that he will consider this two operations instead of one.* He will lift up the old lady's heart without cost to himself or to her. He will forget that the devil is at his task of winning souls and that grace cuts with the sword Christ said he came to bring. *He will try to enshrine the mystery without the fact,* and there will follow *a further set of separations* which are inimical to art. Judgment will be separated from vision; *nature from grace,* and reason from imagination. These are separations which are very apparent today in American life and in American writing. I believe they are less true of the South ... [37]

[5] Blondel's Letter on Apologetics represents one privileged moment in the history of the great Tradition. It recovers the catholic appreciation of human nature as marked by a native connection with the transcendent God. In the process, it frees both humanity and the Spirit of God from shackles of purely human forging: the former by having its immanent integrity reclaimed, the latter by being recognized afresh as beyond the grasp of all arguments, formulas, and orthodoxies. Thus, in Blondel, there takes place the naked encounter between the Enlightenment and the Revelation of the Glory: once again, what is best and bravest and most authentic about humanity at a decisive moment of its history meets the living God it has naturally loved from time immemorial. No wonder this God appeals to humanity and the world by gestures of congruence and consolation, not by dint of dissonance and noise, as if to defeat creation and confound it. God appears, not with the might of dogmatic invasion, but with an invitation to self-transcendence that is as pertinent and penetrating to humanity as it remains ungraspable in its nature and origin. As always, the mystics have best understood this.

[§89] IMMANENCE IN THE EXPERIENCE OF PRAYER

[1] Blondel's cultivation of immanence, with its balanced plea for both human integrity and openness to the supernatural, sounds

strikingly contemporary and hence, convincing; still, it is not an isolated phenomenon. In fact, it must serve to remind us of something that many (if not, indeed, all) times and places have witnessed: the human attempt to reach beyond established creeds and theological and philosophical ideas and practices, even the most cherished and substantial ones, so as to touch God (or the unnameable and unthinkable transcendent) in the most authentic manner imaginable—that is, in naked faith, directly, *without mediation* (cf. §9; §§24-26; §65, 2). Thus the fourteenth-century ascetic and spiritual director who composed *The Cloud of Unknowing* could write to his young friend:

... I bid you, ... let go, as if you did not know that there are any ... means—I mean, [means] to attain God by; for it is true, if you want to be truly contemplative and come to your purpose quickly and effectively, there is no [means] any longer.[38]

Not surprisingly, the attempt to attain the transcendent in immediacy has been, in many religious and philosophical traditions, the principal theme of the wholly dedicated life. In the Christian tradition, the pursuit naturally emerges with particular force in the ascetical movements. Charismatic asceticism has a soul of longing contemplation (cf. §78, 4, a); mysticism is the heart of religious life (§54, 5, c, [n]). It is in striving toward God under the attraction of grace, in a deep longing for transformation, that mystics find out how supernatural grace uncovers and reveals the immanent presence of God as the authentic, long-lost soul of their natural selves (cf. §79, 5-6). *The higher way to the transcendent God turns out to start as a way inward.*

[2] A striking account of the *experiential discovery*, by the soul that longs for God, of God's naturally immanent presence comes to us from the hand of one of the great guides on this way inward. She is the late sixteenth century mystic and reformer, Teresa de Jesús, better known as Saint Teresa of Avila, and the account occurs in the treatise known as *Las Moradas del Castillo Interior* ("The Spaces of the Interior Castle"). She describes the discovery, which she presents as characteristic of "the fourth spaces," as decisive: the way to full union with God is not open to those who do not first find out how the sense of God's presence will well up out of the deepest reaches of their own created selves. The experience is one of *immediacy and closeness*; to those to whom it is granted it becomes clear, all at once, how makeshift, clumsy, and mechanical all their previous experi-

ences of God have been by comparison, caught up as they were in *means* rather than in the thing itself. They also realize how dependent on momentary consolation their experience of the living God has been so far, no matter how strongly they used to feel it—or rather, precisely *because* they used to feel it so strongly. Reviving (but considerably deepening) an image rooted in the fourth Gospel (Jn 4, 14) and found in Gregory of Nyssa's treatise *On Christian Perfection*,[39] Teresa writes:

To understand it better, let us suppose we are looking at two fountains, with basins that fill up with water ... in different ways: the one draws water from a long distance, by means of numerous conduits and much human ingenuity; the other has been built right where the water springs up, and it keeps filling up without any noise. If the spring has a good supply of water (like the one we are talking about), once its large basin is filled up, a great stream starts running from it; no ingenuity is needed, and no building of conduits has to be accomplished, for water keeps running from there all the time. The difference is the following. The water that comes by way of conduits—in my opinion—stands for the joys which, as I have said, are attained by meditation. We come by them by way of thinking, as, in meditation, we avail ourselves of created things and exhaust our understanding; and when it comes at last, as a result of our efforts, it causes a noise every time the soul is to be filled up with some benefit, as I have said.

The other fountain draws the water right from where it springs up, which is God. And just as His Majesty wishes, when He pleases to do some supernatural favor, it comes to us with the greatest peace and quietness and tenderness in our deepest selves—I do not know exactly where, nor how. Nor is this joy and delight felt in the heart, as are those of this world—that is to say, at the outset; for subsequently everything does fill up: this water keeps on overflowing through all the spaces and faculties, until it reaches the body—which is why I said that it begins in God and ends in ourselves. For certainly, as all will see once they have experienced it, the whole exterior person enjoys this pleasure and tenderness.[40]

Here we catch the first, foundational mystical encounter with God in the act: the recovery of the sense of divine immanence in the experience of the unity of deep natural human integrity with gracious divine transcendence. Impelled by grace, the soul in search of God has passed through the introductory, "affirmative" stages. Supported by divine grace, it has advanced, in its dealings with the world and with others, not only in the deliberate pursuit of virtues; it has also availed itself of its own powers of reflection to elevate itself in prayer, laboriously, toward God, by using created things by way of stepping-stones (cf. §67, 2). In doing so, it has indeed experienced the joys of interior growth, though only by sudden spells and surges. Now the person experiences the breakthrough that words can convey but not capture. A "you-know-not-what" (§36, 2) announces itself you-know-not-how, but in any case from an unanticipated source—one deeper than the felt interior self [*jj*]. It is an experience of deep harmony and integration (cf. §79, 2, a). From now on, a delightfully reassuring element of fundamental receptivity and contentment will *permanently* suffuse *the whole* of the person's life. Both the pistic's avid dependence on shared faith and dutiful obedience and the charismatic's earnest reliance on individual or communal commitment and honest spiritual effort (cf. §54, 3-4; §84, 1, b) are quenched, in the God-given assurance of native authenticity graciously discovered and restored, and beginning to fill the whole person to overflowing. In those who begin to walk the way of mysticism, human nature is being renewed from the source on up and from the inside out.

[a]   Using a different set of images, Blessed Jan van Ruusbroec (cf. §90, 1) lucidly lays out the three fundamental characteristics of the experience described by Saint Teresa of Avila: sudden sense of God's inner presence, experience of integration, and experience of liberation. He writes: "There are three things ... that give a person sight in the practice of the inner life. The first is the inward lighting up of divine grace. God's grace in the soul is like the candle in a lantern or other glass vessel, for it warms and makes transparent and brightens the vessel, that is, the good person, and it manifests itself to the person who has it in himself, provided he has the inner resources to attend to himself. It also manifests itself to others through him, by way of virtues and good example. The inner flash of God's grace moves and touches the person inwardly, from within, suddenly, and this quick movement is the first thing that gives us sight. The second results from this quick movement of God. It occurs

---

[*jj*] Teresa terms this "felt interior self" (that is, that part of our interiority that is accessible to sensible experience and conscious observation) the "heart." She goes on to explain, immediately after the passage quoted, that the self that experiences the flood of God's presence lies deeper than the heart: *otra parte aún más interior, como una cosa profunda.* However, like the water in the second fountain, that deeper-seated experience does overflow into the heart, and indeed, into the whole person, the body included, in the form of a sense of authentic freedom and integrity.

on the side of the person, and it consists in the integration of all inner and outer powers, in the unity of the spirit, in the bond of love. The third thing is freedom: the person is able, free from notions and unimpeded, to turn inward as often as he wishes and [as often as] God comes to mind. That is, a person is relieved from worry about weal and about woe, about gain and about loss, about elation and about oppression, about alien cares, about joy and fear, and is not ensnared by any created things."[41]

[3] With an imaginative power that is as distinctively hers as it is deeply catholic, Flannery O'Connor has given dramatic shape to the depth of this native human yearning for God. In *The Violent Bear it Away*, a work as true as only fiction can be, she sets up the figure of Rayber, a principled unbeliever convinced of the sufficiency of reason and rational method, to make her point. Rayber, a teacher, has taken it upon himself to re-educate a tough, enigmatic, uncommunicative boy, young Tarwater. He will do so in an enlightened fashion—that is, first of all, by freeing the boy from the burden of religion. Rayber is convinced that Tarwater's troubled personality is the result of the influence of a fundamentalist relative, the crazed prophet Tarwater—"the old man" who has baptized his great-nephew and commissioned him to carry on his mission after him. Rayber, for his part, has a big personal investment in young Tarwater's upbringing: the boy must give him the satisfaction of being proved right—a satisfaction denied to him by his own young son Bishop, who is physically handicapped and emotionally disturbed beyond upbringing or education. But for all his persistent rationality, Rayber discovers in himself one type of experience he cannot explain; most embarrassingly of all, that experience draws him irresistibly toward the very thing he has taught himself and Tarwater to despise:

His normal way of looking on Bishop was as an *x* signifying the general hideousness of fate. He did not believe that he himself was formed in the image and likeness of God but that Bishop was he had no doubt. The little boy was part of a simple equation that required no further solution, except at the moments when with little or no warning he would feel himself overwhelmed by the horrifying love. Anything he looked at too long could bring it on. Bishop did not have to be around. It could be a stick or a stone, the line of a shadow, the absurd old man's walk of a starling crossing the sidewalk. If, without thinking, he lent himself to it, he would feel suddenly a morbid surge of the love that terrified him—powerful enough to throw him to the ground in an act of idiot praise. It was completely irrational and abnormal.

He was not afraid of love in general. He knew the value of it and how it could be used. He had seen it transform in cases where nothing else had worked, such as with his poor sister. None of this had the least bearing on his situation. The love that would overcome him was of a different order entirely. It was not the kind that could be used for the child's improvement or his own. It was love without reason, love for something futureless, love that appeared to exist only to be itself, imperious and all demanding, the kind that would cause him to make a fool of himself in an instant. And it only began with Bishop. It began with Bishop and then like an avalanche covered everything his reason hated. He always felt it with a rush of longing to have the old man's eyes—insane, fish-coloured, violent with their impossible vision of a world transfigured—turned on him once again. The longing was like an undertow in his blood dragging him backwards to what he knew to be madness.[42]

[4] The question is, How are these testimonies to be interpreted theologically, in line with the great Tradition? On this subject, one of the great mystical theologians of the West can serve as a profound and reliable guide.

[§90] THE FACE OF CHRIST IN THE MIRROR OF HUMAN NATURE

[1] The treatise *Die geestelike brulocht* ("The Spiritual Espousals") is usually taken to have been the second, in order of composition, of the great series of works of mystical theology by Blessed Jan van Ruusbroec (1293-1381), all of them written in his serviceable, limpid Brabant vernacular. Ruusbroec finished it, in all probability, some time towards the end of the twenty-six years he spent as a curate at St. Gudule's Collegiate Church in Brussels, where he had first come to live as an eleven-year-old student, in the quarters of his uncle, a canon at the church. It was there, too, that he had been ordained to the priesthood, in the year 1317, at the age of twenty-four.

The second book of the *Espousals* is devoted to the "interior life"—the Christian life as it is characterized by the inner desire for God. Towards the end of it, the author gets ready to make what he reminds his readers was going to be his fourth point. That is, he will elaborate the meaning of the last words of the text from the Vulgate (Mt 25, 6) that has both inspired and served to organize his entire treatise: "See, the Bridegroom is coming! Go out to meet him!" "*To meet him*": Ruusbroec is about to finish his reflections on the soul's growth in the Spirit, by paying attention to its encounter, in love, with Christ the Bridegroom. That encounter, he will explain, is the substance of the last stage of the life of desire—the stage characterized by *personal union*. This union, in turn, is the prerequisite for the life about to be discussed in the third book of the *Espousals*: the fully contemplative life of union, in "superessential" actuality, with the triune God.

[2]   Our treatment will concentrate on a crucial passage from the second book. In that passage, Ruusbroec *plumbs the presuppositions in the order of nature* of what he will explain in the third book about full mystical union—the flowering of the order of grace. Hence, to understand the former we must appreciate the latter—Ruusbroec's interpretation of grace. That interpretation is part of a broad tradition that goes back to the earliest Greek Fathers and reaches a high point in the fourteenth century, especially (but far from exclusively) in the writings of Meister Eckhart. Hugo Rahner has summed it up as follows:

Christ's special indwelling, *by virtue of grace*, in the hearts of the faithful, who have been united, in the Church, into one single body through Baptism, is a mysterious representation and continuation of the eternal birth of the Logos from the Father and of his birth from the Virgin in time.[43]

In all its stages, in other words, the Christian life occurs in the order of *grace*; it is moved by eschatological aspiration for perfect union with God in Christ—a union that consists in full participation in the inner life of the triune God (cf. §59, 5; §61, 4; §64, 4, b; §66, 2; §82, 1, a). Ruusbroec's vision is no different, except that he is convinced that this perfect union is not just an eschatological promise; rather, its essence is anticipated in the highest stages of prayer, where the life of virtue, and even the loving desire for God, are transcended. Both yield to pure contemplation, and the essence of that contemplation lies in the soul's being actually upheld by the divine Word itself. Thus Ruusbroec can write in *Vanden blinckenden steen* ("The Sparkling Stone") —the treatise he wrote to clarify what he had explained on the subject in the third book of the *Espousals*:

... if, above all things, we are to taste God or experience eternal life in ourselves, we are to enter God above reason, by means of our faith. And there we will abide—made single, vacant, and imageless—lifted up, by means of love, to where our mind is open and bare. For when in love we transcend all things, and in unknowing and darkness we die to every intention, then we are wrought and transformed through the eternal Word, which is the Father's image. And in the vacant being of our spirit we receive the incomprehensible brightness, which encompasses and pervades us, just as the air is pervaded with the sun's brightness. And this brightness is nothing else but a bottomless gazing and seeing. What we are, that we gaze upon; and what we gaze upon that we are; for our mind and our life and our being are, simply and singly, lifted up and united with the truth which is God. And that is why, in this single gazing, we are one life and one spirit with God. And this is what I call a contemplative life.

> We do exercise the best part,
> where through love to God we aspire;
> but where thus, beyond our being, we gaze,
> there we do God possess entire.[44]

[3] Now we can broach and appreciate the passage from the second book of the *Espousals*. For the dynamics of the spiritual life, it was explained long ago, are not cumulative but dialectical (§54, 5, d). That is, the awesome intimacies of mystical union with God in Christ in the actuality of prayer will not leave the human person's native attunement to God behind, as a thing of the past; rather, mystical union will precisely lay bare the breathtaking depth of that original attunement. Far from being obliterated by the actuality of grace, nature is fully revealed only in the light of the supernatural (§82, 4). It is not surprising, therefore, that Ruusbroec, before venturing, in the third book of the *Espousals*, into his account of the mystical union, takes time to fathom human nature. So he writes:

Now we must consider the fourth and last point, which is the meeting with Christ our Bridegroom. For all our inward, spiritual acts of seeing, whether in grace or in glory, and all the virtuous ways in which we move out of ourselves, in whatever practices: all of them are for the sake of a meeting and a union in Christ our bridegroom, for He is our everlasting rest, and the end and reward of all our labor.

As you know, every meeting is a getting together of two persons coming from different places—places contrary and separate in and of themselves. Now Christ comes from on high, as a lord and a generous giver, capable of everything; and we come from below, as poor servants, of ourselves capable of nothing, but in need of everything. Christ comes into us from the inside outward, and we come to him from the outside inward. The result, therefore, will be a spiritual meeting. And this coming and this meeting of ourselves and of Christ occurs in two ways, namely, with intermediary and without intermediary.

Now we must pay attention and seriously concentrate. The unity of our spirit occurs in two ways, namely, essentially and actually [*weselijc ende werke-*

lijc] [*kk*]. You should know that, according to essential [*weselijcken*] being, the spirit receives Christ's coming in [its] bare nature, without intermediary, and without intermission. For the being [*wesen*] [*ll*] and the life that we are in God, in our eternal image, is immediately and indivisibly one with the being and life which we have and which we are in ourselves, in regard to essential [*weselijcken*] being. And therefore, in the most interior, most sublime part of itself, the spirit receives without intermission, in [its] bare nature, the imprint of its eternal image and of divine resplendence; and [it] is an eternal dwelling-place of God, which God occupies with eternal indwelling, and which He visits constantly by coming anew and by illuminating [it] anew with new resplendence of His eternal birth. For wherever He comes, there He is; and wherever He is, there He comes; and where He never was, He will never come, for in Him there is neither chance nor mutability; and in whatever thing He is, it is in Him, for He does not go outside of Himself. And this is why the spirit essentially [*weselijcke*] possesses God in [its] bare nature, and God [possesses] the spirit, for it lives in God and God in it. And by virtue of the higher part of itself, it is capable of receiving, without intermediary, God's resplendence and all that God can accomplish.

And through the resplendence of its eternal image, which shines in it essentially [*weselijc*] and personally, the spirit abandons itself in the highest part of its living soul, to steep itself in the divine essence [*wesen*], and there enduringly possesses its eternal bliss. And it flows out again, along with all

---

[*kk*] Or: by virtue of essence and by virtue of actuality. I have followed the syntax of the original. The real difficulty in translating, however, is not syntax but the interpretation of the Dutch word *werkelijc*. Wiseman (*Ruusbroec*, p. 117) and Rolfson (*Die geestelike brulocht*, p. 470) render *werkelijc* by, respectively, "as it is in its activity" and "actively." The problem with this is twofold. (1) In Middle Dutch *werkelijc* does indeed occur in the sense of "spiritually active," "practicing virtue." However, the ordinary meaning of Middle Dutch *werkelijc* (like modern Dutch *werkelijk*) is not "active," but "actual" in the sense of "real," "effective," "operational." (2) In Ruusbroec's view, while the human spirit's *werkelijc* union with Christ *may* indeed be marked by activity, it may also take forms in which the spirit remains "passive" (that is, actively receptive), yet in which the union is no less *werkelijc*— that is, real, effective, and operational. In my translation, therefore, Ruusbroec's operative pair of matching concepts is taken to be, not so much "essence" and "activity," as "essence" and "actuality"; "essence" then represents what is natural, foundational, transcendental, and potential, and "actuality" what is historical and in that sense "real" (even though provisional, in anticipation of the actuality of eschatological fulfillment). This usage is well instanced elsewhere by Ruusbroec, where he writes, "This simple knowledge and experience of God is possessed in essential love, and exercised and maintained by means of actual love" (*Boecsken der verclaringhe*, p. 130-31). On the issue, cf. J. Alaerts, "La terminologie 'essentielle' dans *Die gheestelike brulocht*."

[*ll*] In Ruusbroec's idiom as in contemporary Dutch, *wesen* (mod. Du. *wezen*) has two meanings. As an abstract term, it means "essence"; as a word, denoting a concrete reality, it means "being."

creatures, through the eternal birth of the Son, and is established in its created being [wesen] by the free will of the Holy Trinity. And here it resembles the image of the supreme Threeness and Oneness in which it is made. And in its created being, it accepts without intermission the impress of its eternal image, just like the untarnished mirror, in which the image constantly remains, and which renews, without intermission, the knowledge of [the image] with new clarity, every time it is looked at anew. This essential [weselijcke] unity of our spirit with God does not exist in and of itself, but it abides in God, and it flows forth from God, and it depends on God, and it reverts into God as into its eternal cause, and, accordingly, it neither parts from God nor will it ever do so. For this unity is in us in [our] bare nature. And were the creature ever to part from God, it would fall into a pure nothing. And this unity is above time and place and is always operative [werct altoes] without intermission—this is how God operates; only it receives the impress of its eternal image passively, inasmuch as it resembles God, but is a creature in itself.

This is the nobility which we have, by nature, in the essential [wesenlicke] unity of our spirit, where it is naturally united with God. This makes us neither holy nor blessed, for all persons, good and evil, have this within themselves. It is, however, the first cause of all holiness and of all bliss. And this is the meeting and the union between God and our spirit in (our) bare nature.[45]

Eschatological union with God by meeting Christ, Ruusbroec knows, is nature's total fulfillment; it is also the soul of all desire for his coming. This eschatological meeting with Christ, therefore, is anticipated in the "actuality" of Christian life in the present. Thus the longing soul's union with Christ becomes, in the depth of the person who has found the grace of mystical prayer, an intensity of repose and contentment. That intensity is not a quiescence; it ebbs and flows, alternating between *freedom and intimacy*. Inasmuch as it is freedom it is *energy*: the person is inwardly moved to "go out," in selfless virtue, into the world, in union with the Word of God, ready to offer service to the visible world and to the neighbor, as they, too, wait to be shaped and remade in the image of the invisible God. Inasmuch as it is intimacy it is *thirst*: the person is inwardly moved to "go in," in selfless love, in union with the Word of God, into the darkness of contemplation—the sanctuary where God dwells.

It is precisely at this point that Ruusbroec takes a decisive reflective step. *The union with Christ in the actuality of action and contemplation is in its turn undergirded at the level of human nature itself: Christian prayer and Christian service are deeply natural.* Thus Ruusbroec confirms, in his own way, the truth of Blondel's (and modern humanism's) anthropological idea ("a very true one at bottom"): "nothing can enter into a person that does not come out of the person, and which does not in some fashion correspond to a desire for development" (§87, 1). In the actual life of growth-by-desire, the essential features of native aspiration are laid bare: humanity is revealed as immanently, indelibly attuned to God, and that attunement turns out to be dynamic—a natural desire for God. Immanent likeness will seek out the original from which it takes its features; made what they are in the divine image and likeness, human persons will seek out the eternal Original that accounts for their deepest selves; in the process, they will find themselves as well. Human integrity turns out to be union with God, and this union turns out to be reunion.

In fathoming this native human desire for reunion with God, Ruusbroec, along with the great Tradition, makes two interpretative moves.

[4] First of all, he affirms that the human attunement to God is what most deeply defines human nature as such. Those who to whom it is given to recover this attunement experientially, in prayer, *have access to the act of continuous creation by which God immediately touches persons;* they are privileged to catch God in the very act of establishing them in the divine image and likeness that defines their created being as such—their "bare essence." That act of creation sets the limits by which the creature, for *its* part, is distanced from God; yet God is not distanced from the creature, but remains immediately active, affirming them in the setting of that very distance (cf. §82, 3, b). As Ruusbroec puts it, the being and the life we *are* in God is identical with the being and the life *we have and are* in ourselves. For that reason, God essentially dwells in the human spirit; the immediacy of the impress that continuously establishes the divine likeness as the hallmark of our being is inalienable in "all persons, good and evil"; nothing short of annihilation can cancel it.

The truly interior life, Ruusbroec explains, consists in actually living by this essential divine likeness. Those who, moved by grace, keep the mirror of human nature untarnished by seeking God with undivided hearts will find the native divine image accessible to experience. In the higher part of their spirit, they will experience the privilege of God's deeply affirming presence, both as the immanent grace that floods the whole person and as the dark luminosity that permeates and deeply assures the understanding.

[5] But Ruusbroec affirms a second, fundamentally *christological* point as well [*mm*]. The mystical encounter with God reveals, in the human person, an essential readiness for the encounter with Christ. For, again, "nothing can enter into a person that does not come out of the person, and which does not in some fashion correspond to a desire for development." Or, in the strictly theological language of Ruusbroec's counterpart to Blondel's principle: "wherever He comes, there He is; and wherever He is, there He comes; and where He never was, He will never come." In other words, the human spirit is created in an utterly "essential" encounter with Christ, *its eternal exemplar,* that basic encounter, therefore, is the transcendental precondition for the spirit's readiness for union with Christ in actuality: we are naturally prepared to meet Christ as he comes to meet us in time. This means that the spiritual *erōs* with which all human persons seek God, in virtue of the divine likeness that is theirs, is not a faceless homing instinct automatically impelling them to reunite with an impersonal divine Prototype (cf. §80, 2). Quite the contrary: it is radically personalized. If the risen Christ affords us a privileged view of the entire world as natively marked by Christ (§40, 2; 3, b), how much more must each human spirit be so marked! For human persons to be created in the image and likeness of God means: to be naturally stamped with the visage of Christ, the divine *Logos*. Ruusbroec is here recovering Irenaeus' christological, and hence, trinitarian theology of creation:

... for [God] made humanity as the image of God [Gen 1, 27], and the image of God is the Son [Col 1, 15], after whose image humanity was

---

[*mm*] The Christian West largely lost sight of this second point as Christian theology began to separate the revealed doctrine of the Blessed Trinity from the exploration of the nature of God and of creation. It did so by increasingly leaving the latter up to philosophy and especially cosmology, as Michael Buckley has explained (§84, 2, a, [*u*]; §86, 1, [*d*]; §99, 3, a). In doing so, modern Christian thought created a serious problem for itself, especially if it is remembered that it also developed a tendency to make the Atonement the center-piece of the Christian faith (cf. §20, 2; §64, 4, b, [*n*]; §72, 2, a; §83, 3, a). The Trinity became associated, not with creation (cf. §60, 2), but only with the economy of salvation. In this way, it began to look like a merely secondary feature of God. That the great Tradition has been impoverished by this development is one of the principal points made by Louis Dupré in his fine little book *The Common Life: The Origins of Trinitarian Mysticism and its Development by Jan Ruusbroec.*

made; that is why, in these last days, he became manifest [1 Pet 1, 20], in order to show that the image resembles himself.[46]

. . .

"No one knows the Son except the Father, nor the Father except the Son, and all those to whom the Son will reveal him" [Mt 11, 27 par. Lk 10, 22]. Now this "will reveal" is not just said with reference to the future, as if the Word began to reveal the Father [only] when he had been born of Mary; it applies generally to all time. For from the beginning the Son stands by [*symparōn*] what he has fashioned, and so he reveals the Father to all to whom the Father wishes him to, and whenever he wishes, and however he wishes.[47]

Irenaeus' seminal theological insight was to become the theology of creation (and hence, the theological anthropology) of Origen, of Athanasius,[48] and of the later Greek Fathers, especially Gregory Nazianzen: the human person "is the image of Christ the image, and has as his duty to 'respect the prototype' image" [*nn*].[49]

Divine grace is capable of empowering the human spirit to sense its total dependence on, and hence, its deep attunement to, the God from whose hand it proceeds; and in that felt dependence, both the eternal genesis of the Logos who is "the reflection of God's glory and the impress of God's nature" (Heb 1, 3) and his incarnation in time are seeking to manifest themselves in human experience. And conversely, in the human spirit's felt unquenchable natural desire for God both the divine Logos' eternal response to God and his return, in time, to "the things of my Father" (Lk 2, 49), are seeking to make the call of the divine mansions (cf. Jn 14, 2) a matter of deep human experience.

The frankest, most single-minded instruments of that revelation and that call are the mystics. They live by virtue of total abandon to, and unconditional desire for, the living God. In this way, they most intimately represent Christ in the Church, and through and in him, the dynamism of the life of the Triune God. This also connects mystics with all of creation. For living by virtue of essential human nature means participating in Christ—that is, participat-

---

[*nn*] Ruusbroec had made this strictly trinitarian point in his first work, *Het rijcke der ghelieven* ("The Lovers' Realm"), under the rubric of the gift of Counsel, understood as intellectual illumination (RW I, pp. 55-59). In this passage, he had also conveyed the experience of God's natural presence in the depth of the person by means of the images of the soul's spark and the flowing fountain (as Teresa of Avila was to do: §89, 2). He was to make the trinitarian point again in his *Een spieghel der eeuwigher salicheit*: RW III, pp. 166-69, 204-05 (ET *A Mirror of Eternal Blessedness*, in *The Spiritual Espousals and Other Works*, pp. 213-15, 238-39).

ing in the Logos' creative sympathy for the whole world. No wonder mystics live for others. In the quiet appeal that emanates from the mystics' dedication to God as a matter of course the divine Logos is charming others into participation in the divine life. In the mystics' spontaneously affirming and healing gestures toward others, the Triune God's creative and redemptive love is pouring itself out, making and remaking the world.[50]

[a] Ruusbroec's christological interpretation of humanity's immanent longing for God as natural foundation of all mystical participation in the life of the Triune God may help modern fundamental theology overcome its "trinitarian timidity."[51] Additional support in this direction may be forthcoming from a better appreciation of the Ignatius of Loyola's trinitarian mysticism.[52] A deeply experiential account of Christ's presence in the human spirit, as its shaping power, is also found in the autobiography of a contemporary of Ignatius, Teresa of Avila: "Once, when I was praying the Office with all the others, my soul suddenly became recollected and appeared to me to be shining like a mirror, all of it, with neither the back, nor the sides, nor the top, nor the bottom being anything but entirely shining. And in the center of it there was the image of Christ our Lord, the way I usually see him. It seemed to me I saw him shining in every part of my soul, as in a mirror, and at the same time this mirror (I do not know how to put it) was all sculptured in the Lord himself, by means of a communication I will never be able to express—most loving."[53]

[b] In the discovery of Christ's hidden lineaments at the heart of the natural order there lies, surprisingly perhaps, a deep connection between Christianity and Judaism. For the Christian conception of Jesus Christ as the Logos Incarnate has its roots in the post-Exilic Jewish cultivation of God's creative *Wisdom*. That Wisdom is present universally and fundamentally, immanent in the design of creation, especially in humanity; and by divine graciousness, it is also present particularly and palpably, in Israel, in the form of the Torah (cf. §98, 2) [*oo*].

[*oo*] On this subject, cf. F. J. van Beeck, *Loving the Torah More than God?*, pp. 59-66.

[c] Here, too, lies the continuing relevance of the second-century apologists' insistence that the Logos Incarnate in Christ simply *is* the very Logos by which God has, from the beginning, established the universe (cf. §60, 2, a). This conception opened the possibility for Justin Martyr to propose a principled Christian universalism: if Christians profess the Logos as Incarnate in Jesus Christ, this is precisely what enables them to see manifestations of the Logos outside the Christian tradition (cf. §23, 3, a). Not surprisingly, this also marked the beginnings of a consistently Trinitarian doctrine of creation.[54]

[d] The catholic Tradition has consistently viewed humanity as originally and ineradicably made in the image and likeness of God (cf. §75, 2).[55] The present section serves to explain that this theme is regularly interpreted christologically. Now the fact that this interpretation turns up in unexpected and charming ways is an indication of its wide acceptance. A reliable witness like Saint Dorotheus of Gaza, in an instruction devoted to the theme of the divine image and likeness, furnishes a good example. The divine likeness, he explains, puts all people, and Christians in particular, under an obligation to honor God by treasuring and caring for the divine image in themselves, for the image in us obliges us to be holy (Lev 11, 44) and merciful (Lk 6, 36). But, he goes on, this theological theme has an immediate communal dimension. Just as, according to the Psalmist, "the Lord is kind [*chrēstos*] to those who patiently wait [*hypomenousin*] for him," so we are to "become kind [*chrēstoi*] to one another" (Eph 4, 32). Dorotheus' full meaning in connecting these two texts escapes us until we realize that he is punning to make his point: in the Greek of his period, *chrēstos* ("kind, gentle") is pronounced *christos* ("Christ"). In the interest of respecting the divine likeness, both in themselves and in each other, Dorotheus is telling his community of monks, they are to drop all habits of passionate self-assertion and "become Christs to one another."[56]

[e] Finally, Karl Rahner's conception of "anonymous Christianity"[57] can be understood in the light of Ruusbroec's notions of essential presence and actual presence. Christians are justified in seeing the presence of Christ *incognito*, not only essentially, in humanity as such, but also actually, wherever human persons and communities live lives of deep congruity with nature.

[6] A final observation. The mystical union explored by Ruusbroec is not the exclusive prerogative of a relatively small number of privileged souls [*pp*]. Mystics continue to derive their faith from the Church (§54, 6); the difference is that they live by it and see it through with far deeper abandon, so that it comes to fuller flower in their individual (and, in cases, communal) lives. Where, then, do we find the Christ-mysticism of the Church at large? How does the Christian community as a whole live by its natural desire for God? How does it bring its natural self, natively marked by Christ, home to God?

The answer, foreshadowed in Jesus' eucharistic discourse in the Fourth Gospel (Jn 6), is as old as Justin Martyr's first *Apology*:

Now this nourishment is called among us "thanksgiving" [*eucharistia*], and the sharing of it is open only to the person who believes that what we teach is true, and who is washed in the bath for the forgiveness of sins and for rebirth, and who lives as Christ handed down [*paredōken*]. For we do not receive these things as ordinary bread and ordinary drink; for just as it was through the Word of God that Jesus Christ our Savior was made flesh and took on flesh and blood for our salvation, so too, we have been taught, the nourishment that has been sanctified by thanksgiving, by means of the prayer whose wording comes from Him—[the nourishment] by which our blood and flesh are nourished by way of transformation—is the flesh and blood of that same Jesus made flesh.[58]

Here are the outlines of the vision that Irenaeus was to elaborate a few decades later (§78, 3). In being made one in Christ and with one another, in a gesture of union that goes beyond comprehensible words and encompasses some of the mute, material elements of the cosmos, Christians are themselves transformed and swept up in a spiritual sacrifice [*qq*]. In them, the whole world and all of humanity, *their native integrity intact*, are even now being graciously, on the strength of God's Spirit, carried up beyond themselves by the Word of God, to be brought home to the God who has

---

[*pp*] This is not to deny that there exist natural predispositions to the graces of mysticism. Thus, in *Vanden gheesteliken tabernakel* ("The Spiritual Tabernacle") Ruusbroec explicitly associates the desire for mysticism with people "who are by nature noble and tender," and adds: "None are capable of supernatural contemplation, except intimate, devout people" (RW II, p. 335).

[*qq*] Cf. Kenneth Stevenson, *Accept this Offering*, pp. 1-15. Stevenson retrieves—successfully, it would seem—the *fundamental* Christian notion of sacrifice from the tangle of post-Reformation debates in which it has been mired all too long. Cf. also his major study of the eucharistic prayer, *Eucharist and Offering*. Cf. also Bishop Mark Santer's deceptively simple *The Church's Sacrifice*.

made them, to whom they find themselves ever so deeply attracted, and who, surpassing all of creation's most deep-seated longings, has promised to be their eternal life.

[7] Thus, once again, we have come around to the nature of Christianity. The third Eucharistic Prayer of the Roman Missal prays for its actualization in a single, characteristically terse phrase:

Ipse nos tibi perficiat munus æternum.
May He bring us to our perfection—an endless offering, for You.

CHAPTER 8

Christian Faith and Credibility: Three Basic Issues

THE PROBLEM OF FUNDAMENTAL THEOLOGY TODAY

[§91] NATURAL AND POSITIVE RELIGION AGAIN

[1] Christianity, it was explained long ago, acknowledges a structural analogy between itself and other great religions. The basis for this analogy is a distinction the Christian faith has in common with these religions: the distinction between, on the one hand, a particular interpretation of the world and humanity embodied in a particular profession of faith and, on the other hand, an acknowledgment of that same world and humanity as a universal order of "nature." We added that this reference to the all-encompassing natural order common to all religions enables Christianity to acknowledge a natural basis for encounter and discussion with them.

But (we went on to explain) from the point of view of Christian theology, interreligious encounter and open dialogue are warranted, not only by this shared natural order, but also by the nature of the Christian community's *particular profession of faith* itself. All particular professions of faith, including the Christian one, are perspectival and hence, interpretative; in the case of the Christian faith this is positively enhanced by the fact that Christianity is professed in an eschatological perspective. The Christian faith, therefore, can never afford to dismiss alternative interpretations of the world and humanity as definitively irrelevant, dated, or unworthy of consideration (§64, 1-2).

[2] The previous chapter, among other things, attempted to *deepen* our insight in both Christianity's universalism and its particularity. It did so by tracing the main thrust of the *anthropology* professed by the great Tradition. To use the language of Blondel, humanity is

defined by "immanence"—a human authenticity that is, ultimately, the reflection of humanity's essential resemblance to God. This takes the shape of a native, dynamic desire for self-transcendence. This desire equips persons, *proximately*, to actively engage in *particular* commitments leading to a sustained growth in the authenticity that is natively theirs. Together, the native desire and the active commitments further equip them, *ultimately*, for two *universal* pursuits, distinct yet correlative: a growing openness to humanity and the world at large [*a*], and in and beyond that, a growing openness to the transcendent God. Both, but especially the latter, come to flower in the acceptance of the offer of the supernatural life of grace and faith, which acknowledges the human spirit's immanence in the very act of enabling it to transcend itself.

In the Christian understanding of the world and humanity, therefore, native resemblance to God equips humanity to stand authentically at the crossroads of all reality. On the one hand, attunement to God equips the human spirit to receive *the presence of God in actuality*—that is, the world of the supernatural—and to represent it to humanity and the world. That supernatural world is announced in the Christian message and professed in the creed, then lived in the Christian life, and ultimately (as well as most importantly) turned to the praise of God in the public and private worship by which the Christian community lives. On the other hand, being made in the image of God the Creator enables the human spirit to appreciate and integrate, in principle, all of *the world and humanity in their natural integrity*, along with their capacity for evolution and development, and to bring them home and offer them to God. In this way, human authenticity ("immanence") mediates the encounter between the world and the living God (cf. §2, 1) [*b*].

In a Christian anthropology, in other words, humanity's native attunement to God is the property by virtue of which human persons have a native capacity to embrace two things as authentically theirs: (1) the *particular* commitments professed by the Christian faith as divinely attested ways to God, and (2) the *universal* commitments to humanity and the world as a whole, along with the

---

[*a*] Blondel saw this openness especially embodied in authentic, unprejudiced philosophy (§§85, 3-4; §87, 1), but authentic commitment to the world and humanity can, of course, take quite a number of other shapes.

[*b*] Henri de Lubac's *The Mystery of the Supernatural*, esp. pp. 97-153, remains a compelling exploration of this deeply Christian anthropology.

transcendent perspectives involved in these commitments. Not surprisingly, therefore, the previous chapter went on to suggest that humanity's essential attunement to both God and the whole universe grounds and authenticates *both* the Christian community's universalism and its particular profession of faith. In other words, in the traditional catholic conception of things, "immanence" (or "native human authenticity") *mediates between positive religion and natural religion.*

This conception puts an end to all "extrinsecism" (cf. §86, 3, c; 6, d) in the understanding of the relationship between positive religion and natural religiosity, faith and reason, grace and nature, the living God and the universe. It upholds the traditional catholic realization that the order of grace, symbolized by the positive Christian profession of faith, transcends humanity and the world in their natural integrity without being alien to them. "Immanence," in other words, bridges the chasm that came to be fixed between positive religion and universal human religiosity, both by the Enlightenment and its aftermath (§§28-30) and by rationalist, preconciliar Catholic theology (§86). This bridging, obviously, works in both directions.

[3] Let us begin by tracing the movement from positive religion towards universalism. Christianity appeals to the Creed—i.e., its *particular* profession of faith—to endorse the "immanence" which natively enables Christians, simply by virtue of their being *human*, to appreciate the whole world and all of humanity in their natural integrity. In other words, the *Creed* demands that we interpret it in such a way as to do justice, both to the demands of humanity and world in their natural integrity (§58), and to the native human demand for integrity in believing. Consequently, the Christian faith involves a commitment to *fundamental theology* with a universalist appeal. This commitment has been especially characteristic of the catholic tradition (§§81-82).

However, just as native, universal human religiosity is not available apart from positive religion of one kind or another (§25, 3, a), so native human intellectual integrity, with its universalist orientation, is not available apart from some positive form of commitment or "faith." In other words, while the *essential capacity* for knowing "the" truth (and hence, for testing each and any particular truth) is the transcendental birthright of every person [c], this capacity is *de facto* available only in partial, "categorical" forms—that is, in reliance on *particular* criteria. Consequently, native human intellectual integrity can never take the shape of an entirely self-sufficient, self-justifying tribunal of last resort, capable of criticizing and putting to the test all commitments and truths while remaining itself beyond the reach of all tests and critiques [d].

Avery Dulles has formulated this most provocatively:

> Everybody . . . operates on some faith or other, and each faith is, in the nature of the case, incapable of being cogently proved. In real life choice is between rival faiths, and there is no neutral ground from which to adjudicate their opposite claims, for every set of criteria presupposes some faith or other. Alternative systems, in religion as in the sciences, threaten each other, since the unbelief of people whom we respect imperils our own convictions. Each faith therefore propagates itself by seeking to win converts. It must overcome or die.[1]

[a] This passage begs for criticism. Dulles, it would appear, is being too exclusively adversarial here. Even if we grant that the particularity of any positive religion sets it up for competition with other positive religions—which, incidentally, makes *controversy* an ordinary (if not always attractive) part of apologetics—Dulles does appear to overlook two related truths.

First, what distinguishes the "faiths" mentioned by Dulles from closed ideological cages holding their adherents hostage to unexamined prejudice, except *some* form of understanding that reaches *across* commitment-boundaries? Such an understanding is not only desirable, but even necessary, if only as a source of appropriate critical *self*-understanding on the part of those sharing a particular faith-commitment. Hence, it is also true that a faith

---

[c] The strength of Blondel's analysis, in *L'Action*, of "immanence" is precisely that it combines a forceful vindication of humanity's real intellectual integrity with an equally forceful affirmation of the proposition that the exercise of this integrity is dependent on an *unquenchable desire for growth*, which shows that, ultimately, the human spirit's autonomy is absolutely conditioned by its reference to the Infinite.

[d] This principle, incidentally, both establishes and sharply limits the possible claims of any form of *Ideologiekritik* ("critique of ideologies"). That all faiths and convictions and opinions should be tested for elements of ideology is clear; that all faiths and convictions and opinions (including, say, Marxism) can serve, in varying degrees, as touchstones by which other faiths and convictions and opinions can be pertinently tested for elements of hidden ideology is equally clear; but that any single set of opinions or convictions or faith-tenets can act as the ultimate tribunal in the critique of ideologies must be steadfastly denied.

"must *understand* or die"—die, that is, of sclerosis brought on by isolation.

Secondly, to the extent that the adherents of a particular "faith" communicate with worlds that lie beyond the boundaries of their own commitments, these commitments often (though not always) turn out to be capable of substantial self-renewal precisely through the encounter with other "faiths." Such renewal (we might think, for example, of development of doctrine) tends to ensure the continued vitality of any particular faith. In this sense, then, it can also be truly said that a faith "must *develop* or die."

[b] However, on the positive side, in writing what he writes, Dulles is *affirming*, not compromising, the legitimacy of fundamental theology as an enduring element in Christian theology. For if we are to believe with intellectual integrity, then fundamental, critical reflection on faith-commitment must occur. But this reflection (and here Dulles is doubtlessly right) can occur only *under the present conditions of humanity and the world.* Under these conditions, all-encompassing, universally attainable truth is available only by way of a *horizon.* That is, it is available only by way of an *ultimate perspective*, and such a perspective is always proportionate to a *particular stance* (cf. §11, 5).[2] Thus, while the whole of being is truly accessible to human understanding, it is so only as an ever-receding reality. That is, an ultimate, universal horizon keeps forever putting in fresh perspective the worlds of those who wholeheartedly commit themselves to a definite, if always provisional, *position*, while straining all the time, with all the dynamism of their being, for worlds beyond their present, necessarily circumscribed world.

[4] What has just been explained enables us now to move in the opposite direction, from universalism towards positive religion. The catholic tradition views the two as strictly correlative (cf. §25, 3, a). No wonder that it appeals to "immanence" in order to establish and commend its *particular* profession of faith as *universally* credible. That is, it appeals to natural human authenticity as the key to an *apologetics* that is reasonable without being absolutely conclusive—that is, an apologetics with a potentially universal appeal (§61, 2).

[a] The points just developed, it would seem, are analogous, if not identical, to the fifth thesis proposed by David Tracy, in his

book *Blessed Rage for Order*, in his proposal for a "revisionist" theology: "To determine the truth-status of the results of one's investigations into the meaning of both common human experience and Christian texts the theologian should employ an explicitly transcendental or metaphysical mode of reflection." Here, it would seem, Tracy's concern with "common human experience" parallels our concern with "universalism," and his "Christian texts" correspond to our "particular profession of faith." Our (or rather, Blondel's) "immanence" sums up the basis on which it is possible to involve ourselves in "an explicitly transcendental or metaphysical mode of reflection," which Tracy, in his treatment, explicitly recognizes as both humane and characterized by a religious dimension.[3] From a fundamental-theological point of view, we have argued, this dimension is given in the essential identity of native human authenticity and divine image.

As we shall see (§92, 5-6), there are significant differences between the fundamental theology elaborated in the present book and Tracy's highly original, wide-ranging, ongoing project in systematic theology. Still, it would appear that the two have at least one central thesis in common. It can be formulated as follows. In the field of tension where Christian faith and common human experience (that is, roughly, Church and Culture) encounter each other, what warrants and blesses, in advance, all responsible conversation about the truth-status of Christianity's positive profession of faith, is the native human "exigence for metaphysical or transcendental reflection."[4] This exigence for reflection, it might be added, goes hand in hand with the native human predisposition to make attempts at interpretative communication with other human beings across any natural and cultural divides (cf. §63, 5, a; §64, 1, a). The latter is also the transcendental precondition for the ongoing interpretative conversation that must keep the Tradition both alive and true to itself (cf. §56, 11, b).

[5] This chapter is designed to round off the first part of the present volume—the part dealing with fundamental theology. It does so by exploring three critical issues not discussed in detail so far. In comparing our treatment with David Tracy's, we have been confronted with the first of these. Not surprisingly, it concerns the very nature of fundamental theology—a question that is frankly contemporary.

[§92] FUNDAMENTAL THEOLOGY A "SEPARATE" DISCIPLINE?

[1] No fundamental theologian who is truly catholic—that is, both particular and universalist, both confessionally committed and open to the culture (§1)—can avoid facing up to a credibility gap that is especially disturbing today. Christianity has always treasured its positive faith tradition not only as *distinctive*, but also as *privileged.* That is, it regards its positive faith-tradition, and in particular its distinctive forms of worship, not only as *superior to natural religiosity* (§31; §62, 1, c; cf. §82, 1, a), but also as *incompatible* with any other positive profession of faith or cult (cf. §32, 3). Christianity, in other words, rejects, not only any universalism alleged to be independent of any positive elements (§25), but also any form of *syncretism*, which would attempt to attain universalism by means of blending elements taken from a variety of positive religions [e].

[a] It is precisely in this way that Christianity has opened itself, more perhaps than other religions, to accusations of barbarism, dogmatism, and bigotry from the side of those devoted to enlightened universalism, both in the ancient (cf. §27, 4, b) and in the modern world (§28, 4; §29, 2; §74, 5) [f]. It has even run the risk of driving into principled atheism those among the civilized who have found themselves weary, both of the irrational strife customary among the adherents of competing religions, and of what it suggests: that God is an oppressive force, not to say a tyrant [g]. Western Christianity today is still forced to take at least some responsibility for the long centuries in which public Christian orthodoxy and oppressive secular power collud-

---

[e] It will be remembered that Christianity's rejection of syncretism does not imply that, by virtue of its own positive profession of faith, Christianity must reject other positive professions of faith as definitively irrelevant, dated, or unworthy of consideration (§64, 1). In fact, Christianity may learn from them, and has, in fact, done so. Consequently, between the two—rejection of syncretism and appreciation of the positive elements of other religions—there lies the uncharted area where *inculturation* and *development of doctrine* must occur.

[f] Most other, non-Christian religions have, of course, done similar things and provoked similar responses. At the very least, they have, like Christianity, attempted to blend their universalist outlook with some form of unconditional, non-negotiable commitment to a particular profession of faith.

[g] In the ancient world, this atheist reaction to the oppressive inhumanity associated with all particular religions is most strikingly expressed by the poet Titus Lucretius Carus, whose famous recital of tales of misguided religious fervor culminates in the line *tantum religio potuit suadere malorum*: "Such is the store of evils that religion has managed to make acceptable" (*De rerum natura* I, 101; ed. Leonard-Smith, p. 212; cf. p. 206).

ed to protect each other's more dubious interests in establishment (cf. §74). That is, modern Christians should not be surprised at the fact that freethinking and roundly atheistic intellectual and political movements should continue to present themselves, even in our own tolerant days, as plausible forms of
liberation from prejudice and oppression, religious and otherwise.

[b] Actual Christian barbarism and bigotry are only a distant
memory today, at least in most of the Western world. Even so,
Christian apologetics still poses a serious *theoretical* problem for
Christians and non-Christians alike. The point is that the *structure* of Christian apologetics has remained suspect. Apologetics
appeals to a *universal order of nature* to make the case for the
credibility of *a particular creed*, but surprisingly, that creed is then
proposed as to be professed *to the exclusion of all other creeds.*
Christian apologetics, in other words, appears first to attract non-
Christians by its appreciation of the universal order of reality,
and then to offer to imprison them in a particular, intolerant,
sectarian profession of faith. This being the structure of the argument, how can apologetics be anything but special pleading,
and hence, a devious exercise in the very prejudice it claims to
overcome?

[c] In North America, the somewhat embarrassing history of
both the political and the religious absolutism of Christian Europe still substantially accounts for the widespread tendency to
suspect dogmatic prejudice and intolerance behind all firmly
held, particular faith-commitments. Still, while it must be granted that such commitments *can* be evidence of bigotry, it must be
insisted that they need not be. In fact, there may be bigotry hidden in tolerance itself, in its skepticism vis-à-vis all firm particular
commitments (cf. §49, 2, d). In this situation Christians must
quietly and peacefully maintain, for example, that, far from necessarily being obstacles to honest interreligious encounter, firm
commitments may in fact enhance it (cf. §62, 1, c).

[2] But there is even more the matter today. The recent knowledge, communications, and technology explosions have brought
about a radical blurring of horizons. This has generated a new,
intensified form of the critical, post-Enlightenment climate. Not
surprisingly, this is especially noticeable in and around the universities. For it is there that the pressure to establish the truth by dint

of producing, storing, retrieving, and taking into account as many data as can be made available is most intense; it is simply impossible not to be affected by this in North American universities, traditionally more briskly experimental and activist than their European counterparts.

What is characteristic of the intellectual climate created by this ongoing eruption of evidentiary and opinionative material is that it tends to cast doubts on the very possibility of any unified understanding of the world and humanity. Overwhelmingly multiple data now defy the proven, widely accepted, predominantly *schematizing* methods characteristic of traditional academic pursuits, and invite approaches that aim at *plasticity* instead. After all, the data are continually changing. This requires a steady supply of new, specialized methods to process and interpret them. No wonder there is, in today's academy, such a nervous discussion of methodology as a vital prerequisite to any possible truth-claims [h].

What this variety of methods also favors is a multiplicity of stances—that is, multiple, and hence provisional, perspectives on reality. This radical plurality of world-views provisionally professed has made the broad-minded world of the classical Enlightenment look naive and provincial by comparison. Any proposed universalism must now face, both at the level of data and in the area of world-views, a plurality of positions that often looks almost aleatory, and ambiguities wholly incommensurable with the certainties derived from past experience.

[3] In such a thoroughgoingly pluralistic climate, any confessional particularism is liable to be experienced as a simplification—that is, as opposed to a religious universalism that can call itself truly contemporary, as well as intellectually and morally responsible [i]. For where the data are felt to be too wild and bewildering to elicit firm commitments, *humane universalism and intellectual integrity are*

---

[h] James Gleick's enlightening book *Chaos* gives a fascinating account of some ways in which the modern scientific understanding of nature along irregular, "chaotic" lines has put in its place the traditional scientific understanding, which entirely operated on the assumption that regularity and linearity were the unmistakable signs of objective truth.

[i] Needless to say, this puts an enormous *cultural* pressure on the churches to be, at the very least, genuinely ecumenical. Serious *secular* scholarship can only shrug its shoulders when theological differences of a derivative nature, which largely reflect past ecclesiastical polemics, continue to be cherished and enforced by anti-intellectualist ecclesiastical agencies and agents, bent on preservation rather than understanding. It is in this light, too, that Jn 13, 35 is to be read!

associated, not with commitments, but with the conscientious suspense of them. This creates a substantially new situation for fundamental theology, as follows.

[4] The bracing atmosphere of creative scholarly skepticism will, of course, stimulate the development of fundamental theology: serious Christians, too, will want to *think*, as well as show that they do so. In such a situation, however, Christian theologians who (rightly) admire academic scholarliness are likely to opt for a new type of fundamental theology. This type will attenuate its traditional correlation, not only with the various Christian orthodoxies but also with the liberal or radical critiques of those orthodoxies. Instead, it will adopt, understandably, a *critical* approach to all doctrinal traditions, and an apologetics that takes its cues from the radically *secular* situation in which we live. It will endorse and adopt standards of integrity current among the truly inquiring; and first among these standards is the scholarly requirement that understanding be autonomous—its only dues are paid to appropriate, critical method. Again, this is especially the case in the universities, where theology most keenly experiences the pressure to adopt a truly scholarly (i.e., neutral, critical, skeptical) stance (cf. §30, 2) [*j*].

With so little in the way of articulate and reliable tradition to guide it, this type of "free" fundamental theology will also be inclined, understandably, to prove its universalism by great respect for empirical data of all kinds and by studied *impartiality*—that is, by ultimately defining religion in profoundly agnostic, fiducial, mainly future-oriented terms. This move may look, to some, like a matter of mere expediency, as if the theologians, unnerved, were simply currying the favor of the prevailing intellectual powers and authorities [*k*]; yet in reality this *epochē* can be both deeply fruitful as well as deeply missionary. For in the minds of many who have opted for this approach, modern fundamental theology establishes its

---

[*j*] In my view, it will be remembered, this pressure has origins that predate the Enlightenment by centuries. They go back at least to the sixteenth century, which saw the rise of the modern, literate, scientific tendency to treat humanity and the world primarily as a set of (material) *objects* that elicit detached, analytic *treatment*, rather than as a complex *presence* that invites committed *responses.* Cf. §56, 12, a, and, further back, §7, 1, a.

[*k*] Archbishop Michael Ramsey (*From Gore to Temple*, p. 7) recalls how William Temple defended himself (as well as the contemporary inquirer after truth) against Ronald Knox' insinuations to this effect. Temple: "I am not asking what Jones will swallow: *I am Jones* asking what there is to eat."

theological credentials precisely by being *separate* [*l*]—that is, kept unrelated to any religious-confessional-theological commitment. For commitments are—of necessity—provisional and hence, partial.

But not only that. The academy is not naive. The world of scholarship tends to be critical, not only in regard to particular, positive faith-commitments, but also in regard of the culture it is part of. Consequently, the new fundamental theology, academic and "separate" as it is, will want, with equal impartiality, to take its distance from the common culture, so as to be able to test it, too. Hence, it is liable to track down and bring to the surface the ways in which, unbeknownst to itself, that culture relates to the transcendent.

Thus the new, independent fundamental theology will attempt to be constructively critical of *both* faith and culture. Typically, this causes it to adopt a two-pronged approach reminiscent of *arbitration*.

[a] The intellectual positions just outlined, it would seem, are most impressively instanced, in the United States, in the careful theological work of David Tracy. In his *Blessed Rage for Order*, transcendental, critical reason distances itself from both Christian doctrine and common human experience, in an attempt to lay the foundations for a "revisionist" theology, capable, by means of autonomous critical inquiry, of interpreting, under-

---

[*l*] Joseph Colombo, in his friendly review of the first volume of *God Encountered*, infers that I view fundamental theology as an abstract moment within systematic theology. This is largely correct. I think of the natural order as an integral moment of the graced world in which we live; hence, I think of fundamental theology as an integral moment (not an abstract one, really) within systematic theology, dialectically correlated to positive theology. Accordingly, I link fundamental theology and systematic theology (as does David Tracy: "The Uneasy Alliance Reconceived," p. 558), and resist the tendency to view fundamental theology as a separate, independent *theological* discipline. However, from my endorsement of Blondel it should be clear that I *also* vigorously resist any tendency, on the part of fundamentalists of every kind, to cast doubts upon the freedom or the legitimacy of *philosophy of religion*; this position is predicated on the (catholic) expectation that a truly free philosophy of religion can be trusted to discover the human "immanence." In this connection, Colombo also observes that the first volume of *God Encountered* never "really" addresses the issue of the *truth* of the Christian faith. Let us assume, for argument's sake, that the truth claims of the Christian faith can be "really" tested only by means of fundamental theology, whether separate or not. In that case, Dr. Colombo's criticism is, of course, correct, though I must recall two things. (1) My decision to postpone fundamental theology till the present volume was a deliberate one (§31, 1-3; cf. already *Christ Proclaimed*, pp. 228-62). (2) I hold (and Dr. Colombo registers this) that the truth claims of the Christian faith can also be properly tested by testing Christianity's constitutive elements ("moments") for their *coherence* (§44).

standing, and testing both of them for meaning and meaningfulness.

The Analogical Imagination broadens the purview. Here, Tracy
cultivates a principled universalism. The reason is not far to
seek. Ultimately, universalism is the only adequate response to
the transcendent God; universalism, therefore, must guide the
theologians' critical probing of the world around them. In that
world, they have to deal and come to terms with three partial,
strongly dissociated "publics": the church, the academy, and society. None of these three has a corner on the truth, for they
have partial agendas of their own; these agendas account for the
existence of three different, separable (?) types of theology: systematic, fundamental, and practical, respectively.

Plurality and Ambiguity, finally, is a fine, sensitive demonstration
of the principal vehicle of ongoing theological-critical inquiry:
conversation. Conversation never ends. It consistently both requires and generates in its practitioners the essential ability to
entertain, test, and try for size a variety of points of view. That
ability is the privilege of the religiously unprejudiced—that is, of
those who have learned how to probe beyond systems and languages and standardized accounts of truth to find the lasting dimension. They are also those who have probed themselves, too,
and in doing so have gone beyond their own egos. Thus they
have become vulnerable to the touch of both the world and
humanity, and in and beyond them, of God.

This overview is too bald and cursory, of course, to do justice
to the delicacy, the depth, the breadth, the coherence, and the
pliancy and sensitivity (the French would call it *la sinuosité*) of
David Tracy's work. Still, even in this summary form it raises two
questions worth discussing.

[5] The first—noted and elaborated, long ago, by Avery Dulles[5]—
can be detailed as follows. In the classic catholic configuration,
which *God Encountered* adopts, God and world, or (more proximately) Religion and Culture, are involved in a *direct* encounter (cf. §§9-
10). This encounter is mediated by humanity's native, transcendental attunement to both God and humanity and the world (§2, 1; §91,
2). Accordingly, the tradition of catholic "systematic" theology places fundamental theology and dogmatic theology in a direct relationship. This relationship is mediated by "immanence," which represents *at once* the human need for integrity in believing, the human

spirit's attunement to all of humanity and the world, and the native human openness to God's gracious self-communication [m].

David Tracy recognizes this tradition and endorses it (cf. §91, 4, a). Yet he also appears to set up, as a matter of principle, the *transcendental capacity* of the human spirit for critical reflection as a *categorical tribunal*, invested with an almost purely *formal* authority, derived from scholarly method. Tracy, it would appear, considers this tribunal capable, in an autonomous, unbiased fashion, of adjudicating the claims of both Faith and Culture—in Tracy's terminology, of Christian texts and common human experience. The merit of this proposal lies in its being empathetic to the credibility gap that *de facto* separates Faith from Culture, and hence, doctrinal theology from fundamental theology. Yet the problem is that the proposal also *ratifies* the gap. The net effect of Tracy's proposal would seem to be that the Christian faith and the common culture are allowed to engage only in a *controlled encounter*, at the bar of autonomous human Reason dressed, for the occasion, in academic attire.

But this raises questions. Where is the guarantee that transcendental human rationality set up as an *autonomous* scholarly tribunal will remain purely formal? That it will remain impartial? And who or what will school the scholar, criticize the critic, accredit the tribunal? And what with the tribunal's claim to authority being billed as formal, what will prevent hidden prejudice from sneaking in by the back door, all the harder to detect for being unacknowledged in advance? Does the actual experience of university life (to which David Tracy's work, it would seem, principally testifies) really bear out the suggestion that unbiased devotion to truth is the *assured* privilege of scholarship and scholarly method [n]?

Most of all, however, in controlling the encounter between Faith and Culture, Tracy's proposal would seem to endorse, at a deeper systematic level, a separation, or at least a dissociation, of God from humanity and the world. To the extent that this is the case, this a-

---

[m] In this construction, it is, in any given situation, a matter of *discernment*, not principle, to determine if the need for a configurative balance between the Church and the Culture demands more emphasis on fundamental theology or on dogmatic theology (§14, 4).

[n] This pointed question must be asked at once whenever it is piously suggested, as sometimes happens in the theological academy, that churches naturally ("understandably") favor unity over truth, while the university characteristically seeks "only the truth."

mounts to an implicit reduction of the human spirit, originally appointed by God as the *mediating participant* in both the divine self-
communication and in the aspirations of humanity and the world,
to the status of a mere *arbitrator*—one who means to moderate the
encounter between grace and nature without sharing in either.
And this in turn suggests that in construing the relationship between Christian faith and human integrity in this way, Tracy is implicitly shying away from the possibility of a clash—that is, a real
crisis-situation.

[6] This is where the second question begins to arise. It concerns
the dominance accorded by David Tracy to critical reflection. Practiced in the interest of human integrity in believing, critical reflection must indeed purify positive faith and thus deepen it. Yet while
it may lay bare the fundamental human thirst for integrity in embracing a positive faith, it cannot and will not *generate* any positive
faith itself. For an orchestra, tuning is a necessary prerequisite, but
not even the most thorough tuning will ever amount to a performance. Eventually, all hesitation has to be overcome, silence must
descend upon the orchestra as well as the audience, the baton has
to come down, and the players have to commit themselves to the
playing of a very particular, positive composition. It makes no real
difference whether the composition gives little or (as in the case of
aleatory music) a great deal of scope to interpretation, improvisa-
tion, and even chance; only a composition justifies the tuning that
precedes. Similarly, no matter how necessary critical reflection may
be, positive faith is the only thing that can show what sense it really
makes. Yet it is notoriously hard to pass from critical reflection to
positive theology.

In this situation, it is helpful to remember that genuine poetry
can communicate before it is understood (cf. §63, 4, c), and that,
in the lived life, appreciation (that is, participative knowledge) precedes critical judgment. In matters of religious faith naked abandon and the positive theology that it inspires (participation again!)
must take precedence over transcendental reflection. This suggests
that there is something to be said for the abiding priority of positive theology understood as *symbolic theology.* In other words, Christianity's positive profession of faith demands that its meaning, its
meaningfulness, and its ultimate reference be *experienced* by willing
participation (which includes the possibility of conflict) before they
are *put to the test* of transcendental reflection. This remains true,
even in the teeth of *the possibility that the encounter between Christian*

faith and modern cultural experience should turn out to be (at least for the time being) *a standoff, or even a conflict.* What if Christianity's positive profession of faith and the understandings resident in it should turn the tables on the common culture and put *its* habits of understanding to a critical test (cf. §31, 4-5) [*o*]?

For all its carefulness and balance, therefore, the problem with David Tracy's critical fundamental theology would seem to be, ironically, that it is a little too preventive. In controlling the encounter between faith and culture, it has not left enough room for *crisis.* Put differently, it fails to reckon with the possibility of a *status confessionis*—a situation when the very faith of the Christian Church is felt to be at stake. Karl Barth may have overstated his witness when he charged that the "conversation" between faith and culture had degenerated into a betrayal of the Word of God; he is still worth listening to. The trail of confessional statements that the Reformed tradition has produced and continues to produce may offend us by its narrow propositionalism (cf. §52, 7) and by the extent to which each individual confession bears the imprint of the situation that provoked it; this does demonstrate the habitual Christian preparedness to interpret a conflict with the culture as a *status confessionis*— that is, as a *kairos* for the kind of effective, articulate witness that furthers the Tradition.[6] Neither Karl Rahner nor Bernard Lonergan were Barthians; both of them did fundamental theology with an abandon that is characteristically catholic. Still, both of them were entirely aware of their dependence, for the viability of fundamental theology as a critical *theological* discipline, on the (potentially hazardous) encounter with what no fundamental theology can produce out of its own store: *positive theology*—the account of the actual life of grace experienced in positive Christian worship, life, and teaching [*p*].

[*o*] Needless to say, if Christianity should extend such a critical challenge to the surrounding culture, this should be done, not with the aggressiveness of those who think they have all the answers, but with the patient, realistic persistence of the poor in spirit who will not be fobbed off with easy answers.

[*p*] In light of this analysis, an observation suggests itself. Robert P. Imbelli has compared volume 1 of *God Encountered* with David Tracy's *oeuvre.* Could it be that the comparison primarily yields a contrast? Are our several efforts, different as they are, related in a fashion parallel to the way in which (at a higher level, of course) the works of, respectively, Odo Casel and Karl Rahner are related (cf. §35, 4, a)? In this context, I remember how my dear friend, the late George Peck, a fine theologian who viewed Catholic thought with the critical sympathy of a kind, orthodox Protestant, once suggested something like this. He joked that, if the theologies of Hans Küng and David Tracy were to set the trend in Catholic

[7] It is time to take our leave from David Tracy's work, and to embark on the final sections of this chapter. We will take on, in the light of today's discussions, two profoundly connected themes in fundamental theology that remain to be considered. We will treat, in three sections, two traditional issues in catholic fundamental theology: the possibilities open to *apologetics* (§93) and the understanding of the crucial concept of *revelation* (§§94-95).

AN APOLOGETICS OF IMMANENCE

[§93] INTERPRETATIVE APOLOGETICS

[1] Apologetics is as old as the Christian Church. Christians have always been encouraged to give an account of the hope that moves them (cf. 1 Pet 3, 15) to the non-Christian world around them, not only by explicit preaching and explanation, but also more simply, by a way of life, whose very unobtrusiveness is naturally persuasive (cf. §32, 2). No wonder a readiness to give an account of the faith has become part of Christian theology, too, in the form of apologetics.

Apologetics as a theological discipline is that branch of fundamental theology that sets out to mount a defense (Gk. *apologia*) of the Christian faith, with the purpose of establishing its credibility before the tribunal of the cultural powers that surround it. It does so on "natural" grounds—that is, it avails itself of whatever *common ground* is available, between Christian and non-Christians, for a meaningful exchange.

Very often, apologetics operates reactively. That is, it will attempt to *correct*—to clear up existing misunderstandings about the Christian faith, or to rebut current attacks on it. But Christians tend to share many of the characteristics of the culture that produces both the misunderstandings and the attacks; hence, they will also feel the need to give an account of the faith for their own benefit. Not surprisingly, therefore, apologetics often operates proactively. That is, it will attempt to *construct*—an exercise that places it in close proximity to fundamental theology. Christian theologians will deliberately entertain serious challenges that are, or could very well be, put to the Creed. The intention behind this exercise is to de-

---

thought, the Catholic Church might well need, not one, but two Barths before the end of the century.

termine if and to what extent such challenges, and the concerns behind them, are legitimate. Should they turn out to be legitimate, it becomes the task of apologetics to explain either in what way the Christian Church, in fact, recognizes them and takes them seriously. And if this should not be the case, apologetics will have to explore how the Church could, and even should, take them seriously.

Between them, correction and construction add up to a broad and varied task. Not surprisingly, therefore, if one thing is clear from Avery Dulles' monograph *A History of Apologetics*, it is this: there is no simple accounting for the variety of approaches that thinking Christians, through the centuries, have taken to Christian apologetics, even though in doing so they have operated on one single, fundamental (if often implicit) assumption.

[2] What is this assumption? It is the proposition that the first seven chapters of this volume have approached and explored in a variety of ways. The Creed is an authoritative statement of the Christian message of God's gracious self-communication, and it addresses humanity and the world in their natural integrity. In doing so, the Creed practices what it professes. It professes that in Christ, God's Word Incarnate, God has lovingly taken on and enhanced the natural order. Authorized by the God whom it professes, *the Christian Creed proceeds to take on humanity, in its reasonable quest for integrity in both believing and understanding, and it appeals to that very quest to obtain a hearing for itself.* For implicit in the quest the Creed recognizes humanity's *immanence*—its native attunement to transcendence. In and beyond the human openness to the world and humanity in their natural, God-given integrity, the Christian faith surmises a native openness to the order of grace (cf. §58, 2-4).

Consequently, Christian theologians, especially in the catholic tradition, have consistently felt that this immanence is on their side. It can be expected to furnish Christian theology with fundamental, natural, and hence universally appealing arguments, such as will commend the faith to unbelievers as naturally attractive and reasonable. This remains true, even if the Christian theologian continues to realize that it takes more than a taste for the naturally attractive and the reasonable to embrace the Christian faith.

[3] Now for the variety. The arguments used in apologetics come in two broad categories: particular (or "positive") and universal (or "rational"). This distinction yields another, well-known distinction: apologetics is either of the confessional or of the fundamental kind.

Confessional apologetics aims at the defense of the Christian faith as an organic whole—that is, the faith as it actually exists in the shape of the communal observance of particular forms of worship, life, and teaching. In other words, confessional apologetics focuses on the defense of the Christian faith as a *positive* religion. Not surprisingly, it operates mostly in situations where the Christian community is surrounded by other, positive non-Christian religions or by positive forms of unbelief (cf. §24, 3; §26). In such a context, the common ground that makes apologetics possible is the fact that all the parties to the debate are in fundamental agreement about the legitimacy of positive elements in religion as such (cf. §30, 2). Availing itself of this agreement, apologetics will attempt to correct misunderstandings and misrepresentations of *particular* Christian beliefs and practices, and to refute *particular* beliefs and practices of other religions or sects (including Christian ones). It will do so by exposing their internal inconsistencies, or by demonstrating their incompatibility, either with accepted human wisdom or with accepted conceptions about true religion. The great second and third century defenses of the Christian faith against both pagan religions and gnostic corruptions of the Christian faith are mainly, although not exclusively, exercises in confessional apologetics,[7] as are some of the earlier medieval *apologias* to refute Jews and "Saracens."

Fundamental apologetics is designed to operate in a rather different environment. It addresses situations in which positive religion is not a pressing public issue, either because there prevails a broad consensus on the positive elements of religion (as in medieval Europe) or because the positive elements of religion are experienced as interesting, intriguing, or curious rather than as true, substantive, or challenging (as in the United States today). In these cases, the problem for theology is not so much that particular, well-defined errors threaten the integrity of the Christian faith; it is, rather, that the credibility of *any* articulate religious faith-commitment *as such*, and of the Christian faith in particular, is in question. Fundamental apologetics, therefore, must seek an anchorage that is deeper and a common ground that is broader and more universal: in its effort to account for Christianity's credibility, it must call on the *natural, universal* human capacity for truth (and in particular, religious truth) as a *radically* authoritative (even if ultimately inadequate) ally. No wonder it tends to be reflective and theoretical—far more so than confessional apologetics, which often operates at close quarters, and thus favors arguments that are practical, and even *ad hominem.*

[4] Saint Thomas Aquinas explains all of this rather well in the second chapter of the first book of his *Summa contra Gentiles.* After pointing out that there is an inherent affinity between love of God and dedication to wisdom, and hence, to disciplined theological thought, he explains that in this work he will endeavor "to clarify, to the best of my modest ability, the truth professed by the Catholic faith, while disposing of the errors opposed to it."[8] Then he proceeds to explain how, *in the situation in which he finds himself,* universal reason provides the most promising approach:

It is hard to argue against the errors of particular [opponents], for two reasons. First, *we are not familiar with the impious propositions of particular teachers of error to such a degree that from the very things they say we can borrow reasons that will serve to demolish their errors.* Now this is precisely how the ancient doctors went about their business, with a view to demolishing the errors of the gentiles. After all, they were in a position to know their views, since they themselves had been gentiles, or at least, they had lived among gentiles and gotten to know what they taught. The second reason is that *some of them, for instance the Mohammedans and the pagans, disagree with us on the authority of any Scripture that might prove them wrong,* the way we can argue against Jews by invoking the Old Testament and against heretics by invoking the New. But these people accept neither. Hence, *we have to have recourse to natural reason, to which all are forced to give their assent,* even though, it must be noted, it is not adequate to the things of God.

In the course of exploring each particular truth we will indicate which errors are eliminated by it, and how the truth that is establishable by argument [*demonstrativa veritas*] is congruent with the faith of the Christian religion.[9]

Thus, given the option between confessional and fundamental apologetics, Aquinas chooses the latter. His choice becomes clearer if we recall that the *Summa contra Gentiles* was designed as a seminary textbook for the training of future missionaries in North Africa, where, besides local forms of paganism, Islam was the dominant religion [*q*]. Yet the *Summa contra Gentiles* clearly has a different

[*q*] It is to be noted that in the course of the Middle Ages, Islam, long accepted as a distant relative of Christianity, and hence, as a serious, if totally misguided, conversation partner, began to be treated, with growing hostility, as a form of aggressive unbelief. Consequently, the tone of confessional apologetics in the encounter with Islam became extremely harsh, and the fundamental-apologetics

audience in mind as well: the leading intellectual circles of mid-thirteenth century Christendom. There, Christianity as a positive religion was, of course, firmly *in possessione*; where the positive teachings of the faith were concerned, the Catholic Church and its theologians had only Judaism and a few marginal anti-establishmentarian heresies to contend with. But while orthodox Christianity's intellectual and practical monopoly was obvious, it went by no means uncontested (cf. §27, 1, a).

[5] Starting from the cathedral schools just shy of the turn of the tenth century, a truly authoritative challenge to the Christian faith had been slowly surfacing. Sir Richard Southern has characterized it as "intellectual restlessness."[10] Initially, it fed on the heady discovery that theological problems could be tackled (if only in a crude fashion) by means of logic—that high point of the early study of the *artes*. But some time in the twelfth century the restlessness took off in earnest. It reached its peak in the thirteenth century, when it settled at the university of Paris as its home *par excellence*. There more than anywhere else it seized upon the best of pagan intelligence and wisdom, principally represented by Aristotle's logic and his universalist nature-philosophy as mediated by the great Arab commentators and interpreters.

By the time Aquinas was writing the *Summa contra Gentiles*, some time between 1261 and 1268, just before he began work on the *Summa theologiæ* (cf. §80, 1), he had moved to Italy. Nevertheless, the book is firmly rooted in the exciting world of the new thinking current in Paris, and in that world it stands out as a truly notable achievement. For one thing, it succeeds remarkably well in confronting the challenge posed by the wave of intellectual restlessness. But more importantly, the underlying secret of its success is that it is itself a mature fruit of that restlessness. In this way, the *Summa contra Gentiles* could become the first, classic example of the fully philosophical type of *apologia* for the Christian faith—of the kind that can take on a culture because it is no stranger to its struggles. No wonder it inaugurated a centuries-long tradition of fundamental apologetics, of which the last truly original work is bishop Joseph Butler's *The Analogy of Religion, Natural and Revealed, to the Constitution and Course of Nature*, first published in 1736.

---

approach became more prominent (cf. A. Dulles, *A History of Apologetics*, pp. 72-111). Vatican II rectified this somewhat, by recognizing the fundamental partnership once again (LG 16; NA 3).

The hallmark of this tradition is the fundamental proposition that the relationship between Christian faith and the understanding available to natural reason is governed by *concordance* or *congruence* (*convenientia*). This concordance, broadly speaking, takes two forms that are as distinctive as they are closely related, and hence, inseparable. The first form of concordance is predicated on the realization that a large number of truths professed in the Christian faith can also be substantially argued by persuasive natural-reason arguments. The second form of concordance is predicated on the conviction that the truths that are substantially of the "revealed" variety, and hence, essentially beyond all demonstration, are nevertheless capable of being deeply pondered and understood by way of investigation by reasonable argument and analysis.

[a] In the *Summa contra Gentiles*, the former type of concordance dominates the first three out of the work's four books; in Butler's *Analogy*, it occupies all of Book I, as well as chapters 1-4 and 8 of Book II. In the *Summa contra Gentiles*, the second type of concordance prevails in the fourth and final book; in the *Analogy of Religion*, chapters 5-7 of Book II are devoted to it.

[b] A caution is in order here. The order of exposition, it must be remembered, is not always a reliable guide to the order of understanding (§7, 2). The structure of both Aquinas' *Summa contra Gentiles* and Butler's *Analogy* appear to imply that the truths of natural religion are to be kept carefully *separate* from those of revealed religion. To draw this conclusion, however, would amount to reading into both of these works a thoroughly modern conception—one which has been commended only by the aftermath of the Reformation and especially by the Enlightenment. In this conception, there is no integration, either between grace and nature, or between faith and reason; they are each placed in a relationship of mere contiguity. And if the two pairs are still claimed to be mutually complementary, that complementarity is understood only in a merely extrinsecist sense (cf. §86, 3, c; 6, d).

Extrinsecism, however, is part neither of Aquinas' nor of Butler's conception. In their order of exposition the treatment of the truths arguable by natural reason does indeed precede the treatment of revealed truths. But this treatment implies that they think of reason and revelation only as *distinct*, not *separate*. For the basic premise of their several apologetics is that the truths of the Christian faith form *an integrated whole, organically ranging from the natural to the revealed.* Hence, what they mean to demonstrate is how human reason can operate *along this entire range,* by virtue of its natural powers of understanding [r]. Reason does so operate by establishing *convenientia* between understanding and the truths of faith, and this *convenientia* varies according to the various relationships that may obtain between Reason's power of understanding and each particular truth under discussion. The *convenientia,* in other words, engages natural human reason at different levels of capacity. At one end of the range, truths expressing religious mysteries arguable by natural reason invite substantial argument; at the other end, truths expressing mysteries of the Christian faith in the strict sense of the word invite abandon to supernatural faith, in willing *docta ignorantia* [s].

[c]   Consequently, Aquinas' appeal, in the first three books of the *Summa contra Gentiles,* to *demonstrativa veritas* must not be construed as a claim to absolute rational certainty about the truths of the Christian faith. We are still centuries removed from the demand that issues be settled by incontrovertible, totally objective argument, geometry being the standard of *all* true (i.e., absolutely certain) knowledge (cf. §7, 1, a). Bishop Butler, on the other hand, is familiar with this demand. It is significant, therefore, that he expressly bases his apologetics, not on absolute, mathematical certainty, but on *probability* as the true guide of life.

[6]   In this classic conception, therefore, there is no chasm fixed between fundamental apologetics and confessional apologetics. Both are firmly set in the same context. In Christian apologetics, the faith as an integral, historic, yet reflective movement attempts to give an account of itself before the tribunal of the cultural powers that be, which are themselves capable of reflection, too. In this encounter between faith and culture, fundamental apologetics does

---

[r] The title of Butler's book brings this out clearly. The Christian religion is *both natural and revealed.* As a whole, the Christian religion is analogous to the natural order ("Nature"), both in its essence ("constitution") and in its functioning ("course"). Hence, Christianity is accessible to exploration by means of the analogies which Reason draws from Nature, which is Reason's natural domain. "Analogy" is Butler's equivalent of what we have termed *convenientia,* concordance, or congruence.

[s] Cf. Blondel's explanation of this in §86, 10.

not present itself as a purely rational pursuit entirely preliminary to, and hence separable from, the historic, positive Christian faith-commitment. Rather, it offers a systematic attempt at interpreting that commitment in its organic integrity. And it does so along reasonable lines and by way of *præparatio Evangelii* [*t*]—that is, by seeking to demonstrate the credibility of the catholic faith to outsiders, by means of culturally appropriate, and in that sense, naturally appealing analogies.

[7]   Rationalism, both of the Enlightened and of the Romantic kind, has tended to treat native human religiosity as both entirely reasonable and entirely autonomous—that is, as better and purer according as it was kept further apart from any positive elements (§25, 4). Something analogous can be said of the rationalism of the Catholic, neo-scholastic kind: it thought of the theses developed in fundamental theology as entirely compelling (§86, 6, a-d). As a result, both Deists and rationalist Christians have imagined that any true fundamental *apologia* for religion had to rely on a set of basic, easily identifiable religious and ethical truths claimed to be timeless and universally valid [*u*].

This conception, we have repeatedly emphasized, amounts to an unwarrantable separation, not only of nature from grace, but also of transcendental human reason from the processes of history and culture that embed and inform it. In this light, it is interesting to observe that, for all their insistence on reasonable argument accessible to outsiders, neither Aquinas nor Butler claims to be arguing transcendental, timeless truths. Instead, their several apologetics look to *cultural situations* as the common ground that invites fundamental argument. That is to say, both Aquinas and Butler offer an apologetics that is predicated on a *reasoned interpretation of the*

[*t*] This has always been true of fundamental apologetics in the Catholic tradition; its admitted aim has consistently been (in the language of the 19th and 20th century manuals of scholastic theology) to develop a reasoned, coherent set of *præambula fidei*. However, as Avery Dulles has pointed out, the problem with this scholasticism was that it conceived of these preambles to the faith in rationalist terms, as "necessary preconditions of the judgment of credibility." Dulles rightly adds that for Aquinas, the *præambula* were "simply those truths of faith that are also within the grasp of natural knowledge" (*A History of Apologetics*, p. 93, note). Cf. also the crucial article by Guy de Broglie referred to by Dulles: "La vraie notion thomiste des 'præambula fidei'," as well as §86.

[*u*] Benjamin Franklin's *Autobiography* is a good example of this kind of apologetics in defense of Deism (cf. §25, 4, c).

surrounding culture, with the help of the *best, profoundest, most authori-tative, most widely shared argument available.*

> [a] In the case of the *Summa contra Gentiles*, that cultural situa-tion is peripherally marked by the increasing ideological and political tension between established European Christendom and the alien world of paganism and Islam. Its central concerns are occasioned by the discovery, among the rising intelligentsia at home, of nature and natural reason as creative challenges to the understanding of the world. In the case of the *Analogy of Re-ligion*, the situation is thoroughly changed. The current intelli-gentsia now view the ideal world as a place where natural reli-gion is nobly and innocently observed by savages untouched by intolerant dogma (cf. §28, 4, a); the old-fashioned relationship of creative tension and reciprocal challenge between Christian faith and the best of culture has turned into one of mutual ali-enation and hostility, as Bishop Butler's opening *Advertisement* makes abundantly clear (cf. §29, 1-4). In this world, Reason and Christian faith have become declared enemies; Reason and Reve-lation have drifted apart. Not surprisingly, the very *possibility of revelation* has become the burning issue—the one that dominates the *Analogy of Religion*. It is still with us today, as the next two sections (§§94-95) will make clear.

[8] But first, in light of what has been explained, we must draw several conclusions. First of all, not only confessional apologetics, but also fundamental apologetics is firmly set within the context of the positive Christian profession of faith. Secondly, every system of Christian apologetics, even the most fundamental and reasonable one, operates, not on timeless, objectively universal truth, but on an interpretation of the prevailing culture. But, thirdly, this implies that apologetics is an exercise in *cultural hermeneutics*; it is one form that the interpretative encounter between Faith and World, Church and Culture takes. In that exercise, confessional apologetics more explicitly represents the concerns of Christianity as a confessional, positive religion, whereas fundamental apologetics is more on the side of the shared wisdom and the integrity of the culture.

[9] This, in turn, leads to yet another conclusion. The themes of confessional apologetics tend to be explicitly theological [*v*];

[*v*] Precisely for that reason, its capacity for naiveté and dogmatism of a mindless,

fundamental apologetics sounds more secular, but *in practice* it is often more properly theological—or rather, christological. For in taking the culture seriously, the fundamental Christian apologist is not bent on currying the favor of the powers that be, but acting on a warrant implicit in the Creed itself (cf. §62, 1, a). In taking on the culture, fundamental apologetics is but acting on the imperative of the Incarnation: in the Christian community's gestures of out-reach to the culture, Jesus Christ, the Word Incarnate, continues to take on humanity and the world with a love that includes every conceivable concern.[11]

This, however, places fundamental apologetics under the scrutiny of the *imitatio Christi*, as follows. Systems of fundamental apologet-ics set out to bolster the credibility of the Christian faith by re-course to cultural concerns. But apologetics are only as authori-tative as the cultural concerns they adopt; for that reason, apologists tend to adopt *dominant concerns* as the arena for their encounter with the culture. But in doing so, they *may* be implicitly—and, worse, uncritically—endorsing the prejudices and inequities of a culture. Then it is time to remember that what qualifies dominant cultural concerns for theological attention and christological inclu-sion is their being *concerns*, and hence, their being *relevant*; it is not their being *dominant* that so qualifies them. Thus the imitation of Christ requires of fundamental apologetics that it be prepared to take on a critical role, *by representing countervailing tendencies overlooked or positively downplayed by the culture at large.* Thus any fun-damental apologetics that wishes to establish the credibility of the Christian faith in a manner consistent with Christ himself, must exhibit a "*critical* sympathy with dominant concerns."[12] In today's skeptical world, it might be added, such a critical edge will add to, rather than detract from, the credibility of Christian apologetics as a realistic interpretation of the culture.

[a] In light of the discussion just completed, it remains wise to recall Dietrich Bonhoeffer's caution that Christian doctrine must be the heart of any Christian theology, not apologetics. For there is danger in apologetics: it may degenerate into a habit of treating Christianity's *relevance* as the measure of its *truth*, which may place the modern theologian on the brink of compromise and betrayal of the faith (§83, 4).

---

non-theological kind must be clearly recognized: §25, 4, a.

[b] Our discussion should also shed some light on *the apologetic foundations of much present-day liberation theology.* Theologians of liberation like Johann Baptist Metz (*Faith in History and Society*), Jon Sobrino (*Christology at the Crossroads*), and Leonardo Boff (*Jesus Christ Liberator*) are obviously justified in appealing to the Scriptures, and more especially, to the life-style of the historical Jesus, in support of their interpretation of the Christian faith as it must take shape in the culture out of which they speak and which they address. But the credibility of their theological efforts depends in no small measure on the fact that they offer a persuasive interpretation—even from a secular point of view—of that culture. In this way, liberation theology is but doing what all sound theology attempts to do, namely, to achieve "discretionary fit" between Church and Culture, true worship and genuine worldliness (§14, 2) [*w*].

[c] One consequence of the discussion just completed remains to be mentioned, in anticipation of a fuller treatment later on in this volume. *God Encountered* proposes to treat the "proofs of the existence of God" offered, since Aquinas, by a host of Christian thinkers, as philosophical approximations of the doctrine of creation, and in that sense as "natural theology." Not surprisingly, it will do so in an interpretative fashion—that is, it will attempt to understand these proofs without claiming timeless significance on behalf of any of them taken by themselves. For simply taking them by themselves, as perennially valid arguments, would amount to lifting them out of the context of the culture that produced them as meaningful arguments.

GOD ENCOUNTERED?

[§94] REVELATION: DIVINE "INTERVENTION"?

[1] In this section and the next we take up a truly basic issue in fundamental theology. It was first mentioned long ago, when it was called a "radical challenge" and "a *crux* of modern systematic the-

---

[*w*] For an important discussion of the problems that beset the relationship between Christian faith and secular (in this case, Marxist) philosophy as it affects the interpretation of culture, cf. the letter "On Marxist Analysis," addressed, in 1980, to the major superiors of the Jesuit communities in Latin America, by the then general superior of the Jesuits, Pedro Arrupe, in the wake of the Puebla convention of the Latin American episcopate a few years earlier.

ology" (§23, 3, b). It can be responsibly regarded as one of the principal intellectual challenges, if not the principal, offered to Christianity by the mentality of the modern era. The treatment of this issue, therefore, can be expected to confront our interpretation of the Creed squarely with the world as we experience it today.

The issue concerns, once again, the interpretation—philosophically as well as theologically—of the relationship between *grace and nature*. In that sense, what is involved is (again) the relationship between positive revelation and natural human religiosity; implicitly, what is also at stake (again) is the possibility of true worship (§35). Besides, Christianity specifically claims the historic person of Jesus Christ, put to death and raised by God, and thus revealed, in the Spirit, as God's Son, as the determinative core of God's self-revelation; hence, what is involved in a special way is the relationship between *historic Christianity and the universal possibility of faith*. Ultimately, of course, what is involved is the truth of the Christian doctrine of God as triune, as well as its theological intelligibility.

[2] At the heart of the issue, strikingly explored in Martin Buber's *Eclipse of God* (§35, 2), lies the forced choice (or so it seems to many) between *integralism* (or fundamentalism) and *modernism* (or reductionism). Must we, theologians, bow our reflective, critical heads before any scandalous facts—before what is often referred to as the "objectivity" of the Christian faith? Are we, in other words, to acknowledge that the *substance* of the Christian religion is a matter of true divine "intervention"? *Or* can we adequately account for Christianity if we reduce Christianity to *historic experiences that are immanently human*—experiences that have yielded, and continue to yield, Christianity's historic self-expression in worship, life, and teaching? The question can be raised, less abstractly, in the form of oft-heard concrete questions, as follows.

Does the Creed mean to affirm that the living God has been, as is being, actually *encountered* in the world? Or can this metaphor be reduced, ultimately, to a dramatic manner of giving symbolic expression to a particular set of *human* religious *experiences?* Does, for example, Israel's Covenant refer to a *reality of partnership*—one that involves, not just historic Israel, but God as well? *Or* is it a naive picture? That is, does it simply convey an intense *experience of partnership* on the part of *Israel*—an experience that is essentially available naturally and universally, to all nations (where, of course, it is liable to be expressed in different, but virtually equivalent, sets of symbols)? Or let us take an explicitly Christian theme. Is it truly

God who is known in the real, historic person of Jesus Christ, and moreover, is God thus known in a wholly unique, definitive, unsurpassable manner? *Or* is it enough to understand Jesus Christ as the symbol of a new, definitive level in the immemorial development of human religious consciousness, and hence, is Christianity reducible to the highest form of humanity's awareness of God? Put differently, is the orthodox interpreter of the Creed forced to opt for the (naive?) acceptance of the order of Christian grace as a genuinely *new reality* or *level of reality*—one that encompasses and perfects the natural order? Or is it legitimate to settle for a *critical reconception* of the order of grace as a mere *reinterpretation of the one, single natural reality that we know as "creation"* (cf. §23, 3, b; §30, 4)?

[a]   Dilemmas like these are explicitly raised by existentialist thinkers, who usually answer them in a reductionist spirit. What comes to mind, for example, is Rudolph Bultmann's rejection of all divine intervention as a throwback to mythology, and his thesis that the historical Jesus' significance must be restricted to the area of personal, existential faith in the present moment;[13] we can also think of Willi Marxsen's reduction of the truth of Jesus' resurrection to a human, if Christian, *Interpretament*.[14] But the question is implicitly raised in the theological positions of the most characteristically *modern* theologians—that is, of all those who have (rightly!) taken the modern "turn to the subject" seriously. Thus Schleiermacher thinks in terms of one *unified* divine plan for the world, carried out in two coordinated developmental stages; yet he barely skirts the reductionist position when he explains that the appearance of Christ marks the coming, not so much of God as of "God-consciousness": the transition of *humanity* (formerly mired in physical existence, with its inherent repetitiousness) to an existence characterized by the spiritual and the creative.[15] Paul Tillich opts for the concept of "correlation" to explain the relationship between divine revelation and human predicament;[16] yet questions remain as to whether that correlation is not, in fact, lopsided [x]; for in his eagerness to protect the divine transcendence, he tends to restrict any possible awareness of God's mystery to the *human experience* of being ultimately concerned, just as he appears to reduce the reality of the

---

[x] Cf. F. J. van Beeck, *Christ Proclaimed*, p. 213: "God's self-revelation in Christ has been limited by the limitations of the human situation."

gift of the Spirit to the "Spiritual Presence"—that is, to the life of faith and love consisting in the *finite spirit's* "state" of being "grasped" and "taken into" the "transcendent union of unambiguous life" [y].[17]

[3] In the Anglo-Saxon and North American world, somewhat less pervious to the existentialist mood, the dilemmas just formulated often explicitly hinge on the neuralgic issue of divine "intervention." This is doubtlessly due to the strong influences that derive, not just from liberal Evangelicalism and Deism (cf. §20, 2-4; §28, 2), but specifically also from the atmosphere created by Newton's theological cosmology (in which the inner coherence and consistency of "the system of nature" bulks so large). As long as the normative world-picture was "pre-modern," it is often suggested, there was relatively little questioning of the possibility of divine intervention ("inbreaking") in the *natural* order; this allegedly made it easy (or at least relatively easy) to accept *supernatural* intervention as well, specifically in the form of scriptural inspiration, miracles, and revelation. But we moderns (so the explanation continues) now live, if not in a closed natural order, "in which miracles no longer happen" (§86, 8, b, [t]), then at least in an autonomous one. This strongly predisposes us to regard grace and revelation as purely alternative, elective, not strictly demonstrable *interpretations* of a world order that is essentially stable (if evolutionary, and in that sense historical: cf. §87, 2, d). Such a world order spontaneously suggests one single, consistent, *natural* divine plan. As a result there is, for many of us, a curious, arbitrary otherworldliness involved in conceiving of the world order as reflecting an integral divine plan of a *supernatural* kind—even if it is one in which grace is carefully coordinated

---

[y] By way of comparison, cf. the careful way in which Bernard Lonergan, in keeping with his interest in exploring the subjective preconditions for the developing life of faith, fully acknowledges the *experience* of divine love, yet refuses to reduce its *reality* to the human capacity for it; cf. *Method in Theology*, pp. 105-07. Not all the authors that have availed themselves of Lonergan are as careful. One wonders, for example, at the end of William M. Thompson's interesting *Christ and Consciousness*, to what extent the Christian faith has been quietly turned into a function of historic human growth. At the end of Daniel A. Helminiak's elegant *Spiritual Development*, one wonders if the Christian faith has been reduced to the status of one particular set of (purely instrumental?) categories by means of which it is possible to express natural human development. This thought especially occurs when one reads, on the last page of the book, that "Spiritual development, whether understood within the philosophic, the theist, or the Christian viewpoint, *is nothing other than human development* according to a particular set of concerns" (p. 211; italics added).

with natural reality. For even in this coordinated scheme, revelation is experienced as opposed to nature. "Nature," after all, evokes a sense of *autonomy*: it sums up the (relatively) *independent* universe *created* by God, knowable by the human mind exercising its native *independence*. "Grace," on the other hand, evokes a sense of *heterono-my*: it sums up the universe of Christian faith, produced by a *mysterious, saving divine intervention in history*, to be acknowledged only by a profession of utter *dependence*. Faced with this dilemma, we moderns are naturally reluctant to fall back upon a naive "interventionism"; as a result, we sometimes find ourselves (only slightly less reluctantly) settling for what really amounts to a form of Deism (cf. §23, 3, b).[18]

[a] The dilemmas just stated are strikingly, as well as representatively, instanced in Maurice Wiles' elegant and stimulating *The Remaking of Christian Doctrine*.[19] In Wiles' view, God, being the creator of the universe, cannot but be committed, foundationally, to its *independence*. This axiom yields a fundamental criterion with which to test the credibility of all religious affirmations: we are to refrain from "claiming any effective causation on the part of God in relation to particular occurrences." In Wiles' proposed reconstruction of Christian theology, this becomes *the* criterion. Together with the two (formal) criteria of coherence and economy (§8, 6, a, [*f*]), it determines the whole "pattern of belief" to be developed; but in doing so, it also determines the *content* of what can be credibly proposed as the true substance of mature belief.[20] The criterion operates *negatively*: like Ockham's razor, it shaves away anything in the profession of faith not required by itself. The motive behind the operation is the classic—and valid!—concern of the apologist: to test the Christian faith by the standard of human intellectual integrity in believing. Many of our thinking contemporaries, Wiles implies, cannot be fairly compelled to give intellectual assent to more than what can survive the application of this principle. He admits that the operation does yield a form of Deism, but one that is still acceptable: it does not cut off all relatedness, on the part of God, to the world, even if it does restrict that relatedness to God's being "source of existence and giver of purpose to the whole."[21]

In keeping with the restrictions demanded by the principle, Wiles proceeds to whittle away at the doctrines of Christ's person and work, as well as the doctrine of the working of the Holy Spirit, till they have become mere *instances* of a single, *universal* proposition: God's "purposive concern" in regard to the world as a whole. Since this proposition is universal, it does not depend, for its validity, on any historic instances, for God's concern for the world—God's "care"—is sufficiently ascertainable *from creation* [z]. That is also why the doctrines themselves can continue to be affirmed as having real meaning. Still, it is understood that any such meaning must be reductively understood: it derives, not from the doctrine claimed as true because revealed in history, but solely from the affirmer's judgment of what can possibly be meant by *any* affirmation concerning God in relation to the world [aa].   In this way, God having been reduced to the status of the provident, caring creator of all that is, the intractable particulars of Christianity's positive profession of faith have ceased to be an embarrassment.

[b] From some of the examples Wiles gives, we may infer, with a fair degree of probability, just where that embarrassment lies. Wiles' rendition of some of Christianity's central doctrinal claims is excessively "interventionist": claims made in behalf of direct biblical inspiration,[22] in behalf of Jesus' divine Sonship viewed as a hard historical fact that should be establishable apart from Christian faith,[23] in behalf of the universal, totally objective atoning efficacy of one particular historical event: Jesus' death on the cross. It must be granted, doctrines thus proposed *are* unbelievable to anyone who prizes, as Wiles does, human freedom, matu-

---

[z] This is a truly rationalist conception, reminiscent of Lessing's *dictum*: "Accidental truths of history can never become the proof of necessary truths of reason." Cf. also the following: "The truth of a historical narrative, however assured, cannot give us the knowledge nor consequently the love of God, for love of God springs from knowledge of him, and knowledge of him should be derived from general ideas, in themselves certain and known, so that the truth of a historical narrative is very far from being a necessary requisite for our attaining our highest good." Quotations from Henry Chadwick, *Lessing's Theological Writings*, pp. 53, 30.

[aa] This recalls a sequence of mid-eighteenth century fundamental-theological developments. Christian Wolff (1679-1754) had still defined the relationship between Reason and Revelation in such a way as to safeguard the relative autonomy of Revelation, which, he maintained, might be above Reason while not being contrary to it. This (rightly) allowed Reason to establish certain criteria of intellectual integrity by which Revelation might be legitimately tested. The situation, however, drastically changed when the Neologians developed two far more radical positions: (1) Regardless whether Revelation is real or not, its content cannot in any case be different from that of universal natural religion establishable by Reason; hence, (2) Reason must positively eliminate doctrines which are not identical with the deliverances of Reason. Cf. Charles H. Talbert's introduction to *Reimarus: Fragments*, p. 5. Cf. also §86, 3, b, [i].

rity, and responsibility.[24] But the question is whether Wiles' versions of these doctrines are not straw men. Is the crude interventionism Wiles finds implicit in these revealed doctrines really integral to them? Or, for that matter, does the great Tradition require it [bb]? The present section means to propose what the next will make it a point to argue constructively, namely, that the answer must be no on both counts, and hence, that Wiles' proposal involves a reduced version of the Christian faith—specifically, a Modernist one (cf. §20).

[4] Before we attempt to develop, in the next section, an understanding of revelation (often misleadingly called "divine intervention") by means of systematic reflection and argument, let us suggest a broad historical and cultural *placement* of the issue, as well as a first philosophical analysis.

Let us start with a few witnesses from the second and third centuries. The apologists, Irenæus, and Origen are obviously innocent, not only of the modern "turn to the subject," but also of the scientific mentality that objects to divine intervention in the chain of cosmic causation. Still, this does not mean that their view of divine self-revelation is naively "interventionist." Thus the *Letter to Diognetus* explicitly insists that God does not intrude by means of physical force of the kind that overcomes opposing forces; rather, God sends the Son in gentleness (§79, 1 and [cc]). Irenæus insists that God, as creator, is at home in the world, and therefore, that God does not need to break to enter; being immanent (that is, immanent in such a fundamental way as only a truly transcendent God can be), the *Logos* does not intervene in the world from outside (§78, 3). Origen draws a conclusion from this. He agrees with Celsus that God does respect the world's integrity, as it develops toward its intended completion. But he reminds Celsus that the road to that completion runs through that particular repository of the *Logos* which is the human person, made in the divine image (cf. §27, 4, c). Hence, if God guides the world,

---

[bb] And since the excessive interventionism that characterizes Wiles' version of these doctrines accounts for his reductionist interpretations, the latter are open to question, too. Wiles' proposal, I wish to suggest, arouses the suspicion that he may be a representative case of liberal Evangelicalism slipping into rationalism. Newman had this very thing in mind when he decried the loss of mystery that results from a one-sided emphasis on the *manifest* character of *select* doctrines (cf. §15, 3; §20, 3).

God does not take care, as Celsus imagines, only of *the universe as a whole,* but in addition to that He takes particular care of every rational being."[25]

A century and a half later, Gregory of Nyssa rounds out the argument. God is not remote, but close to the world, for "the divine is equally in all and it permeates the whole of creation in the same way, and nothing could remain in being apart from the One Who Is" (§75, 2). Hence, unlike the meddlesome gods of the ancient pantheons (cf. §86, 8, b) [*cc*], God does not "intervene." But, Gregory implies, God does relate to each being in accordance with its nature; specifically, God intimately relates to the human person, capable, by virtue of the divine resemblance and the capacity for moral action, of making the perfection of God a matter of inner-worldly experience, by "being perfect as your heavenly Father is perfect" (Mt 5, 48).[26]

The conclusion is obvious. The Church Fathers' notion of God's activity in the world is not rooted in a naive (in Bultmann's language, "mythological") conception of "effective causation on the part of God in relation to particular occurrences." Instead, the Fathers place all divine action in the world in the context of an understanding of divine immanence—*an understanding in which the human person plays a decisive role.* This, it would seem, leads to a hermeneutical ground-rule. In cases where patristic passages do seem to imply or express a naive understanding of the divine activity in the world, the realization that their thought is embedded in a deep sense of God's immanence should temper our eagerness to attribute mechanical, "interventionist" ideas to them [*dd*]. In fact, could it not be argued that the Fathers could afford to sound naive precisely because the theological and cosmological metaphysics they were operating on were anything but naive?

[5] Where, then, in the history of Western culture, are we to place the problematic idea that God "intervenes"? Not in the Middle Ages, which were familiar with divine immanence and recognized

---

[*cc*] Christians had come to agree with the Stoics and other schools of philosophy that the pagan gods sullied the purity of the divine, and hence that they were no more than inferior demons—the powers (elemental and otherwise) that Christ, by virtue of his resurrection, had overcome, at least in principle.

[*dd*] Thus I must disagree, on hermeneutical grounds, with Maurice Wiles, when he alleges that the patristic understanding of scriptural inspiration, with very few exceptions, looked upon the Spirit as a foreign, "additional" factor, and hence, regarded the human author's role as purely instrumental, and consequently, as entirely passive (*The Remaking of Christian Doctrine,* pp. 89-90, 106, 116).

the hand of God in the world, while at the same time enjoying a sophisticated philosophical understanding of the distinction between
God as *causa prima* and the inner-worldly causality exercised by the
whole range of secondary causes. In this understanding, all worldly
causes operate under the sustaining, immanent impulse of the transcendent *causa prima*, understood as the transcendent source, not
just of *efficient* causality, but also, and especially, of *formal* and *final*
causality [*ee*].

The answer, therefore, must be, again (cf. §7, 1; §17, 1, a; §82,
3, [*g*]; §86, 3, b): in the first half of the sixteenth century, which
witnessed the rise of the cultivation of "objectivity" as never before.
The world began more and more to look like an immense collection of discrete, relatively impenetrable objects, all of which offered
themselves for description and definition by means of discrete
truths, capable of being spelled out, objectively, on the printed
page. Mathematics and mechanics began to be the paradigm of
both truth and reality, and even of art, as, among other things, the
laws of optical perspective began to be rigorously enforced (§56, 12,
a, [*i*]). And since all objects began to be thought of as affecting
each other only extrinsically, efficient causality gained an almost
absolute prominence.

[a] The problem is, of course, that efficient causality best explains the mutual relations of solid bodies—*inanimate objects.* But
lifeless things are inert; they are foreign to each other, or at best
contiguous; if they affect each other at all, they do so only extrinsically (at least in the macroscopic world of everyday observation, on which the new cosmology was based). Living beings, by
contrast, exist differently, much though they share many of the
properties of inanimate things. They actively transcend themselves so as to take on their physical environment; they are characterized by an immanent ability, both to communicate with
other beings like themselves and to seek self-actualization by
means of growth and development, both in inner consistency
and in interactiveness—that is, in an interplay of immanence and
transcendence. Human persons are characterized by an immanence that gives rise to an even further transcendence. They
transcend, not only themselves, but also their physical environment, and they do so self-consciously; *though part of the material*

[*ee*] For Aquinas' position on this issue, cf. §86, 1, [*d*].

order, they are *selves*, open to *otherness as such*—other persons and, ultimately, God. Efficient causality fails to account for all these forms of immanence and transcendence; to account for them, both Jewish and Christian philosophical traditions have appealed to formal and final causality (cf. §102, 10), as David B. Burrell has recently explained once again.[27]

[b]   In this light, the English theologian David Jenkins would seem to offer a skewed analysis of cultural developments when he writes: "Christianity, having settled down into its mediaeval moulds, was largely unable to 'take' the strictly neutral and secular approach to everything in the universe (including eventually, man in so far as he is homogeneous with the rest of the universe), which is the essence of the scientific approach and which gives it its liberating and creative effect."[28] As a matter of historical fact, the separation of humanity from the universe is *not* the result of the scientific mentality at all—or at least not initially. It was an *implicit assumption* of that mentality's favorite *method*, which favored the reduction of all causality to efficient causality. The method was immensely successful, and hence, persuasive. In time, however, the method helped drive the synthetic, interpretative spirit out of the world of objectivity; it had to take refuge in a different world [*ff*].

Thus the protest against "divine intervention" is part of scientific method as it arose in the sixteenth century. The mechanization of the Western world picture[29] and its aftermath created a theological problem. Curiously, Christians ended up joining the movement set afoot by the method; many of them became pious Cartesians, too, and withdrew from the world, to save

---

[*ff*] To take one eloquent example, the great anatomist Vesalius (1514-1564), whose anatomical atlases show that he was the first to *see* the body scientifically, clinically, dispassionately, with an eye as keen as his scalpel, is a *Platonist* as well as a Cartesian *avant la lettre*. He completely separates soul from body and spirit from matter, and names God, not *creator*, implying a coherent world, but *opifex* ("craftsman"), implying a world of mere *things*. Vesalius can write: "And thus we will render thanks, singing hymns to God the maker of all things, for having bestowed on us a reasonable soul, which we have in common with the angels (as Plato also suggested, not unmindful of the much-abused philosophers). On the strength of that [soul], if there is but faith, we shall enjoy that eternal happiness, when it will no longer be necessary to inquire into the seat and the substance of the soul by the anatomizing of bodies or by means of reason weighed down by bodily shackles." Quotation in J. H. van den Berg, *Het menselijk lichaam*, II, p. 221, n. 5. On Vesalius, cf. *The Illustrations from the Works of Andreas Vesalius*; cf. also F. J. van Beeck, *Christ Proclaimed*, pp. 41, 45, 525-32.

their purely spiritual souls (cf. §66, 4, a). In light of all this, it would have been more correct, perhaps, for David Jenkins to write that, with few exceptions (Pascal being one of them; cf. §96), Christians failed, not so much to 'take' the undifferentiated scientific and secular approach to everything in the universe, as to take it *on*.

[c] We can now go back to Maurice Wiles' *Remaking*. Wiles fully realizes that efficient causality fails to account for revelation; hence he rejects any notion of special divine presence associated with particular instances of "effective causation" (§94, 3, a). The problem, however, is that he does not confront the defective anthropology implicit in modern culture's unawareness of the concepts of formal and final causality. The concept of revelation that Wiles rejects is neither supernatural nor attuned to humanity (cf. §95, 5, [*pp*]); hence, he is right in rejecting it. But he fails to develop a concept of revelation that is satisfactory: one that accommodates what he so obviously prizes in human beings: freedom, maturity, and responsibility—the very features that are the authentic human correlates of the self-revelation of God, as the next section will argue.

[d] Incidentally, the extent to which the sixteenth and seventeenth century mechanization of the world picture is an intellectual watershed in the understanding of the "effects" of God's saving action is well demonstrated by the fact that Aquinas has, as yet, no problems attributing efficient ("instrumental") causality to both the sacraments and Christ's Passion—even though he adds that formal ("exemplary") causality must play a part in explaining the effects of his Resurrection.[30] By contrast, a modern theologian like Karl Rahner resolutely opts, both in an early essay and in his mature *Foundations of Christian Faith*, for formal causality as the central category to understand grace, which is *communication* of divine life.[31]

[6] The realizations developed in this section must give us our cues to a fresh approach to the problem of divine revelation—an approach that must respect both the Tradition and the culture we live in. The *patristic tradition* suggests that (1) the abiding immanence of the transcendent God in the natural order is an essential key to revelation, and that (2) the presence of the specifically human element in the world is of crucial relevance to both the reality and the understanding of God's immanence in it. The *culture*, for its part, insists that faith be

wedded to human authenticity and integrity; consequently, (3) it wishes to satisfy itself that Christian revelation is not predicated on a naively interventionist concept of divine activity in the world; specifically, too, (4) it raises the issue of Revelation in the context of its experience of the undeniable blessings, intellectual and practical, that have accrued to the human community thanks to the successes of Reason, especially (though far from exclusively) in its scientific and technological applications (cf. §96, 4, [a]).

[a]   Other realizations, previously developed, will have to guide our analysis as well.   Thus, if divine revelation is specially connected with the presence of the specifically human in the cosmos, then our analysis is well advised to pay special attention to the distinctive ways in which the world of *things* functions in communication between and among *persons.*   Incidentally, in doing so, we may discover remedies for some of the painful dichotomies typical of modernity.   One such dichotomy is the Cartesian rift between matter and spirit, which, ever since Kant, has taken the shape of the dreadful dichotomy between nature and freedom.   Nature, we must rediscover, is neither fixed nor a closed circle, but pliable—that is, amenable to historicity and consequently, to freedom (cf., again, §87, 2, d, esp. [gg]; §104, 1).   Another, parallel dichotomy is the Cartesian rift between the world and God, and hence, between human Reason and divine Revelation (§86, 3, c; §93, 7, a).   Thus, since nature is not a purely inert, material prison, Reason is not its prisoner; hence, human understanding really does reach beyond the world of objects (even if Locke and Kant strongly suggest the opposite); Reason is natively open to the presence of spirit in the world and hence, to nature's attunement to the order of grace.   And if this implies (as it does) that grace is not intrusive, then Revelation cannot be narrowly historical—that is, it does not occur, purely adventitiously, in the shape of discrete, readily identifiable historical occurrences wholly wrought by God; rather, it must in some real sense be the flower of nature's immanent aspiration towards transcendence.

[7]   In the next section, therefore, we will attempt to develop a fresh fundamental-theological approach to divine revelation.   We will do so by way of an analysis of the phenomenon of communication between and among persons.   Our expectation that human communication will prove to provide a useful analogy to divine

revelation is based on two well-known claims. First, language about God cannot but avail itself of metaphors borrowed from human concerns and experiences in the world. Secondly, divine revelation is a form of communication.

One final preliminary point. As indicated, we will attempt to understand divine revelation by using processes of human communication as an analogy. However, our analysis will discover that the *reality* of divine Revelation is inseparable from the very processes that serve as analogies towards its *understanding*. Human communication, in other words, will prove to be the *indispensable anthropological infrastructure* of divine Revelation (§95, 10).

[§95] REVELATION AND ITS ANTHROPOLOGICAL INFRASTRUCTURE[32]

[1]   One realization that will easily come to anyone whose experience has been shaped by the experience of encounters with other persons is the following: communication between and among persons involves more than the transmission of content, even though all communication involves some kind of identifiable content [gg]. *Human communication involves more than things communicated*; communication is not a mere transfer of "matter" between and among people. For content to be communicated relatively un-

---

[gg] The *content* of communication consists in the *things* we communicate *to* others. These things are "goods": material goods like merchandise, professional services, money, and gifts; "somatic" goods like handshakes and kisses; "mental" goods (usually conveyed verbally) like birthday wishes, promises, and (especially) ideas and concepts. With regard to the latter, it must be noted that there prevails a real analogy between the verbal communicating of ideas/concepts and the behavioral conveying of things, in that both are interpersonal transactions. Of course, words (especially terms) are *also cognitive;* this gives them a capacity for "impersonalness" and abstraction that things and somatic goods do not have, at least not to the same extent. That capacity lies in the ability of words to *signify*—that is, to represent things and ideas/concepts *outside* the context of particular situations. In that sense, words enable us to take our *distance* from interpersonal situations so as to transcend them intellectually; for that reason, verbal communication, being cognitive, often favors the content of communicative activity at the expense of its interpersonal elements. But we must remember that in using words we not only *know* things but also *handle* them, especially by using words to *name* them—that is, verbally point to them; and in the interpersonal sphere, we use words (even abstract ones) *performatively*, as J. L. Austin has shown in his classic *How to do Things with Words* (Cambridge: Harvard University Press, 1962). Consequently, *all* communication, *including verbal communication that is chiefly cognitive*, is a form of *behavior*, it is "gestural" (cf. Augustine, *Confessions*, I, VIII, 13; also, F. J. van Beeck, *Christ Proclaimed*, pp. 85-98). From this it follows that *all* content—including material and somatic goods—functions symbolically, as will be explained.

distorted from one person *to* another, what is required on the part of both is an interpersonal context—an awareness of *mutual presence*, of actively and receptively being *with* one another [*hh*]. Such a context, in fact, is not only required for the satisfactory *conveying* of content already possessed by one person involved in the encounter; in intellectual communication, we also require a context of interpersonalness in order to succeed in satisfactorily *articulating* the content we are conveying [*ii*]. Thus, to repeat Martin Buber's insight, communication as encounter ("I-Thou") is the matrix of communication as articulation and sharing of content ("I-It"), or, *communication-with is the matrix of communication-to.* Or again, in communicative activity, elements taken from the world of things are meaningfully integrated into encounters between or among persons.

[a] It follows that interpersonal encounter and content-sharing are not two discrete events, related to each other in a merely occasional fashion—events that only happen to occur simultaneously. In actual communication, the personal encounter and the content conveyed are *intrinsically correlated*; if they were not, it would be impossible to tell the difference between appropriate and inappropriate communication.

Whenever human communication is experienced as *appropriate*, the content communicated is harmoniously integrated into the encounter. In appropriate communication, therefore, there is *broad symbolic consonance* between the quality of mutual presence and the content communicated, both at the giving and at the receiving end. That is, the content positively *carries and conveys* the encounter, while at the same time *shaping, tempering, and regulating* it. Thus appropriate communication ranges from the simple kindness that is fitting when, say, a travel agent gives a customer the required information about airline schedules, to the deep

---

[*hh*] That experience is often connected with *affect* as distinguished from mere knowledge. Basic training in human relations makes use of this distinction, when participants are encouraged, *for purposes of training*, to *separate* feelings from thoughts and focus, for the time being, on the former. Still, the goal of the training is neither the canonization of affect nor its separation from thought, but their integration: "I sense how you feel, so I can see what you say." It is precisely in and behind the integration of thought and affect that we surmise, and thus encounter, the person in his or her integrity.

[*ii*] That context may be remote. Think, for example, of the "audience" that any author imagines, whether implicitly or explicitly, while writing with a view to publication.

tenderness that suits the encounter between, say, two persons sharing their love of God.

Needless to say, there is a wide area of possibilities for *inappropriate* communication; human communication is essentially precarious; in most instances, communication involves a struggle with elements of inappropriateness. Inappropriate communication is characterized (not by integration but) by *alienation*—that is, by *appreciable symbolic dissonance*. Among countless possible instances, we can think of drastic ones, like the case of the frustrated lover angrily shouting, "But I love you!" or, at the other extreme, the case of the bank teller who, disconcertingly, seems to put his very soul into the cash he counts out to me [*jj*].

[2] Let us now begin gradually to take our distance from the element of content-sharing in communication, so as to focus mainly on the element of personal encounter. A first point to be made is that in every act of content-sharing, I always share more than *what* I share. In actual communication-situations, there is, inherent in all content, a surplus value—a reality that (mostly) remains unstated; for in whatever I do and say, I also express *my own reality*. Thus in communicating, I always do more than just exactly what I do, always say more than just exactly what I say; for in and beyond what I do and say, I convey *myself*, albeit symbolically. This communication of self remains limited, of course; nothing that we manifestly do or say ever succeeds in conveying the full, integral reality of our selves. That is, if symbolic communication reveals us, it also falls short of wholly giving us away; what we do and say manifests us, but something about us is bound to remain implicit in the manifesting.

[*jj*] Here, in the experience of communication that fails due to symbolic dissonance, lie the experiential roots of Jean Paul Sartre's thesis that interpersonal communication is nothing but a bitter illusion, which illustrates the absurdity of human existence. Our struggle to communicate amidst the intractable world of things is perpetual; tiresomely, we humans find ourselves forever attracted to others, yet without ever being positively capable of reaching them, *as others*. This shows that we are ultimately doomed, as persons, to remain alienated. Locked up inside ourselves, we are as isolated as things, but worse off, for our self-consciousness prevents us from being at peace within ourselves. For self-consciousness means *inner dividedness*, down to the core of our being; our selves give us no respite from our selves, yet we cannot help dealing with ourselves either (*pour-soi*). Our thus being at loggerheads with ourselves prevents us from reaching out to others freely, without being bothered by our selves; in fact, others serve but to remind us of our isolatedness. And with the weariness characteristic of *ressentiment*, Sartre suggests that the simple, undivided, un-self-conscious reality of things (*en-soi*) is a far more appealing form of being than human existence.

In fact, what is thus left implicit about us is often accentuated by the manifest: persons we have come to know really well are often more mysterious to us than others whom we know only superficially. All of this leaves the full reality of "*who* we really are" a perpetual mystery, never to be either expressed or captured in any particular act of communication.

This combination of self-manifestation and persistent hiddenness is carried ("symbolized") at the level of content. *What* we communicate is always necessarily limited. No matter how much content I communicate, it is never exhaustive: I could have thought of a different gift; to the handshake, I could have added a kiss; I remember I left an important point of information to my partner's imagination. Thus the very limits of what we make manifest in communicating suggest the many goods not shared and the untold things that remain unstated; the content that I manifestly communicate also serves to symbolize the content that remains recessive.

But this means that I reveal and conceal myself not only in what I manifestly communicate, but also (and, in fact, often more eloquently) in the things I leave undone and unstated. And thus it is in the *chiaroscuro* created by what we do and do not do, say and do not say, that we most adequately communicate—that is, both reveal and conceal, both surrender and hold back—*two realities, distinct yet integrated: our personal selves and what we mean to communicate.*

This leads to one further, more radical step. In communication, the interpersonal conveying of self is the active, originating element: it undergirds and sustains what occurs at the level of content. For even if I withhold content—that is, if I communicate "nothing in particular"—I cannot help conveying *myself*, somehow. That is, while we are physically with others, we are bound to convey something. Among other things, this accounts for the unpleasant fact that absent-minded persons can be ever so annoyingly present; it also explains why, in any encounter, those who are not involved, whether by design or out of impotence, have such a frustrating way of obstructing communication among those who are. As persons, therefore, we cannot *not* communicate; we cannot help "revealing," or "manifesting," ourselves, if always incompletely, and hence, never without at least some puzzlement. In any situation, we are players and participants, like it or not. This holds even when we absent ourselves physically: we cannot help suggesting some kind of message, even if we do not always articulate just what it is, in which case we leave it to others to second-guess what we might mean. Thus, whether by action or by default, we always communicate something, and in that "something" we also symbolically communicate ourselves. To exist as a person is to self-communicate, if always in particular, and hence partial, ways [*kk*].

[3] Now in communicating ourselves, both in what we manifest and in what we leave undone and unstated, *we invite a response in kind.* That response is the self-communication of others. Every act of self-communication is an *appeal*—a plea addressed to others to render themselves present to me in actuality. These moves, of course, involve sizable risks on both sides, for full symbolic consonance between what I communicate and who I am is never insured in advance, neither in my offer of self-communication nor in others' response to it. Unintentionally, I may botch the way I come across; equally unintentionally, others may misinterpret me. Worse still, my invitations and appeals can meet with deliberate indifference and cold rejection on the part of others; and I myself have it in me to turn devious in addressing myself to others and seek to manipulate them.

Still, all these ominous realizations serve only to reinforce, rather than detract from, a fundamental truth: we can no more help appealing to others to communicate themselves to us than we can help communicating ourselves to them. To exist as a person is to invite the self-communication of others, if always in particular, and hence partial, ways.

But this is where a *fundamental human responsibility* emerges, and inseparable from it, *a fundamental human freedom.* This can be explained in two successive moves, as follows.

[4] At the interpersonal level, communication involves more than one bare personal existent acknowledging, in and through what he or she communicates, the bare existence of another person. Our orientation, as persons, to other persons, is an original given (§64, 2, [*l*]); hence all other persons are valuable, not just derivatively, by reference to an extrinsic set of moral norms, but originally and inherently. The simple givenness of a person, therefore, is not a bare, neutral fact; it creates an ethical situation; each and every per-

---

[*kk*] Readers of the first two paragraphs will recall Newman's parallel images and expressions to convey a parallel point (§15, 3); in the last paragraph, they will have noticed echoes of Karl Rahner's "Zur Theologie des Symbols" (ET "The Theology of the Symbol").

son intrinsically demands to be responded to, in a way each and every thing does not; among persons, *factual availability for response establishes moral responsibility* [*ll*].

In the self-communication by which I invite others to convey themselves to me I must acknowledge this responsibility. My self-communication should suggest an offer of positive regard and acceptance of the other as such. The self-revealing plea, "be there for me" must imply some form of commitment, "I will be there for you." My offer of self-communication, no matter how implicit, must always intimate that, in the actuality of communicative behavior, I will encounter the other person, no matter how clumsily, in accordance with his or her intrinsic worth as a person.

This means that in every particular communication-situation, *symbolic consonance in communication* is not just a pragmatic issue, that touches on the orderly transfer of content; it is a moral issue predicated on the abiding nature of personhood. Both my own integrity as a person and the integrity of the other demand that, in and through whatever we communicate, we do justice, both to each other and to our own authentic selves.

Needless to say, this justice is an elusive pursuit, since the personal integrity of both ourselves and others is beyond full comprehension or expression; the selfhood of persons—our own as well as others'—and our mutual presence are indeed available to us, but only in symbol—that is, precariously and tentatively, in the ongoing experience of patient negotiation and interpretation [*mm*]. But it is precisely in thus seeking to do justice that we empower each other to overcome our inherent trepidation in the face both

---

[*ll*] Readers of Emmanuel Lévinas will recognize in this proposition my deep indebtedness to his central thesis that the personal identity we bring to our encounters with others is not self-constituted, but responsive. That is, it is fundamentally beholden to the unconditional, *essentially unilateral* demand for justice that resides in the face—both utterly vulnerable and sovereignly authoritative—of *the other*, who *precisely as other* reveals God. Our treatment differs from Lévinas' in that it places personal relatedness, and the responsive identity-experience that is inseparable from it (cf. §35, 1), in the context of communication among fundamentally equal—and hence, equally responsible—partners. As a result, we understand the inescapable imperative inherent in personal encounter in terms of fundamental symmetry and mutuality. This implies an understanding of encounter (and the moral obligation inherent in it) as a matter of *sympathy*, and ultimately, of God as *compassionate love*, demanding the active pursuit of justice without limits.

[*mm*] The reader will recall a proposition developed much earlier in this volume: no information without participative knowledge, and hence, without (the need for) interpretation (cf. §63).

of what we are and of what are meant to be more fully: persons responsively and responsibly present to one another.

Communicating our selves and inviting the self-communication of others, therefore, is not something we can suspend at will; it is inherent in our existence as persons. Hence, the demand for justice and integrity in interpretative communication is coextensive with human life itself; it is always with us, even though it surfaces only in particular communicative interactions, in the form of a demand for symbolic consonance. Thus personal integrity—our own and others'—ceaselessly urges us to do justice to others, by sharing with them such things as we have at our disposal, and to do so in such a way as to share, in some fashion, our authentic selves with them as well. This sharing encompasses, on our part, a morally authoritative appeal extended to others to do justice to us in turn; thus we invite them to share with us of such things as they have at their disposal, so as in some fashion to share themselves with us as well [nn].

[5] Inseparably from the exercise of this fundamental responsibility between and among persons we become conscious of *a fundamental freedom* as well. As persons, we have seen, we are living gestures of responsible communication extended to others, as well as appeals for responsible communication in turn. Yet every time *appropriate* communication comes off, we are delighted and surprised—even thankful, so much so that we will want to talk about it, to the point of bearing witness to it. Much as appropriate communication is an obvious and natural thing to engage in, we apparently find it is not to be taken for granted. This begs for further reflection.

[nn] The opposite of all this is the disregard of others. This occurs in pardonable (if often culpable) ways when, to whatever extent, I treat another person inconsiderately—that is, as infrahuman, as a *thing*. But even things are entitled to an appropriate level of positive regard; between persons and things, true encounters (if sub-verbal ones) do occur; "mere things" do not exist. For this reason, inconsiderateness, however immoral, still involves that minimal form of positive regard that consists in the acknowledgment of the other's existence as part of the world. The ultimate immorality, and the true source of all violence against humanity as such, consists in *actively ignoring human personalness as such*—treating persons as non-persons that are not worth a thing. This frightening possibility looms on the horizon of any world view to the extent to which it is enslaved to *mere* things and desensitized to the whole range of the universe's spiritual ingredients. As a result, such a world view is liable to recognize as really real only "the right things," especially its own favorite ideas, ideologies, prejudices, and idols.

At the heart of the issue lies the following experience: *in the presence of other persons, we never feel neutral.* We feel either in touch or out of touch, basically connected or largely alienated. How to account for this?

To exist with other persons is to self-communicate and to invite self-communication. This is a given; we cannot suspend it at will. Being with others is tantamount to being called to responsiveness; others call upon us willy-nilly; we are responsible to each other's personalness. No wonder factual inability or, worse, refusal to engage in appropriate communication strikes us as a moral failure—a failure of fundamental mutual justice. Not surprisingly, when, in a particular situation, we sense that communication is failing, we are liable to feel driven into some form of personal isolation; a curious self-consciousness (of a self-centered, non-liberating kind) may take a hold of us; by way of cover, we may strike a pose or two, deliberately or instinctively; but the posturing only further checks the flow of encounter, or blocks it altogether. Symbolic dissonance has set in; inappropriate communication further invades the atmosphere; we start pretending to communicate rather than communicating; it may even occur to us that is probably the best we can do for now; we are becoming actors—something akin to hypocrisy takes over.[33] Somehow the suspicion may come to us that we are being unpleasantly and unfairly judged, and found wanting, so we try a bit harder, but to no avail. And underneath it all, we are conscious, vaguely or keenly, that *we are betraying what we are*, namely, persons responsibly present to persons. In failing to communicate appropriately, we are falling short of what is morally incumbent on us as persons, as well as being deprived of what is morally owed to us as persons.

But thank goodness, there is the other experience, too. Few things are so satisfying, exhilarating, or touching as "hitting it off," at *any* level of appropriateness, with other persons. Yet, curiously, whenever communication comes off, it will strike us as somehow *unexpected*—as a bounty we cannot wholly account for, let alone take credit for. We are satisfied, and in giving expression to our satisfaction, we are likely to recount, with gratitude, elements that contributed to the positive experience; but the elements never quite seem to fully explain why "it clicked." This drives home the realization that appropriate communication, while the most natural and pertinent thing in the world as well as a fundamental moral imperative, can never be compelled; it is a *free interpersonal gift.* How can this be?

In self-communicating, I freely extend to others what it is my deepest duty to extend to them as persons: my very self—that is, that which it is my sole as well as deepest privilege to extend. Others may jeopardize this freedom; they may succeed in tricking the gift of myself out of me by feigned love, or even in extorting it from me by violence; but it would be immoral for them even to try to do so. Others may also enhance this freedom. They can accept the gift of myself from me. They can even elicit it from me, by freely communicating themselves with me. In fact, it is precisely in response to acts of free self-communication that I find myself encouraged and empowered to communicate myself in turn. Without the inviting presence of others drawing me out of myself, and without myself agreeing to be drawn out, I might end up finding myself unmoved—habitually powerless to extend myself to anyone. *That* would be moral impotence indeed! Abandoned by others, or worse, having myself abandoned others [*oo*], I would find myself powerless freely to choose to be what I can neither deny I am nor help being: myself. Destined for an open identity cherished and seasoned by habits of relatedness, I would find myself mired in futile self-concern—my identity turned, perversely, into a prison.

Thus in the very act of appropriate communication we find ourselves personally exercising and enjoying, in constructive mutuality, a gracious, liberating inner freedom. This freedom is as integral to our life together as persons as the obligation to respond to each other; in appropriate communication, in other words, we freely agree to empower each other. Thus we freely endorse and enhance what we cannot help being: our selves—that most precious of things which we are also free to diminish and even reject, in self-defeating and ultimately unsuccessful self-contradiction [*pp*].

[*oo*] Note Martin Buber's observation that there is a decisive difference between these two forms of failure of relatedness: "the one who is abandoned by those to whom he uttered the true *Thou* is accepted by God, not the one who himself abandoned them" (*Ich und Du*, p. 123; ET, p. 152).

[*pp*] Here we have laid bare the anthropological infrastructure of the experience of supernatural grace. Limiting communication to the conveying of content involves a neutral treatment of persons, as if they were mere agents designed only to manipulate the world of things by efficient causality. On account of their immanent authenticity, however, human persons are transcendent; they operate on formal and final causality as well. Hence, persons are owed gestures of communication, which involves a degree of benevolence; mere correctness, we feel, amounts to a slight; it is morally deficient. Yet actually encountering others in keeping with their inherent nature as persons is an activity that can only be freely undertaken, and in that sense gracious—something none can extort from any as

To sum up, to exist as persons is to communicate, and this communication consists in the actualization of ourselves and each other as persons dynamically present to each other; this actualization is successful to the extent that it is inspired by mutual empowerment freely given and accepted.

This is where a twofold issue arises. We are impotent to communicate without at least some others to draw us out; our mutuality in communicating, in other words, is shot through with *dependence*, and what is more, dependence *on the part of all.* This dependence is at once ontic and actual, the former being foundational, the latter at least partial. It is *ontic* inasmuch as, for any communication to occur, *all* persons are dependent on the givenness of other persons—that is, on their factual availability for response; it is *actual* inasmuch as, in particular situations, at least *some* are at least partly dependent on the free initiative of particular others. We must explore the implications of both. Let us begin by reflecting on the latter—the phenomenon of actual dependence, in two consecutive steps.

[6] *Appropriate communication constantly needs free initiative;* it is neither self-originating nor self-sustaining. Whenever and wherever two or more persons are available to each other for encounter, all are indeed summoned to respond, but the question is who will grasp the opportunity. Or when an actual process of communication flags, the question is who will make the decisive move to revive it. Who will freely and creatively respond, and to whom, to actuate the process of mutual empowerment?

Many of us can name persons who have been *personally* significant to us. Not infrequently, they are people who have also been *functionally* significant to us; they gave us many things we are grateful for. More importantly, they had a way with things: the seemingly effortless way in which they did things suggested they were in control of what they had to give. Yet their real significance for us lies in the fact that they had a way with *us,* that suggested what kind of *persons* they were. Thus we have come to remember them, thankfully, as part of *who we have become;* they are integral to our autobiography—to the story of such enlightenment and self-awareness as has become ours. If they did train and model us, it was not in *their*

---

owed by right. In the interpersonal world, therefore, there is no such thing as "pure nature"; in dealing with each other, *we either fail to meet the just demands of "nature" or we graciously and freely exceed them.*

favorite mold; in fact, they discouraged admiration and smiled at our self-conscious attempts at mimicry. Instead, they were creative, functionally and personally—thus they helped us find a shape of our own. Curiously, if they made problems for us (as quite often they did), they usually turned out not to be part of them. That is, they managed to *identify* with us without *interfering* with us; we sensed they were concerned, but in such a way as to let us be; we felt free. They may have added to our self-knowledge by sharing with us (in a way we could accept) their informed judgments about us; yet they seemed less interested in *what* they understood *about* us than in understanding *us.* Apparently undaunted by the disparateness and incoherence of our experience of ourselves, of others, of our world, and of God, they succeeded in providing us with a welcoming, searching, illuminating presence. That presence felt like a pledge of acceptance. Thus we were enabled to let our philosophy of life and our self-knowledge, our judgments and our convictions take shape in our own minds; they were instrumental in revealing us to ourselves. And so, here we are, having grown into tolerably self-accepted and well-integrated persons, with a fairly comfortable sense of self-identity, and hence, with a reasonable ability (as well as a quiet courage) to reach out to others as scattered and confused now as we once were.

Invariably, we remember such persons as remarkably well-integrated and hence, as quite self-sufficient. While they obviously enjoyed dealing with our immature or impotent selves, they did not seem to revel in helping us; *if* they were at all dependent on us, our dependence on them was far greater—we really *needed* them. Yet what seemed to matter to them was not so much our need as our selves—our inner potential for freedom and identity. In fact, what made them especially capable of enhancing us was that they clearly did not expect to be enhanced by us. Modest without self-abasement, engagingly un-self-conscious, and clearly unimpressed by their own level of personal integration, they were carefree enough to be freely present to our struggling selves, penetratingly yet unobtrusively [*qq*].

[*qq*] The thumbnail sketch just drawn owes a debt, not only to personal experience of significant others, but also to Abraham Maslow's phenomenology of the fully actualized person, in such books as *Toward a Psychology of Being* and *Religions, Values, and Peak Experiences.*

Persons like this illustrate a fundamental thesis. The actual event of appropriate interpersonal communication is always a matter of *mutual* presence and empowerment. But to initiate and sustain both the presence and the empowerment, what is needed is personal presence freely—that is, onesidedly—undertaken, which is the fruit of personal identity come to maturity. *The generous inner freedom of the mature is the soul of constructive communication.*

This can also be formulated as follows: to the extent that persons acquire a habit of integrating the world of things, and thus, a habit of transcending their immediate involvement in it, to that extent they will attain their true *personal* selves. To that extent they will also be capable of personal presence to others, of freely identifying with them, and of communicating themselves to others in such a way as to enhance the latter's identity. Put more radically: *the more transcendent persons are, the more immanent they are liable to be.*

[7] This has an important consequence: encounters in which significant others reveal themselves to us are appreciated by us only to the extent that, in encountering them, *we find ourselves revealed to ourselves.* This can be rephrased in the form of another crucial thesis: *encounters in which we meet significant others as truly other are inseparable from authentic self-experience.* Unlike the self-awareness predicated on various forms of self-analysis, self-examination, and introspection, authentic self-experience is responsive; in it, we find, in ways inaccessible to our autonomous egos, self-enlightenment, self-recovery, self-correction and conversion, and growth. Even more pertinently, responsive self-experience guarantees and authenticates to us *the reality of the significant other's presence.* From the depth of our self-experience, therefore, we should never draw the conclusion that we are only experiencing ourselves. Rather, what we experience in our self-experience is the other *precisely as other*—that is, as one who encounters us without our ever being able to fully accounts for his or her identity [rr].

Responsive self-experience becomes manifest in the phenomenon of *witness.* Most commonly, witness involves two levels of affirmation. First, we pay tribute, in both word and deed, to significant others on account of *what* they have given us. But secondly and more pertinently, we witness to significant others on account of *who*

[rr] On this crucial subject, cf. an illuminating article by Stephen Watson: "Reason and the Face of the Other."

they have been for us; they are integral to *ourselves* inasmuch as we have become *authentic, creative persons.* Thus in "testimonial autobiography" (§41, 2; §45, 2; §46, 2), we tend to place whatever *things* others have given us in the context of *who* they have been for us; *what* they did and said has come to symbolize *who* they are *for us as persons.* Grateful self-awareness rather than functional indebtedness prompts us to bear witness to significant others.

Not surprisingly, however, in testimonial autobiography we will also find ourselves attributing to significant others *things* which, as a matter of naked fact, they may not have done or said, but which it would have been most characteristic of them to have done or said. But then, in giving a thankful account of ourselves we are not interested in naked facts; it is out of the fullness of our responsive self-experience that we make the attribution; there are certain *things* which we cannot imagine we would do or understand here and now if we had not encountered *them* there and then.

All of this can be put more theoretically. The self-revealing presence of significant others originally occurs in interpersonal encounters freely animated by *initiators.* Still, it is the *recipients* that will proceed to cherish the encounter as an abiding element of their self-awareness; they, therefore, are also the ones that will proceed to *witness* to it in the form of *content*—that is, by means of definite actions and articulate statements. Typically, they will credit these doings and sayings not so much to themselves (even though they are authentically theirs) as to the significant others who continue to inspire them.

All of this serves to make a point crucial to our analysis. *Significant (self-)communication that comes to us from others is never experienced as a mere intervention from outside.* In interpersonal encounter, when the free (and in that sense, transcendent) presence of another person communicates itself to us, it does so with an impact that is *immanent.* In interpersonal encounter, the inner testimony of self-experience matches the testimony of outward engagement with otherness. Not surprisingly, our best touchstone of the significance of any encounter is immanent: it consists in the experience of finding our deeper, authentic selves engaged, actuated, restored, enhanced—surprisingly yet unmistakably.

[8] So much for our analysis of the fact that all appropriate interpersonal communication is *actually* dependent on the mature freedom of significant others. Now we must explore the implications of the fact that we are *ontically* dependent on others for commu-

nication. It involves two levels of experience, of which the first is an experience of *tradition*.

Appropriate communication, we have said, is neither self-originating nor self-sustaining. This implies that whenever it occurs, not even the mature persons capable of authentically identifying with less mature others completely account for its occurrence. The reason for this is that mature persons that animate appropriate communication are not wholly self-made. Those to whose mature freedom and generosity we bear witness once encountered others to whom they came to bear witness; typically, significant others will acknowledge their dependence on the positive regard once freely extended to them by others significant to them—others not actually present. For mature persons, therefore, to engage in a communicative encounter is not the reinvention of the wheel every time they do it. Rather, the opposite is the case. As we encounter more and more persons as truly other, we discover that they become, in us, a quiet company of friends who equip us for encounters with yet others [*ss*]. Significant others, in other words, are *active participants in a tradition of freely undertaken benevolence to others*.

However, there is something comparable on the receiving end as well. Those *to whom* significant others communicate themselves are not *tabula rasa*; no matter how immature they may be, they are not without an identity of their own to start with. Interpersonal communication invariably builds on what is *given*; and we know from experience that this givenness includes an observable initial preparedness for interpersonal communication.

[*ss*] True encounter, in other words, enhances our disposition to engage in further encounters. It is enlightening to contrast this experience with the experience of accumulating *things* (that is, all that fits the category of content; cf. §95, 1, [*gg*]). While it is entirely human to collect things both material and mental out of interest and affection, things also lend themselves to mere accumulation. Not surprisingly, people will collect every kind of item: stamps, but also match-books, egg-cups, firearms, cat figurines, signatures of influential persons, limericks, jokes and puns, word-etymologies—the more trivial, the more collectible. But as we go on collecting, we find we cannot keep up with things; they tend to crowd each other out (not only in our houses, but also in our memories, our minds, and especially our hearts). And what is more, we find the person in us will get lost in the press of multiplicity; accordingly, we doubt the full personal maturity of obsessive collectors, whether of objects or of knowable things. It is to be noted, too, that the category of things can include persons, to the extent that we (attempt to) collect them as if they were objects. Finally, these observations are of some consequence towards the understanding of integralism, which is the reduction of the faith to an accumulation of manifest elements (cf. §19, 1).

We conclude that *authentic capacity for interpersonal communication is at least partly habitual—a matter of pre-existing tradition.* Our factual availability to each other for responsive and responsible encounter—the ground for our ontic dependence on each other for communication—is never completely formless.

[a] Lest we make the mistake of casting the dynamic we are analyzing in narrowly (inter-)personalist terms, an important point must be made here. Recipients of the mature presence of significant others, it was explained, will *witness* to that presence to others in word and deed, and they will do so also in the form of *content*—that is, by means of definite actions and articulate statements that convey the freshness of the experience. Typically, it was added, they will attribute these doings and sayings to the significant others that inspired them. Witness to the creative maturity of significant others, in other words, will breed new communication, not only of the live *interpersonal* variety, but also of the *instrumental, institutional* kind—the kind that promises *stability. Testimony borne by trustworthy witnesses founds reliable schools of action and thought*; it tends toward the structuring of traditions (and eventually of a fairly unified *culture* with a distinctive *sensus communis*), in the twin forms of *organized common life* and *traditional community wisdom* [*tt*]. Still, neither shared practices nor shared wisdom are, in and of themselves, sure-fire devices; they will function as means of appropriate communication only to the extent that they function *symbolically*—that is, as vehicles of a truly communicative, responsive life together (cf. §56, 12-13). For such a meaningful life any community and any culture needs symbolic consonance; shared norms for action and the truths that enshrine shared wisdom must be experienced as meaningful and authentic. But this means that they have to be regularly reestablished and reinterpreted. Thus all practices and all wisdom depend for their meaningfulness on *interpretation by authentic witnesses.* All communities and cultures, therefore, need prophets—people who creatively shape and reshape the intractable here and now out of an affinity with the *soul* of the common tra-

---

[*tt*] Note that the relationship between interpersonal encounter and witness to significant others in deed and word is analogous to the relationship between the worship of God and Christian witness in conduct and teaching (§47, 5). Note, too, that any kind of common life and any community wisdom must be *learned* to be understood, as George Lindbeck has well explained in *The Nature of Doctrine.*

dition. In the long run, tradition is kept alive by authentic communicators, not by critics, and certainly not by taskmasters, letter-worshipers, and hacks.

[9] Traditions, both of live interpersonal benevolence and of life-shaping institutional structures of communication, go a long way to account for the actual occurrence of constructive interpersonal communication. Still, it would be rash to conclude that they adequately account for it. It is surely pointless to deny that people do indeed grow in freedom and generosity from the benevolence shown to them, at the strictly interpersonal level, by others. Still, it is primitive to think of sustained traditions of interpersonal communication solely in terms of chain-reactions of strictly personal empowerments [*uu*]; and in any case, we know from experience that any such imagined chains have weak links: we find ourselves also failing to live up to the positive regard extended to us by others, and thus we interrupt the flow of constructive communication. And at the level of institutions, it is true that people are indeed right to rely on stable traditions for appropriate communication; but we know that traditions can also harden and become a hindrance to communication rather than a help.

Thus we are faced with the fact that *ultimately* we find ourselves presented to each other for appropriate communication simply as we are, naked and without ado; just by being around each other, we mutually invite constructive ("creative") acceptance, and we discern each other's habitual capacity for it; in the final analysis, what we must respond to in communicating is our naked, unadorned selves, presented to each other in our irreducible otherness.

Yet the fact is that *we do actually respond*, and with a spontaneity that is never quite *reducible* to the merely appropriate. True encounters with others do occur, transcending the world of things; others get the best out of us—that is, the truly unexpected response we did not know we had inside us. When truly appropriate communication—the free mutual sharing of ourselves—does occur, it somehow reveals a spiritual wealth that surpasses the expectations prompted by the merely given. Living—immature as we are—in a pre-

---

[*uu*] Moreover, such a move leads to a variant of Traditionalism (§12, 1, a). Logically, the chain-idea involves an endless regression of the chicken-and-egg variety, which explains nothing. But non-explanation is precisely what lies at the root of the traditionalist claim that God started all authentic communication with an historic "primordial self-communication."

carious world, here we are, actually communicating; while not creating one another in any absolute sense, we do decisively affect
each other as we grow as persons. Thus the fact that fruitful interpersonal communication animated by freedom and personal maturity does occur, *even in the midst of chance and immaturity*, is a marvel
that eludes complete rationalization. There is something about the
experience of interpersonal communication that suggests that, ultimately, it is simply a *gift*—one that will forever surprise the anticipa-
tions of even the most mature.

[10] Not surprisingly, therefore, the free, mature, truly integrated,
self-giving person is experienced, in some religious traditions, as a
witness to a better world. Secure personal identity freely, unselfcons-
ciously, and indeed unselfishly shared with others in both action
and thought, we sense, must be somehow prompted by, embedded
in, and encompassed and supported by, a larger Presence that is in-
effably free, eternal, generous, indefeasible, and mysteriously self-
manifesting,

> Ground of being, and granite of it: pást áll
> Grásp Gód, throned behind
> Death with a sovereignty that heeds but hides, bodes but abides.[34]

Ultimately, that is, it must be a transcendent, gracious, self-com-
municative Presence that inspires and guarantees the freedom with
which the good among us communicate themselves to other persons. Only an unconditional, all-enabling Presence is transcendent
enough to move our innermost immanence to open itself to others
without anxiety about ourselves [*vv*].

[*vv*] We can think of persons of extraordinary maturity and commitment like
Dag Hammarskjöld, whose reflections, collected in *Markings*, have led many to a
renewed, truly responsible sense of God. Fictional characters may come to mind
as well: Prince Leo Nikolayevich Myshkin in F. Dostoevsky's *The Idiot*, consciously
modeled after Jesus Christ by its author; Tarrou in Albert Camus' *The Plague*, who
has decided to identify with victims rather than join the cause of violence by
fighting evil; and, in the novels of the emphatically non-Christian, non-theistic contemporary British novelist Iris Murdoch (b. 1919), figures like Max Lejour in *The
Unicorn* (1963), with his mature belief in the non-violence of the Good, or more
recently, in *The Message to the Planet* (1989), the eccentric Marcus Vallar, who, after
remarkable early careers as a mathematician and a painter, sets out on a tightrope
search for the truth beyond the cosmic network, until at length he charms others
by a wordless, enigmatic kindness, to which, however, he himself succumbs because
it leads to "pure suffering," which is an attribute of God alone (cf. §110, 4, b). On
the truly adult person as a witness to the living God, cf. Thomas Merton's observations on "final integration": *Contemplation in a World of Action*, pp. 205-17; cf. also

But in that case that same Presence must also be so penetrating as to ground the deepest identity of *all* persons, in an acceptance so unconditional as to be wholly creative. There, at the core of each person, it establishes, not only the unconditional demand for positive regard that marks all persons as persons, but also their irresistible attractiveness. That is, God's everlasting offer of self-communication must be the transcendent precondition for the immanent appeal that invites us to touch and affect others so close to the core of their identities. By way of a variation on a theme played, long ago, by Aquinas, we might say, "All those who encounter others encounter God implicitly in whomever they encounter" (cf. §8, 8; cf. also §102, 10). God's (self-)communication, therefore, could not possibly be experienced as a mere intervention from outside; it graciously addresses us at the core of our identity, where we are made in the divine image and likeness—that is, where we are made in the image of Christ (cf. §§89-90).

But in *that* case the divine Presence also encompasses our *failures* in communication—that is, it patiently and faithfully holds out hope for a restoration and renewal of encounter even when those involved in interpersonal communication prove inadequate or even downright misleading, and when the traditions that support it languish and lapse. *Dios escrive derecho con líneas torcidas*—"God writes straight on crooked lines."

A well-known passage in Augustine's *Confessions* illustrates this insight. Now firmly in communion with God in and through the community of the Church in which he is a newly-appointed bishop, Augustine is free, finally, to recall all the implications of his experience of being the Prodigal Son. He recalls how, completely at a loss, he had wandered among the poets and philosophers; none of them had connected and communicated with him in such a way as to nourish him and lead him to a mature sense of identity; he had been

... a stranger in a faraway land, barred from You as much as from the husks of the pigs, whom I was giving the husks to eat, ... struggling and straining, short of truth.

Now he has become a witness. With profound gratitude he recalls the significant others he has encountered on his slow, winding road

---

his *Faith and Violence*, pp. 111-18. I am indebted to Walter E. Conn's anthology *Conversion* for the last two references.

to the Church: Monica, Alypius, Nebridius, Ambrose. They have been to him, not only reliable supporters of his authentic, long-lost self, but also faithful and effective witnesses to God's enduring presence. But that is not the whole story. Participation in the community of faith has enabled Augustine to discover the real power at work behind the communicative impasses and failures in his earlier life, as long as all he had to go by was elegant but unsubstantial pagan myths (the staple of classroom practice in late antiquity), scraps of improbable Manichaeism, and the skepticism of the Academy. Ultimately, it is God, transcendent and immanent, who has led him to the truth, both by the banality of illusion and error and by the faithfulness of trustworthy friends. So he can conclude, in a Neo-Platonist vein:

Yet You were inside, deeper than my innermost self, and above, higher than my uppermost self.[35]

[11] Here it is—the core of the catholic understanding of revelation. The divine self-communication comes from on high, yet it is inseparable from authentic human immanence. But far from simply becoming a matter of self-experience, the God who reveals the divine Self becomes more, not less, adorable and ungraspable for being so intimately manifest (cf. §34, 2). Thus divine self-communication makes witnesses of human persons: God is "the God of Abraham, the God of Isaac, and the God of Jacob," and ultimately, "the God of Jesus Christ." Yet while touching us as persons, God bids us reshape the world of both persons and things [ww]. In that world, we cannot hope ever to convey or understand God's self-revelation fully, whether in action or in speech, whether as a Church community or as individual Christians; so we treasure such ways as the Tradition has tried and found proven, while we keep on seeking inspiration to try new ways as we travel.

[a] Students of the Second Vatican Council will have noticed that the analysis of the concept of Revelation proposed in this

---

[ww] Here lies the root of the catholic tradition's claim, well explained by Aidan Nichols, that divine revelation exists in articulate deliverances (and, he might have added, in particular rules of life) from the outset. (For the anthropological basis of this thesis, cf. §95, 1-2.) At no time, therefore, is revelation shapeless and non-propositional, as the Modernists, who were willing to settle for a divorce between an immutable, wholly transcendent essence of Christianity and its mutable, fundamentally non-authoritative expressions in place and time. Cf. *From Newman to Congar*, esp. pp. 71-176.

chapter is substantially indebted to the anthropology enshrined in the Pastoral Constitution on the Church in the Modern World (cf. esp. GS 12-18). On a more strictly theological front, it is beholden to the description of Revelation in salvation-historical terms proposed by the Dogmatic Constitution on Divine Revelation (DV 2-4).

[b] Explicit Catholic doctrine on divine Revelation as such is a late development; it did not occur until the nineteenth century. Accordingly, the theological reflections associated with it took their cue, not from the great Tradition, but almost exclusively from an eighteenth-century agenda: the deadlock between Reason and *Christian* Revelation (cf. §86, 3, c; §93, 5, b; 7, a; §94, 6, a) [xx]. Practically speaking, therefore, "revelation" had come to be identified exclusively with the *mysteria proprie dicta* of the Incarnation and the mysteries directly connected with it (cf. DS 2779; 3015-20; 1341; CF 110; 131-37). This had led to two interconnected theological positions, misleading both because of their unnecessary rigidity and on account of their being out of touch with the great Tradition.

In the first place, the understanding of the "mysteries" of the faith, and of the way in which they had been delivered to the Church, had become far too content-oriented and rational. "Mystery" had long ceased to be understood as a matter, both of God's self-communication to humanity and of the corresponding revelation, *in history*, of humanity's authentic nature and destiny. Instead, it had come to be understood as a "deposit" of absolute truths, inaccessible to Reason by definition, and hence, acceptable only by God-given faith, upon the sole authority of the *magisterium*—an authority ultimately guaranteed by the revealing God [yy].

[xx] In the seventeenth and eighteenth centuries, which witnessed a widespread Jewish revival in Western Europe, the Christian habit of downplaying the reality of God's self-revelation to Israel was reinforced by the tendency of *liberal* Judaism, represented by leaders like Moses Mendelssohn (cf. §28, 4, a, [d]), to abandon the claim that Judaism involved, not only ceremonial traditions, but also *revealed truths*. This paved the way for the assimilation of an appreciable number of prominent Jewish families into the liberal Christian establishment. Orthodox Judaism was never part of the cultural debate about the relationship between Reason and Revelation.

[yy] A side-effect of this was the tendency towards a tight demarcation of the *limits* of revelation: since divine Revelation became definitive with the person of Jesus Christ, it had to be complete with the death of the last of Jesus' associates, the apostles (cf. DS 3421).

Secondly, in making the divinity of Jesus Christ into the sole determinative truth of Revelation, Catholic doctrine and theology separated the historical Jesus from the mystery inherent in Israel's faith-tradition and in the "cloud of witnesses" (Heb 12, 1) it had produced. The "pioneer and accomplisher of our faith" (Heb 12, 2), the "faithful witness" (Rev 1, 5; cf. 1 Tim 6, 13), disappeared almost entirely behind "the Word made flesh" (Jn 1, 14). As a result, any christology from below became impossible, whether of the transcendental kind (§31, 1, b) or of the kind that could take the historical life of Jesus the Jew seriously. Vatican II made essential corrections in this area. It recalled God's self-revelation to Abraham and to the People of Israel through Moses and through the Prophets (DV 14; cf. 4), and it insisted on salvation-historical revelation, by means of which "the deepest truth regarding both God and human salvation has shone forth to us in Christ, who is the mediator as well as the fulfillment of all of revelation" (DV 2).

[c] In his important monograph *Models of Revelation*, Avery Dulles has explained that revelation takes many forms, and hence, that it allows for a variety of partial, yet convergent, theological approaches. Thus it can be viewed as doctrine, history, inner experience, dialectical presence, and new awareness. Readers familiar with Dulles' treatise will have noticed that the above analysis attempts to do justice to the models proposed by Dulles, in their organic interconnectedness. They will also have noticed that the present treatment endorses Dulles' own constructive proposal: revelation is God's self-revealing presence mediated symbolically [zz].

[d] Finally, the fundamental analysis of Revelation just offered is consistent with two sets of insights developed by Karl Rahner.

First, there is Rahner's refusal to restrict divine Revelation to the events of *special* (that is, Judaeo-Christian) revelation. By

---

[zz] On the subject of symbolism and the usefulness of "dialogue" as a model of revelation, cf. also David Brown's "God and Symbolic Action," with this proviso, however, that the author's opening appeal to telepathy and telekinesis (p. 104) is an *argumentum ex ignoto*. It suggests (mistakenly, I think) that we are dealing with reliably established experiences and what is more, with reliable insight into their structure. Even more pertinently, Brown's appeal to paranormal phenomena is not essential to his argument.

virtue of the essential human openness to the self-communication that comes from others and ultimately from God, human history *as such* is both salvation history and revelation history; to reduce universal world history to mere *Naturgeschichte* ("history of nature") flies in the face of theological anthropology in the catholic tradition [*aaa*].[36] Just as reflection on the positive profession of Christian faith lays bare humanity's native orientation to God (§59, 3), and thus mandates *theological* reflection on history and nature as such (§59, 6, a), so reflection on Judaeo-Christian revelation in its particularity lays bare the universality of salvation and revelation.

Secondly, there is our contention that significant (self-)communication that comes to us both from others in their relative transcendence (§95, 7) and from the utterly transcendent God is never experienced as a mere intervention from outside. This endorses an important thesis of Karl Rahner's: only those whose authenticity has been transformed by God's self-communication can interpret the historic symbols of Revelation—that is, understand divine Revelation as it has taken shape in concrete, "categorical" forms.[37]

[12] And so, finally, our fundamental-theological reflections have reached the point where this second volume of *God Encountered* can introduce its central theme: the divine *exitus*—the Revelation of the divine Glory. In keeping with the Tradition as well as with the professed intentions of this theological system (§23, 4), this self-revelation of the living God will be treated in two coordinated stages: God and Creation (Part II) and God and Redemption (Part IV), with a section on Creation and Fall in between (Part III).

Our opening move must be one which both the Holocaust and modern cultural anthropology have conspired to raise as, conceivably, the most fundamental question for Christian theology today. It concerns the central issue of Christian theology: the Christian conception of God. The issue can be put in the form of questions. Is authentic Christian faith in God rooted in the historic faith of Is-

---

[*aaa*] In fact, there are good philosophical and theological reasons to doubt that even *Naturgeschichte* can be adequately distinguished (let alone separated) from world history viewed as an essentially anthropological and hence, theological reality; cf. §80, 3, [*c*]; §87, 2, d, [*gg*]. After all, the real world is essentially anthropic; that is, for all their intractability, things essentially function in the world of persons, and cosmic processes become part of human history.

rael or in an allegedly universal, and even perennial, natural philosophy? Or, better perhaps, is Christian thought indebted to Israel's faith for its rational understanding of the relationship between God the Creator and the created order, and if so, how?

These questions were raised with tremendous urgency by a great seventeenth-century Christian: Blaise Pascal. He was among the first to appreciate the cultural watershed that was to determine (as this chapter has attempted to show) the theological agenda of modern times: the scientific approach to the world and humanity.

When, therefore, in the remaining three parts of this second volume, we treat the central Christian doctrines of God, Creation, the Fall, Jesus Christ, and the Blessed Trinity, we will first turn to Pascal.

Notes

Introduction

1. Cf. Ps 91 (90), 6, in the Vulgate. For the probable origin of the usage, cf. the edition of Evagrius Ponticus' *Praktikos* in *SC* 171, p. 521, n. 12. Cf. also John Eudes Bamberger's translation, pp. 18, n. 26, and p. 26, n. 43.
2. Cf. Donnah Canavan Gumpert and others, *The Success-Fearing Personality*.
3. "*Si parva licet componere magnis*": Virgil, *Georgica* IV, 176.
4. Letter of Piet Schoonenberg, S.J. to the author, November 9, 1989.
5. ET Barry, pp. 1001-08.
6. Cf. Verna E. F. Harrison, "Male and Female in Cappadocian Theology," esp. 468-69 and note 93. In a reference to von Balthasar's theology of the sexes as explained in a *Communio* article ("Die Würde der Frau," *Internationale Theologische Zeitschrift "Communio"* of July, 1982, pp. 346ff.), Ulrich Ruh notes that von Balthasar has a twofold approach that attempts to reconcile the essential unity of the sexes (which is based on natural-ontological mutual indebtedness and receptivity, and hence, which prohibits the dominance of one sex over another), with the affirmation of the archetypical primacy of the male (which results in the natural affinity of masculinity in theology, christology, and sacramental theology). Cf. "Als Mann und Frau schuff er sie," p. 577. This position, though highly debatable and certainly unknown to the Church Fathers, deserves to be taken seriously.
7. Quotations from Gerald P. Fogarty, *American Catholic Biblical Scholarship*, pp. 337-39 (italics added).
8. In *La Tradition et les traditions* (ET *Tradition and Traditions*).
9. Cf. H. Schelsky, "Ist die Dauerreflektion institutionalisierbar?"
10. Cf. "Konsensfindung als hermeneutisches Problem," esp. pp. 50-51.
11. *Hermeneutik—ein ökumenisches Problem*, p. 186.
12. Cf. *Hermeneutik—ein ökumenisches Problem*, p. 144.
13. *The Presence of the Word*, p. 223 (italics added).

Chapter 1

1. *Metaphysics* A, 1 (980^{a}22).
2. Cf. David E. Aune, *The Cultic Setting of Realized Eschatology in Early Christianity*.
3. *The Courage to Be*, pp. 176-83; cf. p. 26-27.
4. Incidentally, Jos 6, 17 and 1 Sam 4, 4 present textual problems.
5. Cf. David Novak, *Jewish-Christian Dialogue*, pp. 39-41.
6. On the subject, cf. also Heinrich Schlier, *Mächte und Gewalten im Neuen Testament* (ET *Principalities and Powers in the New Testament*).
7. Cf. Frances M. Young, *The Making of the Creeds*, pp. 16-32.
8. Cf. F.J. van Beeck, *Christ Proclaimed*, p. 88-93.
9. Cf., e.g., *S. Th.* I, 25, 3, *in c.*

10. Cf. J. N. D. Kelly, *Early Christian Doctrines*, pp. 83-108.

Chapter 2

1. For many details and insights in the present section and in §64 I am profoundly indebted to conversation with, and suggestions from, Charles Hallisey and Francis X. Clooney, S.J., both of them capable scholars in the history of religions as well as loyal friends, and hence, reliable and constructive critics.
2. Cf. *Jewish-Christian Dialogue*, esp. pp. 26-41; (quotations pp. 26, 35; italics added). Novak's exhaustive treatment of the subject can be found in his *The Image of the Non-Jew in Judaism.*
3. For a good summary of the issues involved, cf. Ninian Smart, *The Philosophy of Religion*, pp. 99-137.
4. Cf. Huston Smith, *The Religions of Man*, pp. 154-55; quotation p. 154.
5. Cf. Wilhelm Halbfass, *India and Europe*, pp. 349-68.
6. On the characteristic differences between neo-Hinduism and traditional Hinduism in their several evaluations of other religions, cf. Wilhelm Halbfass, "Śaṅkara and Kumārila on the Plurality of Religious Traditions," in *Studies in Kumārila and Śaṅkara*, pp. 85-105. Also, cf. his *India and Europe*, pp. 403-18.
7. Cf. Fazlur Rahman, *Major Themes of the Qur'ān*, pp. 23-25, 166-67. Cf. also Annemarie Schimmel's elegant *Islam: An Introduction.*
8. On this "rhetoric" of "inclusion," "obedience," and "hope," which has its origin in the risen Christ, cf. F. J. van Beeck, *Christ Proclaimed*, esp. pp. 145-262. Cf. also "Ten Questions on Soteriology and Christology," pp. 277-78.
9. Cf. F. J. van Beeck, "Professing the Uniqueness of Christ."
10. Cf. F. J. van Beeck, *Loving the Torah More than God*, pp. 69-77.
11. *Kritik der reinen Vernunft*, B 377-96, A 321-338.
12. *S. Th.* II-II, 45, 2, *in c.*: "Rectitudo autem iudicii potest contingere dupliciter, uno modo, secundum perfectum usum rationis; alio modo, propter connaturalitatem quandam ad ea de quibus iam est iudicandum."
13. Cf. F. J. van Beeck, *Christ Proclaimed*, pp. 66-70, 85-98.
14. Cf. Ian Ramsey, *Religious Language*, esp. pp. 11-48.
15. *Selected Essays 1917-1932*, p. 200.
16. Cf. *The Nature of Doctrine*, esp. pp. 32-41, 73-84.
17. For a discussion of the Jewish parallel to this, cf. David Novak, *Jewish-Christian Dialogue*, pp. 14-25.
18. Cf. *Wahrheit und Methode*, pp. 289-90, 356-57, 375 (ET *Truth and Method*, pp. 273-74, 337-38, 358).
19. Peter Hünermann, "Das Lehramt und die endliche Gestalt der Glaubenswahrheit," p. 373: "... daß der Kirche diese Wahrheit nicht in seiner Vollendungsgestalt, sondern im Zeugnis Jesu Christi gegeben ist. Er ist gekommen, 'von der Wahrheit Zeugnis abzulegen' (Joh 18, 37). Der Glaube ist trotz seiner eschatologischen Unbedingtheit eine vergehende, endliche Gestalt der Wahrheit (vgl. 1 Kor 13, 8-12)."
20. Cf. F. J. van Beeck, *Christ Proclaimed*, pp. 308-09, 331-42.
21. Cf. F. J. van Beeck, "Professing the Uniqueness of Christ," esp. pp. 32-35.
22. Gerd Theißen, *Der Schatten des Galiläers*, p. 55 (cf. ET *The Shadow of the Galilean*, p. 36).

23. David Novak, *Jewish-Christian Dialogue*, p. 80.
24. "Mankind's Religiously Divided History Approaches Self-Consciousness," in *Religious Diversity*, p. 111 (italics added). Feminists reading this passage might see a connection between the male idiom and the implication of superiority, or at least control.
25. "The World Church and the World History of Religion: The Theological Issue," pp. 54, 63 (italics added for emphasis).
26. Cf. Tom F. Driver's "The Case for Pluralism," the final essay in *The Myth of Christian Uniqueness* (pp. 203-18; quotation p. 206), discussing a highly critical response by Kenneth Surin to the essays in that collection. Cf. also Michael Barnes, "Beyond Inclusivism."
27. The last phrase suggested by remarks in Tom F. Driver's "The Case for Pluralism," p. 205.

Chapter 3

1. Flannery O'Connor, Letter of 2 August 1955; *Collected Works*, pp. 943-44.
2. Cf. Jean Daniélou's introduction to Chrysostom's *On the Incomprehensibility of God*, in *SC* 28, esp. pp. 15-29.
3. *In Eccles. Hom.* VII; *PG* 44, 729-32; Jaeger, vol. 5, pp. 412/6-414/9; 415/17-19 (cf. ET Gregory of Nyssa, *From Glory to Glory*, pp. 127-29). Cf. also *De vita Moysis* II, 110-11 (*PG* 44, 359; Jaeger, vol. 7/1, pp. 66/15-67/8; ET pp. 79-80).
4. *Comm. in Eccles.* VII; *PG* 44, 732; Jaeger, vol. 5, pp. 416/1-8 (ET cf. Gregory of Nyssa, *From Glory to Glory*, p. 129).
5. Quoted by Nicholas Lash, *Easter in Ordinary*, p. 171.
6. Quoted (from his 1907 book *The Doctrine of the Trinity*, pp. 109-10) in *Words about God*, (Ian T. Ramsey, ed.), p. 18; italics added.
7. Cf. Michael Buckley, *At the Origins of Modern Atheism*, pp. 71-99. Cf. also Eberhard Jüngel, *Gott als Geheimnis der Welt*, pp. 146-67 (ET pp. 111-26).
8. "Desiderium sinus cordis": St. Augustine, *Tract. in Joh.* 40, 10; quoted in Peter Brown, *Augustine of Hippo*, p. 156. Cf. §49, 1.
9. *Epist.* 130 (*Ad Probam*), XIV-XV (27-28); *CSEL* 44, p. 72: "... quoniam ipsa est pax, quæ præcellit omnem intellectum, etiam ipsam in oratione poscendo, quid oremus, sicut oportet, nescimus. quod enim, sicuti est, cogitare non possumus, utique nescimus, sed, quicquid cogitanti occurrerit, abicimus, respuimus, inprobamus, hoc non esse, quod quærimus, nouimus, quamuis illud nondum, quale sit, nouerimus. Est ergo in nobis quædam, ut ita dicam docta ignorantia sed docta spiritu dei, qui adiuuat infirmitatem nostram." Cf. *Confessions* XII, V, 5 for an earlier, less developed version of the same insight.
10. Quoted by Nicholas Lash, *Easter in Ordinary*, p. 167.
11. *In I Sent.*, 8, 1, 1, *ad 4*: "... ideo dicit Damascenus, quod [nomen 'qui est'] non significat quid est Deus, sed significat quoddam pelagus substantiæ infinitum, quasi non determinatum. Unde quando in Deum procedimus per viam remotionis, primo negamus ab eo corporalia; et secundo etiam intellectualia, secundum quod inveniuntur in creaturis, ut bonitas et sapientia; et tunc remanettantum in intellectu nostro, quia est, et nihil amplius: unde est sicut in quadam confusione. Ad ultimum autem etiam hoc ipsum esse, secundum quod est in creaturis, ab ipso removemus; et tunc remanet in qua-

dam tenebra ignorantiæ, secundum quam ignorantiam, quantum ad statum viæ pertinet, optime Deo conjungimur ... et hæc est quædam caligo, in qua Deus habitare dicitur." The last phrase of this passage alludes to Solomon's words at the temple dedication according to the Vulgate (2 Chron 6, 1): "Dominus pollicitus est, ut habitaret in caligine."

12. *S. c. G.* 3, 49, *Cognoscit tamen:* "... hoc est ultimum et perfectissimum nostræ cognitionis in hac vita ... *cum Deo quasi ignoto coniungimur.* quod quidem contingit dum de eo *quid non sit* cognoscimus, quid vero sit penitus manet ignotum. Unde et ad huius sublimissimam cognitionis ignorantiam demonstrandam, de Moyse dicitur, quod *accessit ad caliginem in qua est Deus.*"

13. Cf. *Deonise Hid Divinite,* pp. 48-59, esp. 52/12-53/9.

14. David B. Burrell, *Knowing the Unknowable God,* p. 1; italics added for emphasis.

15. Moses Maimonides, *Guide for the Perplexed,* Pt. 1, Chaps. 59-60; ed. Friedländer, pp. 83-89; quotation, p. 88 (italics added). Quoted in Ian T. Ramsey (ed.), *Words about God,* p. 35.

16. In *Werke* (Ed. Wilpert), vol. 1, pp. 2-100; ET *Of Learned Ignorance* (ed. Heron).

17. On this subject, cf. especially Book 3, Chapter 3 of *Of Learned Ignorance.*

18. *Philosophisch-Theologische Schriften,* p. 300: "*Et ait Gentilis:* Video te devotissime prostratum et fundere amoris lacrimas non quidem falsas, sed cordiales. Quaero, quis es? *Christianus:* Christianus sum. *G:* Quid adoras? *C:* Deum. *G:* Quis est Deus, quem adoras? *C:* Ignoro. *G:* Quomodo tam serio adoras, quod ignoras? *C:* Quia ignoro, adoro. *G:* Mirum video hominem affici ad id, quod ignorat. *C:* Mirabilius est hominem affici ad id, quod se scire putat. *G:* Cur hoc? *C:* Quia minus scit hoc, quod se scire putat quam id, quod se scit ignorare."

19. Fritz Stippel, Epilogue to *Der verborgene Gott,* pp. 44-46. For Stippel's comparison of Cusanus' attitude with the agenda of the vitalist philosophers, cf. Otto's similar comparison of Schleiermacher with the idealism of Herder, Goethe, Kant, and Fichte: §25, 4, d.

20. Thus, for example, Carol Klein in *The Credo of Maimonides.*

21. Such is David Hartman's contention (*Maimonides: Torah and Philosophic Quest*). Interestingly, Hartman's thesis runs parallel to Moses Mendelssohn's in *Jerusalem oder über religiöse Macht und Judentum* (cf. §28, 4, a, [d]), except that Hartman utterly rejects what Mendelssohn is willing to embrace: the recognition of the remote God of Deism as the God of Israel.

22. Jacob Haberman, *Maimonides and Aquinas,* p. 40.

23. Cf. John Coulson, *Religion and Imagination,* pp. 63ff.; cf. also pp. 115ff.

24. Cf. F. J. van Beeck, *Christ Proclaimed,* pp. 198-202.

25. "... inter creatorem et creaturam non potest similitudo notari, quin inter eos maior sit dissimilitudo notanda."

Chapter 4

1. *Catech.* V, 12 (ed. Reischl-Rupp, vol. I, pp. 148-50).

2. The English-speaking world is now fortunate in having an authoritative account of this discovery, in the form of R. P. C. Hanson's *The Search for the Christian Doctrine of God.*

3. *Van den gheesteliken tabernakel,* §XLI; RW II, pp. 75-76.

4. David Brown, *Invitation to Theology*, p. 128.
5. In the essay "Wer ist die Kirche?": *Sponsa Verbi*, pp. 148-202; quotation pp. 181-82 (italics added for emphasis).
6. Letter of November 1, 1519, to John Slechta (*Opvs Epistolarvm Des. Erasmi Roterodami*, vol. 4, p. 118, ll. 228-37; quoted by H. Wagenhammer, *Das Wesen des Christentums*, pp. 45-6): "Porro philosophiae Christianae summa in hoc sita est, vt intelligamus omnem spem nostram in Deo positam esse, qui gratis nobis largitur omnia per Filium suum Iesum. Huius morte nos esse redemptos, in huius corpus nos insitos esse per baptismum, vt mortui cupiditatibus huius mundi ad illius doctrinam et exemplum sic viuamus, vt non solum nihil admittamus mali verumetiam de omnibus bene mereamur; et si quid inciderit aduersi, fortiter toleremus, spe futuri praemii quod omnes pios haud dubie manet in aduentu Christi: vt ita semper progrediamur a virtute in virtutem, vt nihil tamen nobis arrogemus, sed quicquid est boni Deo transcribamus."
7. Cf. Jared Wicks, "Lutero e la religiosità vissuta," p. 124.
8. Cf. Hans Wagenhammer, *Das Wesen des Christentums*, pp. 93-104. Unfortunately, Wagenhammer does not appear to have noticed similar issues in the works of the women mystics.
9. Quotations from Hans Wagenhammer, *Das Wesen des Christentums*, p. 52.
10. Hans Wagenhammer, *Das Wesen des Christentums*, pp. 47-77.
11. Cf. John Bossy, *Christianity in the West 1400-1700*, esp. pp. 167-71.
12. I have had no opportunity to consult Friedrich Lücke, *Über das Alter, den Verfasser, die ursprüngliche Form und den wahren Sinn des kirchlichen Friedensspruches In necessariis unitas, in non necessariis libertas, in utrisque caritas: Eine litterarhistorische Studie; nebst einem Abdrucke der Paraenesis votiva pro pace ecclesiae ad Theologos Augustanae Confessionis, auctore Ruperto Meldenio* (Göttingen: Dieterich, 1850).
13. Cf. Hans Wagenhammer, *Das Wesen des Christentums*, pp. 114-66.
14. Hans Wagenhammer, *Das Wesen des Christentums*, pp. 181-252.
15. In what follows, I am indebted to the attractive, coherent, and well-documented interpretation of Lessing's thought on the nature of Christianity proposed by Hans Wagenhammer (*Das Wesen des Christentums*, pp. 236-50).
16. Cf. "Über den Beweis des Geistes und der Kraft," *Gesammelte Werke* 8, pp. 9-16 (ET "On the Proof of the Spirit and of Power," in *Lessing's Theological Writings*, pp. 51-56).
17. Letter of February 2, 1774 to Karl Lessing: *Gesammelte Werke*, vol. 9, pp. 595-99; quotation p. 597.
18. Letters of July 23 and August 9, 1778 to his brother, Karl Lessing, and to Elise Reimarus: *Gesammelte Werke*, vol. 9, pp. 786-87, 795-96.
19. "Die Religion Christi": *Gesammelte Werke*, vol. 8, pp. 538-39 (ET "The Religion of Christ, 1780," *Lessing's Theological Writings*, p. 106).
20. Letter of November 28, 1780: *Gesammelte Werke*, vol. 9, pp. 876-78.
21. BT Sanhedrin 46*b*.
22. Timothy Ware, *The Orthodox Church*, pp. 26-43, 210.

Chapter 5

1. For the dimensions of this predicament in the West, cf. Robert Markus' fine monograph *The End of Ancient Christianity*.

2. Literally, "On the Question: What is the Profession of the Christian?" [*Peri tou ti to tou Christianou epaggelma*]: Jaeger, vol. 8/1, pp. 129-142 (cf. ET Saint Gregory of Nyssa, *Ascetical Works*, trans. Virginia Woods Callahan; *FC* 58, pp. 77-89). The Latin title usually given is *De professione christiana* ("On the Christian Profession"). The letter is also briefly treated by Hans Wagenhammer, *Das Wesen des Christentums*, pp. 86-89.

3. "So, as someone might explain the idea of Christianity by means of a definition, we will put it as follows." (*Oukoun hōs an tis horōi tou christianismou tēn dianoian hermēneuseien, eroumen houtōs:* Jaeger, vol. 8/1, p. 126/6-7; ET, cf. *FC* 58, p. 85).

4. Cf. *The Dead Come to Life, or, The Fisherman*, 36 (*Lucian*, vol. 3, pp. 54-55).

5. Jaeger, vol. 8/1, pp. 135/6-137/1. Cf. *FC* 58, pp. 84-85.

6. On the indebtedness to Stoicism, on the part of the Church Fathers, including Gregory of Nyssa, in their accounts of divine providence, cf. M. Pohlenz, *Die Stoa*, vol. I, pp. 428ff.

7. Jaeger, vol. 8/1, pp. 138/27-139/4; cf. *FC* 58, p. 87.

8. Jaeger, vol. 8/1, pp. 141/14-142/3; cf. *FC* 58, p. 89.

9. "Die Mitteilung des Heiligen Geistes ist Bedingung der Aufnahme des Christentums in uns; er vereint alle Gläubigen zu einer geistigen Gemeinschaft, durch welche er sich den noch nicht Gläubigen mitteilt [: die innere Tradition]; durch die Liebe, die in der Kirche durch Aufnahme des in ihr waltenden [höheren geistigen] Lebens in uns erzeugt word, ist Christus mitgegeben; nur in der Gemeinschaft der Gläubigen werden wir Christi bewußt." (*Die Einheit in der Kirche*, p. 5; words in square brackets supplied from the text as it appears in the table of contents, p. [9]).

10. Cf. F. J. van Beeck, *Christ Proclaimed*, pp. 471-79, 507-18.

11. *Hij is een God van mensen*, pp. 9-48 (ET *The Christ*, pp. 13-49).

12. The so-called "Second Epistle of Clement to the Corinthians," XIV, 5 (*AF* I, pp. 152-53). For the theme of eternal design, cf. the reference to the "spiritual Church," created before the sun and the moon: XIV, 1 (pp. 150-51).

13. *Adv. Hær.* 5, 2, 1-3 (*SC* 153, pp. 30-41).

14. *S. c. G.* IV, 49: "Quod autem anima et corpus in Christo ad personalitatem Verbi trahuntur, non constituentia aliquam personam præter personam Verbi, not pertinet ad minorationem virtutis, ... sed ad dignitatem maiorem. Unumquodque enim melius esse habet cum suo digniori unitur, quam cum per se existit: sicut anima sensibilis nobilius esse habet in homine quam in aliis animalibus, in quibus est forma principalis, non tamen in homine."

15. The full text runs: *Ex Umbris et Imaginibus in Veritatem.* Cf. Meriol Trevor, *Newman: Light in Winter*, p. 646.

16. *LThK* VII, coll. 829ff.; cf. H. Vorgrimler, *Sacramententheologie*, pp. 27-28, for some further references.

17. "Reply to Interpretation and Criticism," p. 333.

18. "Theology and Symbolism," pp. 110-11 (italics added for emphasis).

19. On this subject, cf. James D. G. Dunn, *Christology in the Making*.

20. Cf. F. J. van Beeck, *Loving the Torah More than God?*, pp. 60-62.

21. Cf. M.-D. Chenu, "Vérité évangélique et métaphysique wolffienne à Vatican II."

22. *Letter to Diognetus*, 7, 2-5 (italics added); *AF* II, pp. 364-65 (cf. Barry, pp. 40-41). Cf. also F. J. van Beeck, *Christ Proclaimed*, p. 462.

23. Cf. Augustine's *Confessions*, VI, III, 4, for this central conviction of both Neo-Platonism and the Jewish-Christian tradition.

24. Cf. *Spiritual Exercises*, nrs. 315, 330-35.

25. Cf. Peter Brown, *Augustine of Hippo*, pp. 40-60.

26. *De fide et symbolo*, 7 (*CSEL* 41, p. 11): "Ex quo iam spiritalibus animis patere confido nullam naturam deo esse posse contrariam. si enim ille est et de solo deo proprie dici possit hoc uerbum—quod enim uere est, incommutabiliter manet, quoniam quod mutatur, fuit aliquid quod iam non est, et erit quod nondum est—nihil habet deus contrarium. si enim quaereretur a nobis, quid sit albo contrarium, responderemus nigrum; si quaereretur, quid sit calido contrarium, responderemus frigidum; si quaereretur, quid sit ueloci contrarium, responderemus tardum, et quaecumque similia. cum autem quaeritur, quid sit contrarium ei quod est, recte respondetur: quod non est."

27. "Aimer la Thora plus que Dieu" (*Difficile liberté*, pp. 189-193), p. 193: "... avoir créé un homme capable de répondre, capable d'aborder son Dieu en créancier et non point toujours en débiteur—quelle grandeur vraiment divine! ... Dans quelle vigoureuse dialectique s'établit l'égalité entre Dieu et l'homme au sein même de leur disproportion." Cf. F. J. van Beeck, *Loving the Torah More than God?*, p. 39; cf. the discussion on pp. 51-52.

28. For examples of fourth-century challenges to the claims to superiority implicit in the ascetical life, cf. Robert Markus, *The End of Ancient Christianity*, pp. 37-43.

29. Robert Markus, *The End of Ancient Christianity*, pp. 38, 36.

30. *Confessiones*, IX, III, 5.

31. *Confessiones* XIII, XXXIX, 49, quoted by Henry Chadwick, "The Ascetic Ideal in the History of the Church," p. 10.

32. Peter Brown, *The Body and Society*, pp. 256-58.

33. Peter Brown, *The Body and Society*, p. 387.

34. Cf. Peter Brown, *The Body and Society*, pp. 292-98.

35. Peter Brown, *The Body and Society*, pp. 33-34, quoting Justin's *Apology* I, 15, 1-5. For a sensitive account of the strands that went into the making of Western monasticism, cf. *ibid.*, pp. 63-83.

36. Cf. John P. Meier, *A Marginal Jew*, vol. I, pp. 336-45 for a survey with a wealth of bibliographical information.

37. St. John Chrysostom, *On Virginity*, 73, 4 (*PG* 48, 587[326]; *SC* 125, pp. 354-55); quotation also used by Peter Brown, *The Body and Society*, p. 307.

38. Cf. Robert Markus, *The End of Ancient Christianity*, pp. 181-97.

39. Cf. Peter Brown, *The Body and Society*, pp. 345-56.

40. Cf. Peter Brown, *The Body and Society*, pp. 279-84.

41. The monk Horiesius, quoted by Peter Brown, *The Body and Society*, p. 236.

42. *The Body and Society*, pp. 165-66.

43. *The Body and Society*, p. 239.

44. Henry Chadwick, "The Ascetic Ideal in the History of the Church," p. 23.

Chapter 6

1. For an up-to-date account of the life and work of St. Thomas Aquinas, cf. James A. Weisheipl, *Friar Thomas d'Aquino*.

2. Aquinas is quoting the text as he finds it in the Latin translation of Aristotle's *Physics* he is using; cf. *In Octo Libros de Physico Auditu sive Physicorum Aristotelis Commentaria*, II. *Lectio* 13, *Secundam rationem*, [500]. For the original, cf. Aristotle, *Phys.* 199ª11.

3. *S. Th.* I, 60, 5 *in c.* (italics added for emphasis): "*Inclinatio enim naturalis in his quæ sunt sine ratione, demonstrat inclinationem naturalem in voluntate intellectualis naturæ.* Unumquodque autem in rebus naturalibus, quod secundum naturam hoc ipsum quod est, alterius est, principalius et magis inclinatur in id cuius est, quam in seipsum. Et hæc inclinatio naturalis demonstratur ex his quæ naturaliter aguntur, quia 'unumquodque sicut agitur naturaliter, sic aptum est agi,' ut dicitur in II *Physic..* Videmus enim quod naturaliter pars se exponit, ad conservationem totius, sicut manus exponitur ictui absque deliberatione, ad conservationem totius corporis. Et quia *ratio imitatur naturam*, hujusmodi imitationem invenimus in virtutibus politicis; est enim virtuosi civis ut se exponat mortis periculo pro totius reipublicæ conservatione; et si homo esset naturalis pars huius civitatis, hæc inclinatio ei esset naturalis. Quia igitur bonum universale est ipse Deus, et sub hoc bono continetur etiam angelus et homo et omnis creatura, quia *omnis creatura naturaliter, secundum id quod est, Dei est*; sequitur quod naturali dilectione etiam angelus et homo plus et principalius diligat Deum quam seipsum. Alioquin, *si naturaliter plus seipsum diligeret quam Deum, sequeretur quod naturalis dilectio esset perversa; et quod non perficeretur per charitatem, sed destrueretur.*"

4. *In IV Libros Sent.* III, 29, 1, 3, *in c.* (italics added for emphasis): "Quia ergo bonum nostrum in Deo perfectum est, sicut in causa universali prima et perfecta bonorum, ideo bonum in ipso esse magis naturaliter complacet quam in nobis ipsis; et ideo *etiam amore amicitiæ* naturaliter deus ab homine plus seipso diligitur. Et *quia caritas naturam perficit, ideo etiam secundum caritatem deum supra seipsum homo diligit, et super omnia alia particularia bona.*"

5. Sebastian Moore, "Ratzinger's 'Nature' Isn't Natural," p. 51.

6. Letter of 2 August 1955; *Collected Works*, pp. 943-44 (cf. §65, 2 and note 1).

7. ".... deificata non est perempta, salvata est autem magis." In the original text (the dogmatic definition of the third Council of Constantinople of A.D. 681) this expression refers to the human will of Christ. However, from the context, as well as in view of the parallel with the definition of Chalcedon, it is clear that the expression can be responsibly applied to Christ's human nature as such.

8. Cf. P. Smulders, "Dogmengeschichtliche und lehramtliche Entfaltung der Christologie," p. 492, n. 96.

9. Cf. *LThK* 10, coll. 437-40 for a survey. Cf. also *NDT*, p. 995.

10. "Über das Verhältnis von Natur und Gnade," pp. 327-28; cf. also pp. 340-45 (ET, pp. 301-02, revised; cf. also pp. 313-15).

11. *Systematic Theology*, I, pp. 61-62.

12. Cf. F. J. van Beeck, *Christ Proclaimed*, pp. 202-17.

13. On the entire issue in Bonhoeffer, cf. F. J. van Beeck, *Christ Proclaimed*, pp. 232-51.

14. "... nicht in der Reflektion auf sich selbst, sondern im Aktbezug auf Gott versteht sich der Mensch, d.h. nur dort, wo er wirklich vor Gott steht. Nicht wo er Möglichkeiten in sich vorfindet, kraft deren er vor Gott stehen kann" ("Die Frage nach dem Menschen in der gegenwärtigen Philosophie und

Theologie," p. 80; cf. ET p. 61).

15. "Wo aber die Frage nach der Vergegenwärtigung zum *Thema der Theologie* wird, dort können wir gewiß sein, daß die Sache bereits verraten und verkauft ist ("Vergegenwärtigung neutestamentlicher Texte," p. 305; cf. ET "The Presentation of New Testament Texts," p. 305). For the entire passage, cf. F. J. van Beeck, *Christ Proclaimed*, p. 248.

16. "Die Mündigkeit der Welt ist nun kein Anlaß mehr zu Polemik und Apologetik, sondern sie wird nun wirklich besser verstanden, als sie sich selbst versteht, nämlich vom Evangelium, von Christus her." Cf. *Widerstand und Ergebung*, pp. 158-63; quotation p. 163 (cf. ET *Letters and Papers from Prison*, 167-72; quotation p. 172).

17. For an illuminating analysis, cf. Walter Brueggemann, "The Triumphalist Tendency in Exegetical History."

18. Cf. esp. *Systematic Theology*, I, pp. 83-86, 147-50; III, pp. 249-75.

Chapter 7

1. Some of Blondel's own reflections on the circumstances that prompted him to write the Letter, recorded about 35 years after the event, can be found in *Le problème de la philosophie catholique*, pp. 11-15. The present quotation ("... pour dégager l'apologétique des anciennes argumentations et pour l'amener sur le terrain proprement et purement psychologique") is on p. 13.

2. Quotation from Brunschvicg's anonymous review of *L'Action* in the November, 1893 supplement to the *Revue de Métaphysique et de Morale* (*Le problème de la philosophie catholique*, pp. 15): "Il convient d'ajouter, tout en rendant hommage à la sincérité, à la largeur de conception, à la subtilité dialectique de M. Blondel, qu'il trouvera parmi les défenseurs des droits de la Raison, des adversaires courtois, mais résolus." Cf. also Jean Lacroix, *Maurice Blondel*, p. 32.

3. Cf. *Le problème de la philosophie catholique*, pp. 13-14 (italics added for emphasis): "Ces diverses interprétations, tout en m'apportant de précieux encouragements, me faisaient sentir, par leurs éloges mêmes comme par leurs flottements et leurs réserves, l'extrême péril auquel était exposée ma pensée si l'on déplaçait le dessein tout rationnel que j'avais conçu du terrain philosophique *où il devait se limiter.* Je n'avais pas voulu aborder, je n'abordais pas, en une thèse de Doctorat soutenue devant la Sorbonne, les pentes glissantes de l'apologétique. Je ne prétendais nullement, comme déjà on paraissait le craindre, tirer de la nature et de la raison quelque chose des vérités révélées, ni postuler la réalité de l'ordre de grâce."

4. "... dans l'ordre des certitudes rationnelles, [cette question de méthode] est de première importance. J'expliquerais pourquoi la philosophie apologétique, *dans l'intérêt même des conclusions qu'elle prépare ou permet, ne doit pas devenir une apologétique philosophique.* n'est philosophique, à vrai dire, rien de ce qui est simplement un instrument ou un moyen." Cf. "Lettre de Maurice Blondel à l'Abbé Denis," in *Les premiers écrits de Maurice Blondel*, pp. 3-4; quotation p. 3 (italics added for emphasis).

5. "Lettre sur les exigences de la pensée contemporaine en matière d'apologétique et sur la méthode de la philosophie dans l'étude du problème reli-

gieux." The letter was republished in *Les premiers écrits de Maurice Blondel*, pp. 5-95 (ET in *The Letter on Apologetics* and *History and Dogma*, pp. 127-208). For brief explanations, cf. Avery Dulles, *A History of Apologetics*, pp. 204-05, and Gregory Baum, *Man Becoming*, pp. 1-23.

6. Cf. *Les premiers écrits de Maurice Blondel*, p. 27 (ET in *The Letter on Apologetics* and *History and Dogma*, p. 146): "... comme un inventaire, mais non comme une invention capable de justifier, par le dynamisme qui les suscite, les ascensions de la pensée."

7. *Les premiers écrits de Maurice Blondel*, p. 28 (ET in *The Letter on Apologetics* and *History and Dogma*, pp. 146-47): "Ne nous épuisons pas à ressasser les arguments connus, à offrir un *objet*, alors que c'est le *sujet* qui n'est pas disposé. Ce n'est jamais du côté de la vérité divine, c'est du côté de la préparation humaine qu'il y a défaut et que l'effort de la démonstration humaine doit porter. Et ce n'est point là simple affaire d'adaptation ou pur expédient temporaire; car ce rôle de préparation subjective est de première importance, it est essentiel et permanent, s'il est vrai que l'action de l'homme coopère, dans toute son étendue, à celle de Dieu."

8. *Les premiers écrits de Maurice Blondel*, p. 28 (ET in *The Letter on Apologetics* and *History and Dogma*, p. 147): "... déviations, «intelligences faussées» ou «maladies de la raison». ... Des erreurs individuelles, des vues incomplètes et des défaillances particulières à tel ou tel esprit, resort peu à peu le dessein de Dieu dans la conduite de l'humanité..."

9. Cf. *Les premiers écrits de Maurice Blondel*, p. 29 (cf. ET in *The Letter on Apologetics* and *History and Dogma*, p. 147): "Ou bien, en cherchant à discerner le travail d'enfantement qui secoue perpétuellement l'humanité, on s'attache à profiter de cet immense effort, à l'éclairer, à le faire aboutir, à allumer la mèche qui fume déjà, à ne pas croire aisément que, dans les doctrines les plus opposées à la nôtre, il n'y a rien de salutaire pour nous-mêmes, à nous faire aux autres pour les faire à nous. Et c'est trouver la source de la fécondité intellectuelle."

10. The paragraphs under [1] sum up and interpret points 2-5 of the first part of the *Lettre*. cf. *Les premiers écrits de Maurice Blondel*, pp. 9-26 (ET in *The Letter on Apologetics* and *History and Dogma*, pp. 131-45).

11. ET Barry, pp. 1001-08. Cf. James Hennesey, "Leo XIII's Thomistic Revival: A Political and Philosophical Event."

12. Gerald P. Fogarty, *American Catholic Biblical Scholarship*, pp. 311, 344, 350.

13. Cf. Peter Raedts, "De christelijke middeleeuwen als mythe," which makes good use of, among other things, John Van Engen, "Christian Middle Ages as an Historiographical Problem."

14. "Ut nihilominus fidei nostrae 'obsequium rationi consentaneum' esset, voluit Deus cum internis Spiritus Sancti auxiliis externa iungi revelationis suae argumenta, facta scilicet divina, atque imprimis miracula et prophetias, quae cum Dei omnipotentiam et infinitam scientiam luculenter commonstrent, divinae revelationis signa sunt certissima et omnium intelligentiae accommodata."

15. Cf. *Les premiers écrits de Maurice Blondel*, pp. 26-27 (ET in *The Letter on Apologetics* and *History and Dogma*, p. 145): "Cette argumentation, celle même qu'on donne au commencement de toute théologie dans le traité de la religion, on nous la résume justement en ses termes: «La raison démontre l'existence de Dieu. Ce Dieu a pu se révéler. L'histoire prouve le fait de la révélation; elle

prouve aussi l'authenticité des Livres Saints, l'autorité de l'Église. Le catholicisme se trouve donc établi sur une base rationnelle véritablement scientifique.»"

16. *HG*, pp. 30-31.
17. *HG*, pp. 16-17.
18. *HG*, pp. 30-33.
19. *HG*, pp. 18-19, 30-33.
20. ET *HG*, pp. 28-35. The reference to the *philosophia perennis*—neo-scholasticism's proud (if unhistorical) self-designation as the philosophy whose truth is assured and beyond all vicissitudes and fashions—occurs in *Humani generis* just after the point where the quotation in DS 3894 breaks off.
21. *HG*, pp. 16-17; 30-31.
22. Cf. *VatIIPr* III/I, pp. 15-23, 54-89.
23. *VatIIPr* II/II, pp. 279-423; quotations pp. 284-85.
24. *VatIIPr* II/I, pp. 523-63, esp. 541-49.
25. *VatIISyn* I/III, pp. 32-36.
26. Cf. Joseph Ratzinger's essay in *Commentary on the Decrees of Vatican II*, vol. 3, p. 155-66; cf. also Gerald P. Fogarty, *American Catholic Biblical Scholarship*, pp. 334-50.
27. Cf., for instance, the clear account of the issue in *Neues Glaubensbuch*, pp. 547-60 (ET *The Common Catechism*, pp. 553-67).
28. *De vita Moysis* II, 47 (*PG* 44, 344; Jaeger vol. 7/1, p. 51/17-19; ET pp. 68-69).
29. Cf. *Les premiers écrits de Maurice Blondel*, pp. 29-30 (cf. ET in *The Letter on Apologetics* and *History and Dogma*, pp. 147-48; some italics added in the translation): "Au point de départ, c'est-à-dire pour la scolastique, l'ordre naturel at l'ordre surnaturel, subordonnées en une hiérarchie ascendante, *se superposent* en se touchant; et il y a comme trois zones étagées: au bas ... la raison est tout à fait chez elle ...; au haut ... la foi seule nous révèle le mystère de la vie divine et celui de la vie humaine conviée au banquet de la divinité; au milieu un terrain d'entente ou de rencontre mutuelle, la raison découvrant imparfaitement ce que la foi éclaire et confirme des vérités naturelles les plus importantes. Et c'est là, grâce à cette communauté *d'objets* reconnus, que confluent deux courants issus d'origines médiatement différentes, et mêlant leurs eaux sans les confondre. ...

Bientôt pourtant ce dualisme devait apparaître moins comme une solution que comme l'énoncé d'un problème, du problème philosophique et religieux par excellence. Dans un esprit de violent réaction contre l'intellectualisme ... de la scolastique, le protestantisme ... supprime ... la zone mitoyenne, comme si, au lieu d'être le terrain de la concorde, elle risquait de devenir le champ des conflits et de la guerre. Les ordres qu'on avait *superposés*, sont dès lors *juxtaposés sans communication possible ni lien intelligible*, unis seulement, prétendait-on, dans la mystérieuse intimité de la foi individuelle. En sorte que du jour où la raison, laissée seule maîtresse du connaissable, prétend trouver, immanentes en elle, toutes les vérités nécessaires à la vie, elle exclut radicalement ce monde de la foi; il n'y a plus juxtaposition, mais *opposition*, mais incompatibilité."

30. Cf. *Les premiers écrits de Maurice Blondel*, pp. 32-34 (ET cf. *The Letter on Apologetics* and *History and Dogma*, pp. 150-52): "Si les formes usitées de l'apologétique dite philosophique n'ont plus aucune prise aujourd'hui sur une raison

incrédule, ce n'est pas, on vient de le voir, sans une cause profonde. ... la critique sévère à laquelle j'ai été obligé, je n'aurais pu l'entreprendre ... si je n'étais convaincu que la crise dont je parle ... sera salutaire à tous, par ce qu'elle exige d'intelligence nouvelle et par ce qu'elle prépare de bien futur.
...

Il ne se fait rien de bien à contre-coeur, par concession pénible et onéreuse, par accommodement contraint, comme si l'on y perdait au lieu d'y gagner de part et d'autre. Peut-être, en terminant cet examen, estimerons-nous que les exigences accrues de la pensée contemporaine sont légitimes, sont utiles, sont conformes autant à l'esprit philosophique qu'à l'esprit même du catholicisme.
...

En deux mots qu'il faudra expliquer, mais qui marquent d'emblée la gravité du conflit, la pensée moderne avec une susceptibilité jalouse considère la notion d'*immanence* comme la condition même de la philosophie; c'est-à-dire que, si parmi les idées régnantes il y a un résultat auquel elle s'attache comme à un progrès certain, c'est à l'idée, très juste en son fond, que rien ne peut entrer en l'homme qui ne sorte de lui et ne corresponde en quelque façon à un besoin d'expansion, et que ni comme fait historique, ni comme enseignement traditionnel, ni comme obligation surajoutée du dehors, il n'y a pour lui vérité qui compte et précepte admissible sans être, de quelque manière, autonome et autochtone. Or, d'autre part, il n'y a de chrétien, de catholique que ce qui est *surnaturel*, — non pas seulement transcendant au simple sens métaphysique du mot, parce qu'enfin on peut supposer des vérités et des existences supérieures à nous dont l'affirmation, procédant de notre fond, serait immanente elle-même, — mais proprement surnaturel; c'est-à-dire qu'il est impossible à l'homme de tirer de soi ce que pourtant on pretend imposer à sa pensée et à sa volonté."

31. For a fine survey of the issue, along with a bibliography, cf. *LThK, s.v.* "Desiderium naturale." For Aquinas' explanation, cf., for example, *S. c. G.* III, 25; 51-53; 57; *Q. D. de Veritate* 22, 2, *in c.* and *ad 5.* Cf. also William R. O'Connor's careful analysis of Aquinas' teaching in *The Eternal Quest*, as well as his 1948 Aquinas Lecture on the same subject, *The Natural Desire for God*, and Venant Cauchy, *Désir naturel et béatitude chez saint Thomas*.

32. Cf. *L'intellectualisme de Saint Thomas*, esp. pp. 201-29 (ET *The Intellectualism of Saint Thomas*, pp. 197-216).

33. Cf. esp. *Le point de départ de la métaphysique*, Cahier V ("*Le Thomisme devant la philosophie critique*"), pp. 273-353; for a competent English translation of the most important passages these pages, cf. *A Maréchal Reader*, pp. 163-98.

34. Cf., for example, the essays "The Natural Desire to See God," "Openness and Religious Experience," "Metaphysics as Horizon," and "Cognitional Structure," in Bernard Lonergan's *Collection*.

35. Quoted by James M. Somerville, *Total Commitment*, p. 7.

36. *Hij is een God van mensen*, p. 30 (cf. ET, pp. 35-36). Cf. F. J. van Beeck, *Christ Proclaimed*, pp. 286-92.

37. "The Catholic Novelist in the Protestant South," in *Collected Works*, pp. 862-64 (with the exception of the first italicized word, all italics added for emphasis).

38. *A Pistle of Discrecioun in Stirrings*, in *Deonise Hid Divinite*, p. 73/7-10.

39. Cf. *PG* 46, 284-85; Jaeger vol. 8/1, pp. 212/4-16 (cf. *FC* 48, p. 121): "Whatever

is free from every passionate disposition reflects the pioneer of freedom from passion—Christ. Those who draw their thoughts and feelings from him, as from a pure and uncontaminated wellspring, will exhibit in themselves the resemblance to the original, just as there is resemblance between water and water—running well-water and water that comes from there, in a jar. For the purity that exists in Christ is of one and the same kind as the purity observed in the person sharing it. Still, the one comes straight from the well, the other is drawn from it, and carries along attractiveness of thoughts and feelings, which it introduces into the person's life. In this way there is harmony between the hidden person and the visible person, as our lives exhibit the gracefulness that corresponds to, and is animated by, thoughts and feelings that derive from Christ."

40. The original (*Las Moradas*, Quartas Moradas, Cap. 2, 2-4, pp. 380-81 [cf. ET *Interior Castle*, pp. 236-37]): "Hagamos cuenta, para entenderlo mejor, que vemos dos fuentes con dos pilas que se hinchen de agua ... de diferentes maneras; el uno viene de más lejos por muchos arcaduces y artificio; el otro está hecho en el mesmo nacimiento del agua, y vase hinchendo sin nengún ruido; y si es el manatial caudoloso, como este de que hablamos, después de henchido este pilón, procede un gran arroyo; ni es menester artificio, ni se acaba el edificio de los arcaduces, sino siempre está procediendo agua de allí. Es la diferencia que la que viene por arcaduces es—a mi parecer—los contentos que tengo dicho que se sacan con la meditación, porque *los* traemos con los pensamientos ayudándonos con las criaturas en la meditación y cansando el entendimiento; y como viene, en fin, con nuestras diligencias, hace ruido cuando ha de haver algún hinchimiento de provechos que hace en el alma, como queda dicho.

Estotra fuente viene el agua de su mesmo nacimiento, que es Dios, y ansí como Su Majestad quiere cuando es servido hacer alguna merced sobranatural, produce con grandísima paz y quietud y suavidad de lo muy interior de nosotros mesmos, yo no sé hacia donde, ni cómo, ni aquel contento y deleite se siente como los de acá en el corazón; digo en su principio, que después todo lo hinche; vase revertiendo este agua por todas las moradas y potencias, hasta llegar al el cuerpo, que por eso dije que comienza de Dios y acaba en nosotros; que, cierto, como verá quien lo huviere probado, todo el hombre esterior goza de este gusto y suavidad."

41. *Die geestelike brulocht*, pp. 296-99; cf. 284-87 (cf. *The Spiritual Espousals and Other Works*, pp. 75-76; cf. 71-72). Note that Ruusbroec uses the image of the spring as well: pp. 453-57 (cf. *The Spiritual Espousals and Other Works*, pp. 112-13).

42. *Collected Works*, p. 401 (*The Violent Bear it Away*, chapter 4).

43. *Die Gottesgeburt*, p. 13 (italics added): "Die *durch die Gnade gegebene* besondere Einwohnung Christi im Herzen der in der Kirche durch die Taufe zu einem einzigen Leib zusammengefügten Gläubigen ist eine geheimnisvolle Nachbildung und Fortsetzung der ewigen Geburt des Logos aus dem Vater und der zeitlichen Geburt aus der Jungfrau."

44. *Vanden blinkenden steen, etc.*, pp. 146-49 (ET cf. *The Spiritual Espousals and Other Works*, pp. 170-71). The text restates what Ruusbroec had explained in *Die geestelike brulocht*, pp. 581/64-583/84 (*The Spiritual Espousals and Other Works*, p. 147). I read the final sentence of the Dutch text as an instance of Ruus-

broec's habit of summarizing his teaching in vaguely rhyming lines; hence the free translation.

45. Cf. *Die geestelike brulocht*, pp. 468-75 (*The Spiritual Espousals and Other Works*, pp. 116-18).

46. *Demonstration of the Apostolic Preaching*, 22 (*SC* 62, pp. 64-65; ed. Robinson, pp. 89-90); cf. the elaboration of this in *Adv. Haer.* V, 16, 1-2 (*SC* 153, vol. 2, pp. 212-17).

47. *Adv. Hær.* IV, 6, 7 (*SC* 100, vol. 2, pp. 454-55).

48. Cf. esp. *Contra Gentes*, 40-47 (ed. Thomson, pp. 108-33).

49. Quotation from R. P. C. Hanson's discussion of Gregory Nazianzen, in *The Search of the Christian Doctrine of God*, p. 709.

50. On the themes treated here, cf. P. Mommaers' introduction to the critical edition of Ruusbroec's *Boecsken der Verclaringhe*, esp. pp. 27-42.

51. The expression is Harvey D. Egan's: *Ignatius Loyola the Mystic*, p. 66, footnote 1.

52. Cf. the recent treatment by Harvey D. Egan: *Ignatius Loyola the Mystic*, esp. pp. 66-85.

53. *Libro de la vida*, 40, 5; pp. 869-70.

54. Cf. J. N. D. Kelly, *Early Christian Doctrines*, pp. 83-137.

55. For an encyclopedic treatment of the theme in the Greek Fathers, cf. *DictSp* 6, coll. 813-22; on the consequences of the theme for the understanding of contemplation, cf. *DictSp* 2, 1827-1911.

56. *Instruction* 12, §134 (*SC* 92, pp. 396-97; the editor overlooks the fact that the text Dorotheus attributes to the "Psalmist" is a conflation of Ps 144 (145), 9 LXX and Lam 3, 25; cf. Nahum 1, 7).

57. Cf. "Anonymes Christentum und Missionsauftrag der Kirche" (ET "Anonymous Christianity and the Missionary Task of the Church") and the related treatments by Rahner and others referred to in the footnotes of that essay.

58. *Apol.* I, 66, 2 (Goodspeed, pp. 74-75; ET Bettenson, pp. 66-67; Barry, p. 35).

Chapter 8

1. "Fundamental Theology and the Logic of Conversion," p. 183.

2. Cf. also F. J. van Beeck, *Christ Proclaimed*, pp. 185-88.

3. *Blessed Rage for Order*, pp. 52-56; quotation p. 52 (capitalizations omitted).

4. *Blessed Rage for Order*, p. 53.

5. Cf. "Method in Fundamental Theology: Reflections on David Tracy's *Blessed Rage for Order*." Cf. also, *Models of Revelation*, p. 288.

6. I am indebted to Professor Daniel L. Migliore of Princeton Theological Seminary for this observation.

7. Cf. Avery Dulles, *A History of Apologetics*, pp. 22-50.

8. *S. c. G.* I, 2: "... veritatem quam fides Catholica profitetur, pro nostro modulo manifestare, errores eliminando contrarios."

9. *Summa contra Gentiles*, I, 2 (italics added): "Contra singulorum autem errores difficile est procedere, propter duo. Primo, quia *non ita sunt nobis nota singulorum errantium dicta sacrilega ut ex his quae dicunt possimus rationes assumere ad eorum errores destruendos.* Hoc enim modo usi sunt antiqui doctores in destructionem errorum gentilium, quorum positiones scire poterant quia et

ipsi gentiles fuerant, vel saltem inter gentiles conversati et in eorum doctrinis eruditi. — Secundo, quia *quidam eorum, ut Mahumetistae et pagani, non conveniunt nobiscum in auctoritate alicuius Scripturae, per quam possint convinci,* sicut contra Iudaeos disputare possumus per Vetus Testamentum, contra haereticos per Novum. Hi vero neutrum recipiunt. *Unde necesse est ad naturalem rationem recurrere, cui omnes assentire coguntur.* Quae tamen in rebus divinis deficiens est.

Simul autem veritatem aliquam investigantes ostendemus qui errores per eam excludantur; et quomodo demonstrativa veritas fidei Christianae religionis concordet."

10. Cf. R. W. Southern, *The Making of the Middle Ages,* pp. 184-208; quotation p. 186.
11. Cf. F. J. van Beeck, *Christ Proclaimed,* pp. 154-62.
12. Cf. F. J. van Beeck, *Christ Proclaimed,* pp. 486-501.
13. Most succinctly in the essay "New Testament and Mythology."
14. Esp. in *The Resurrection of Jesus of Nazareth.*
15. Cf. *Der christliche Glaube* (ET *The Christian Faith*), §94, 3.
16. Cf. *Systematic Theology,* I, pp. 59-66.
17. Cf. *Systematic Theology,* I, esp. pp. 12-14, 108-11; III, pp. 111-138; cf. p. 274.
18. Cf. David Brown, *The Divine Trinity,* esp. pp. 3-158.
19. For Wiles' dilemmatic approach to the issue and for his proposal for a "middle way," cf. *The Remaking of Christian Doctrine,* esp. pp. 115ff.
20. Cf. Paul Wignall, "Patterns in Theology."
21. *The Remaking of Christian Doctrine,* pp. 38; 17-19.
22. *The Remaking of Christian Doctrine,* pp. 106, 116.
23. *The Remaking of Christian Doctrine,* pp. 41-60.
24. Cf. *The Remaking of Christian Doctrine,* p. 116ff., also quoted by Paul Wignall, "Patterns of Belief," p. 101.
25. *C. Celsum* IV, 99; ET (Chadwick) pp. 262-63.
26. Jaeger, vol. 8/1, pp. 137/12-138/24; cf. *FC* 58, p. 86.
27. Cf. his "Divine Practical Knowing: How an Eternal God Acts in Time."
28. *The Glory of Man,* p. 62.
29. Cf. E. J. Dijksterhuis, *The Mechanization of the World Picture.*
30. Cf. e.g., *S. Th.* III, 62, 5, *in c.* and *ad 1;* 56, 1, *ad 3.*
31. Cf. "Zur scholastischen Begrifflichkeit der ungeschaffenen Gnade" (ET "Some Implications of the Scholastic Concept of Uncreated Grace"), and *Grundkurs des Glaubens,* pp. 127-29 (ET, pp. 120-22).
32. For this section, I am substantially indebted to the sensitive and constructive criticisms of my friends and colleagues Jill N. Reich and James J. Walter, both of Loyola University, Chicago.
33. Cf. Gerard S. Sloyan, *Jesus in Focus,* pp. 32, 94-95.
34. Gerard Manley Hopkins, *The Wreck of the Deutschland,* stanza 32.
35. *Confessiones* III, VI, 11; *CSEL* 33, pp. 52-3: "longe peregrinabar abs te exclusus et a siliquis porcorum, quos de siliquis pascebam"; "laborans et aestuans inopia veri"; "tu autem eras interior intimo meo et superior summo meo." Chadwick (*Confessions,* p. 42, n. 20) suggests that the first quotation conveys how, at an early stage in his teaching career, Augustine was already bored with the texts that academic tradition was forcing him to teach to his students—"the pigs"! Cf. also *Confessiones* X, VII, 11.

36. Cf. *Grundkurs*, pp. 147-53 (ET *Foundations of Christian Faith*, pp. 142-48).

37. *Grundkurs des Glaubens*, pp. 154-55; ET *Foundations*, p. 149-50: "This transcendental knowledge ... must be distinguished from verbal and propositional revelation as such. ... [It] is a modification of our transcendental consciousness produced permanently by God in grace. ... And as an element in our transcendentality which is produced by God's self-communication, it is already revelation in the proper sense. ... Only when God is the subjective principle of the speaking and of man's hearing in faith can God in his own self express himself."

Bibliography

Adam, Karl. *Das Wesen des Katholizismus.* Second edition. Düsseldorf: Verlag von L. Schwann, 1925 (ET of the fourth [1927] edition: *The Spirit of Catholicism.* New York: The Macmillan Company, 1929).

Alaerts, J. "La terminologie 'essentielle' dans *Die gheestelike brulocht.*" *Ons Geestelijk Erf* 49(1975): 225-47, 337-65.

Altizer, Thomas J. J. *The Gospel of Christian Atheism.* Philadelphia: The Westminster Press, 1966.

Arrupe, Pedro. "Sobre el «análisis marxista»." *Acta Romana Societatis Jesu* 18(1980-83): 331-38 (ET "On Marxist Analysis," 347-54).

Athanasius, [Saint]. *Contra Gentes* and *De Incarnatione.* Edited and translated by Robert W. Thomson. Oxford: Clarendon Press, 1971.

Auerbach, Erich. *Mimesis: The Representation of Reality in Western Literature.* Princeton, NJ: Princeton University Press, 1953.

Augustine, Saint. *Confessions.* Translated with an Introduction and Notes by Henry Chadwick. Oxford: Oxford University Press, 1991.

Aune, David E. *The Cultic Setting of Realized Eschatology in Early Christianity.* Leiden: E. J. Brill, 1972.

Austin, J. L. *How to do Things with Words.* Cambridge: Harvard University Press, 1962.

Baillie, Donald M. *God Was in Christ: An Essay on Incarnation and Atonement.* New York: Scribner's, 1948.

Balthasar, Hans Urs von. *Cordula oder der Ernstfall. Kriterien,* 2. Second edition. Basel: Johannes-Verlag, 1967 (ET of the first [1966] edition: *The Moment of Christian Witness.* Glen Rock, NJ: Newman Press, 1969).

———. *Sponsa Verbi: Skizzen zur Theologie II.* Einsiedeln: Johannes Verlag, 1961.

Barnes, Michael. "Beyond Inclusivism." *The Heythrop Journal* 30 (1989): 325-27.

Barth, Karl. *Credo.* New York: Charles Scribner's Sons, 1962.

———. *The Faith of the Church: A Commentary on the Apostles' Creed According to Calvin's Catechism.* Edited by Jean-Louis Leuba; translated by

Gabriel Vahanian. New York: Meridian Books, 1958; London and Glasgow: Collins, 1960.

Baum, Gregory. *Man Becoming: God in Secular Experience.* New York, Herder and Herder, 1970.

Baxter, Richard. *The True and Only Way of Concord, Of all the Christian Churches: The desirableness of it, and the detection of false dividing Terms.* London: John Hancock, 1680.

Beeck, Frans Jozef van. *Catholic Identity after Vatican II: Three Types of Faith in the One Church.* Chicago: Loyola University Press, 1985.

————. *Christ Proclaimed: Christology as Rhetoric.* New York, Ramsey, NJ, and Toronto: Paulist Press, 1979.

————. *Loving the Torah More than God? Towards a Catholic Appreciation of Judaism.* Chicago: Loyola University Press, 1989.

————. "Professing the Uniqueness of Christ." *Chicago Studies* 24(1985): 17-35.

Berg, J. H. van den. *Het menselijk lichaam: Een metabletisch onderzoek.* Two vols. Nijkerk: G. F. Callenbach, 1965.

[Blondel, Maurice.] *L'Être et les êtres: Essai d'ontologie concrète et intégrale.* Bibliothèque de philosophie contemporaine. Paris: Librairie Félix Alcan, 1935.

————. *The Letter on Apologetics* and *History and Dogma.* Translated by Alexander Dru and Illtyd Trethowan. New York, Chicago, and San Francisco: Holt, Rinehart and Winston, 1964.

————. *Les premiers écrits de Maurice Blondel.* Paris: Presses universitaires de France, 1956.

————. *Le problème de la philosophie catholique. Cahiers de la nouvelle journée,* 20. Paris: Librairie Bloud & Gay, [1932].

————. Cf. also Teilhard de Chardin, Pierre.

Boff, Leonardo. *Jesus Christ Liberator: A Critical Christology for Our Time.* Maryknoll, NY: Orbis Books, 1978.

Bonhoeffer, Dietrich. *Akt und Sein: Transzendentalphilosophie und Ontologie in der systematischen Theologie. Theologische Bücherei,* 5. München: Chr. Kaiser Verlag, 1964 (ET *Act and Being.* New York and Evanston: Harper & Row, 1961).

————. "Die Frage nach dem Menschen in der gegenwärtigen Philosophie und Theologie." In *Gesammelte Schriften,* 3. Edited by Eberhard Bethge. München: Chr. Kaiser Verlag, 1966, pp. 62-84 (ET "Man in Contemporary Philosophy and Theology." In *No Rusty Swords,* 1. Edited by Edwin H. Robertson. Revised translation. The Fontana Library. London: Collins, 1970, pp. 46-65).

————. "Vergegenwärtigung neutestamentlicher Texte." In *Gesammelte Schriften,* 3, pp. 303-24 (ET "The Presentation of New Testament Texts." In *No Rusty Swords,* 1, pp. 302-20).

————. *Widerstand und Ergebung: Briefe und Aufzeichnungen aus der Haft.* Edited by Eberhard Bethge. München and Hamburg: Siebenstern

Taschenbuch, 1966 (ET *Letters and Papers from Prison.* Edited by Eberhard Bethge. Revised edition. New York: Macmillan, 1967).

Bossy, John. *Christianity in the West 1400-1700.* Oxford and New York: Oxford University Press, 1987.

Broglie, Guy de. "La vraie notion thomiste des 'præambula fidei'." *Gregorianum* 34(1953): 341-89; 36 (1955): 291-92.

Brown, David. *The Divine Trinity.* London: Duckworth, 1985.

———. "God and Symbolic Action." In *Divine Action: Studies Inspired by the Philosophical Theology of Austin Farrer.* Edited by Brian Hebblethwaite and Edward Henderson. Edinburgh: T. & T. Clark, 1990, pp. 103-22.

———. *Invitation to Theology.* Oxford and Cambridge, MA: Basil Blackwell, 1989.

Brown, Peter. *Augustine of Hippo: a Biography.* Berkeley, Los Angeles, and London: University of California Press, 1969.

———. *The Body and Society: Men, Women and Sexual Renunciation in Early Christianity.* New York: Columbia University Press, 1988.

Brueggemann, Walter. "The Triumphalist Tendency in Exegetical History." *Journal of the American Academy of Religion* 38 (1970): 367-80.

Buber, Martin. *Gottesfinsternis: Betrachtungen zur Beziehung zwischen Religion und Philosophie.* In *Werke*, vol. 1, *Schriften zur Philosophie.* München: Kösel; Heidelberg: Lambert Schneider, 1962, pp. 503-603 (ET *Eclipse of God: Studies in the Relation Between Religion and Philosophy.* New York: Harper & Row, 1957).

———. *Ich und Du.* Second edition. Köln: Verlag Jakob Hegner, 1966 (ET *I and Thou.* Translated by Walter Kaufmann. New York: Charles Scribner's Sons, 1970).

Buckley, Michael J. *At the Origins of Modern Atheism.* New Haven and London: Yale University Press, 1987.

Bultmann, Rudolph. "New Testament and Mythology." In *Kerygma and Myth: A Theological Debate.* Edited by Hans Werner Bartsch. New York: Harper & Row, 1961, pp. 1-44.

Burrell, David B. "Divine Practical Knowing: How an Eternal God Acts in Time." In *Divine Action: Studies Inspired by the Philosophical Theology of Austin Farrer.* Edited by Brian Hebblethwaite and Edward Henderson. Edinburgh: T. & T. Clark, 1990, pp. 93-102.

———. *Knowing the Unknowable God: Ibn Sina, Maimonides, Aquinas.* Notre Dame, IN: University of Notre Dame Press, 1986.

Butler, Joseph. *The Analogy of Religion, Natural and Revealed, to the Constitution and Course of Nature.* Introduction by Albert Barnes. New York: Jonathan Leavitt; Boston: Crocker and Brewster, 1833.

Buren, Paul M. van. *The Secular Meaning of the Gospel: Based on an Analysis of its Language.* New York: Macmillan; London: Collier-Macmillan, 1966.

———. *A Theology of the Jewish-Christian Reality.* Part 1. *Discerning the Way.*

Part 2. *A Christian Theology of the People Israel.* Part 3. *Christ in Context.* San Francisco: Harper & Row, 1980, 1983, 1987.

Calvin, John. *Institutes of the Christian Religion.* Edition of 1559. Grand Rapids, MI: Wm. B. Eerdmans Publishing Company, 1983.

Camus, Albert. *La Peste.* In *Théâtre, Récits, Nouvelles.* Edited by Roger Quilliot. *Bibliothèque de la Pléiade,* 61. [Paris]: Gallimard, 1962 (ET *The Plague.* New York: Alfred A. Knopf, 1971).

Canavan Gumpert, Donnah, and others. *The Success-Fearing Personality: Theory and Research, with Implications for the Social Psychology of Achievement.* Lexington, MA: Lexington Books, 1978.

Casas, Bartolomé de las. *The Only Way to Draw All People to a Living Faith.* Edited by Helen Rand Parish. Translated by Francis Patrick Sullivan. New York: Paulist Press, 1992.

Cauchy, Venant. *Désir naturel et béatitude chez saint Thomas.* Montréal, Paris, and Saint Boniface: Fides, 1958.

Chadwick, Henry. "The Ascetic Ideal in the History of the Church." In *Monks, Hermits and the Ascetic Tradition.* Edited by W. J. Sheils. [Oxford:] Basil Blackwell, 1985, pp. 1-24.

Chenu, M.-D. "Vérité évangélique et métaphysique wolffiennne à Vatican II." *Revue des sciences philosophiques et théologiques* 57(1973):632-40.

Chesnut, Glenn F. *The First Christian Histories: Eusebius, Socrates, Sozomen, Theodoret, and Evagrius.* *Théologie historique,* 46. Paris: Beauchesne, 1977.

Chitty, Derwas J. *The Desert a City: An Introduction to the Study of Egyptian and Palestinian Monasticism under the Christian Empire.* London and Oxford: Mowbray's, 1977.

Clooney, Francis X. "Christianity and World Religions: Religion, Reason, and Pluralism." *Religious Studies Review* 15(1989): 197-204.

———. "In Joyful Recognition: A Hindu Formulation of the Relationship Between God and the Community and its Significance for Christian Theology." *Journal of Ecumenical Studies* 25 (1988): 358-69.

———. "The Study of Non-Christian Religions in the Post-Vatican II Roman Catholic Church." *Journal of Ecumenical Studies* 28 (1991): 482-94.

———. "Liturgical Theology in a Comparative Context: Some Hindu Perspectives on Lex Orandi/Lex Credendi." *Worship* 63(1989): 341-50.

The Cloud of Unknowing. Introductory Commentary and Translation by Ira Progoff. Delta Books. New York: Dell Publishing, 1957.

The Cloud of Unknowing and the Book of Privy Counseling. Edited by William Johnston. Image Books. Garden City, NJ, and New York: Doubleday, 1973.

The Cloud of Unknowing and the Book of Privy Counselling. Edited by Phyllis Hodgson. *Early English Text Society,* 218. Revised 1958. Reprinted 1981. London, New York, and Toronto: Oxford University Press,

1944 (for 1943).

Cohn, Norman. *The Pursuit of the Millennium: Revolutionary Millenarians and Mystical Anarchists of the Middle Ages.* Revised edition. New York: Oxford University Press, 1970.

Colombo, Joseph A. Book Review of *God Encountered*, vol. 1. *Horizons* 16(1-990): 388-89.

Commentary on the Decrees of Vatican II. Edited by Herbert Vorgrimler. New York: Herder and Herder, vol. 3, 1969.

Congar, Yves. *La Tradition et les traditions.* Vol. I, *Essai historique,* vol. II, *Essai théologique.* Paris: Librairie Arthème Fayart, 1960, 1963 (ET *Tradition and Traditions: An historical and a theological essay.* New York: Macmillan, 1966).

Conn, Walter E. *Conversion: Perspectives on Personal and Social Transformation.* New York: Alba House, 1978.

Cotter, A. C. *The Encyclical "Humani Generis", with a Commentary.* Weston 93, MA: Weston College Press, 1951.

———. *Theologia Fundamentalis.* Weston, MA: Weston College, 1940.

Coulson, John. *Religion and Imagination: 'in aid of a grammar of assent'.* Oxford: The Clarendon Press, 1981.

Cox, Harvey. *The Secular City: Secularization and Urbanization in Theological Perspective.* Revised edition. New York, NY: The Macmillan Company, 1966.

Deonise Hid Divinite and Other Treatises on Contemplative Prayer Related to The Cloud of Unknowing. Edited by Phyllis Hodgson. *Early English Text Society,* 231. Reprinted. London, New York, and Toronto: Oxford University Press, 1958.

Devivier, Walter. *Christian Apologetics: A Rational Exposition and Defense of the Catholic Religion.* Translated, edited, and augmented by Joseph C. Sasia. 2 vols. New York: Joseph F. Wagner; London: B. Herder, 1924.

Dewart, Leslie. *The Future of Belief: Theism in a World Come of Age.* New York: Herder and Herder, 1966.

Dijksterhuis, E. J. *The Mechanization of the World Picture.* Oxford: Clarendon Press, 1961.

Dorotheus of Gaza, St. (Dorothée de Gaza). *Oeuvres spirituelles. Sources chrétiennes,* 92. Paris: Éditions du Cerf, 1963 (ET *Discourses and Sayings. Cistercian Studies Series,* 33. Kalamazoo, MI: Cistercian Publications, 1977).

Dostoyevsky, Fyodor. *The Idiot.* Translated by David Magarshack. Illustrated by Charles Keeping. London: The Folio Society, 1971.

Dürer, Albrecht. *The Painter's Manual.* New York: Abaris Books, 1977.

Dulles, Avery. *Apologetics and the Biblical Christ. Woodstock Papers,* 6. Westminster, MD: The Newman Press, 1963.

———. "Fundamental Theology and the Logic of Conversion." *The Thomist* 45(1981): 175-193.

————. *A History of Apologetics.* New York: Corpus; Philadelphia: Westminster; London: Hutchinson, 1971.

————. "Method in Fundamental Theology: Reflections on David Tracy's *Blessed Rage for Order.*" *Theological Studies* 37 (1976): 304-16.

————. *Models of Revelation.* Garden City, NY: Doubleday, 1983.

Dunn, James D. G. *Christology in the Making: A New Testament Inquiry Into the Origins of the Doctrine of the Incarnation.* Philadelphia: Westminster Press, 1980.

Dupré, Louis. *The Common Life: The Origins of Trinitarian Mysticism and its Development by Jan Ruusbroec.* New York: Crossroad, 1984.

————. "The Dissolution of the Union of Nature and Grace at the Dawn of the Modern Age." In *The Theology of Wolfhart Pannenberg.* Edited by Carl Braaten and Philip Clayton. Minneapolis: Augsburg, 1989, pp. 95-121.

Dupuis, J. "Le débat christologique dans le contexte du pluralisme religieux." *Nouvelle revue théologique* 113(1991): 853-63.

Ebeling, Gerhard. *Dogmatik des Christlichen Glaubens.* Tübingen: J. C. B. Mohr (Paul Siebeck), 1982.

————. *Einführung in theologische Sprachlehre.* Tübingen: J. C. B. Mohr (Paul Siebeck), 1971 (ET *Introduction to a Theological Theory of Language.* Philadelphia: Fortress Press, 1971).

————. *Das Wesen des christlichen Glaubens.* Tübingen: J. C. B. Mohr (Paul Siebeck), 1959 (ET *The Nature of Faith.* Philadelphia: Fortress Press, 1961).

————. *Wort und Glaube.* Tübingen: J. C. B. Mohr (Paul Siebeck), 1960 (ET *Word and Faith.* Philadelphia: Fortress Press, 1963).

Egan, Harvey D. *Ignatius Loyola the Mystic. The Way of the Christian Mystics,* 5. Wilmington, DE: Michael Glazier, 1987.

Eliot, T. S. *Selected Essays 1917-1932.* New York: Harcourt, Brace and Company, 1932.

[Erasmus of Rotterdam]. *Opvs Epistolarvm Des. Erasmi Roterodami.* Revised edition by P. S. Allen and H. M. Allen. Vol. 4. Oxford: Clarendon Press, 1922.

Evagrius Ponticus. *The Praktikos* and *Chapters on Prayer.* Edited by John Eudes Bamberger. Spencer, MA: Cistercian Publications, 1970.

Fenton, Joseph Clifford. "The Case for Traditional Apologetics." *American Ecclesiastical Review* 141(1959): 406-16.

Feuerbach, Ludwig. *Das Wesen des Christentums. Gesammelte Werke.* Edited by Werner Schuffenhauer. Vol. 5. Berlin: Akademie-Verlag, 1973 (ET *The Essence of Christianity.* Translated by George Eliot. *Harper Torchbooks.* New York: Harper and Row, 1957).

Fiorenza, Elisabeth Schüssler. *In Memory of Her: A Feminist Historical Reconstruction of Christian Origins.* New York: Crossroad, 1983.

Fiorenza, Francis Peter, and Metz, Johann Baptist. "Der Mensch als Einheit von Leib und Seele." Vol. II of *Mysterium Salutis,* edited by

Johannes Feiner and Magnus Löhrer. Einsiedeln, Zürich, and Köln: Benziger Verlag, 1967, pp. 584-636.

Fogarty, Gerald P. *American Catholic Biblical Scholarship: A History from the Early Republic to Vatican II*. San Francisco, Harper & Row, 1989.

[Franklin, Benjamin]. *The Autobiography of Benjamin Franklin*. Edited by Richard B. Morris. New York: Washington Square Press, 1955.

Gadamer, Hans-Georg. "Geschichte des Universums und Geschichtlichkeit des Menschen." In *Geisteswissenschaften—wozu?* Beispiele ihrer Gegenstände und ihrer Fragen: Eine Vortragsreihe der Johannes Gutenberg-Universität Mainz im Wintersemester 1987/88. Edited by Hans-Henrik Krummacher. Stuttgart: F. Steiner Verlag Wiesbaden, 1988.

———. *Philosophical Hermeneutics*. Berkeley, Los Angeles, and London: University of California Press, 1976.

———. *Wahrheit und Methode: Grundzüge einer philosophischen Hermeneutik*. Second edition. Tübingen: J. C. B. Mohr (Paul Siebeck), 1965 (ET *Truth and Method*. London: Sheed & Ward, 1975).

Gleick, James. *Chaos: Making a New Science*. New York: Penguin Books, 1987.

Gregory of Nyssa, Saint. *Ascetical Works*. Translated by Virginia Woods Callahan. *The Fathers of the Church*, 58. Washington: The Catholic University of America Press, 1967.

———. *Catechetical Oration*. Edited by James Herbert Srawley. Cambridge: Cambridge University Press, 1956 (ET *NPNF*, Second Series, vol. 5, pp. 471-509).

———. *From Glory to Glory: Texts from Gregory of Nyssa's Mystical Writings*. Introduced by Jean Daniélou. Translated by Herbert Musurillo. New York: Charles Scribner's Sons, 1961.

———. *In Inscriptiones Psalmorum. In Sextum Psalmum. In Ecclesiasten Homiliae*. Edited by James McDonough and Paul Alexander. *Gregorii Nysseni Opera*, vol. 5. Leiden: E. J. Brill, 1962.

———. *Gregorii Nysseni Opera Ascetica*. Edited by Werner Jaeger. *Gregorii Nysseni Opera*, vol. 8, part 1. Leiden: E. J. Brill, 1952.

———. *Gregorii Nysseni De Vita Moysis*. Edited by Herbert Musurillo. *Gregorii Nysseni Opera*, vol. 7, part 1. Leiden: E. J. Brill, 1964 (ET *The Life of Moses*. Edited by Abraham J. Malherbe and Everett Ferguson. New York: Paulist Press, 1978).

Grenet, P. B. *Les vint-quatre thèses thomistes (De l'évolution à l'existence)*. Second edition. Paris: P. Téqui, 1962.

Haberman, Jacob. *Maimonides and Aquinas: A Contemporary Appraisal*. New York: KTAV Publishing House, 1979.

Halbfass, Wilhelm. *India and Europe: An Essay in Understanding*. Albany: State University of New York Press, 1988.

———. Studies in *Kumārila and Śaṅkara. Studien zur Indologie und Iranistik*, Monographie 9. Reinbek: Verlag für orientalistische Fachpublikationen, 1983.

Hammarskjöld, Dag. *Markings.* Translated by Leif Sjöberg and W. H. Auden. London: Faber & Faber, 1964.

Hanson, Richard P. C. *The Search for the Christian Doctrine of God: The Arian Controversy 318-381.* Edinburgh: T. & T. Clark, 1988.

Harrison, Verna E. F. "Male and Female in Cappadocian Theology." *Journal of Theological Studies,* N.S. 41(1990): 441-71.

Hartman, David. *Maimonides: Torah and Philosophic Quest.* Philadelphia: The Jewish Publication Society of America, 1976.

Haubst, Rudolf. *Die Christologie des Nikolaus von Kues.* Freiburg: Herder, 1956.

Hawking, Stephen M. *A Brief History of Time: From the Big Bang to Black Holes.* Toronto, New York, London, Sidney, and Auckland: Bantam Books, 1988.

Helminiak, Daniel A. *Spiritual Development: An Interdisciplinary Study.* Chicago: Loyola University Press, 1987.

Hennesey, James. "Leo XIII's Thomistic Revival: A Political and Philosophical Event." in *Celebrating the Medieval Heritage: A Colloquy on the Thought of Aquinas and Bonaventure.* Edited by David Tracy. *The Journal of Religion* 58(1978): Supplement, pp. 185-97.

Hettinger, Franz. *Revealed Religion.* Edited by Henry Sebastian Bowden. London: Burns & Oates, 1895.

————. *An Interpretation of Religion: Human Responses to the Transcendent.* Houndmills, Basingstoke, Hants. and London: The Macmillan Press, 1989.

Hünermann, Peter. "Das Lehramt und die endliche Gestalt der Glaubenswahrheit: Überlegungen zur römischen Instruktion über die kirchliche Berufung von Theologen." *Herder-Korrespondenz* 44(1990): 373-77.

Hugon, Édouard. *Principes de philosophie: Les vint-quatre thèses thomistes.* Fifth edition. Paris: Pierre Téqui, 1927.

Hulsbosch, A. *De schepping Gods: Schepping, zonde en verlossing in het evolutionistische wereldbeeld.* Third edition. Roermond: J. J. Romen en Zoon, 1964 (ET *God in Creation and Evolution.* New York: Sheed and Ward, 1965).

Illingworth, J. A. *The Doctrine of the Trinity Apologetically Considered.* London: Macmillan, 1907.

Imbelli, Robert P. Book Review of *God Encountered,* vol. 1. *Theological Studies* 51(1990): 145-47.

James, William. *The Varieties of Religious Experience.* Ninth edition. New York: Collier; London: Macmillan, 1974.

Jenkins, David. *The Glory of Man.* New York: Charles Scribner's Sons, 1967.

John Paul II, Pope [Karol Wojtyla]. *The Acting Person. Analecta Husserliana,* 10. Dordrecht and Boston: D. Reidel Publishing Co., 1979.

Jüngel, Eberhard. *Gott als Geheimnis der Welt: Zur Begründung der Theologie des Gekreuzigten im Streit zwischen Theismus und Atheismus.* Third edition. Tübingen: J. C. B. Mohr (Paul Siebeck), 1978 (ET *God as the Mystery of the World: On the Foundation of the Theology of the Crucified One in the Dispute Between Theism and Atheism.* Grand Rapids, MI: William B. Eerdmans, 1983).

[Kant, Immanuel.] *Immanuel Kant's Critique of Pure Reason.* Translated by Norman Kemp Smith. New York: St. Martin's Press, 1965.

―――. *Werke in sechs Bänden.* Edited by Wilhelm Weischedel. [Wiesbaden]: Insel-Verlag, 1956-64.

Kelly, J. N. D. *Early Christian Doctrines.* Revised edition. San Francisco: Harper & Row, 1978.

Klein, Carol. *The Credo of Maimonides.* New York: Philosophical Library, 1958.

Knauer, Peter. *Der Glauben kommt von Hören: Ökumenische Fundamentaltheologie.* Graz, Wien, and Köln: Verlag Styria, 1978.

Knitter, Paul F. "Making Sense of the Many." *Religious Studies Review* 15 (1989): 204-07.

―――. *No Other Name? A Critical Survey of Christian Attitudes Toward the World Religions.* Maryknoll, NY: Orbis Books, 1985.

Knox, Ronald. *Enthusiasm: A Chapter in the History of Religion.* New York: Oxford University Press, 1961.

Kristensen, W. Brede. *The Meaning of Religion: Lectures in the Phenomenology of Religion.* Introduced by Hendrik Kraemer. The Hague: M. Nijhoff, 1960.

Lacroix, Jean. *Maurice Blondel: Sa vie, son oeuvre, avec un exposé de sa philosophie.* Paris: Presses Universitaires de France, 1963.

Lash, Nicholas. *Easter in Ordinary: Reflections on Human Experience and the Knowledge of God.* Charlottesville: The University Press of Virginia, 1988.

Lawrence, Frederick. "Method and Theology as Hermeneutical." In *Creativity and Method.* Edited by Matthew L. Lamb. Milwaukee: Marquette University Press, 1981, pp. 79-104.

Lessing, Gottlob Ephraim. *Gesammelte Werke.* Edited by Paul Rilla. 10 vols. Berlin and Weimar: Aufbau-Verlag, 1954-58.

―――. *Lessing's Theological Writings,* Selected and introduced by Henry Chadwick. Stanford, CA: Stanford University Press, 1957.

Levie, Jean. *La Bible, parole humaine et message de Dieu. Museum Lessianum: Section biblique,* 1. Paris and Louvain: Desclée de Brouwer, 1958 (ET *The Bible, Word of God in Words of Men.* Reprint. New York: P. J. Kenedy & Sons, 1964).

Lévinas, Emmanuel. *Difficile liberté: Essais sur le judaïsme.* Second edition. Paris: Albin Michel, 1976.

Lindbeck, George A. *The Nature of Doctrine: Religion and Theology in a Postliberal Age.* Philadelphia: Westminster Press, 1984.

Norbert Lohfink. *Der niemals gekündigte Bund: Exegetische Gedanken zum christlich-jüdischen Dialog.* Freiburg, Basel, and Wien: Herder, 1989 (ET *The Covenant Never Revoked: Biblical Reflections on Christian-Jewish Dialogue.* New York: Paulist Press, 1991).

[Lonergan, Bernard J. F.] *Collection: Papers by Bernard Lonergan, S.J.* Edited by F. E. Crowe. New York: Herder and Herder, 1967.

———. *Grace and Freedom: Operative Grace in the Thought of St. Thomas Aquinas.* Edited by J. Patout Burns. London: Darton, Longman & Todd; New York: Herder and Herder, 1971.

———. *Insight: A Study of Human Understanding.* New York: Philosophical Library, 1970.

———. *Method in Theology.* Second edition. New York: Herder and Herder, 1973.

Loosen, Loed. "Geen christendom zonder joodse Jezus." *De Heraut* 118 (1987): 260-65.

Lott, Eric J. *Vedantic Approaches to God.* Foreword by John Hick. New York: Barnes & Noble, 1980.

Louth, Andrew. *Discerning the Mystery: An Essay on the Nature of Theology.* Oxford: Clarendon Press, 1983.

de Lubac, Henri. See Teilhard de Chardin, Pierre.

———. *Catholicisme: Les aspects sociaux du dogme.* Paris: Éditions du Cerf, 1938 (ET of the fourth [1947] edition: *Catholicism: A Study of Dogma in Relation to the Corporate Destiny of Mankind.* New York: Longmans, Green and Co., 1950).

———. *Christian Faith: The Structure of the Apostles' Creed.* London: Geoffrey Chapman, 1986.

———. *The Drama of Atheist Humanism.* Meridian Books. Cleveland and New York: The World Publishing Company, 1963.

———. *The Mystery of the Supernatural.* New York: Herder and Herder, 1967.

Lucian. [*Works.*] With an English Translation by A. M. Harmon. 8 vols. Cambridge, MA: Harvard University Press; London: William Heinemann, 1960.

Lucretius. *T. Lucreti Cari De Rerum Natura Libri Sex.* Edited by William Ellery Leonard and Stanley Barney Smith. Madison, Milwaukee, and London: The University of Wisconsin Press, 1968.

Maimonides, Moses. *The Guide for the Perplexed.* Translated by M. Friedländer. Second edition. New York: Dover Publications, 1956.

Maréchal, Joseph. *Le point de départ de la métaphysique: Leçons sur le développement historique et théorique du problème de la connaissance.* Cahier V: *Le Thomisme devant la philosophie critique.* Louvain: Museum Lessianum; Paris: Librairie Félix Alcan, 1926.

———. *A Maréchal Reader.* Edited and Translated by Joseph Donceel. New York: Herder and Herder, 1970.

Markus, Robert A. *The End of Ancient Christianity.* Cambridge: Cambridge

University Press, 1990.

Marxsen, Willi. *The Resurrection of Jesus of Nazareth.* Philadelphia: Fortress Press, 1970.

Maslow, Abraham H. *Religions, Values, and Peak-Experiences.* Columbus, OH: Ohio State University Press, 1964.

――――. *Toward a Psychology of Being.* Second edition. New York, Cincinnati, Toronto, London, and Melbourne: Van Nostrand Reinhold, 1968.

McCool Gerald A. *Catholic Theology in the Nineteenth Century: The Quest for a Unitary Method.* New York: Seabury, 1977.

McKenna, John. "Symbol and Reality: Some Anthropological Considerations." *Worship* 65(1991): 2-227.

Meier, John P. *A Marginal Jew: Rethinking the Historical Jesus.* Vol. I, *The Roots of the Problem and the Person.* The Anchor Bible Reference Library. New York: Doubleday, 1991.

Merton, Thomas. *Contemplation in a World of Action.* Garden City, NY: Doubleday, 1971.

――――. *Faith and Violence: Christian Teaching and Christian Practice.* Notre Dame, IN: University of Notre Dame Press, 1968.

Metz, Johann Baptist. *Glaube in Geschichte und Gesellschaft: Studien zu einer praktischen Fundamentaltheologie.* Mainz, Mathias-Grünewald-Verlag, 1977 (ET *Faith in History and Society: Toward a Practical Fundamental Theologie.* Crossroad Books. New York: Seabury Press, 1980).

――――. *Zeit der Orden: Zur Mystik und Politik der Nachfolge.* Freiburg, Basel, and Wien: Herder, 1977 (ET *Followers of Christ: Perspectives on the Religious Life.* London: Burns & Oates; New York and Ramsey, NJ: Paulist Press, 1978).

――――. See Fiorenza, Francis Peter.

Möhler, Johann Adam. *Die Einheit in der Kirche, oder das Prinzip des Katholizismus, dargestellt im Geiste der Kichenväter der drei ersten Jahrhunderte.* Edited by J. R. Geiselmann. Darmstadt: Wissenschaftliche Buchgesellschaft, 1957.

Monden, Louis. *Signs and Wonders: A Study in the Miraculous Element in Religion.* Foreword by Avery Dulles. New York: Desclée Company, 1966.

Mooney, Christopher F. "The Anthropic Principle in Cosmology and Theology." Unpublished paper, to appear in *Thought.*

Moore, Sebastian. "Ratzinger's 'Nature' Isn't Natural: Aquinas, Contraception and Statistics." *Commonweal* 117(1990): 49-52.

Muck, Otto. *Die transzendentale Methode in der scholastischen Philosophie der Gegenwart.* Innsbruck: F. Rauch, 1964 (ET *The Transcendental Method.* New York: Herder and Herder, 1968).

Murdoch, Iris. *The Message to the Planet.* London: Chatto & Windus, 1989.

――――. *The Unicorn.* London: Chatto & Windus, 1963.

The Myth of Christian Uniqueness: Toward a Pluralistic Theology of Religions.

Edited by John Hick and Paul F. Knitter. Maryknoll, NY: Orbis, 1987.

Neues Glaubensbuch: Der gemeinsame christliche Glaube. Edited by Johannes Feiner and Lukas Vischer. Freiburg, Basel, and Wien: Herder; Zürich: Theologischer Verlag, 1973 (ET *The Common Catechism: A Book of Christian Faith.* New York: The Seabury Press, 1975).

Newman, John Henry. *An Essay in Aid of a Grammar of Assent.* Edited by Nicholas Lash. Notre Dame and London: University of Notre Dame Press, 1979.

Nicholas Cusanus. *Of Learned Ignorance.* London: Routledge & Kegan Paul, 1954.

[————.] Nikolaus von Kues. *Werke.* Edited by Paul Wilpert. 2 vols. *Quellen und Studien zur Geschichte der Philosophie,* 5. Berlin: Walter de Gruyter, 1967.

————. *Philosophisch-Theologische Schriften.* 2 vols. Edited by Leo Gabriel; translated by Dietlind and Wilhelm Dupré. Wien: Verlag Herder, 1964.

————. *Der verborgene Gott: Ein Gespräch zwischen einem Heiden und einem Christen.* Latin and German. Translation and epilogue by Fritz Stippel. Third edition. Freiburg im Breisgau: Erich Wewel Verlag, 1952.

Nichols, Aidan. *From Newman to Congar: The Idea of Doctrinal Development from the Victorians to the Second Vatican Council.* Edinburgh: T. & T. Clark, 1990.

Nolthenius, Hélène. *Duecento: Zwerftocht door Italië's late middeleeuwen.* Utrecht and Antwerpen: Het Spectrum, 1951 (ET *Duecento: The Late Middle Ages in Italy.* New York: McGraw-Hill, 1968).

Novak, David. *The Image of the Non-Jew in Judaism: An Historical and Constructive Study of the Noahide Laws.* Toronto Studies in Theology, 14. New York and Toronto: The Edwin Mellen Press, 1983.

————. *Jewish-Christian Dialogue: A Jewish Justification.* New York and Oxford: Oxford University Press, 1989.

Nygren, Anders. *Agape and Eros.* Philadelphia: The Westminster Press, 1953.

————. *Essence of Christianity: Two Essays.* Grand Rapids, MI: William B. Eerdmans, 1973.

O'Connor, Flannery. *Collected Works.* Edited by Sally Fitzgerald. *The Library of America,* 39. New York: Literary Classics of the United States, Inc., 1988.

O'Connor, William R. *The Eternal Quest: The Teaching of St. Thomas Aquinas on the Natural Desire for God.* New York, London, and Toronto: Longmans, Green and Co., 1947.

————. *The Natural Desire for God.* [The Aquinas Lecture, 1948; Under the Auspices of the Aristotelian Society of Marquette University.] Milwaukee, WI: Marquette University Press, 1948.

Ong, Walter J. *Fighting for Life: Contest, Sexuality, and Consciousness.* Ithaca and London: Cornell University Press, 1981.

———. *The Presence of the Word: Some Prolegomena for Cultural and Religious History.* New York: Simon and Schuster, 1970.

Origen. *Contra Celsum.* Translated by Henry Chadwick. Third edition. Cambridge: Cambridge University Press, 1980.

Owens, Joseph. *The Doctrine of Being in the Aristotelian* Metaphysics: *A Study in the Greek Background of Mediaeval Thought.* Second revised edition. Toronto: Pontifical Institute of Mediaeval Studies, 1963.

Paul VI, Pope. "Mysterium Fidei." *Acta Apostolicæ Sedis* 57(1965): 753-74 (ET Pope Paul VI. *Encyclical Letter Mysterium Fidei: On the Holy Eucharist.* Washington, DC: National Catholic Welfare Conference, 1965).

Philosophiæ scholasticæ summa ad mentem Constitutionis Apostolicæ "Deus Scientiarum Dominus." A professoribus Societatis Iesu facultatum philosophicarum in Hispania. 3 vols. Madrid: Biblioteca de Autores Cristianos, 1952-55.

Pohlenz, Max. *Die Stoa: Geschichte einer geistigen Bewegung.* 2 vols. Third edition. Göttingen: Vandenhoeck & Ruprecht, 1964.

Raedts, Peter. "De christelijke middeleeuwen als mythe: Ontstaan en gebruik van een constructie uit de negentiende eeuw." *Tijdschrift voor Theologie* 30(1990): 146-58.

Rahman, Fazlur. *Major Themes of the Qur'ān.* Minneapolis and Chicago: Bibliotheca Islamica, 1980.

Rahner, Hugo. "Die Gottesgeburt: Die Lehre der Kirchenväter von der Geburt Christ aus dem Herzen der Kirche und der Gläubigen." In *Symbole der Kirche: Die Ekklesiologie der Väter.* Salzburg: Otto Müller Verlag, 1964, pp. 11-87.

———. "Die Grabschrift des Loyola." In *Ignatius von Loyola als Mensch und Theologe.* Freiburg, Basel, and Wien: Herder, 1964, pp. 422-40.

Rahner, Karl. "Anonymes Christentum und Missionsauftrag der Kirche." In *SchrzTh,* 9, pp. 498-515 (ET "Anonymous Christianity and the Missionary Task of the Church." In *TheoInv,* 12, pp. 161-78.

———. "Zur Enzyklika «Humanae Vitae»." In *SchrzTh,* 9, pp. 276-301 (ET "On the Encyclical 'Humanae Vitae'." In *TheoInv,* 11, pp. 263-87).

———. *Geist in Welt: Zur Metaphysik der endlichen Erkenntnis bei Thomas von Aquin.* Second edition, revised and augmented by Johannes Baptist Metz. München: Kösel-Verlag, 1957 (ET *Spirit in the World.* Translated by William Dych. New York: Herder and Herder, 1968).

———. *Grundkurs des Glaubens: Einführung in den Begriff des Christentums.* Third edition. Freiburg, Basel, and Wien: Herder, 1976 (ET *Foundations of Christian Faith: An Introduction to the Idea of Chris-*

tianity. Translated by William V. Dych. New York: Seabury, 19-78).

―――. *Hörer des Wortes: Zur Grundlegung einer Religionsphilosophie.* Revised by J. B. Metz. Munich: Kösel, 1963 (ET *Hearers of the Word.* Translated by Michael Richards. New York: Herder and Herder, 1969. Partial translation in *A Rahner Reader.* Edited by Gerald A. McCool. New York, Seabury, 1975).

―――. "Zur scholastischen Begrifflichkeit der ungeschaffenen Gnade." In *SchrzTh,* 1, pp. 347-75 (ET "Some Implications of the Scholastic Concept of Uncreated Grace." *TheoInv,* 1, pp. 319-46).

―――. "Zur Theologie des Symbols." In *SchrzTh,* 4, pp. 275-312 (ET "The Theology of the Symbol." *TheoInv,* 4, pp. 221-52).

―――. "Theologische Bemerkungen zum Zeitbegriff." In *SchrzTh,* 9, pp. 302-22 (ET "Theological Observations on the Concept of Time." *TheoInv,* 11, pp. 288-308).

―――. "Über das Verhältnis von Natur und Gnade." In *SchrzTh,* 1, pp. 323-45 (ET "Concerning the Relationship Between Nature and Grace." In *TheoInv,* 1, pp. 297-317).

―――. "Ein Weg zur Bestimmung des Verhältnisses von Natur und Gnade." *Orientierung* 14(1950): 141-45.

Ramsey, Arthur Michael. *From Gore to Temple: The Development of Anglican Theology between* Lux Mundi *and the Second World War 1889-1939.* London: Longmans, 1960.

Ramsey, Ian T. *Religious Language: An Empirical Placing of Theological Phrases.* Second edition. London: SCM Press, 1967.

[―――.] *Words about God: The Philosophy of Religion.* Edited by Ian T. Ramsey. New York: Harper & Row, 1971.

Ratzinger, Joseph. *Einführung in das Christentum.* München: Kösel-Verlag, 1968 (ET *Introduction to Christianity.* London: Burns & Oates, 1969).

[Reimarus, Hermann Samuel]. *Reimarus: Fragments.* Edited by Charles H. Talbert. Lives of Jesus Series. Philadelphia: Fortress Press, 1970.

Robinson, John A. T. *Honest to God.* London: SCM Press, 1963.

Rousselot, Pierre. *L'intellectualisme de Saint Thomas.* Second Edition. Paris: Beauchesne, 1924. (ET *The Intellectualism of Saint Thomas.* New York: Sheed & Ward, 1935.

Ruh, Ulrich. "Als Mann und Frau schuff er sie." *Herder-Korrespondenz* 42 (1988): 574-78.

Ruusbroec, Jan van. *Boecsken der verclaringhe.* [*Little Book of Enlightenment;* Ioannis Rvsbrochii *Samvel sive Apologia*]. *Corpus Christianorum, Continuatio Mediaevalis,* 101. Tielt: Lannoo; Turnhout: Brepols, 1989.

―――. *Die geestelike brulocht.* [*The Spiritual Espousals;* Ioannis Rvsbrochii *De ornatv spiritvalivm nvptiarvm*]. *Corpus Christianorum, Continuatio Mediaevalis,* 103. Tielt: Lannoo; Turnhout: Brepols, 1988.

————. *Vanden blinkenden steen. Vanden vier becoringen. Vanden kerstene ghe-love. Brieven.* [*The Sparkling Stone. The Four Temptations. The Christian Faith. Letters.* Ioannis Rvsbrochii *De calcvlo sev perfectione filiorvm Dei. De qvattvor svbtilibvs tentationibvs. De fide et ivdicio. Epistolae.*] *Corpus Christianorum, Continuatio Mediaevalis,* 110. Tielt, Lannoo; Turnhout: Brepols, 1991.

————. *Vanden seven sloten.* [*The Seven Enclosures;* Ioannis Rvsbrochii *De septem cvstodiis*]. *Corpus Christianorum, Continuatio Mediaevalis,* 102. Tielt: Lannoo; Turnhout: Brepols, 1989.

————. *The Spiritual Espousals and Other Works.* Introduced and translated by James A. Wiseman. The Classics of Western Spirituality. New York, Mahwah, and Toronto: Paulist Press, 1985.

————. *Werken.* 4 vols. Edited by J. van Mierlo, J. B. Poukens, L. Reypens, M. Schurmans, and D. A. Stracke. Mechelen: Het Kompas; Amsterdam: De Spiegel, 1932-34.

Sacræ theologiæ summa: iuxta Constitutionem Apostolicam "Deus Scientiarum Dominus." 4 vols. Madrid: Biblioteca de Autores Cristianos, 1955-56.

Santer, Mark. *The Church's Sacrifice.* Fairacres Publications, 47. Fairacres, Oxford: SLG Press, 1975.

Scheler, Max. *Wesen und Formen der Sympathie.* In *Wesen und Formen der Sympathie. Die deutsche Philosophie der Gegenwart. Gesammelte Werke,* 7. Bern and München: Francke Verlag, 1973, pp. 3-258 (ET *The Nature of Sympathy.* New Haven: Yale University Press, 1954).

Schelsky, Helmut. "Ist die Dauerreflexion institutionalisierbar? Zum Thema einer modernen Religionssoziologie." *Evangelische Ethik* 2(1967): 153-174.

Schimmel, Annemarie. *Islam: An Introduction.* Albany: State University of New York Press, 1992.

Schleiermacher, Friedrich. *Der Christliche Glaube.* 7th edition. Edited by Martin Redeker. 2 Vols. Berlin: Martin de Gruyter, 1960 (ET *The Christian Faith.* Translated by H. R. Mackintosh and J. S. Stewart. Edinburgh: T. & T. Clark, 1928).

Schlette, Heinz Robert. *Die Religionen als Thema der Theologie: Überlegungen zu einer « Theologie der Religionen».* Quaestiones Disputatae, 22. Freiburg, Basel, and Wien: Herder, 1963. (ET *Towards a Theology of Religions.* Quaestiones Disputatae, 14. Freiburg: Herder; London: Burns & Oates, 1966).

Schmaus, Michael. *Vom Wesen des Christentums.* Westheim bei Augsburg: Wiboradaverlag, Abt. G. Rost, 1947 (ET *The Essence of Christianity.* Chicago, Dublin, London: Scepter, 1961).

Schneiders, Sandra M. *The Revelatory Text: Interpreting the New Testament as Sacred Scripture.* San Francisco: HarperSanFrancisco, 1991.

Schoonenberg, P. J. A. M. *Gods wordende wereld: Vijf theologische essais.* Woord en beleving, 13. Tielt: Lannoo, 1962 (ET *God's World in the*

Making. Duquesne Studies: Theological Series, 2. Pittsburgh, PA: Duquesne University Press; Louvain: Editions E. Nauwelaerts, 1964).

―――. *Hij is een God van mensen: Twee theologische studies.* 's-Hertogenbosch: L. C. G. Malmberg, 1969 (ET *The Christ: A Study of the God-Man Relationship in the Whole of Creation and in Jesus Christ.* New York: Herder and Herder, 1971).

Schwager, Raymund. *Der wunderbare Tausch: Zur Geschichte und Deutung der Erlösungslehre.* München: Kösel, 1986.

Sertillanges, A. G. *Les grandes thèses de la philosophie thomiste. Bibliothèque catholique des sciences religieuses*, 15. Paris: Bloud & Gay, 1928.

Sloyan, Gerard S. *Jesus in Focus: A Life in its Setting.* Mystic, CT: Twenty-Third Publications, 1983.

Smart, Ninian. *The Philosophy of Religion.* New edition. New York: Oxford University Press, 1979.

Smith, Huston. *The Religions of Man.* New York: Harper & Row, 1965.

[Smith, Wilfred Cantwell.] *Religious Diversity: Essays by Wilfred Cantwell Smith.* Edited by Willard G. Oxtoby. New York, Hagerstown, San Francisco, and London: Harper & Row, 1976.

―――. "The World Church and the World History of Religion: The Theological Issue." In *The Catholic Theological Society of America: Proceedings of the Thirty-Ninth Annual Convention* 39(1984): 52-68.

―――. "Dogmengeschichtliche und lehramtliche Entfaltung der Christologie." In: *Mysterium Salutis.* Edited by Johannes Feiner and Magnus Löhrer. Vol. 3/I. Einsiedeln, Zürich, and Köln: Benziger Verlag, 1970, pp. 389-476.

Snow, C. P. *The Two Cultures and the Scientific Revolution.* New York: Cambridge University Press, 1959 (Expanded edition: *The Two Cultures: And a Second Look.* Cambridge: Cambridge University Press, 1963).

Sobrino, Jon. *Christology at the Crossroads: A Latin American Approach.* Maryknoll, NY: Orbis Books, 1976.

Somerville, James M. *Total Commitment: Blondel's L'Action.* Washington and Cleveland: Corpus Books, 1968.

Southern, R. W. *The Making of the Middle Ages.* London: Hutchinson University Library, 1967.

Squire, Aelred. *Asking the Fathers: The Art of Meditation and Prayer.* Second edition. Wilton, CT: Morehouse-Barlow; New York and Ramsey, NJ: Paulist Press, 1976.

Stevenson, Kenneth. *Accept this Offering: The Eucharist as Sacrifice Today.* Collegeville, MN: The Liturgical Press, 1989.

―――. *Eucharist and Offering.* New York, Pueblo Publishing Company, 1986.

Stobbe, Heinz-Günther. *Hermeneutik—ein ökumenisches Problem: Eine Kritik der katholischen Gadamer-Rezeption.* Zürich and Köln: Benziger Verlag; Gütersloh: Gütersloher Verlagshaus Gerd Mohn, 1981.

————. "Konsensfindung als hermeneutisches Problem." In *Theologischer Konsens und Kirchenspaltung.* Edited by Peter Lengsfeld and Heinz-Günther Stobbe. Stuttgart, Berlin, Köln, and Mainz: Kohlhammer, 1981, pp. 31-51.

Sudbrack, Joseph. "Die »Anwendung der Sinne« als Angelpunkt der Exerzitien." *Ignatianisch: Eigneart und Methode der Gesellschaft Jesu.* Edited by Michael Sievernich and Günter Switek. Freiburg, Basel, and Wien: Herder, 1990, pp. 96-119.

Sykes, Stephen. *The Identity of Christianity: Theologians and the Essence of Christianity from Schleiermacher to Barth.* London: SPCK; Philadelphia: Fortress Press, 1984.

Teilhard de Chardin, Pierre, and Blondel, Maurice. *Correspondence.* Edited by Henri de Lubac. New York: Herder and Herder, 1967.

Teresa de Jesús. *Libro de la Vida.* In *Obras completas.* Edited by Efrén de la Madre de Dios and Otilio del Niño Jesús. Vol. 1. Madrid: Biblioteca de Autores Cristianos, 1951, pp. 595-877.

————. *Moradas del Castillo Interior.* In *Obras completas.* Edited by Efrén de la Madre de Dios. Vol. 2. Madrid: Biblioteca de Autores Cristianos, 1954, pp. 307-495 (ET In *The Complete Works of Saint Teresa of Jesus.* Translated by P. Silverio de Santa Teresa. Edited by E. Allison Peers. Vol. 2. New York: Sheed & Ward, 1946, pp. 199-351).

Theißen, Gerd. *Der Schatten des Galiläers: Historische Jesusforschung in erzählender Form.* Fifth impression. München: Chr. Kaiser, 1988 (ET *The Shadow of the Galilean: The Quest of the Historical Jesus in Narrative Form.* Philadelphia: Fortress Press, 1987).

Thérèse de l'Enfant Jésus. *Histoire d'une Âme: Conseils et Souvenirs, Prières, Lettres, Poésies.* Paris: Office Central de Lisieux, 1950 (ET *Story of a Soul: The Autobiography of St. Therese of Lisieux.* Translated by John Clarke. Washington, DC: ICS Publications, 1975).

Thompson, William M. *Christ and Consciousness: Exploring Christ's Contribution To Human Consciousness—The Origins and Development of Christian Consciousness.* New York, Ramsey, and Toronto: Paulist Press, 1977.

Tillich, Paul. *The Courage To Be.* The Fontana Library. London: Collins, 1962.

————. "Reply to Interpretation and Criticism," in *The Theology of Paul Tillich.* Edited by Charles W. Kegley and Robert W. Bretall. New York: Macmillan, 1956, pp. 329-49.

————. *Systematic Theology.* Three volumes in one. Chicago: The University of Chicago Press, 1967.

————. "Theology and Symbolism," in *Religious Symbolism.* Edited by F. Ernest Johnson. Reissue. Port Washington, NY: Kennikat Press, 1969, pp. 107-16.

Tracy, David. *The Analogical Imagination: Christian Theology and the Culture of Pluralism.* New York: Crossroad, 1981.

———. *Blessed Rage for Order: The New Pluralism in Theology.* New York: The Seabury Press, 1975.

———. *Plurality and Ambiguity: Hermeneutics, Religion, Hope.* San Francisco: Harper & Row, 1987.

———. "The Uneasy Alliance Reconceived: Catholic Theological Method, Modernity, and Postmodernity." *Theological Studies* 50(1989): 548-70.

Trevor, Meriol. *Newman: Light in Winter.* Garden City, NJ: Doubleday, 1962.

Vahanian, Gabriel. *The Death of God: The Culture of our Post-Christian Era.* New York: George Braziller, 1961.

———. *No Other God.* New York: George Braziller, 1966.

———. *Wait Without Idols.* New York: George Braziller, 1964.

Van Engen, John. "Christian Middle Ages as an Historiographical Problem." *American Historical Review* 91(1986): 519-552.

[Vesalius, Andreas.] *The Illustrations from the Works of Andreas Vesalius.* Edited by J. B. deC. M. Sauders and Charles D. O'Malley. New York: Dover Publications, 1973.

Vorgrimler, Herbert. *Sakramententheologie.* Leitfaden Theologie, 17. Düsseldorf: Patmos Verlag, 1987

Wagenhammer, Hans. *Das Wesen des Christentums: Eine begriffsgeschichtliche Untersuchung.* Tübinger Theologische Studien, 2. Mainz: Matthias-Grünewald-Verlag, 1973.

Ware, Timothy [Kallistos]. *The Orthodox Church.* Revised Reprint. Harmondsworth: Penguin Books, 1983.

Watson, Stephen. "Reason and the Face of the Other." *Journal of the American Academy of Religion* 54(1986): 33-57.

Weisheipl, James A. *Friar Thomas D'Aquino: His Life, Thought, and Works.* With *Corrigenda* and *Addenda.* Washington, DC: The Catholic University of America Press, 1983.

Wetering, Jan Willem van de. *The Empty Mirror: Experiences in a Japanese Monastery.* New York, Ballantine Books, 1987.

Wicks, Jared. "Lutero e la religiosità vissuta." *Gregorianum* 70 (1989): 121-26.

Wignall, Paul. "Patterns in Theology." In Stephen W. Sykes. *The Integrity of Anglicanism.* New York: The Seabury Press, 1978, pp. 101-09.

Wiles, Maurice. *The Remaking of Christian Doctrine.* Second edition. London: SCM, 1975.

Wingren, Gustav. *Credo: The Christian View of Faith and Life.* Minneapolis, MN: Augsburg, 1981.

Young, Frances M. *The Making of the Creeds.* London: SCM Press; Philadelphia: Trinity Press International, 1991.

Zalba Erro, Marcelino. *Theologiæ moralis summa.* Second edition. 3 vols. Madrid: Biblioteca de Autores Cristianos, 1957-58.

Subject Index

(Italics refer to footnotes.)

Action, 235, *235*
Adam, 152
Agent intellect, *234*
Agnosticism, 77, 84, 90-91, *92*
Alienation, 43, *90,* 101
Anglicanism, 122
Anthropic principle, *180*
Anthropology, 77, *179, 200,* 210, *237,* 258, 259; theological, 233, 253
Anxiety, 8
Apologetic(s), 44, 182, 205, 207, 210, 213, 219, 228, *228, 233,* 262, 273, 281; confessional, 275-276, 279; fundamental, 275-276, 279
Apophatic(ism), 81, 93, *93*
Asymmetry, asymmetrical, 23, 95, 113, 185, *186*
Atheism, *89,* 102
Authenticity, 73, 204, 235, 244, 259
Authority, *16*
Autonomy, 36, 196-198, *198,* 202

Baptism, 26
Buddhism, 44, *45,* 46-47, *48;* Mahayana, 44, *46*

Caritas, 55
Cataphatic(ism), 80, 93
Catechesis, 100, 116
Catechisms, 117
Catholic tradition, 92
Catholicism, 122, 141-142, *184;* Roman, *109*
Catholicity, 14, 30-31, 222
Celibacy, 169
Charismatic(s), *46, 91, 144,* 145, 198
Christendom, 51, 120, 277, 281
Christian Tradition, 76
Christianity, 41-44, 47, *48,* 51-52, 99, 107, 120, 159; anonymous, 66, *200,* 255; essence of, 103; nature of, 24, *60,* 98; as transition(al), 65, 139-140
Church, 32, 34, *46,* 51, *64,* 65-66, 72; pilgrim, 70; and State, *91;* undivided Christian, 24, 155, 189, 194
Cloud of Unknowing, 81, 82, 84-85, *83-86,* 242
Communication, 61-62, 295, *295,* 297, 309;

to, 296; with, 296
Comprehension, 55
Conduct, 26, 99
Confessio, 18
Conquista, 52
Consolation, 163
Contemplation, 72, 78, *96,* 242
Convergence, 56-57
Cosmology, 77, *179, 237*
Cosmos, *154*
Councils: ecumenical, 132; Nicaea, *9,* 39, 134; Constantinople I, 134; Lateran IV, 96; Trent, *239;* Vatican I, 158, 213-14, 218; Vatican II, 5, 10, 42, 50, *91, 109,* 141, 145, 210, *158,* 213-14, *221,* 224-25, 228, 277, 313, 315
Counter-Reformation, 117
Covenant, 48, *60;* New Covenant, *60*
Convenientia, 278-79, *279*
Creator, 40
Creature, *62*
Credibility, 280
Creed, 21-24, 26-36, 39-41, 44, 49-51, *65,* 70, 72-75, 92, 98-99, 104, 107, 109, 114, 130, 147-48, 173, 183, 260, 265, 284; Apostles', 22; of Bangor, *39;* baptismal, 23; conciliar, 103; Nicene-Constantinopolitan, *10,* 105, 132; trinitarian, 35; trinitarian-christological, 106
Crisis, 272
Critique of ideologies, *261*
Culture, 263, 269-70, 281, 293

Death-of-God theology, *102*
Deism, Deist(s), 91, 93, *180,* 199-200, *200-01,* 205, 280, 286
Demiurge, 40, 151
Desire for God: humanity's natural, *64*
Devotio moderna, 116
Dialogue, 15, 49, 53, 59-60, 67
Diaspora, 131
Discernment, 227, *270;* of spirits, 163
Disintegration, 114
Dissociation, 114, 125
Dissonance (symbolic), 297
Docta ignorantia, 38, 78-79, 81, 87-88, *93,* 279
Doctrine, *28,* 69, 107
Dogma, 74

Dualism, dualistic, *157, 169*

Ecumenism, *110, 115*
'El Šadday, 37
Encounter(s), 29, 53, 59, 195, 297, 306, *308*, 312
Encratites, 168, 170
Enlightenment, *62*, 84-85, 100, 104, 124, 160, 190-91, 197, *201*, 241, 260, 266, *267*

Eschatology, eschatological, 35, 74-75, 78, 137, 140, 250, 258
Essence, *138*; 251; doxological, 72; (normative), 112
Establishment, 130
Eucharist, 105, 153-55, *223*, 256
Evangelicalism, 286, *289*
Exegesis, 108, *108*
Existential (supernatural), *233*
Exitus, 22-24, 26, 97
Extrinsecism, 260, 278

Faith and Order, *109*
Faith, 83, 229
Fideism, fideists, 92, 129, 213, *223*
Force, physical, 262
Forgiveness of Sins, 35
Fundamentalism, fundamentalist(s), 92, 94

God, 37-41, 63, 68, 71, 73, 75; the Father, 36, 39, Israel's; *46*
Gospel, 40
Grace, 25, *26*, 34, 52, 71-72, 75, 84, 98-99, 100, 140, 149-50, 164, 180-183, 185, 189, 200, 216, 238, 247-48; and nature, 25-27, 146, *166, 229*, 239, 284

Hermeneutics, hermeneutical, 15, 106
Heteronomy, 196-98, *198*
Hierarchy of truths, 23, 112
Hinduism, 44, 46-47, *48*; neo-Hinduism, 47
History, 11, 35-36, 237, *237-38*, 316; salvation, of salvation, 18, 23, 25, 73; of the universe, *237*
Holy Spirit, 34, 88
Horizon(s), 58-59; fusion of, 63
Humanism, 188
Humanity, 44, 54, 63

Idealism, *62*
Identity, 130; responsive, 238
Idiom, 28
Ignorance, *see Docta ignorantia*
Illative sense, *57*
Imitatio Christi, 116, 282
Immanence, 78, 208, 231, 234, 241, 243, 259-60, 263, 269, 273-74, 292, 306, 311
Imperialism, 69
Inspiration of Scripture, *290*

Integralism, integralist(s), 12, 31, 94, 106, 110, 118, 284
Integrity, 14, 30-31, 112, 208, *244*, 251, 259, 267; in believing, 30; intellectual, 74, 262; human, 210, 251
Interpersonalness, 62
Interpretation, 4, 8, 12, 27-28, *29*, 30, 53, 56, 58-62, 65, 71, 111, 143, 147, 236, 300, *300*
Intervention, *155*, 288, 293
Islam, 47-49, *48, 60, 67*, 159, *276*, 281
Israel, 35-36, 66, 131, 158-59, 165, 284, 317

Jansenism, *150*
Jesus (Christ), 4, 30, 32, 34, 39-40, 50, *51*, 65, 72-73, *75*, 101, 119, 139, 222, 246, 248, 254, 274, 282, 285, *314*; historical, 51, 66-67, *94*, 129-30, 283, 285; resurrection, 35-36; risen, 35, 64
Judaism, 41-43, *48, 60, 102*, 159, *160*, 277, *314*

Kerygma, 33, *111*
Knowledge, 54-56; objectifying, 56, 58-59; participative, 53, 56-58, *223*, 227, *300*; practical, 55

Language, 61; performative, 139, 145, *295*
Law of nature, 227; natural, *235*
Logos, 39, 50, *64*, 66, 155, *155*, 158, 183, 252-56, 289
Love, 176

Magisterium, 4-5, 7, 10, 12, *12, 94*, 220, 314
Marcionism, 150, 176
Marriage, 170
Martyrdom, 7
Method, 16
Mimesis, 136
Miracle, 219-20, *221, 226, 227*, 286
Mission, 49-50, 66
Modernism, 30, 94, 106, 143, 209, 223, 284, 289
Mohammedanism, 44
Monotheism, *42, 48*, 86
Mystagogy, 18
Mystery, 72, 75, 93, 100, 147, 314
Mysticism, mystic(s), *46, 144*, 173, 199, 242, 244, 248, 256

Narrative: christological, 35; realistic, 240
Natural order, 44, 73
Naturalism, 154, 189, 192, *192*, 196, 201-02, 217
Nature, 24, 35, 40, 44, 149, 165, 180-186, *190*, 216, 237, 239, *279*; divine, *185*; and grace, 25-27, 146, *166, 229*, 239, 284; human, 50, *190*; order of, 25, 44, 54, 73; pure, 184, 187-88, *191*

Neo-Protestantism, 190
Neo-Thomism, 207, *209*, 215, 233
Neutrality, *17*
North America, 90, 107, 110, 131-32, *158, 195, 197*, 199-200, *221*, 265-266, 286

Objectivity, 16
Omnipotence, *38*
Openness, 14, 31, 66
Opinions, 31
Orthodoxy, 92, 125

Pantokratŏr, 36-38, *39*
Paradox, 186
Participation, 55
Particularity, 100
Patience, 114, 146, *146*
Perichŏrēsis, 25
Perspective, 56-58, 65
Pietism, 150, 217
Pistic(s), *46*, 96, *144*, 198
Platonism, 179
Pluralism, pluralistic, *50*, 63, *64, 67*, 68-69, 266
Potentia absoluta, 38
Potentia oboedientialis, 199
Præambula fidei, *280*
Prayer, 79, 82, 96, 241
Prejudice, *51*
Presence, 296
Profession of faith, 13, 18, 24, 28, 30-31, 34, 44, *51*, 61, 65, 74, 97, 138, 182, 258; baptismal, 23
Projection, *64*
Prophecy, 219, 225
Prospect (cognitive), 24
Protestant(ism), 109, *158*; evangelical, 108

Rationalism, 125, 211, *221*, 230, 280
Reason, 126-27, 229, 270
Reditus, 23-24, 26
Reflection: fundamental theological, 34, 73; natural theological, 35
Reformation, *89*, 100, *102*, 104, 106-07, 117, 159, *184*, 188, 190-92, 194, 229, 233
Regulae Fidei, 23, 29, 126, 130
Relation, 16
Relativism, 4, 30
Religion(s), 41-42, 44, 49-50, *51*, 52, *52*, 54, 60, 66, 101, 258; natural, 53-53, 260; positive, 34, 260-61,   ; positive elements, 52
Religious life, 167, 242
Renaissance, 233
Responsibility, 299-300
Resurrection: of the flesh, 35; Christ's, *76*. *See also* Jesus (Christ)
Retrospect (cognitive), 24
Revelation, 13, *13*, 44, *109*, 200, 212, 216, 218-19, 224, 241, 273, 281, *288*, 294-95,

313-315, *314*
Romanticism, 84
Rule(s) of faith, *see Regulæ fidei*

Sabaoth, 37
Sacraments, 156; natural, *52, 157*
Sacrificium intellectus, 95
Salvation, *64, 102*, 119
Scripture(s), 104-08, *109, 158*, 221, 225; and Tradition, 5, 11, 106
Secularization, *102, 212*
Self-Absorption, 192
Self-Communication, 24-25, 299-300, 316; divine, 25, 97, 274, *310*
Self-Transcendence, 210
Sexuality, 169
Shema, 37
Sin, 11, 166, *189*, 202
Soteriology, *94*
Spirit, 72, *75*, 79
Status confessionis, 272
Stoicism, Stoics, *48*, 137, 161, *290*
Structure(s), 29, 59, 72
Supernatural, 183-84, 231, 238, 286
Symbol(s), symbolic, 29, 73, 105, 148, 155-57, *156, 158, 299, 309*
Syncretism, 264
Systematics; systematician(s), 7

Teaching, 8, 23, 99, 272
Testimonial autobiography, 139, 307
Theological reflection: fundamental, 34, 73, 260
Theology: fundamental, *268*, 272-73; natural, 34, 181, 183, 188, 283; positive, 272; symbolic, 271
Theonomy, 198
Things, *295, 301, 307*
Thomism, 213, 215-17
Torah, 43
Tradition, *64*, 73, 107, 110, 209, 224, 293, 308; great, 1-2, 4-18, *12*, 24, 33, *64*, 103, *155*, 189, 194, 202, 231-32, 241, 289; catholic, 132
Traditionalism, traditionalist(s), 92, 129, 213, 228
Transcendence, 78, 162-63, 166, 191, 232, 238, *238*, 311; God's, 76, 98, 162, 274, 285, 291-92, 306
Trinity, 25, *39*, *252*
Triumphalism, 209

Understanding, 27, 33
Universalism, universalist, 35, *48*, 69, 72, 98, 100, 131, 139, *145*, 183, 260, 264, 266; Christian, 32; eschatological, 74; natural, 32; protological, 35, 44; subsidiary, 49
Universe, 37

Veda, Vedanta, 46-47

Ways: illuminative, purgative, unitive, *45*
Wisdom, 159, 254
Witness, 18, 29, 306-07, 309

Word as address, 195
Word of God, 11
World, 29, 54, 63
Worship, 23, 26, 34, 72, 74-75, 82, 88, 97, 99, 104-05, 147, 272

Name Index

(Italics refer to footnotes.)

Adam, Karl, 142
Alaerts, J., *249*
Albert the Great, *184*
Alberti, Leone Battista, *17*
Alfrink, Bernard, 225
Altizer, Thomas J., *102*
Alypius, 313
Ambrose of Milan, St., 168, 171, 313
Andrewes, Lancelot, 123
Anselm of Canterbury, 79, 84
Aristotle, 33, *138*, *161*, 177, 179, 181, *184*, 186, *234*, 277, 325
Arminius, Jacobus, 124
Arrupe, Pedro, *283*
Athanasius, St., 253
Auerbach, *136*
Augustine, St., 3, 78-80, 87-88, 90, *157*, 161, 164, 167-68, *169-70*, 179, 181, *189*, *223*, *295*, 312-13, 320, 324
Aune, David Edward, 318
Austin, Joseph L., *295*

Baillie, Donald M., *172*
Balthasar, Hans Urs von, 4, 6-7, *6-7*, 114, 118, 140, 145, *158*, 318
Bamberger, John Eudes, 318
Barnes, Michael, 320
Barth, Karl, 5, 110, *140*, 145, *192*, 193, 272, *273*
Baum, Gregory, 327
Bautain, Louis, *219*
Baxter, Richard, 120, *121*
Bea, Augustine, 225
Beeck, Frans Jozef van, *25*, *51*, *60*, *102*, *110*, *121*, *136*, *158*, *184*, *197*, *200*, *254*, *285*, *292*, *295*, 318, 319, 321, 323, 324, 325, 326, 329, 331, 332
Benedict XV, *215*
Berg, J. H. van den, *292*
Bergius, Conradus, *121*
Bérulle, Pierre de, 78
Blondel, Maurice, 204-05, *206-08*, 207-14, 219, *221*, *226*, 228-34, *233*, *235*, 241, 251-52, 258, *259*, *261*, 263, *268*, *279*, 326, 327, 328

Boehme, Jakob, 122
Boff, Leonardo, 283
Bonaventure, St., *189*, *198*, *214*
Bonhoeffer, Dietrich, 190, *192*, 192-96, 212, 282, 325
Bossuet, Jacques-Bénigne, 123
Bossy, John, 322
Broglie, Guy de, *280*
Brown, David, *102*, *315*, 322, 332
Brown, Peter, *151*, *154*, *168-69*, *171*, 172, 320, 324
Brueggemann, Walter, 326
Brunschvicg, Léon, 205, 326
Buber, Martin, 16, *16*, *59*, *62*, *159*, 284, 296, *303*
Bucer, Martin, 119
Buckley, Michael J., 3, *89*, 200, 211, *252*, 320
Buddha, Gautama, *64*
Bullinger, Heinrich, 119, 124
Bultmann, Rudolph, 285, 290
Buren, Paul van, *43*, *102*
Burrell, David B., 292, 321
Butler, Joseph, 277-81, *279*

Cajetan, Thomas Vio, Cardinal, *184*,
Callahan, Virginia Woods, *215*, 323
Calvin, John, 110
Camus, Albert, *311*
Canavan, Donna — Gumpert, 318
Casas, Bartolomé de las, *52*
Casaubon, Isaac, 122
Casel, Odo, 272
Cassian, St. John, 168, 170
Celsus, *227*, 289
Chadwick, Henry, *126*, *168*, *170*, *288*, 324, 332
Chenu, M.-D., *216*, 323
Chestnut, Glenn F., *144*
Chitty, Derwas J., 167
Chrysostom, St. John, 168, 170, 320, 324
Clement of Alexandria, St., 7, 77
Climacus, St. John, 172
Clooney, Francis X., *67*, *69*, *157*, *196*, 319
Cohn, Norman, 114
Colombo, Joseph A., *12*, *268*
Congar, Yves, 12, *109*, *313*

Conn, Walter E., *312*
Constantine, Emperor, *144*
Cotter, A. C., *220-21*
Coulson, John, 321
Cox, Harvey, *102*
Cusanus, *see* Nicholas of Cusa
Cyprian, St., 168
Cyril of Jerusalem, St., 103

Damascene, St. John, 77, 81
Daniélou, Jean, 320
Dante Alighieri, 58, 90
Denis, Charles, 204, *233*
Descartes, René, 78, *121, 179*
Devivier, Walter, *220*
Dewart, Leslie, *102*
Dijksterhuis, E. J., 332
Diognetus, 289
Dionysius the Areopagite, Pseudo-, 79-84, *79-80, 84*
Dorotheus of Gaza, St., 255, 331
Dostoevsky, Feodor, *311*
Driver, Thomas, 319
Dulles, Avery, *219, 226, 228,* 261-62, 269, 274, 277, 280, 315, 327, 331
Dunn, James D. G., 323
Dürer, Albrecht, *17*
Dupré, Louis, *229, 252*
Dupuis, J., *50*

Ebeling, Gerhard, 110-11, 195
Eckhart, Meister, 117, 247
Egan, Harvey D., 331
Eliot, George (Mary Ann Evans), *101*
Eliot, T. S., 58
Engen, John van, 327
Erasmus, Desiderius, 115-16, *116,* 145
Eusebius of Caesarea, *144*
Evagrius Ponticus, *81,* 318

Fénélon, François de Salignac de La Mothe —, 123
Fenton, Joseph Clifford, *221*
Festugière, A. J., *169*
Feuerbach, Ludwig, 101-02, *101-02,* 129, 144
Fichte, Johann Gottlieb, 321
Fiorenza, Elisabeth Schüssler, *171*
Fiorenza, Francis Peter, *156*
Fogarty, Gerald, *158, 221,* 318, 327, 328
Franklin, Benjamin, *280*
Franzelin, Johann, *158*
Freud, Sigmund, 102, *102,* 129
Fries, Heinrich, *10, 110*
Frings, Joseph, 225
Frost, Robert, xvii

Gadamer, Hans-Georg, xvii, *13,* 14-16, *62, 63, 237*
Gleick, James, *266*

Goethe, Johann Wolfgang von, 321
Grenet, P. B., *215*
Gregory Nazianzen, St., 253, 331
Gregory of Nyssa, St., 76, 135, 135-39, *135-36, 139,* 141, *144,* 145, 163, 168, 171, 226, 241, 243, 290, 320, 323

Haberman, Jacob, 321
Halbfass, Wilhelm, 319
Hallisey, Charles, 319
Hammarskjöld, Dag, *311*
Hanson, R. P. C., 321, 331
Harnack, Adolph von, *140,* 159
Harrison, Verna E. F., 318
Hartman, David, 321
Haubst, Rudolf, 87
Hawking, Stephen M., *180*
Hegel, G. W. F., 204
Helminiak, Daniel A., *286*
Hennesey, James, 327
Herder, Johann Gottfried, 321
Hettinger, Franz, 220
Hick, John, 48, *52, 69, 124*
Hill, William J., *158*
Hinrichs, J. C., *121*
Hodgson, Phyllis, *81, 84, 96, 199*
Hopkins, Gerard Manley, 332
Horiesius, 324
Hügel, Baron Friedrich von, 14, 77, 81, *159*
Hünermann, Peter, 319
Hugon, Édouard, *215*
Hulsbosch, A., *237*

Ignatius of Loyola, St., *154,* 163, 254
Illingsworth, John Richardson, 77
Imbelli, Robert P., *272*
Irenaeus of Lyons, St., 150-51, *152,* 153, *154,* 162, 176, 186, 252, 256, 289

Jaeger, Werner, *135,* 320, 323, 329, 332
James, Henry, 74
James, William, *159*
Jefferson, Thomas, xiv
Jenkins, David, 292-93
John XXIII, Pope, 210
John of St. Thomas, 215
John Paul II, Pope, *235*
Johnston, William, *96*
Julian the Apostate, 134
Jüngel, Eberhard, 320
Justin Martyr, St., 169, 255-56, 324

Kant, Immanuel, 54, *179, 198, 212, 233, 237,* 294, 321
Kelly, J. N. D., 319, 331
Klein, Carol, 321
Knitter, Paul F., *50-52, 64, 124*
Knauer, Peter, 195
Knox, Ronald, 114, *267*

Küng, Hans, 272

Lacroix, Jean, 326
Lash, Nicholas, 9, 159, 197, 320
Laud, William, 123
Lawrence, Frederick, 13, 29
Leo XIII, Pope, 4, 215
Lessing, G. E., 104, 109, 124, 125-129, 126, 129, 227, 288, 322
Lessing, Karl, 322
Lessius, Leonard, 89, 200, 233
Levie, Jean, 158
Lévinas, Emmanuel, 102, 165, 300
Liénart, Achille, 225
Lincoln, Abraham, xiv
Lindbeck, George, 28, 61, 309
Locke, John, 294
Lohfink, Norbert, 60
Loisy, Alfred, 140
Lombard, Peter, 3, 176, 178
Lonergan, Bernard, xiv, 62, 70, 184, 189, 233, 272, 286, 329
Loofs, Friedrich, 159
Loosen, L., 64
Lott, Eric J., 48
Louth, Andrew, 17
Lubac, Henri de, 6, 8, 102, 111, 142, 184, 228, 233, 259
Lucian, 135
Lücke, Friedrich, 322
Lucretius, Titus — Carus, 264
Luther, Martin, 116, 119, 192

Maimonides, Moses, 86, 90, 321
Marcion, 151, 151, 176
Marcus, Robert, 170, 322, 324
Maréchal, Joseph, 209, 233, 233
Marx, Karl, 102, 102, 129, 144
Marxsen, Willi, 285
Maslow, Abraham, 305
Maximus Confessor, St., 7, 146
McCool, Gerald A., 216
McKenna, John, 157
Meier, John P., 108, 128, 324
Meldenius, Rupertus, 121
Mendelssohn, Moses, 125, 314, 321
Mersch, Émile, 142
Mersenne, Marin, 200, 211, 233
Merton, Thomas, 311
Metz, Johann Baptist, 62, 145, 156, 283
Meyer, Albert, 10
Migliore, Daniel, 331
Möhler, Johann Adam, 142, 142
Monden, Louis, 226
Monica, St., 313
Mooney, Christopher F., 180
Moore, Sebastian, 184, 189, 325
Mozart, Wolfgang Amadeus, 17
Muck, Otto, 209

Murdoch, Iris, 311
Murray, John Courtney, 91

Nebridius, 313
Newman, John Henry, xviii, 9, 12, 57, 140, 156, 159, 219, 223, 234, 289, 299, 313, 323
Newton, Isaac, 211
Nicholas of Cusa, 87-89, 87, 321
Nichols, Aidan, 313
Nietzsche, F. W., 102
Nolthenius, Hélène, 179
Novak, David, 43, 198, 318, 319, 320
Nygren, Anders, 111, 150

Ockham, William, 287
O'Connor, Flannery, 74, 182, 240, 245, 320
O'Connor, William R. 329
Ong, Walter J., 16, 123
Origen, 67, 152, 172, 227, 253, 289
Otto, Rudolph, 321

Pascal, Blaise, 293, 317
Paul VI, Pope, 223
Peck, George, 272
Perrone, Giovanni, 219
Pétau (Petavius), Denis, 122
Philo, 76, 90
Pius X, Pope St. 214
Pius XI, Pope, 214
Pius XII, Pope, 64, 158, 233
Plato, 138, 161, 292
Polenz, M. 323
Proba, 79-80, 87
Progoff, Ira, 85-86

Raedts, Peter, 327
Rahman, Fazlur, 319
Rahner, Hugo, 247
Rahner, Karl, xiv, 5-6, 10, 62, 66, 110, 116, 156, 187, 187, 190-91, 200-01, 208-08, 233, 233, 238, 255, 272, 272, 293, 299, 315
Ramsey, Arthur Michael, Archbishop, 211, 267
Ramsey, Ian T., 319, 320, 321
Ratzinger, Joseph, 111, 184, 189, 325, 328
Reich, Jill, 332
Reimarus, Elise, 128-29, 216, 288
Renckens, H., 36
Robinson, John A. T., 102
Rolfson, Helen, 249
Rousselot, Pierre, 209, 233, 233
Ruh, Ulrich, 318
Ruusbroec, Jan van, Blessed, x, 85, 112, 117, 244, 246-48, 249, 250-52, 252-53, 254-256, 256, 330, 331

Santer, Mark, 256
Sartre, Jean-Paul, 297
Scheler, Max, 150

Schelsky, H., 318
Schimmel, Annemarie, 319
Schleiermacher, Friedrich, *140, 142, 159,*
285, 321
Schlette, Heinz Robert, *52*
Schlier, Heinrich, 318
Schmaus, Michael, 142
Schneiders, Sandra M., *109*
Schoonenberg, Piet, 148, *237,* 239, 318
Schopenhauer, Arthur, 90
Schwager, Raymund, *152*
Scotus, Johannes Duns, Blessed, *214*
Semmelroth, Otto, 157
Sertillanges, A. G., *215*
Shakespeare, William, xiv
Slechta, John, 322
Sloyan, Gerard, 332
Smart, Ninian, 319
Smith, Huston, 319
Smith, Wilfred Cantwell, *52,* 67-68, *67-68*
Smulders, P., *325*
Snow, C. P., *233*
Sobrino, Jon, 283
Sommerville, James, 329
Socrates, *161*
Southern, Richard, 277, 332
Speyr, Adrienne von, 7
Spinoza, Baruch, 90
Squire, Aelred, *186*
Stevenson, Kenneth, *256*
Stippel, Fritz, 321
Stobbe, Heinz-Günther, 14-15, *16*
Strauss, David Friedrich, *101*
Suarez, Francisco, *214*
Südbrack, Joseph, *233*
Surin, Kenneth, 320
Suso, Henricus, 117
Sykes, Stephen, *140*

Talbert, Charles H., *216, 288*
Tauler, Johann, 117
Teilhard de Chardin, Pierre, *154, 233, 237*
Temple, William, *267*
Teresa of Avila, St., 242-44, *244, 253,* 254

Tertullian, 152
Theißen, Gerd, *41,* 67, 319
Theodore of Mopsuestia, 184
Thérèse of Lisieux, St., xiv
Thomas Aquinas, St., 3, 7, 38, 55, 58, 79,
80, 81, 83-84, *84,* 86, 90, 155, *157,* 161,
176-81, *179-81, 184, 186, 209,* 212, 215,
215, 216, 216-17, 229, 232, *233,* 234, 276-
80, *280,* 283, *291,* 293, 312, 324, 325, 329
Thomassin d'Eynac, Louis, 123
Thompson, William M., *286*
Tillich, Paul, 36, 157, *158, 190,* 190-91, *197-
98,* 285
Toland, John, 122
Tracy, David, xv-xvii, 262-63, *268,* 268-73,
272, 331
Trevor, Meriol, 323
Troeltsch, Ernest, *140*

Vahanian, Gabriel, *102*
Verecundus, 167
Vesalius, Andreas, *292*
Virgil, 318
Vorgrimler, Herbert, 323

Wagenhammer, Hans, 118, *140, 145,* 322,
323
Walter, James J., 332
Ware, Timothy, 322
Watson, Stephen, *306*
Weisheipl, James A., 324
Wetering, Jan Willem van de, *45*
Wicks, Jared, 322
Wignall, Paul, 332
Wiles, Maurice, 287-89, *289-90,* 293
Wingren, Gustaf, 111
Wiseman, James, *249*
Wolff, Christian, 216, 288

Young, Frances M., 36, 318

Zalba, Marcelino, *214*
Zwingli, Ulrich, 119

Scripture Index

(Italics refer to footnotes.)

Genesis 1, 226, 232; **1, 12,** *150;* **1, 18,** *150;*
1, 21, *150;* **1, 25,** *150;* **1, 26,** 152; **1, 27,**
137, 252; **1, 31,** *150;* **2, 4,** 36; **2, 23,** 153
Exodus **20, 21,** 82
Leviticus **11, 44,** 255

Deuteronomy **4, 19,** 37; **6, 4,** 37; **32, 39,** 13
1 Samuel **17, 31-47,** *236*
Psalms **35, 3,** *135;* **42, 7,** 30; **62, 2,** *135;* **89,**
6-9, 37
Proverbs **3, 19-20,** 159; **8, 22-31,** 159
Wisdom **1, 7,** 153; **7, 26,** x; **8, 1,** 232; **9,** 226
Ecclesiastes **3, 7,** 76

Sirach **17, 17**, 37; **24, 3-4**, 159; **24, 7**, 159
Isaiah **40, 12-28**, 182; **42, 3**, 209; **66, 18-21**, 66
Zephaniah **2, 9**, 36
Zechariah **1, 3**, 36
Matthew **5, 48**, 290; **6, 19-21**, 137; **7, 12**, 209; **10, 19**, 8; **11, 27**, 253; **12, 20**, 209; **25, 6**, 246; **28, 20**, 13, 32
Mark **4, 19**, 8; **5, 34**, 226; **10, 52**, 226; **13, 22**, 226
Luke **2, 49**, 253; **6, 36**, 255; **10, 22**, 253; **12, 11**, 8; **13, 23-24**, *64*; **13, 24-29**, 66; **22, 19**, 153; **22, 20**, 152; **24, 39**, 153
John **1, 1**, 39; **1, 3**, 39; **1, 10**, 39; **1, 11**, 39, 151-52; **1, 14**, 315; **3, 1-3**, 226; **3, 16**, 149; **3, 34**, *75*; **4, 14**, 243; **4, 48**, 226; **6**, 256; **11, 25**, *135*; **12, 24**, 153; **13, 35**, *266*; **14, 2**, 253; **14, 6**, *135*; **16, 13**, 18; **17, 5**, 39; **18, 37**, 65
Acts **9, 2**, 141; **16, 17**, 141; **17, 24-28**, 182; **17, 34**, 79; **18, 25-26**, 141; **19, 9**, 141; **19, 23**, 141; **23, 6**, 127; **24, 14**, 141; **24, 22**, 141
Romans **1, 19-20**, 226; **1, 20**, 182; **4, 17**, *56*; **5, 5**, 178; **5, 6-8**, 149; **8, 19-22**, 209; **8, 25-27**, 79; **8, 26**, 79; **8, 32**, 178; **10, 17**, *239*;

11, 35, 152; **12, 1**, 218; **14, 9**, 65
1 Corinthians **1, 24**, *135*; **1, 30**, *135*; **2, 9**, 138, 149; **5, 4-5**, *65*; **6, 15**, 152; **7, 25-35**, 166; **8, 6**, 39; **10, 16**, 152; **11, 24**, 153; **11, 25**, 152; **15, 28**, 100; **15, 53**, 153
2 Corinthians **5, 6-10**, 141; **6, 16-18**, 37; **12, 9**, 153
Galatians **1, 6**, 111
Ephesians **2, 19-21**, 141; **4, 32**, 255; **5, 30**, 151-53
Philippians **2, 11**, 153; **3, 15**, 4; **4, 7**, 79
Colossians **1, 14**, 152; **1, 15**, 252; **1, 16-17**, 39; **1, 19**, *75*; **1, 20**, 152; **2, 9**, *75*; **3, 4**, *135*
1 Timothy **2, 4**, 100; **6, 13**, 315
Hebrews **1, 2-3**, 39; **1, 3**, x, 253; **8, 1**, *111*; **11, 13-16**, 141, **12, 1**, 141, 315; **12, 2**, 315; **13, 8**, 72
1 Peter **1, 1**, 141; **1, 20**, 253; **2, 11**, 141; **3, 15**, 32, 273
1 John **1, 1-2**, 39; **3, 23**, *111*
Revelation **1, 5**, 315; **1, 8**, 37; **4, 8**, 37; **5, 1-5**, 70; **5, 12**, 70; **9, 16**, 37; **11, 17**, 37; **15, 3**, 37; **16, 7**, 37; **16, 14**, 37; **19, 15**, 37; **21, 22**, 37

Franz Jozef van Beeck, S.J., Ph.D., is the author of eight books and about forty essays and articles. In the area of theology, examples are "Towards an Ecumenical Understanding of the Sacraments" (1966); "Sacraments, Church Order, and Secular Responsibility" (1969); *Christ Proclaimed: Christology as Rhetoric* (1979); *Fifty Psalms: An Attempt at a New Translation* (with Huub Oosterhuis and others; 1969); *Grounded in Love: Sacramental Theology in an Ecumenical Perspective* (1981); "Professing the Uniqueness of Christ" (1985); *Catholic Identity after Vatican II: Three Types of Faith in the One Church* (1985); "The Worship of Christians in Pliny's Letter" (1988); *God Encountered: A Contemporary Catholic Systematic Theology,* Volume I, *Understanding the Christian Faith* (1989); *Loving the Torah More than God? Toward a Catholic Appreciation of Judaism* (1989); "Tradition and Interpretation" (1990); "Divine Revelation: Intervention or Self-Communication? (1991); "Professing Christianity Among the World's Religions" (1991); "Two Kind Jewish Men: A Sermon in Commemoration of the Shoa" (1992). In the area of literature, there are pieces like *The Poems and Translations of Sir Edward Sherburne (1616–1702)* (1961); "Hopkins: *Cor ad Cor*" (1975); "A Note on *Ther* in Curses and Blessings in Chaucer" (1985); "The Choices of Two Anthologists: Understanding Hopkins' Catholic Idiom" (1989). He is working on the second part of the second volume of *God Encountered*. Personal predilections include liturgy, spiritual direction, preaching, as well as music (he used to be a decent violinist) and some bird watching.